AIRPORTS

The Challenging Future

Proceedings of the 5th World Airports Conference
on technological and economic change

5 - 7 May, 1976

THE INSTITUTION OF CIVIL ENGINEERS LONDON 1976

Conference sponsored jointly by the Institution of Civil
Engineers, the Royal Institute of British Architects, the
Royal Aeronautical Society, the Chartered Institute of
Transport, the Royal Town Planning Institute and the
Aerodrome Owners' Association

ORGANIZING COMMITTEE

G. Edwards (Chairman)
D. Allford
P.W. Brooks
E. Davies
W.M. Hargreaves
E.G. Sibert
A.H. Stratford

EDITOR

Mary Monro

Published by Thomas Telford Limited, for the Institution
of Civil Engineers.

CONTENTS

Opening address

Guy Barnett, MP
Permanent Under Secretary of State, Department of the Environment

It gives me great pleasure to welcome you on behalf of the Government and to have the honour to
open the proceedings of this conference. I
would like to congratulate the Institution of
Civil Engineers for organizing and sponsoring it
and the Royal Institute of British Architects,
the Chartered Institute of Transport, the Royal
Town Planning Institute and the Aerodrome Owners'
Association as the other sponsors.

The impressive list of sponsors, the distin-
guished speakers and guests from the UK and many
other countries, and the many organizations represented testify not merely to the importance
of aviation and of airports. They reflect, I
suggest, the wide spread of disciplines and interests of those concerned in and affected by
air transport; and of the relevance at this time
of the theme of the conference.

The last two or three years have been a test-
ing time in many fields of endeavour, not least
in aviation. For airport planners and policy
makers it has been a time for rethinking and developing new approaches, both by the airport
authorities and by government.

For a couple of decades, which witnessed, for
example, the introduction of commercial jet airliners and the explosive growth of package tours,
there seemed to be a certainty that there was an
imminent need for vast new four runway airports.
This apparent certainty culminated in the Maplin
project for the third London airport, which appeared as a bold and imaginative initiative capable of meeting the UK's long-term requirements,
offering unfettered scope for the introduction
of the latest advances in design and layout, and
providing a solution to the problems of noise
around airports.

In a period of world wide economic difficulties - but also of technological change - we in
Britain have had to question such concepts.
With uncertainty over the future growth of demand and with a need for financial economies,
the Maplin project had to be critically viewed
as a project with a long lead time, and requiring very heavy capital investment in its early
stages with no possibility of any early returns.
At the same time it became clear that the introduction of larger aircraft had diminished what
had been an almost unquestioned need for additional runway and air traffic control capacity
in the London area. Finally, the availability
of quieter aircraft, coupled with the prospect
that there could be large-scale fleet replace-

ments during the 1980s, meant that before any
major new airport could become operational on an
effective scale the noise problems at the existing airports would be sharply reducing.

In all these circumstances it became generally
accepted that opportunities for making the most
effective use of existing airports and of their
already available ground access and other infrastructure must be sought. But while there is
the need for cost effectiveness, and for solutions which in the face of change can be flexible rather than monolithic, there is another
dimension. That is the relationship between a
major international airport and the community:
a dimension whose significance is now acknowledged by airport authorities in many countries,
not least I am glad to say by Britain's own airport authorities.

Today, air transport is not an activity of a
few specialists or of minority interests. It
has now to be seen as a major public transport
industry, an image which it seems to me the recent introduction of shuttle services from the
London airports may significantly foster. It is
an important source of employment and of economic benefit to many; but at the same time, particularly in the London area, it can contribute
to local shortages of labour which can affect
local services. A major airport is a substantial
traffic generator which can impose risks of congestion on local road and rail systems. Such
traffic congestion can harm both the airport and
the community, and airport planning cannot proceed without careful studies with the local highway and transport authorities and without a development of a mutual understanding of what may
be practicable and acceptable. At Heathrow, for
instance, London Transport are even now complet-
ing an extension to the London underground which
will link the central terminal area direct to
central London and to the whole of the London
underground system. Gatwick has always had a
first class and convenient direct rail link to
London Victoria, and improvements to the airport
railway station are planned as a component part
of that airport's current expansion. Again
there are the impacts which an airport, like any
other major employer, must have on housing demand and planning in the surrounding areas, all
of which must be taken into account before major
investments in airports are committed. Lastly,
but by no means least, there is the important
consideration of community reaction to aircraft
noise, to which technology is responding by

providing quieter aircraft.

It is because of these many external relationships, and because, in a mature democracy, large and possibly intrusive developments cannot and should not be imposed without explanation and understanding, that the Government has embarked on a wide ranging consultation exercise before settling on the major lines of a possible future national airports policy. In November 1975 a consultation document on the London area airports was published and there will shortly be a second document covering airports in the rest of Great Britain. Significantly, the consultations are being conducted jointly by the Department of Trade, which has responsibilities for civil aviation and aircraft noise, and by the Department of the Environment with its wider interests in access, housing, planning and the environment generally. It is desired that these consultations should not be confined to specialists, but should involve the authorities and organizations which represent those who use, who obtain their livelihood from, and who are affected by airports. Only after these consultations have been completed and the results carefully assessed will the Government put proposals before Parliament. It is recognized that this might seem to impose yet further uncertainties and delays. But I believe that this process, which I may say demands patience and adaptability from the airport planners, is both inevitable and right.

Turning now to the more direct problems affecting airport operators, planners and designers, there is first the general question of the role of each airport. This is central to the consultations now in train. In this connexion Heathrow will remain Britain's premier airport, certainly for the plannable future. Its status as a major international airport has recently been given an important boost with introduction into commercial service of Concorde, the world's first supersonic passenger aircraft. British Airways twice weekly service to Bahrain will be expanded to include regular flights across the Atlantic to Washington. But Heathrow is not the UK's only airport. Until the recent recession in air travel the regional airports had been steadily increasing the volume of traffic they handle. It is possible that the 1980s may see a small number of them emerging as substantial international airports in their own right, with a range of services to foreign destinations at acceptable frequencies. Increasingly the Government's thinking on national airport strategy is taking this regional dimension into account, following some admirable pioneering studies carried out for us by the Civil Aviation Authority. This is a subject where there is much to be learned by the pooling of knowledge from other countries.

In the London area, Gatwick is currently in the course of a major expansion programme which will take its capacity up to 16 million passengers annually. When this expansion is completed in 1978 it will be necessary for the balance and mix of traffic between Heathrow and Gatwick to change in order to obtain the best use of available facilities, while at the same time causing minimum disruption to airline operations. I am sure that this problem of allocating traffic be-

tween two or more airports serving the same city or region will become more widespread in the future and is one worthy of consideration by conferences such as this.

Within airports, the problem of providing extra capacity has changed noticeably in the last few years. In particular, with larger aircraft it has become technically possible to achieve much higher passenger throughputs without the need for additional runways. For example, the London area consultation document examines the possibilities for handling 38 million, or even 53 million passengers a year at Heathrow and 25 million at Gatwick without the need for any additional runways. Such possibilities would involve solving problems of designing compact and efficient terminals and related facilities at airports which were originally laid out for much lower levels of traffic. At Heathrow the island site in the central area already copes with a greater number of aircraft movements in a smaller area than any other major international airport. It is a tribute to the skill of the British Airports Authority and their staff that they are able to plan to raise the capacity of the central area by a half over the next few years. Indeed over the last 10 years the Authority has acquired great expertise in making effective use of available space, in maintaining services while carrying out major improvements and expansion, while at the same time running their enterprise at a profit. Abilities and experience in these fields will I am sure be in demand around the world in the years to come and I expect to see the British Airports Authority giving an increasing amount of advice and assistance.

I would like to say a few words about one vital aspect of airport planning and operation - and that is security. Present day terminals were designed when there was much less need for security than now: it is vital that future planning recognizes the need for it. It is also vital that there should be close co-operation between governments and their security forces, airlines, airport authorities and all others who use and work in airports. The Government welcomes the increasing number of accessions to the Tokyo, Hague and Montreal aviation security conventions.

This conference is being held at a time of ever growing awareness of change - changes in technology, changes in economic circumstances, and may I add changes in attitudes. But this great industry of aviation - and I include those who run the airports, the airlines, the aircraft and equipment manufacturers, the travel industry and tour operators - is in the van of change. It is itself one of the greatest innovators of all time and one which is having an enormous influence on the way of life and outlook of peoples throughout the world. That is why I expect, and find, this conference addressing itself not to fears of uncertainty but to the challenge which changes offer. This conference, the fifth in the series, will follow the high standards of previous years. I feel sure that the many excellent papers which are being presented, and the high level of the forthcoming discussions will provide a first rate contribution. It is with full confidence that I wish your conference great success.

1. The new economic environment and its effect on air transport

K. Hammarskjold
Director General, International Air Transport Association

External economic and other factors are forcing air carriers to look more closely at traditional operating philosophies. The paper outlines the effect of recent worldwide recession on airlines and airports, and urges closer co-operation for restoring growth.

It is a pleasure to be with you today to explore some aspects of our common new economic environment and its effects on air transport. Economic changes have in recent years not only been the preoccupation of specialists, but also of the man-in-the-street, and it is therefore timely that as partners in the provision of the public service air transport system, airports and airlines take stock of the common pressures which are now confronting them. This is such an opportunity.

I believe that the central characteristic of today's economic situation is the rapid pace of change in all areas. From the end of the Second World War to the late sixties, economic development occurred in an evolutionary fashion. Broadly speaking, during this period strong economic expansion in some industrialised nations generally offset cyclical downswings in the economies of others. We had become used to steady expansion, controlled inflation, relatively stable monetary exchange rates and a predictable business cycle. In these circumstances, Keynsian principles provided a familiar and accepted tool for the management of the principal economies of the world.

All this changed in the seventies when sustained growth abruptly turned into severe recessions. The 'swings and roundabouts' pattern of national economic activity gave way to the massive parallel swings of interdependent economies. Naturally, the risks are greater, the impact is more pronounced and, instead of evolution, we have what is seemingly a form of revolution: simultaneous inflation and recession - 'stagflation' as it is popularly known - high unemployment and wild currency gyrations all occurring at the same time. And the old domestic demand management principles don't seem to work.

It is these developments and their impact on air transport - and impact they most assuredly do - that I want to consider today. I should also like to offer some thoughts on the future outlook.

For the purposes of comparison, let us look briefly at the pre-1970 evolutionary period of economic development.

The economic climate of the sixties offered enormous promise for air transport development. It was a decade of almost uninterrupted strong economic growth, moderate inflation and comparatively stable exchange rates in most regions. Consumer income increased regularly and international trade and travel showed substantial gains. The introduction of jet equipment at the beginning of the period itself revolutionised the economics of air transport pushing up average speeds from three hundred to five hundred miles per hour, doubling capacity per aircraft and pushing down unit operating costs at current prices by twenty percent from 1963 to 1969. This cost reduction and improved productivity was a feature of the sixties and provided an incentive for the carriers to introduce a wide variety of lower yielding promotional fares.

It has been estimated that the average scheduled air fare throughout the world decreased by almost nine percent in current dollars between 1960 and 1970. In terms of 1960 constant dollars the decline was in the order of thirty to forty percent. In markets such as the North Atlantic and the Pacific the reduction was even greater. Total world tonne kilometres performed by the scheduled airlines increased approximately fourfold during the decade. Additional aircraft capacity was added on existing routes, more routes were opened and the birth of new nations meant new carriers and new destinations. Meanwhile, airports were improved and expanded to handle the increased passenger and cargo flows.

By the mid-sixties the airlines' future looked assured - booming world economies, widebodied jets on the horizon, seemingly endless growth forecasts in the area of fifteen to twenty percent per annum for passengers and cargo and the so-called mass travel market waiting to be served. Moreover, for the first time in their comparatively brief history, the airlines were beginning to produce adequate financial returns. In 1966 they had attained a modest but promising profit equal to six percent of revenue - a fact not unnoticed in the stock market.

Yet with the benefit of hindsight we can now see how easily this euphoric bubble was to burst. 1966 was the peak profitability year for the air transport industry. In the last sixties the first signs of creeping inflation had begun to emerge, pressures against continued growth in the form of commodity scarcities and rising prices could be discerned. On top of this, commitments to high capacity aircraft severely strained carrier finances, the aircraft themselves failed in their early years to produce the promised cost reductions and they helped induce what has now become our bête-noire - overcapacity on certain routes. The mass travel market certainly materialised, but with it came unbridled and wasteful competition between scheduled and schedulised charter carriers which resulted in undercutting of agreed tariffs, yield dilution and growth without profit.

Nor can I over-emphasise the impact of this latter development on air transport economics. In a recent speech I expressed the view that: "while world economic recovery will clearly help to restimulate travel demand and prop the sagging finances of air carriers, on its own it will not produce a healthy air transport system. For that we need a return to regulatory sanity". I would therefore be remiss if I failed to draw attention to the effect of the breakdown which has occurred in the air transport regulatory framework during the past decade. This framework was established by governments in the mid-1940s at Chicago and Bermuda to provide some equilibrium between market entry, pricing and capacity growth on international air transport routes.

These rules, which worked efficiently in the interest of consumer and carriers for twenty years, began to be eroded in the mid-sixties. Market entry is no longer strictly controlled due to the mushrooming of schedulised charter operations outside the Chicago/Bermuda system, and the proliferation of unregulated indirect air carriers. This, in turn, has nullified the effectiveness of the pricing mechanism as a growing portion of the market has moved outside the government-supported conference machinery. Meanwhile, and not the least as a result of this partial regulation, capacity has expanded out of phase with traffic demand spurred by the perhaps too rapid introduction of wide-bodied aircraft and the traffic slump of recent years. This process has led to a breakdown of the system and virtually all carriers, scheduled and schedulised charter, are operating close to or below the bottom line.

And this was the state of the air transport industry at the end of what I call the evolutionary phase of economic development. Air

carriers were no longer in the pioneering game, they were no longer the high flyers of the stock market. They were fighting for economic survival.

And then came the seventies and our new environment of economic revolution. The extraordinary world-wide inflation, the oil price explosion which both compounded that inflation and contributed to the worst economic recession of post-war years, and the wild currency gyrations which followed the breakdown of the Bretton Woods monetary regime. This highly volatile economic climate which has slowed down all commerce has had a particularly adverse effect on air transport.

Inflation has forced up transport and tourism costs while, at the same time, reducing consumer purchasing power and sentiment. Consumer price increases in the twenty-four OECD countries - the major air traffic generators - were up 10.6 percent in 1975, more than triple the average 1960-70 rates. As you well know, in some countries - and most particularly the developing nations who can least afford it - the inflation rate has been in excess of 20 percent. Despite some fall-off from the 1974 peak, many OECD countries continue to experience double digit rates of inflation in 1976. Recession in 1974 and 1975 has meant increased private savings, reduced trade and reduced travel demand. In 1975 real GNP in western industrialised countries as a whole declined by 2 percent and unemployment reached record post-war levels. Figures for the United States show this unemployment is still above 7 percent, despite the fact that the economic recovery is well under way in that country.

The currency gyrations of the seventies have played havoc with international pricing structures, dismembering painstakingly negotiated fares and rates agreements, drastically changing transportation and ground costs and causing uncertainty in consumer decision making. In the past year we have continued to witness wide swings in major currency exchange rates, and the recent IMF Jamaica agreements have now formalised floating.

The effect on air transport of this new economic environment has simply been to knock another nail into the financial coffin of many carriers - scheduled and schedulised charter.

It is hardly a secret that many air carriers have incurred very substantial financial losses in recent years. Throughout the seventies, return on air carrier investment has declined steadily as operating results have hovered around the break-even point only. 1975 produced one of the worst overall air carrier financial results in the history of the industry. To take only one example, operating revenues for international services of IATA carriers were some 0.3 percent below operating costs, let alone providing for any return on investment. The worst problem is on the so-called blue ribbon North Atlantic. With an earnings deficiency on required investment in the order of Two thousand million dollars over the past five years, this rates as one of the great all-time loss leaders for any industry. I don't want to give the impression that this financial problem exists only for IATA carriers. It is common to virtually every airline operating in international markets.

As you know, cost pressures have been a serious concern for air carriers since 1969 when the habitually declining cost trend began to reverse. Costs became the major preoccupation following the massive fuel price escalation which forced up unit costs of IATA carriers by 23 percent in 1974. Since that time, fuel prices have stabilised somewhat, but labour, capital, environmental costs, and of course - as I can scarcely fail to add to this gathering - airport charges continue their upward spiral.

I well recognise that airlines have no monopoly on cost escalations. Airports have also suffered in recent years from mounting construction and operational costs coincident with increasing labour and interest charges. Unfortunately, the resultant increases in airport charges have been at a far higher rate than hitherto experienced, and at a time when the rest of the air transport industry has been suffering from recession. Indeed, user charges for IATA carriers have increased nearly five-fold during the past decade.

In the United Kingdom for example, the Government has set a target for the British Airports Authority of 15.5 percent return on net assets, a return which is readily achievable because to a large degree carriers are captive customers. Yet, as I have indicated earlier, rates of return of this nature are completely unheard of for the vast majority of international air carriers. I might add that this target does not exist for British roads, British rail and British ports and harbours.

Similarly, the Eurocontrol programme for accelerated cost recovery for en-route facilities has been a marked feature of airline cost increases since 1971. For example, the fifty million dollars paid in charges in 1974 was simply increased by some two hundred percent for the present year by ministerial decision. Can you imagine the public reaction to an IATA Traffic Conference fare proposal along similar lines? What makes matters worse is that many of the countries participating in this programme are acting in direct conflict with international charging policies which they themselves have supported in ICAO as recently as 1974, and which air carriers have therefore taken into account in their own planning.

The situation becomes more difficult to comprehend when one looks at the total system - for example in Europe where governments either own or financially control the airports, the en-route facilities and the airlines. Surely it is time for some form of constructive policy to be developed which adequately balances the interests of all three components, rather than as the expression goes "taking from Peter simply in order to pay Paul". Such policies are even more urgently needed at a time when Peter is lingering on the verge of bankruptcy.

In fact, I go a stage further and suggest that provision of the necessary infrastructure should be considered as the government contribution to the public service of air transport. The economic and social benefits of civil aviation are well-known and the infrastructure is no less worthy of government support than its surface counterpart, which is already getting such support on a massive scale.

In the face of this cost escalation air transport, like other industries, has had no alternative but to increase prices. Carriers have nevertheless been reluctant to take such action in recent years when traffic growth has been slight, thereby risking the possible further depression of the market. Even where governments have been asked to approve essential tariff adjustments there has been a significant time lag between agreement and implementation. Thus, while fares have risen, the increase has still been insufficient to cover corresponding rises in cost.

Just to compound matters, our traditional traffic growth patterns have also been changed by the economic environment. The rate of growth on most routes has declined during the past two year period. 1975 ICAO figures show a 2 percent increase in scheduled passenger kilometres, compared to an annual average of 13 percent during the 1960s. This overall figure again masks the real weakness which is the North Atlantic, where scheduled passengers actually declined by some 6 percent and cargo tonnes by some 12 percent in 1975. The message is clear: the era of double-digit traffic growth is behind us on most routes. We must plan our equipment acquisition and infrastructure development on this new basis.

Regrettably, one cannot dismiss the impact of a decade of double-digit capacity growth so easily. We already have the equipment and infrastructure based on the traffic growth forecasts of our evolutionary economic phase. During the sixties, unutilised aircraft capacity expanded more than five times, that is at an annual average rate of over 18 percent. Recognising the consequences of this development in the early seventies, air carriers have been taking measures within their control to adjust their capacity to the changing traffic patterns.

Between 1970 and 1974 total traffic of the world's airlines increased at 8.6 percent per annum, while capacity grew at 7.2 percent.

This control on capacity build-up is a positive development, but it makes little impact on the existing excess. Regrettably, the airlines are prevented from effectively combatting that excess because of traditional opposition in certain quarters in the United States to carrier co-operative arrangements such as pooling capacity agreements and scheduling agreements which would allow seat supply to be more suitably tailored to demand. I am hopeful that, in the not too distant future, such views will be reconsidered in the light of the obvious public benefit derived from such arrangements. I simply mean the fact that higher load factors must ultimately result and these will be reflected in prices to the consumer.

So there you have the contemporary air transport economic situation. Financial results are unacceptable. Revenues are inadequate to cover costs, traffic growth has slowed significantly, overcapacity still exists on many routes.

But if I sound pessimistic about the present, let me hasten to say I am cautiously optimistic about our future outlook. For the first time in many years, our regulatory prospects seem somewhat brighter. Key governments are now in the process of intensive re-examination of the post-war rules, prompted, if you like, by the financial situation of air carriers in the new economic environment. Hopefully, despite all the talk and flirtation with deregulation, commonsense will prevail - at least in the international field - and we will see rational reregulation. All carriers will be brought within the same government policy - some prefer to call it regulatory - system, artificially discriminating devices to protect one type or another will be eliminated and some balance will be restored between capacity and market need. I believe these actions will be taken in the not-too-distant future - I do not see how anyone involved in this industry, and that includes the politicians and regulators, can justify the continuing waste of excess capacity in today's economic environment.

At the same time, I am hopeful that the worst of the adverse economic trends are behind us and that the industry will capitalise on this fact. The world-wide general economic outlook is more favourable at this moment than at any time during the past two years. The major countries seem to be regaining some control over inflation, and there are clear signs that a broad-based recovery has begun. The critical US economy is expected to grow by some 6 percent this year and disposable income is forecast to increase by 5 percent. Despite predictions of a slackening in 1977, most forecasters still see a healthy growth in the years ahead.

The recovery in Japan and many European countries is proceeding more slowly than in the United States, but there are hopes that the expansion will be sustained longer. Thus, for the balance of this decade, we can anticipate moderate economic growth in the industrialised nations as a group somewhere between 3 and 4 percent, and inflation rates remaining comparatively high, but more stable than in recent years.

In these circumstances, we look forward to improving consumer confidence and with it increased air passenger traffic growth - but at levels which are more directly aligned to overall GNP development than in the past. We forecast growth in total scheduled international passenger traffic in the order of 7 to 8 percent per year through 1981. We also foresee some shift in global travel patterns during the next five years. Developing routes such as the mid and south Atlantic, or Europe to the Middle East, will have a higher than average rate of growth and this will be counter-balanced by lower growth rates in more mature markets, such as intra-Europe and the North Atlantic.

These changing trends are of course vitally important to airport planners, so let me quickly add a caveat. Forecasting is an inexact science and even the best projections can be rendered meaningless overnight by, for example, political developments. Undoubtedly the actions of the OPEC nations in 1973 overturned virtually every economic forecast in existence, including the prediction for seemingly limitless air transport growth of 15 to 20 percent per annum. I believe that we must all approach long-term planning based on such forecasts with a degree of caution. We must minimise commitments to expensive projects to ensure that our common resources achieve maximum utilisation. This is as important in respect of airport facilities as it is to aircraft themselves. To cope with accelerated economic change, I believe that air carriers, airport authorities, manufacturers, tourism authorities and government departments must strive to improve and co-ordinate their forecasts. Major problems will occur if any one party goes out on a limb with unco-ordinated development plans involving high capital expenditure. We must face up to the fact that this capital may just not be available in the future to anyone - and I say this with the trepidation of a man who has recently seen a manufacturer's forecast which stated that some 46 billion dollars would be required for new aircraft during the next decade. This from an industry that is not only burdened with over-capacity but is unable to even cover its operating costs in many cases.

Fortunately, the air carriers and the airport authorities at the national and international level have been involved for many years in co-operative programmes which include traffic forecasting at international airports. I believe that these programmes, which should be intensified, form a solid base for co-ordinated airport planning and development in the years ahead. We are therefore in a good position to respond jointly to our chang-ing economic environment, and quickly to ad-just our planning.

Such co-operation and flexibility is essen-tial if we are effectively to manage our resources in today's 'revolutionary' economic environment. Airports, manufacturers, tourism authorities and airlines - we are all comple-mentary pieces of the public service air trans-port system. If that system is to function efficiently, we have to operate in co-ordina-tion and with a full understanding of each other's problems - planning, financing and operating. I hope that by outlining some of the economic problems facing air transport today, I have contributed to this essential co-operative process.

Vote of thanks

H. E. Marking
Deputy Chairman and Managing Director, British Airways

Mr Hammarskjold has given us an admirable run down on the 'before' and 'after' situation of the airline industry in the world - before and after the watershed of the oil crisis.

The 'before' situation was one of cost production, improving productivity and lower fares. He also put into the before situation the time of the breakdown of international regulatory processes, and spoke of the blurring between scheduled services and schedulized charter services. That is certainly something which has been intensified since then, and I think there is a great need now for a rethink. Something has to be done if the airline industry of the world is not to remain forever in the economic doldrums in which it now finds itself.

Rationalization of services between carriers and between scheduled and what Mr Hammarskjold calls 'schedulized charter carriers', is essential I believe if there is not to be wasteful and unprofitable duplication of services. At the moment there are hundreds of thousands of empty seats flying around the world, and all of them money thrown down the drain, for there is no more perishable product than an aircraft seat Once the aircraft door is closed, the sale is gone forever. The number of empty seats must be reduced if the airlines of the world are to make reasonable financial returns and reasonable profits, and so enable cheaper fares to be offered to the public. All have the same objective whether in the scheduled service or the charter service. All want to offer the public a good deal and, at the same time, keep out of the bankruptcy court. But cheaper fares are only possible with a sound economic basis on which to run the businesses.

Mr Hammarskjold mentioned airport charges, and I could scarcely forbear to cheer him. When an Airport Authority tells me that it is making a profit of £X million, I can only say it is disgraceful that it is not £2X million which could easily be done by charging the captive users twice as much, for all profit comes out of the users. There is no other source of revenue. I do not blame the British Airports Authority in this case, because I think they have been set an unreasonably high target by Her Majesty's Government. At the same time I do not blame the Minister for the target because it was set many years ago. But where an industry is operating in an entirely captive market, I think it is unreasonable to expect them to make returns of this sort which can only come from the users, namely, the airlines who pay landing fees, and the other concessionaires who have work on the airport.

I would not even exclude from my remarks the Civil Aviation Authority. This has been ordered to be self-supporting by 1977-78. I am not in a position to say that the CAA charges are too high. But where I do make a point about the Civil Aviation Authority's charges is that when the charges are in respect of duties which are for the benefit of airlines, then the airlines should pay. But when the charges are part of the regulatory processes imposed by the State, then the State should bear the cost of that work. That is a distinction which has not been made by government in requiring the CAA to be self-supporting. I think that is something that ought to be looked at.

Many years ago, Mr C. R. Smith, who was then Chairman of American Airlines, said that the airlines of the world live on growth; growth has a wonderful way of covering up mistakes, and when there is no growth all the things done badly stand out like a sore thumb. Airlines are in that position now of very small growth, and all the mistakes are standing out.

Mr Hammarskjold remarked that the years before the oil crisis were years of increasing productivity. We have to get back to increasing the productivity of airlines. Indeed, our plan in British Airways over the next five years is to increase staff productivity by 55%. It is a hard and a demanding target. It certainly will not be easy to achieve, and can only be achieved by co-operation of the work force and trade unions. But I believe there is a reasonable chance of doing it.

'Consultation' was the watchword on which Mr Hammarskjold finished his remarks. I believe that consultation between the UK Government and BA is good, though I am sure it is capable of a great deal of improvement. But the pattern that is set in the UK is not necessarily that which happens elsewhere, and all too often, even in this country, capital is spent which afterwards is found not to have been as well spent as it ought to have been. There must be consultation between all interested parties and IATA, the body which represents the scheduled airlines of the world.

Mr Hammarskjold thought we could look forward to the future with cautious optimism. I share that view. There will not be boom times ahead, but I think we are beginning to draw out of the period of heavy loss. I hope that those who build and operate airports can help the operators in offering as economic a service as possible.

2. Airport planning in the UK: past, present and future

The Rt Hon. Lord Boyd Carpenter
Chairman, Civil Aviation Authority, London

The paper traces the development of post-war airport policy from the period when society and aviation were in general accord, through the period when concepts of the environmental airport became popular, to the needs, and most practical method of dealing with them of today and the next two decades.

Since the end of the Second World War one is aware of passing through two distinct eras in the development of aviation in the UK. One can also look forward with some certainty to the end of the second era and the dawn of a third. There will however be no consensus of agreement on the precise date at which the first era gave way to the second nor on the year in which the present, second era will give way to the third. A useful analogy might be the progression from day to night and then back to day. Before reaching the end of this paper I hope to demonstrate the more precise relevance of this simple analogy to the subject of this paper.

2. The first era was one of general accord between aircraft and airports upon the one hand and people and environment on the other. It was pre-eminently the age of the propeller-driven piston-engined aircraft. Whether this era extended until the end of the 1950s, and included the period of pre-eminence of the turbo-prop aircraft - in particular the Viscount - must remain in dispute. It is easy for most people to forget the public uproar over the decision in 1954 to develop Gatwick Airport. I remember it very well because I was Minister of Transport and Civil Aviation at the time, and was responsible for the decision. An old friend who lived near there never spoke to me again, and another, on being told I had flown over the area in a helicopter prior to taking the final decision expressed regret that he had missed the opportunity to shoot me down. At the same time there was a continual stream of protests from anti-noise groups around Heathrow. To many people at that time the high-pitched scream of the turbo-prop though different from the whine and roar of the jet, was just as unpopular. The golden age in which aviation lived in a state of amity with all its neighbours was relatively short-lived.

3. In other respects, the image of aviation was by no means unattractive. The typical airport was a rather modest affair and not the conglomeration of marble halls and multi-storey car parks to which we have now had to accustom ourselves. Airport terminals were still the traditional single storey building with doors back and front, one set opening on to the airport apron, others on to the car park. One could actually see the aircraft. Some of us may recall with nostalgic pleasure flying into Heathrow (North) and driving out of the airport gates in an incredibly few minutes - by current standards - after one's plane had come to rest.

4. In several other respects aviation was able to live happily with the rest of society. Civil aviation in that period had much in common with the Service flying of war-time days. Most if not all the civil aerodromes had served as bases for the RAF or USAF. A high proportion of civil aircrew looked, talked and dressed very much like the heroes of a few years before. A number of the civil aircraft in use were similar to, or closely derived from, military machines. In general, aviation was accepted by local communities as being a good employer and a useful support to local service industries and to commerce. Although major problems had already been encountered in the development of new and existing airports, for example Gatwick and Heathrow, the term Airport Planning, with its wider connotation, was as yet unknown.

5. Whether the Viscount - that most gentlemanly of aircraft - marked the final stages of the golden age of aviation, or the beginning of the second era is open to question; what is not in dispute is that with the introduction of the Boeing 707 in 1960, the golden age was clearly behind us. This period might be called the age of the low by-pass jet. Among the aircraft most closely associated with this period, in addition to the 707 were the DC-8, VC-10, the Trident, the Caravelle, and the BAC 1-11. From a British standpoint, this period was pre-eminently that of the Rolls-Royce Spey, an engine justifiably acclaimed for its efficiency and reliability and in course of time used in a multitude of aircraft throughout the world.

6. In many ways this was a period of spectacular aviation progress. There was a marked increase in flying speed, though not as dramatic then as the introduction of Concorde in our own time. From the operator's point of view the increase in speed produced a roughly equivalent increase in the number of miles an aircraft could fly within a given period, and substantially reduced aircraft amortization costs per aircraft mile. At the same time, much larger aircraft were coming into use producing substantial economies in both capital and operating cost per seat mile. The culmination of higher speeds and larger planes

enabled the cost of air travel to be substantially reduced, and triggered off the growth of a whole new market of leisure and holiday flying. The development of the inclusive Tour and the Affinity Group Charter enabled the industry to capitalize still further on the technical developments achieved earlier in the decade.

7. With traffic growing at around 15% per annum, it is perhaps not surprising that runway capacity began to come under pressure. With few exceptions, the system of runways released for civil use in the years following the end of the Second World War was adequate to meet civil needs for many years. A number of these runways had to be strengthened and lengthened; but up to the middle 1960s, the laying down of new runways was not a major issue. The rate of growth of traffic in the middle and late 1960s brought to an end this happy state of affairs in the UK. The question of a third London Airport became a major public issue.

8. To the general public, this second period of post-war aviation was pre-eminently that in which aircraft noise became a national, as distinct from a purely local issue. Engines such as the Spey, the Conway and the JT3D were strikingly more noisy than their predecessors. Furthermore the particular quality of noise made by the low by-pass jet was highly objectionable to many people. Moreover even when coming into land at relatively modest power-settings, the high-pitched whine of the compressor gave rise to widespread complaint. The use of reverse-thrust after touch-down was yet one more source of irritation.

9. Furthermore at a time when the new low by-pass jet engines were coming into increasing use, the rate of movement of aircraft during peak periods at a number of airports, including Heathrow, was such as to produce a continuous stream of over-flying aircraft at approximately $1\frac{1}{2}$ minute intervals for hours on end.

10. At the same time the 1960s saw the birth of public concern for the environment more generally although aviation remained the prime target. It was the accepted judgement of the day that the generation of aircraft then flying was unable to 'live with people' and should be banished as far as possible from the haunts of civilized man. Few people pursued this idea to the logical conclusion of proposing the closure of airports in built up areas such as Heathrow. But the idea was applied with full rigour in the consideration of new airports. It figured significantly in the long-drawn out consideration of Stansted for development as the third London Airport – first proposed in the report of the Interdepartmental Committee of 1964 and accepted with reservations as Government policy in the White Paper of 1967. It was largely if not entirely on environmental grounds that the Government later decided to have the whole matter re-examined by a

Commission under Mr Justice Roskill (as he then was). Environmental factors figured very significantly in the choice of the short-listed sites subsequently considered by the Roskill Commission, and they were an equally important element in the then Government's rejection of the Commission's recommendation and choice of a coastal site at Maplin, although as some of us thought and said at the time failing to appreciate that environmental objections to the necessary ground connections outweighed the alleged environmental advantages, to all save the Brent goose, of the site itself.

11. Before considering the implications of this widespread assumption that aviation was not compatible with civilised living, we might perhaps note other respects in which aviation was developing an image unlikely to endear it to the country at large. For better or worse the industry's advertising agencies hit upon the concept of what is now derisively termed the 'Jet Set' typified by the thrusting young executive in his crumpled light-weight suit and with his high blood pressure, surveying the world with a mixture of distaste and disdain, and the leisured if not necessarily idle rich flying in first-class cabins to equally expensive destinations. Happily, we now see rather less advertising of this kind. In two particular respects the concept of the Jet Set has been highly damaging. First of all, it has reinforced public suspicion that aviation is a pursuit of the relatively well-off, if not the positively rich. Paradoxical as it may sound at a time when the development of the Inclusive Tour and low-fare charter flight was bringing flying within the reach of millions of ordinary people, it was not uncommon to find aviation being attacked on grounds of social privilege and injustice.

12. There was secondly a substantial group of comfortably off people in the UK and in a number of other countries who were temperamentally unsympathetic towards aviation – who were more attracted by slow modes of transport than by fast; who placed an exceptionally high value on peace and quiet; who, without being passionately chauvinistic, looked askance at holidays abroad and particularly at those with minimal cultural content; whose attitudes tended to the conservative – with a small c – or in the modern idiom, 'square'. To this body of opinion aviation was something not to be encouraged, and if ways could be found by which it could be positively discouraged e.g. by failing to provide the necessary airports, then this was not a matter for regret.

13. One may now summarise the main features of the 1960s, in terms of their repercussions on airport planning. Firstly, they were years of very rapid growth of aviation, both in terms of passenger numbers, and in terms of aircraft movements. It was therefore very plausible to predict increasing pressure on existing runways, and the need for additional capacity. Secondly, aircraft noise levels

were high, and there was no firm evidence that aviation either could or would produce remedies quickly enough to be of relevance to the new airports under consideration. Furthermore, the anti aircraft-noise interest, which had so far been predominantly local in nature, now began to receive wide if sometimes eccentric support. Lastly, aviation was developing an image which rendered it highly unpopular with some sections of the population.

14. The most important outcome of these conflicting pressures was the concept of the 'environmental airport'. If it was accepted that aircraft both were and would remain unable to co-exist with people, and should be banished as far as possible from the haunts of civilised man, this was perhaps the only logical outcome. One should also note that the 'environmental airports' conceived at this time were generally large multi-runway developments. Given the rate of growth of air traffic in the 1960s, and the absence of firm grounds for predicting any levelling-off in the growth curve, it would have been short-sighted to look for new sites unable to accommodate at least two main runways. The terms of reference of the Roskill Commission specifically required a site suitable for four fully independent runways. The search for sites for large airports on this scale took place in many parts of the world. In North America, the most extensive effort to find a site suitable for a large environmental airport was of course at New York. Similar exercises took place, however, in Texas, in California, and across the border at Montreal. The search for a new airport at Tokyo was more traumatic. In Australia, investigations of a very similar nature were carried out to find a suitable site for the second Sydney airport.

15. The concept of the environmental airport has not been entirely without fruit, and many countries suffer from at least one airport of this kind. But generally speaking, the concept has failed to justify the facile optimism of its proponents. At London and New York, two of the major world centres of international aviation, it would be fair to say that those responsible for airport planning have now decisively rejected the concept. This is in vivid contrast with the enthusiasm with which the idea was espoused only a few years before. On examination, however, the grounds for the demise of the environmental airport are not hard to identify.

16. The most obvious explanation, namely the difficulty of finding suitable sites, is certainly too facile. It has not been impossible to find prospective airport sites in remote areas, where only a relatively few people would have been directly affected. In most if not all of the areas referred to above, it has been possible to draw up a short-list of possible sites causing minimal impact on the locally resident population. Moreover, there has been no difficulty in identifying sites of no marked recreational value, measured in terms

of the number of visitors attracted from neighbouring towns and cities.

17. Airport planners, hoping to locate new airports in areas of uninhabited and untouched natural wilderness were, however, rapidly disillusioned. No sooner were such prospective sites identified than a whole new set of environmental interests and protection-groups sprang to their defence. It was immediately asserted, contrary to the accepted wisdom of only a year or so before, that coastline, and particularly coastline reasonably accessible to large centres of population, was of supreme recreational value, and the most unsuitable place of all to consider siting an airport. Airport planners found themselves caught in a bewildering cross-fire between contradictory environmental factions. They had been forbidden to consider prospective airport sites within or near areas of significant population, either urban or rural; at the same time, they found equally if not greater environmental values being attached to wide areas of countryside and coastline, these values tending to increase in inverse proportion to the number of human beings found there. Perhaps the most extreme example of this type of environmental pressure is the action taken against the proposed third Los Angeles Airport at Palmdale - situated in a desert! It is perhaps not surprising that there was a measure of public support for the suggestion that it might be better to abandon the quest for new airports altogether.

18. The second weakness in the concept of the environmental airport was that it would in the nature of things have to be situated at some distance from its traffic catchment area. This necessitated the famous 'umbilical cord' between the airport and the centre of the city or conurbation it served. Clearly this would represent a major disadvantage to the air traveller, and serious difficulties were anticipated in persuading airlines to operate from such airports. Equally importantly however, the construction and use of the long road and/or rail transport links required would themselves be environmentally damaging. For example, the full operation of Maplin Airport, on the Thames Estuary and so far from central London would have been impossible without a new direct airport-only rail link, which, at the London end, would have had to run through densely populated areas, and further out through suburbs and countryside. In addition it was planned to construct a motorway which would have run from the airport as far as the outer suburbs of London. The prospect of continuing this motorway to its logical destination through the densely populated communities of London's East End was however too daunting for the planners even to contemplate and still more so, I would guess for the politicians national and local.

19. It is perhaps surprising that this dilemma arose so unexpectedly. A substantial proportion of the traffic at any major international airport comes from, or is heading to, the

centre of some metropolitan area. This is
particularly true of overseas business and
leisure travellers, but it is also true of many
local residents who, if they have to use public
transport to get to the airport, must travel
into the city centre, from their homes, before
they can proceed onwards by public transport
to the airport. Where airports are situated
close to the city centre, or at the edge of the
built-up area, these surface journeys are
relatively short, and many air travellers are
able to proceed directly to the airport, either
by private car or by public transport. These
journeys will therefore give rise to modest
demands for surface transport capacity, and a
correspondingly modest degree of noise nuisance.
By contrast, the environmental airport requires
much longer surface access journeys, and these
have frequently to be routed through the city
centre, where surface transport capacity is
likely to be under most serious pressure, and
where noise from road or rail transport is
likely to impinge on the maximum number of
human ears. The environmental airport, by
definition, directly imposes aircraft noise
on relatively few people - but at a cost of
imposing a considerably greater load on the
surface transport system, and of imposing
considerably more surface transport noise on to
neighbouring residents over many miles of town
and country. All this on top of great
inconvenience to the air traveller who is
compelled to undertake a long journey before
he can even get to his aircraft and it of
course deprives air travel of some of its
advantage, i.e. speed. It is fair to add that
there were some of us who foresaw these
objections from an early stage. Like Cassandra
we were not listened to.

20. A third and final problem of the environmental airport is that of labour requirements.
Airports situated in or close to existing
metropolitan areas normally have little difficulty
in recruiting an adequate labour force. In such
areas the ebb and flow of business activity will
usually enable an airport to build up its labour
force from the existing working population. If,
in addition, there are whole industries undergoing
long-term decline, then the growth of an airport
is an unmixed blessing. An environmental airport,
distant from any large town or city, cannot
recruit its labour force locally, nor can it
easily attract it away from the metropolitan
area itself. A new airport-city will have to be
created requiring much more land than the
airport itself, and the environmental
implications of which will often be as far-
reaching as those of the airport itself. Hence
the common phenomenon of an immediate rise in
land values in the vicinity of newly designated
airport sites. The implication may be therefore
of a major and irreversible change in the
character of a wide area of countryside or
coastline.

21. At first sight, it might seem to be an
unfortunate quirk of history that so many far-
reaching decisions on airport planning were
under consideration in many of the world's

leading centres of aviation at a time when
aircraft were generally held to be incompatible
with civilised residential living. It might
however be truer to say that it was the
presumption of incompatibility which largely
created the problems in airport planning so
widely encountered during this period. The
environmental airport was the apparent solution
to the problem of incompatibility. The concept
was not completely without fruit, and the
Aeroport de Paris was able to develop such an
airport at Roissy en France with few of the
serious disadvantages discussed above. But
more generally this solution to the airport
planning problem has proved unsatisfactory, not
only on the more conventional grounds of cost
and efficiency, but paradoxically as it has
undoubtedly appeared to many local anti-noise
interests, on wider environmental grounds than
they themselves were prepared to contemplate.
Fortunately, we in the U.K. in common with many
other countries, drew back before it was too
late from embracing the concept of the
environmental airport. There can surely be few
areas of human affairs in which such costly
mistakes are possible. Even the Channel tunnel
could hardly have been worse.

22. The second era of post-war aviation is of
course still with us, and may well last for up
to further decade. However the main features
of the succeeding era are already becoming
apparent and given the long time-span within
which airport planning has to be conducted, it
is to these characteristics that attention must
now be addressed. Three principal issues merit
discussion.

23. The first is the future rate of growth of
demand for air transport. Over the next year
or two, we may expect a pause in the growth of
activity, and it may be a year or more before
the peak traffic levels of 1973 are passed.
After that time, most experts appear to agree
that the annual growth rates of around 15%
experienced during the 1960s are unlikely to
re-appear. Nevertheless, I am not numbered
among those who consider that aviation will by
the end of the present decade have reached some
sort of equilibrium or ceiling level. As
people once again become better-off in real
terms, as they surely will, they will tend, as
in the past, to spend a higher proportion of
their income on holidays and travel generally,
of which aviation will continue to get an
increasing share. As in the past, technological
advances will continue to reduce total costs
per seat mile, although these advances may well
be less dramatic than those of the last 15
years, and may be off-set in part by factors
outside our control. Finally, we would expect
to see the further development of air fares and
types of service better matched to the needs of
the travelling public, and tapping potential
new markets in many different parts of the world.
Aviation has made tremendous progress in this
direction over the past decade; no one should
assume that we are nearing the end of the road.

24. After a short pause therefore, one would

expect the factors conducive to the growth of aviation to re-assert themselves. No one can be certain how powerful these forces will be. On our own current estimates, it seems unlikely that the long-term growth rate of passenger demand will return to the levels reached during the late 1960s and early 1970s. (In the non-scheduled field, the growth of traffic during this period was in part based on artificially low fares and tour prices - policies which have subsequently been drastically and painfully corrected.) A long-term growth rate within the range 7%-10% now appears more likely, modest perhaps by previous aviation standards, but one which all but a handful of other industries would regard with envy.

25. In the past, the need for new airports has been due to increasing pressure on runway capacity during peak periods. This is not to suggest that airport terminal and other ground-handling facilities are always indefinitely extendable. But in practice runways have proved to be the significant bottle-neck. With passenger demand traditionally increasing at some 15% per annum, and with the average number of seats per passenger aircraft increasing at around 5%-6% per annum, passenger Air Transport Movements tended to increase, over the years, by some 8%-10% per annum, to which had to be added any increase in all-cargo operations. If, as suggested above, the rate of growth of future passenger demand may fall below 10% per annum, this has important implications for runway capacity. Admittedly, the more modest predicted increase in passenger demand will tend to reduce the willingness and ability of airlines to re-equip with larger aircraft, and this in turn may reduce the effort devoted to the design and development of new generations of aircraft. However, a number of other factors seem likely, over the next five-ten years, to increase the average number of passengers per aircraft handled at UK airports. Firstly international air traffic is forecast to increase much more rapidly than domestic. Generally speaking, aircraft on international services are larger than those on domestic sectors. Secondly, a high proportion of the predicted future growth of demand is in the leisure rather than the business sector. A proportion of this traffic will be carried in charter aircraft at load-factors of some 85%. At the same time that proportion of leisure traffic which is carried on scheduled flights, on various types of discounted fare, and under part-charter arrangements, will raise scheduled service load factors. Irrespective therefore of whether the additional leisure traffic flies on charter or scheduled flights, one would expect it to be carried at the relatively high load factor implied by the relatively low level of the fares charged. Moreover, the long-haul market appears likely to be more buoyant than the short-haul, a further factor conducive to the acquisition by airlines of relatively large aircraft. Finally, airlines are likely to be under considerable pressure during the next few years, on grounds both of fuel economy and of noise, to accelerate the retirement of their older aircraft from main-line service. Despite, therefore, the problems facing the industry in the short term, it appears very unlikely that the future increase in average passengers per plane will fall below 5% per annum. On these assumptions, much the greater part of the increase in passenger demand will be met by an increase in average passenger loads per aircrafts. The resulting increase in passenger Air Transport Movements may therefore be small indeed, possibly around $2\frac{1}{2}$% per annum.

26. No great powers of imagination are required to appreciate the significance of the situation in which the rate of increase of passenger demand comes within striking distance of the rate of increase in the average number of passengers per plane. At the very least it materially moderates the increasing pressure on existing runways and the ensuing need for additional runway capacity. Furthermore, it needs no more than the most rudimentary arithmetic to deduce that if the rate of increase in average passenger loads can be raised to equality with the rate of increase in passenger demand, then (other things being equal) the effective capacity of existing runways becomes, for a short time ahead, adequate until load factors reach their highest practical level. (A number of problems arise under the ceteris-paribus assumption - including the increased use of all cargo aircraft, and the effect on runway capacity of turbulent wake created by these large aircraft resulting in larger separation standards at landing and take-off. While these problems are not unimportant they do not affect the basic principle of the above argument.) If, at the same time, there are no physical constraints on the extension of passenger terminals and other passenger and freight handling facilities, nor on the development of improved road and/or rail access to the terminal area, it follows that the capacity of the airports in question has a very considerable, in not an indefinite, degree of stretch, particularly if aircraft continue to get bigger. This situation, in which investment in new larger aircraft effectively removes the need for investment in new airports, might be described, for obvious reasons, as the 'Boeing Equilibrium'.

27. Some may be inclined to dismiss this idea as far-fetched - though one may doubt whether they include our friends in Seattle! But perhaps it should not be completely over-looked. From time-to-time one hears it asserted by one of the many self-styled experts in airport planning - more in anger than in sorrow - that the big metropolitan areas of the world cannot accept any new major civil airports. Like it or not, aviation must make do with what it already has. If, however, there is any truth in the idea that at least some of our airports may not be very far from the state of equilibrium in aircraft movements analysed above, the threat to have to make the best of the airports we have might turn out to be, not perhaps an entirely empty one, but very much less daunting than some might expect.

This argument cannot of course be used to justify the decision taken a short while ago voluntarily to abandon the possibility of building the second runway at Gatwick Airport for which the original plans made such careful provision. This is not the place to discuss at length the 'little local difficulties' of airport planning in the London area. Suffice it to say however that a situation in which scheduled operations in the world's most important centre of international aviation have to be contained within the capacity of three independent runways (if one disregards Stansted for this purpose) for the indefinite future, is one which we in the UK are likely to regret. Moreover to seek to build up traffic to the levels at which current investment at Gatwick is aimed on the basis of a one runway airport would appear to involve risks which no one else appears to be prepared to face anywhere in the world.

28. Before summarising the main features of the third age of post-war aviation, some reference must be made to the field of aircraft noise. There is no need to discuss the matter in detail. There is now firm evidence that by about 1985 the aircraft using large international airports will, on average, be no more than half as noisy as those now flying, and that the noisiest types, such as the early Boeing 707s, the VC 10s, and the Tridents, will have been withdrawn from front-line service. By 1990 further advances can be expected. The full meaning of these developments is well brought out in the consultation document on London Airports published a few months ago by Her Majesty's Government, from which the following data are extracted. The significance of this material does not lie in the particular level of traffic postulated, nor in the distribution of the traffic between the three London Airports in question (both of which must at this moment remain uncertain) but in the dramatic contrast between the growth of traffic and the decimation of the number of resident population exposed to serious aircraft noise.

Postulated Passenger Traffic Levels and
Population Exposed to Noise Above the 35 NNI
Level at British Airport Authority Airports in
the London Area

	1974 (actual)	1980	1985	1990
Postulated passenger traffic (million)	26	39	58	79
Population resident within the 35 NNI contour (million)	2.06	1.55	0.99	0.23

The striking feature of this data is that over a period when total passenger traffic at the airports in question might increase three-fold, the number of people living within the 35 NNI contours would decline by nearly 90%. It should be noted that these estimates assume the operation of super-sonic transport aircraft, and also assume no specific Government measures to assist the hush-kitting or retirement of existing noisy aircraft. That is to say, they reflect what might reasonably be expected to follow from the independent initiative and efforts of the aviation industry itself.

29. It is perhaps too early to predict that, by the latter part of the 1980s, the problem of aircraft noise around London's major airports will have been reduced to the proportions experienced during the first Post-War era of aviation. (As noise contouring had not then been invented, we have no means of finding out.) But clearly the seriousness of the problem will have very materially diminished, despite a substantial growth in air traffic. Nevertheless, it does not seem unreasonable to predict that by the late 1980s, air travel may have become accepted as an integral part of civilised life, along with the other modes of mass transport. There is indeed in both absolute and relative terms an increasing need for steps to quieten heavy road traffic, and to reduce its pollution of the atmosphere.

30. If the above analysis is valid, it helps to resolve the question raised in paragraph 17 above, namely whether airports are more compatible with urban or with rural environments. A number of grounds clearly favour the urban location. The first is the level of background noise. It is generally agreed that aircraft noise, in common with other noise sources, becomes a nuisance insofar as it stands out above the background noise level. This is particularly apparent where aircraft flight paths traverse heavily industrialized areas, with major rail or road arteries. Even without any aircraft noise, the environment in many of those areas would be significantly affected by transport and other industrial noise. This phenomenon does not have to be explained to many people who work in city centres, but live in the suburbs or the neighbouring countryside. According to the measures of aircraft noise in general use, such as our own Noise and Number Index, aircraft noise levels are frequently higher at one's place of work than at one's residence. One's subjective measurement of aircraft noise, on the other hand, quite often reverses this comparison, aircraft noise at one's place of work being lost in the roar of city traffic.

Secondly quite apart from the question of back-ground noise, it seems reasonable to assume that aircraft noise is more intrusive in a rural area than in towns and cities where mechanical noises of many kinds have become an accepted feature of the environment. For example, a moderately high level of background traffic noise is not considered inappropriate to high-class residential areas in the West End of London. A similar level of traffic noise, would, on the other hand, be completely inappropriate to a manor house or a cottage in the depths of the country. Not surprisingly, aviation has more in common with other industries, and particularly with transport industries, than with rural pursuits.

The above considerations will become all the more powerful when aircraft noise, both in volume and in quality, is reduced to such an extent that it merges naturally into the background of our urban areas.

In airport planning terms, the main features of the third age of Post-War aviation can be very briefly listed.

(a) A considerable expansion of passenger throughput at existing airports, met largely for some years by an increase in the average number of passengers per plane, and to a much lesser extent by more aircraft movements

(b) The very substantial reduction in aircraft noise around existing major airports, which will go far to remove environmental objections to the above indicated growth of passenger throughput.

(c) The rejection of large new 'environmental airports', as being both undesirable on more broadly defined environmental grounds, and in the light of (a) and (b) above, unnecessary.

(d) Serious problems in developing the terminal capacity of existing airports to match the 'stretch' in the effective (passenger) capacity of the runways.

(ε) Equally serious problems in channeling peak flows of traffic into and out of existing airports, and the consequent value of, if not an outright need for, rail access of a high standard.

31. If these prophesie contain any element of truth at all, the third era of Post-War aviation is unlikely to represent the restoration of any past Golden Age, if such ever existed! A new set of problems will confront us. These problems have an air of reality which has been lacking among the problems posed to airport planners during the present, second era. During this latter period those engaged in airport planning have often felt that they were being asked to find answers to problems defined in such a way as to be insoluble. To return to the analogy with which this paper began, one would hope that the new era would see an end to the night of gloom through which airport planners seem to have been groping their way for so long.

To the airport planner it is of course self-evident that it will be against the parameters of the third era rather than those of the present, second era, against which his efforts will finally be judged. I only wish the same

could be said about all those who participate in the grand public debate on airport policy. Many including substantial numbers of the planning profession, seem almost unaware that the 1960s are no longer with us. For example, the imposition of increasingly strict night curfews on aircraft movements at Heathrow and Gatwick may possibly have made sense in the past, and, if restricted to the noisy types of aircraft typical of that period, can still be argued for despite their economic cost. What must cause concern is restrictions applied indiscriminately to noisy aircraft and quiet alike, and the common assumption, which governments have done little or nothing to refute, that night curfews will become more restrictive during future years just when aircraft are becoming increasingly quiet. Very little attention seems to be given to the fact that the lifting of night curfews for quiet aircraft would give airlines an incentive to speed up the replacement of noisy aircraft by quiet ones, and so reduce noise by day.

As a second example one might instance the noisy local opposition to the use of Stansted as a civil airport. No doubt during the 1960s, when Stansted was being considered as the site for a major two-runway international airport, fulfilling a parallel role to those of Heathrow and Gatwick, such opposition would have been entirely natural, and understandable. However, there can be no such justification for resurrecting the arguments of the mid-1960s against the vastly different nature and scale of development proposed by the British Airports Authority for Stansted in the 1980s. And indeed in the interests of the good employment which development of an airport brings, my Authority has from time to time had requests for help in building up traffic there!

Finally, if anything at all has been learned from Cublington and Maplin, it is that airports, like most other industries, are urban rather than rural phenonema, and find their place more naturally on the outskirts of our towns and cities than in the untouched countryside. Yet despite this, considerable weight is placed both in airport planning and in the development of what we in the UK paradoxically call Minimum Noise Routes, on the precise number of people residing within pre-determined noise contours. (For the information of our guests from overseas. Minimum Noise Routes are planned to overfly quiet places such as - Cublington and Maplin!) Among future problems, that of ridding ourselves of the unfortunate inheritance of the second era of Post-War aviation is by no means the least.

3. Germany

Prof.Dr.- Ing. W.Treibel
Director, German Airports Association

Airports in the Federal Republic of Germany are organized as private companies, and there is no overall national airport planning authority. The German Airports Association acts in an advisory
capacity. The paper analyses the development of this multi-central network, and the necessary advance
planning proposed to deal with future increases of traffic, especially international.

FORM OF ORGANISATION OF THE AIRPORTS IN THE
FEDERAL REPUBLIC OF GERMANY AND BERLIN (WEST)
1.   Compared with Great Britain and Canada,
the international airports in the Federal
Republic of Germany are, since more than
50 years, private stock companies (AG) or private
companies with limited liability (GmbH). That
means that the Federal Republic of Germany has
no national airport planning authority. The
federal government is competent for the international representation including the grant of
traffic rights, the air traffic control and air
traffic security and the implementation of all
kinds of aviation laws and rules, including
specifications for airport design and operation.
The licence for planning, construction and
operation of airports is, however, within the
competence of the states, in Germany called
"Länder". This splitted competence of federal
government and 11 states has disadvantages and
advantages.

2.   The German Airports Association (ADV)
- members of which are all international airports and 30 regional airfields - advises,
according to its articles, federal government
and states, as to "the preparation and execution
of all laws and other official regulations concerning the common interests of its members".
ADV outlines airport planning requirements by
forecasting demand and associated investment
for the airports in periods of five years each.
The results are published, as for example in
"The traffic development, expansion planning
and investment demand of the German airports
up to 1977", and their impact on local planning
activities and political decisions must not be
underestimated. (fig. 1)

3.   The liberal form of cooperation of the airports in the Federal Republic of Germany including Berlin (West) is fundamentally supported
through the consultative and coordinating
activity of six ADV expert committees. Members
of these committees are about 200 experts
of the airports and ADV's head office
together with representatives of the federal
government and the states. These are the

ADV expert committees "Law and Security",
"Economics", "Operation and Technics", "Planning
and Construction", "Traffic" and "Environment".
They serve for the exchange of experience and
mutual assent. The questions which are important
for the self-administration are coordinated in
a Special Committee comprising all directors of
the major international airports. The German
Airports Association does, however, not control
the business activity of its members.

4.   The form of organisation of the German
airports as stock or limited liability companies
has not been changed since decades. Today the
federal government is, together with states and
cities, a shareholder of the airports Berlin,
Frankfurt, Hamburg, Köln/Bonn and München. All
other international airports in the Federal
Republic of Germany have the respective state
and city as shareholders. On 30.6.1975 the share
capital of all international airports in the
Federal Republic of Germany and Berlin (West)
amounted to approx. DM 580 million. In terms
of money, the federal government holds a share
of 21 %, the states 50 % and the cities 29 %.
(fig. 2)

THE AIRPORT NETWORK IN THE FEDERAL REPUBLIC OF
GERMANY
5.   It is the generally recognised endeavour of
the German transport policy "to secure the
equality of chances of all citizens in all areas
and regions" through a suitable transport infrastructure. Since many years the Federal Republic
of Germany has, therefore, a close network of
international airports. The airport companies
exist in most of the cases since the beginning
of scheduled civil air traffic. They still serve
the same regions; in other words, the commercial
traffic demand of these regions with the highest
economic concentration as well as highly
populated areas in our country. These are from
north to south: Hamburg, Bremen, Hannover,
Düsseldorf, Köln/Bonn, Frankfurt, Saarbrücken,
Nürnberg, Stuttgart and München(fig. 3)
In some cases the site of the airport was
changed due to the higher physical requirements
of modern aircraft.

ARBEITSGEMEINSCHAFT DEUTSCHER VERKEHRSFLUGHÄFEN e.V.

STUTTGART-FLUGHAFEN

The traffic development, expansion planning and the investment demand of the German airports to 1977

Stuttgart, August 1967

Fig.1. The traffic development, expansion planning and the investment demand of the German airports up to 1977

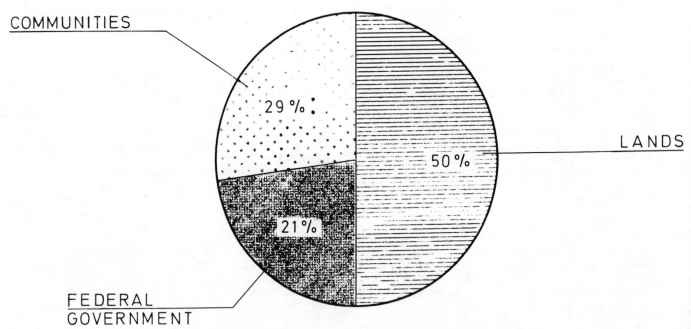

Fig.2. Percentage of capital share at all German airports

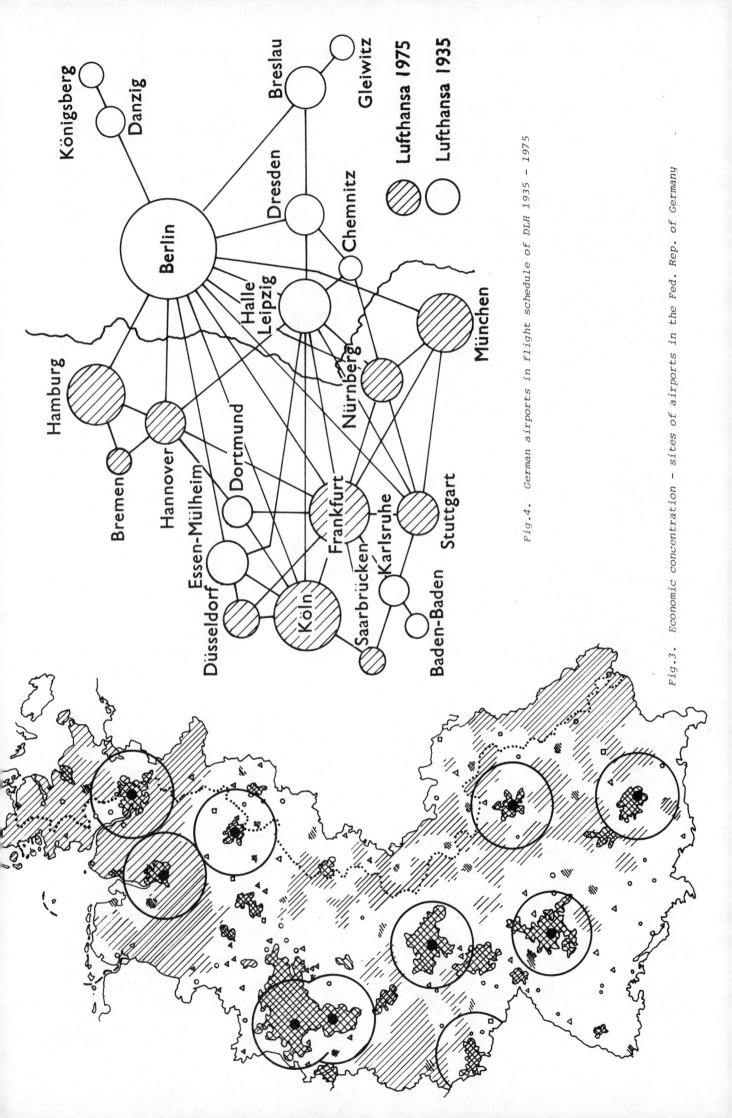

Fig.4. German airports in flight schedule of DLH 1935 – 1975

Fig.3. Economic concentration – sites of airports in the Fed. Rep. of Germany

Fig.4 labels:

Königsberg
Danzig
Breslau
Gleiwitz
Dresden
Chemnitz
Berlin
Halle
Leipzig
Nürnberg
München
Hamburg
Hannover
Bremen
Dortmund
Essen-Mülheim
Düsseldorf
Köln
Frankfurt
Karlsruhe
Saarbrücken
Stuttgart
Baden-Baden

Lufthansa 1975
Lufthansa 1935

6. A comparison of the airports in the Luft-hansa flight schedule of summer 1935 with today's international airports in the Federal Republic of Germany confirms the useful site planning of our airports. The service of the national airline is the basis of our multi-central airport network. Some airports of the pre-war airport system, as for example Dortmund and Essen-Mülheim in the west, Mannheim and Baden-Baden in the south have lost their inter-national status. Today they serve as airfields for the general aviation. (fig. 4)

7. The traffic results of the German airports can be taken from fig. 5 (fig. 5). In detail the 11 airports of the Federal Republic of Germany registered in 1974 a total of 963.149 commercial aircraft movements, i.e. 2,6% more than in the previous year. The number of air passengers (including transit) increased, compared with 1973, by 4,4% to 36,5 million. About one third of the total air passenger volume was registered at Frankfurt Airport.

INTERNATIONAL ORIENTATION OF THE AIR TRANSPORT
8. The German air transport has an international orientation. The economy of the Federal Republic of Germany and the prosperity of the population is directly influenced by the export. More than half of all air passengers are international and almost 90% of the outbound air freight goes to foreign destinations.

9. Fig. 6 gives a breakdown of local passengers in % according to destination in 1974. This shows that 42,5% of all air passengers are transported within the Federal Republic and to and from Berlin, 45,8% have their final destination in Europe and 11,7% fly to destinations outside Europe. The international traffic share there-fore amounts to 57,5%. Local passengers depar-ting to non-European destinations have a share of 23,5% in Frankfurt, 11,4% in München and 10,0% in Köln/Bonn. In absolute air passenger figures this means for example for the airport Frankfurt that about 3,2 million air passengers departed in 1974 to foreign destinations, including a share of 1,14 million air passengers to non-European destinations. On the long run this means that the share of domestic air passenger traffic decreases slightly, mainly due to the drastic reduction of the air transport to and from Berlin in the past three years.

10. The breakdown of air freight according to destination in 1974 is shown in fig. 7. Statistics indicate that 89% of the departing air freight is international freight. The share of the freight with non-European destination is 50,7% in total; in Frankfurt it amounts to almost 60%.

11. These figures show that the orientation of traffic flows from and to German airports is mainly international. This means a manifold connection of the German airports to the European and world air transport network, being an essen-tial condition for the multi-central airport concept in the Federal Republic of Germany which has grown over the years.

TRANSPORT DEVELOPMENT
12. The transport development of the past 15 years has confirmed the multi-central structure of the German airport network (fig. 8). Since more than 15 years, the shares of the German airports in the total air passenger volume (arr + dep) have remained nearly constant. Berlin with its continuously decreasing share is an exception. The reasons are - as everybody knows - of political nature.

13. Four airport categories are the result of the long-term analysis:
- small airports with a share of less than 2,5% of the total volume; these are Bremen and Nürn-berg. In 1974 this corresponded with less than 1 million air passengers per airport,
- medium airports with a share of less than 7,5% of the total volume. These are Köln/Bonn, Hannover and Stuttgart. In 1974 this correspon-ded with less than 3 million air passengers per airport,
- major airports with a share of less than 15% of the total volume. These are Hamburg, München, Berlin and Düsseldorf. In 1974 this corresponded with about 5 million air passengers per airport, and
- one big airport with a share of more than 30% of the total volume. This is Frankfurt. In 1974 this share corresponded with a traffic volume of more than 12 million air passengers.

AIR PASSENGER FORECAST 1985
14. The German Airports Association (ADV) has recently presented an air passenger forecast for the German airports up to 1985 based on an annual growth rate of 6,7%. For the first time no minimum resp. maximum values were published. Instead of these values, a medium value was estimated with possible variations of ± 10% in the 10th year of the forecast. The forecast is checked every year and, if necessary, adjusted to the market and transport development.

15. Fig. 9 shows a comparison of the BAA and ADV air passenger forecasts. The British fore-casts show a spectacular growth break beginning in 1982 with annual growth rates of 6,3% to 8,9% compared with 4,2% to 8,7% in the period from 1974 to 1982. In total the British fore-cast is based on a more optimistic transport development than the German forecast.

16. Following the air passenger forecast and the empiric rates, seven international airports in the Federal Republic of Germany and Berlin (West) must be able to handle in 1985 a traffic volume between 4 and 10 million air passengers each and one airport must have a capacity of more than 20 million air passengers.

17. Due to this forecast, all airport operators check from time to time whether the existing and/or planned airport facilities on the air- and landside will be at disposal in due time or whether bottlenecks are to be expected. Within the scope of ADV, comparative surveys have been carried out for the air- and landside in the first half of 1975. Some results from these studies give a survey on the judgment of

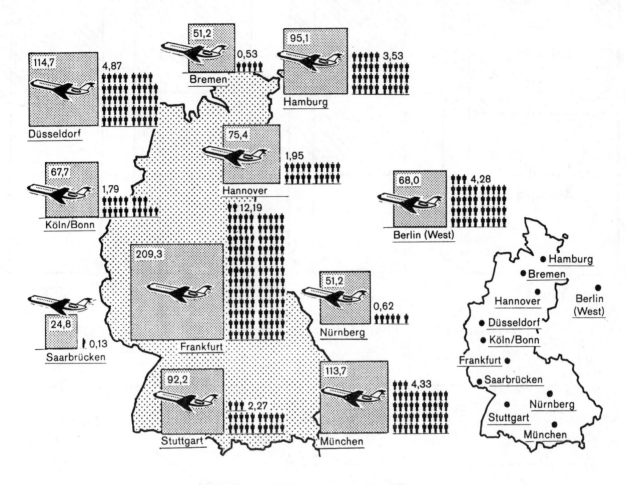

Fig.5.   *Traffic at airports 1974*

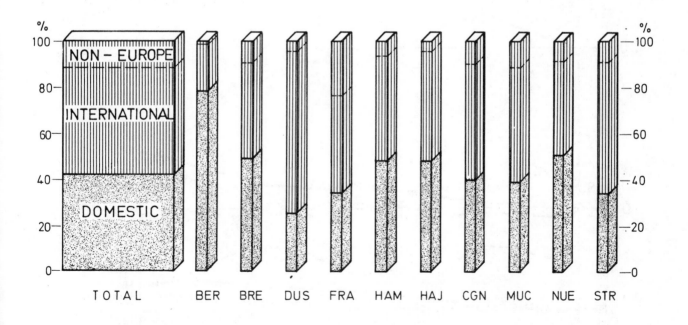

Fig.6.   *Breakdown of local passengers in % according to destination, 1974*

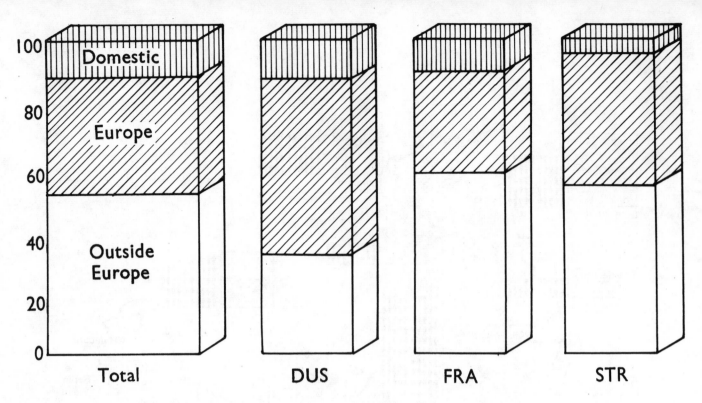

Fig.7. Breakdown of air freight in % according to destination, 1974

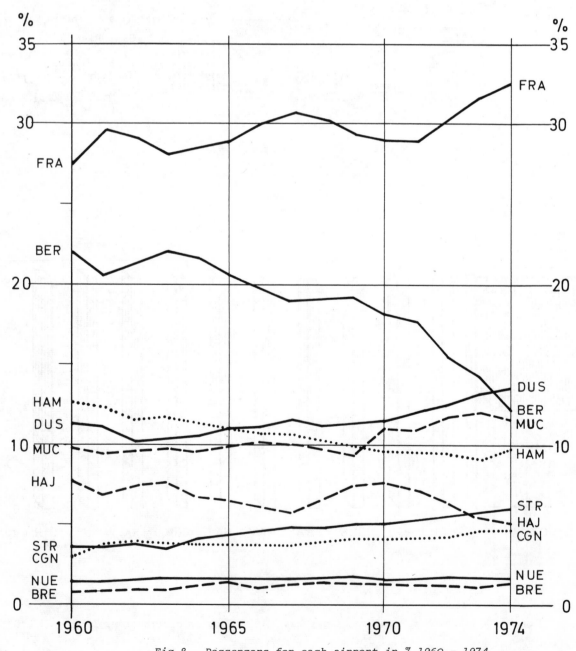

Fig.8. Passengers for each airport in % 1960 - 1974

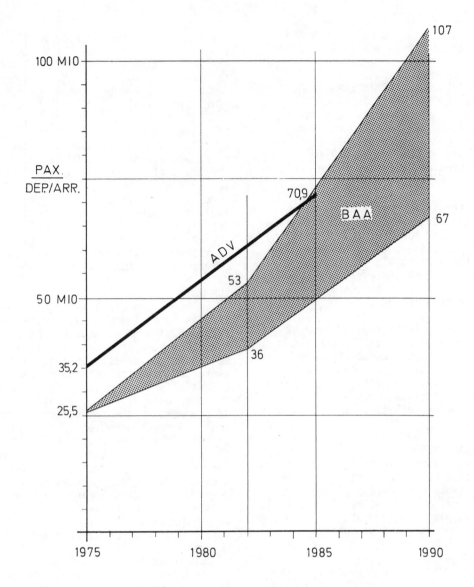

Fig.9. Passenger forecast ADV-BAA

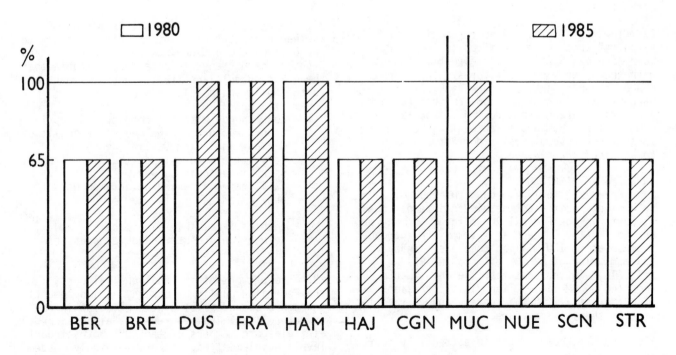

Fig.10. Future runway capacity at German airports

our airport terminals including the planned expansions for the two five years periods until 1985.

CAPACITY EXPLOITATION OF THE INTERNATIONAL AIRPORTS IN THE FEDERAL REPUBLIC OF GERMANY
18. If the planned new airports München II and Hamburg II cannot be built in due time, the result would be severe bottlenecks in runway capacity (fig. 10). München-Riem will already have a lack of capacity in the early eighties.

19. As to the terminals, difficulties in the passenger handling are to be expected at Stuttgart Airport and for the freight handling at the airports Nürnberg and Saarbrücken (fig. 11), if the approval for the expansion is not given in due time. As everywhere, the environmental problems play a considerable negative role in this process.

20. In total, however, the expected growing transport demand in Germany can be handled through the expansion and new construction plans of the individual airport operators. If there are difficulties and delays in the realisation of the construction, this is certainly not within the responsibility of the airport operators.

ACCESS BY RAIL AND ROAD
21. Fig. 12 "Rail connections of airports" shows that at present the airports Frankfurt and Düsseldorf dispose of direct railway connections. The connection of Hannover Airport is in construction and plans for Hamburg II, Köln/Bonn, München II and Stuttgart are presently in preparation.

22. The present road connections of the German airports are, according to the opinion of the airport operators, only sufficient for the airports Köln/Bonn and München-Riem.

23. The next fig. 13 "Road connections of airports" shows that the airports Frankfurt, Köln/Bonn and Stuttgart are directly connected with the network of the motorways (Autobahn). New Autobahn-connections for Frankfurt and Hannover are in construction. Further Autobahn-connections are planned for the airports Bremen, Hamburg I and Hamburg II as well as München II. In addition several less important road connections are planned.

INVESTMENT/TRAFFIC UNIT
24. From 1960 to 1974, about DM 4,600 million have been invested at the eleven international airports in the Federal Republic of Germany and Berlin (West). The annual investments increased from about DM 100 million to a preliminary maximum value of DM 790 million in 1971 (fig. 14). In the past year the investments amounted to DM 316 million. This corresponds almost exactly with the average annual investment of the last 15 years.

25. The breakdown of the investments by source is as follows:

the federal government approx. 10%
the states   "   20%
the communities   "   11%
the airport companies "   59%
   through revenues, funds and outside credits (fig. 15).

26. The medium investment expenditure in the past 15 years for all German airports amounted to an average of about DM 12,50/traffic unit, whereby traffic unit means 1 air passenger resp. 100 kg freight or mail. This is a low expenditure in the international comparison. The number includes, however, only a part of the investment for air traffic control installations, since the German airports only have to pay for the immobile ATC-facilities serving the take-off and landing process and the visual landing aids.

SUMMARY
27. The German airport organisation takes efforts to realise an optimum over-all economic solution with an expenditure as small as possible. I am convinced that our liberal airport organisation which is based on local initiative - connected with the voluntary coordination of essential principle decisions - has facilitated the adaptation to the aircraft and transport development in the past 15 years. Neither the short-term introduction of the jets at the end of the fifties nor the broad use of wide-bodied aircraft in the last three years have found the German airports unprepared. Even the difficulties of the beginning have been avoided by means of advance-planning which was recommended by the German Airports Association. At other occasions as well, the ADV observes its task as an autonomous body. This includes among other things
- mutual charges policy
- preparation of operational recommendations
- and active cooperation in international aviation organisations like AACC and IIWG.

28. Recent discussions in the German public whether a concentration of the air transport to one or few international airports in the Federal Republic of Germany would be more suitable than the existing multi-central airport network led to the following conclusions:
The multi-central German airport network
   - corresponds with the economy and population structure of the Federal Republic of Germany including Berlin (West),
   - serves the interests of the air transport users in an optimum way,
   - facilitates a demand-orientated use of public funds,
     and last not least
   - enables a flexible air space use and secures an undisturbed development of civil aviation.

29. The network of international airports in the Federal Republic of Germany is supplemented through a second level of the aviation infrastructure (fig. 16). 30 regional airports and airfields are members of the ADV. Both airport levels supplement each other. In highly-loaded

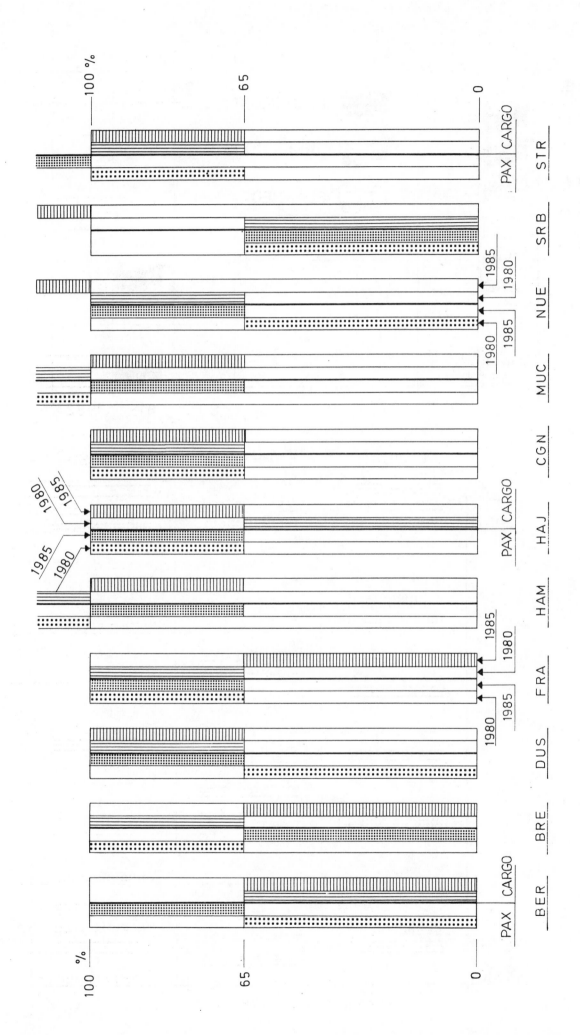

Fig.11. Future terminal capacity

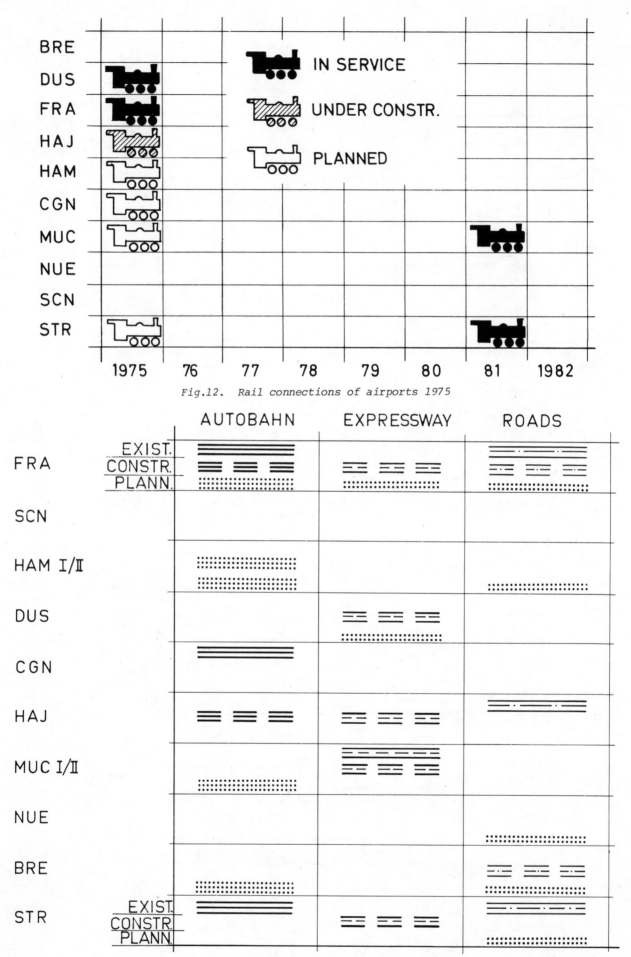

Fig.12. Rail connections of airports 1975

Fig.13. Road connections of airports 1975

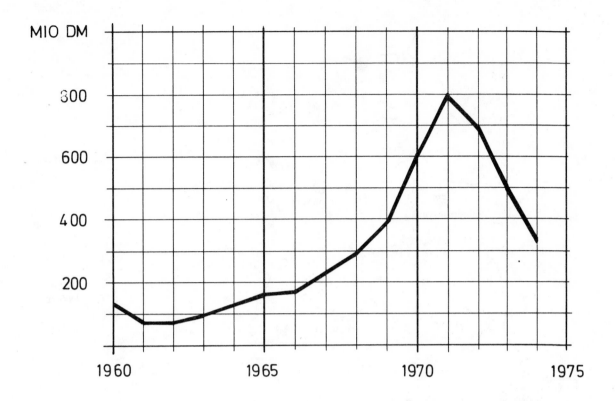

Fig.14.   Yearly airports investments

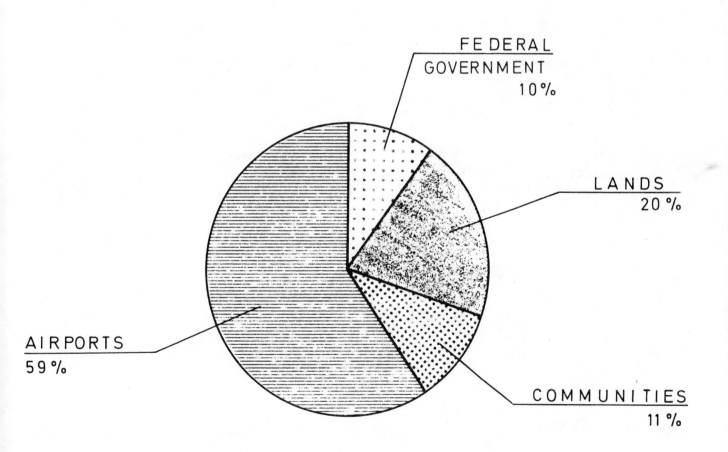

Fig.15.   Financing of investments 1960 - 1974

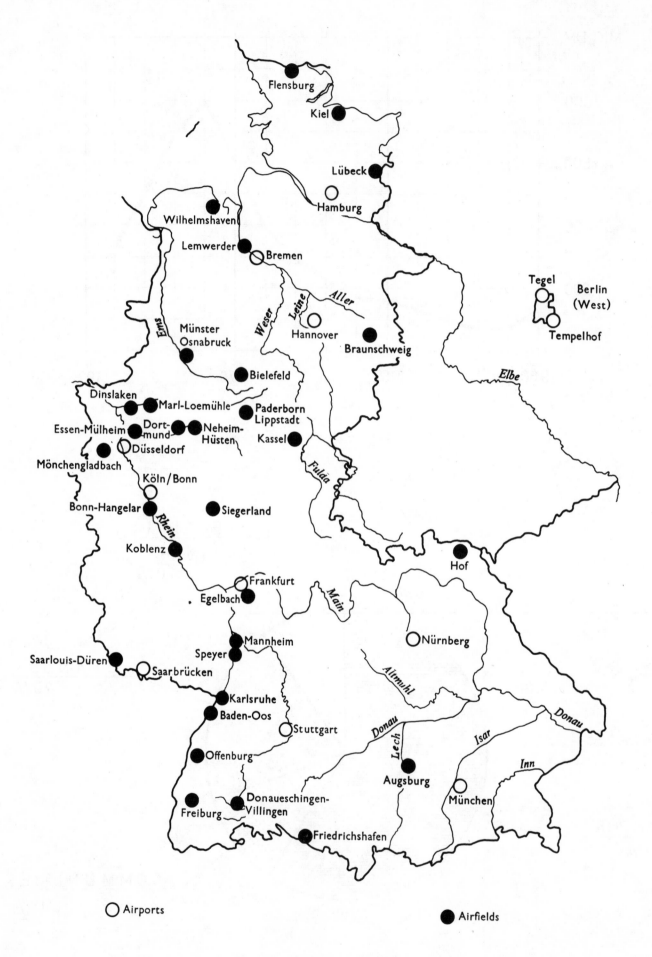

Fig.16. Airports and airfields in the Fed. Republic of Germany

regions, neighbouring airfields ease the transport load as satellites to the international airports. From the planning point of view, this guarantees an additional flexibility of the total airport system in Germany.

30. I hope that my remarks have given a survey on the German airports and their organisation.

The system of a coexistent development of individual self-responsible airport companies in a common conception is certainly not easy to realise. The past 25 years of German airport development, however, are for me a proof for the usefulness of our principle decision for this liberal airport system.

4. Development concept for a Canadian national airports plan

H. Young
Director of Planning, Airports and Construction Services, Canadian Air Transportation Administration

The social and economic development of Canada has historically been keyed to the provision of transportation facilities. The development of civil aviation in the 20th Century has adhered to this pattern and a National Plan for Airports is deemed to be of great significance. This paper deals with a concept for the development of a National Plan, with concentration on airport facilities needed over the foreseeable future.

INTRODUCTION

1.   The various water and surface transportation modes which facilitated European settlement in Canada and which provided an immense contribution to the assimilation and unification of our vast territories, all have a continuing role from the perspective of our nation's development. Air transportation has an equally dramatic role, on the one hand being characterized by a steady shift in travel patterns both between cities and with other nations, and, on the other hand, by providing transportation links which other modes cannot cater for.

2.   Canada is the second largest country in the world with territories much larger than Europe. Long distances are the norm. Our political and economic centres are widely scattered and with the coming of aviation in the 20th Century it became a matter of geographic, social and economic necessity to build more and more airports. Much of this need is reflected in the development of 11 International airports which contribute to Canada's traditional role as a trading nation; in addition, however, aviation demand has resulted in the construction of aerodromes for isolated communities or in support of industrial development in previously uninhabited or sparsely populated areas of the country.

3.   Today, there are more than 1800 land, water and heliport aerodromes in Canada. Of these, nearly half are licensed as airports and they range in size from a few acres with a gravel or natural landing strip to our 17,000 acre Mirabel International Airport which has enough space and facilities to handle the largest and most sophisticated air traffic. The Ministry of Transport owns and operates 110 airports and another 66 owned by the Ministry are operated by local communities or organizations on our behalf. The remainder are owned and operated by Provincial, Municipal, Military or private agencies.

4.   The Ministry of Transport plans, designs, and constructs airport facilities and manages, operates and maintains plant, equipment and services at the various airports. Our obligation for non-Ministry owned airports extends through the range from specialist advice to financial assistance for operation and capital contributions - in whole or part. During the fiscal year 1975-1976 the airports segment of the Ministry budget involved approximately $670.0M including over $340.0M capital expenditures. Revenue expectancies approximate $188.0M - and the gap between expenditures and revenues is a serious problem. This problem is compounded by the fact that most of our airports are not and, with very few exceptions, probably never will be self-supporting.

5.   While the imbalance between expenditures and revenues constitutes our largest single problem, we have others of equal or greater complexity. Many airports require extensive up-dating or replacement of existing facilities, a large proportion having been in service since World War II or shortly thereafter. Deterioration of buildings and surface structures is commonplace and this is further aggravated with respect to the accommodation of high speed and large passenger volume aircraft for which many airports are undersized. Other problems such as security needs have resulted in utilization of comparatively large public areas for purposes not considered in original designs for passenger terminals.

6.   Our problems, of course, are mirrored by problems being encountered by the air carriers. The air industry has serious financial difficulties; competition between carriers, traffic peaking, proportionately lower budgets and revenues, costly equipment and escalated costs for other resources have adversely affected the carriers. We, therefore, have an additional resultant problem, that is to say, we are searching for lower standards - both in services we provide and in design of facilities. Lower standards are not appreciated by airport users and cause many chain reaction problems.

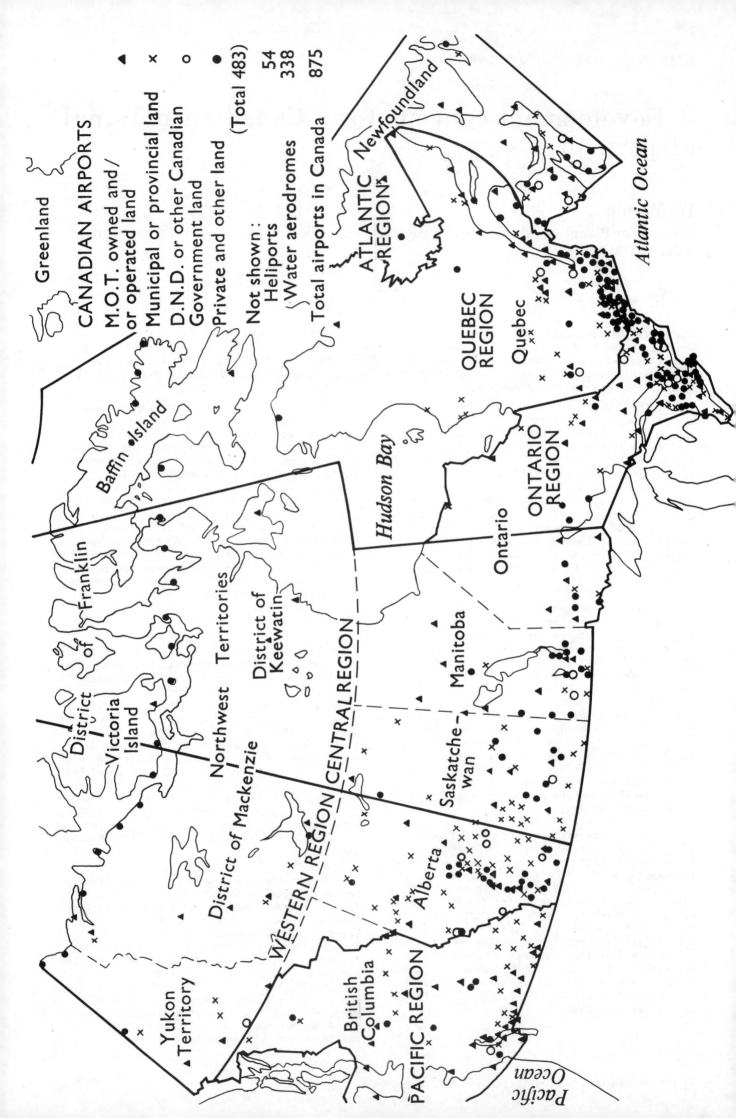

CANADIAN AIRPORTS

◄ M.O.T. owned and/
or operated land

✕ Municipal or provincial land

○ D.N.D. or other Canadian
Government land

● Private and other land   (Total 483)

Not shown : Heliports   54
            Water aerodromes   338
            Total airports in Canada 875

Greenland

Baffin Island

District of Franklin

Victoria Island

District of Mackenzie

Northwest Territories

District of Keewatin

Yukon Territory

WESTERN REGION CENTRAL REGION

British Columbia

PACIFIC REGION

Alberta

Saskatche-wan

Manitoba

Hudson Bay

Ontario

ONTARIO REGION

QUEBEC REGION

Quebec

Newfoundland

ATLANTIC REGION

Atlantic Ocean

Pacific Ocean

7.   It will be seen, therefore, that the National Plan for Airports must adhere to the underlying objective of achieving the most for the least cost and to the satisfaction of three levels of government as well as airport users. In addition to and in confirmation of this objective the Plan will necessarily adhere to new transportation policy announced in June 1975 which stated "Transport policy is now directed toward development of a total transportation system for Canada based on the principle of competition, but providing accessibility and equity of treatment for users as an essential instrument of support for the achievement of national and regional economic and social objectives".

FUTURE DEVELOPMENT OF AIRPORTS
8.   The national system of airports in Canada requires a complete overhaul and we are approaching this need very cautiously because of underlying social as well as economic considerations. In common with other countries, we continue to experience relatively unrestrained urban development adjacent to airports and, conversely, the environmental impact of airport operations has become a matter of great and common concern. We are thus faced with a variety of solutions regarding the future development of individual airports which can best evolve from local study and dialogue. In recognition of this, a programme aimed at the development of individual Airport Master Plans has been installed.

9.   Concurrent with the development of Airport Master Plans, the Ministry has launched an inter-related programme relative to the development of Area Master Plans; the latter being preponderately aligned to airways and airspace control and the former being largely concerned with ground facilities and services. An Area Master Plan, by definition, should precede the development of individual Airport Master Plans because the safety of aircraft operations and the roles of individual airports in the area concerned are paramount factors for consideration. Because of expediency concerning individual airports and also due to the lack of certain specialist resources, we have, however, proceeded with the development of some individual Airport Master Plans without the benefit of related Area Master Plans.

10.   The Canadian Air Transportation Administration (CATA) is divided into 6 Regions which are geographically defined on the accompanying "Canadian Airports" illustration. Responsibilities for development of Area Master Plans and Airport Master Plans are assigned to each of the Regional Administrators. Each Regional Headquarters has a number of Branches which generally comprise duplicates of the CATA Headquarters Branches located in Ottawa. Thus, while our management philosophy is largely geared to decentralization of responsibilities, CATA Headquarters supports Regional counterparts - particularly in respect of long range planning, but also with regard to the implementation of short and intermediate range development plans.

11.   For a variety of reasons the development of Area Master Plans involves a general disregard of ownership of individual airports. That is to say, airspace and air traffic control problems and solutions are equally applicable regardless of who owns and operates individual airports within the area concerned. In respect of Airport Master Plans, however, our programme is aligned to an overall priority for Ministry owned airports during immediate future years, with a few exceptions which are aligned to political expediencies or in support of important local economic development plans. Within this context, therefore, the objectives of Area Master Plans and Airport Master Plans are defined as follows:

Objective - Area Master Plan
To develop the most appropriate alternative locations and roles, for a system of airports and aeronautical components, that meet future operational, environmental, economic and social requirements for a specific area. The selected plan will have a time horizon of 20 years and will be periodically analyzed for effectiveness.

Objective - Airport Master Plan
To develop the most appropriate intermediate and long range plans relative to facilities and resources needed to satisfy the designated future role of the subject airport: the sum total of these plans to be defined within a Master Plan document which is up-dated periodically to provide justification for the planning and implementation of capital, operating and maintenance projects.

12.   Despite the fact that our overall priorities in the Airport Master Plan development programme are preponderately aligned to Ministry owned airports, our ultimate aim is to encompass all airports in Canada. In large measure this is an almost impossible task; from the viewpoint of resources needed to do the job and in light of the current economic situation and related controls, our objective appears to be entirely impractical. Nevertheless, the programme has been launched with considerable enthusiasm and forces both within and external to the Ministry of Transport are providing support and impetus to the seemingly impossible workload. Before defining those forces, however, it would be appropriate to summarize the action being taken to ensure that the future development of Canadian airports proceeds as quickly and efficiently as possible. In summary, therefore;

(a) A programme for the development of Area Master Plans and individual Airport Master Plans was effectively launched in 1975 by the 6 Regional Administrators in CATA - i.e. at the first level of organization.

(b) The Master Plan development programme is largely concerned with Ministry owned airports in the initial phase but will ultimately encompass all airports within the National Airport System - i.e. all aerodromes in Canada which are licensed as airports.

(c) The programme will provide a natural and continuing source of information and data needed for the development of national plans.

THE NATIONAL AIRPORTS SYSTEM

13. Within Canada airports fit into three categories broadly defined as National, Community, and Arctic Groups. It is sufficient for purposes of this paper to merely define them as airports of national interest, local interest and Arctic location respectively.

14. The majority of the most active airports in the National Group are Ministry owned and operated; for example, of the 25 airports ranking highest in passenger traffic, 24 are owned and operated by the Ministry of Transport. The sole exception is an Industrial Airport owned and operated by the City of Edmonton which, because of its location, has an important role in respect of local and regional traffic as well as access to the North West Territories. There are 88 National Group Airports including the 11 International.

15. The majority of the Community Group airports are owned and operated by municipalities or private agencies. These airports include some feeders to National Group airports but all are of predominantly local interest and generally support business, industry or tourism with some being defined as Remote; the latter are required to relieve isolation in non-Arctic communities or settlements not served by reliable surface transportation on a year-round basis. 724 airports fall within the Community Group category.

16. There are 63 airports in the Arctic Group. They are located in the Yukon and North West Territories as well as the northernmost segment of the Province of Quebec - all being North of the 60th parallel.

17. In general, the main segments of the National Airport System are aligned to the various airport groups National, Community and Arctic in descending order of importance from an economic (commercial) perspective and largely in reverse order of importance from a social perspective. There are notable exceptions to these orders of importance, for example, some Arctic airports are almost solely for the purpose of facilitating oil exploration; in addition, a few National and many Community Group airports are aligned to a role of equal social and economic importance.

18. I previously mentioned some internal and external forces and influences which have or will give impetus and support to our Regional Master Plan development programme. It is appropriate that these be brought into focus in context of the National Airports System and before proceeding with the National Airports Plan scenario.

SOCIO-POLITICAL INFLUENCES

19. In varying degrees the 10 Canadian Provinces have all exhibited an increased interest in air transportation during recent years. This interest transcends the previous natural concern which Provincial governments traditionally expressed in support of development proposals

affecting airports located within their respective Provinces. Much of the new interest has stemmed from social and economic studies and activities which have generated specific justifications for transportation facilities. New interest has also been born of concern related to the clash of urban development programmes with the operation and development of airports.

20. The increased interests of Provincial governments in civil aviation have been paralleled by socially oriented policies and programmes installed and being implemented by other Federal government Ministries or agencies. In these respects there has been considerable cohesion between the Federal and Provincial agencies concerned and it is worthwhile mentioning some cases to exemplify how socio-political programmes must be given serious consideration when preparing plans for development of airports.

21. Many Federal or Provincial or cost-shared Federal-Provincial efforts to uplift or sustain the economy of specific regions in Canada have, by intent, caused population shifts, new or increased industrial development, development of new or revived tourist centres, or any of a host of new activities in locales which were previously depressed, sparsely populated, and even uninhabited. Without exception such efforts incorporate or result in the generation of a need for new transportation facilities. In many cases, an airport is an adjunctive or an alternate need - or expansion of the airport where one already exists becomes an integral need.

22. There are many other socio-political influences which must be given serious consideration by the airport planner. In Canada these generally comprise two groups which can be broadly defined in their relationships to airports which on the one hand are in or adjacent to large population centres, or, on the other hand, are relative to airports in sparsely populated locales.

23. With reference to airports in or adjacent to large population centres, airport planners face much more complex problems than those which existed 15 or 20 years ago. Dominant issues in those days were preponderately oriented to aeronautical considerations; other issues, where they existed, were of little or no consequence in the face of the energy and pressures of the booming aviation industry. Prior to the mid-1960s, airport planners were thus concerned with a limited number of issues. These generally related to locations that could meet technological and safety requirements related to the operation of aircraft, sites that were relatively inexpensive, located close to the city or market area served and were topologically suitable for construction purposes.

24. As we proceeded through the 1960s the adjacency of airports to their prime market areas gave impetus to the dynamic and virtually unrestricted land development which has occurred around all our towns and cities. Whereas

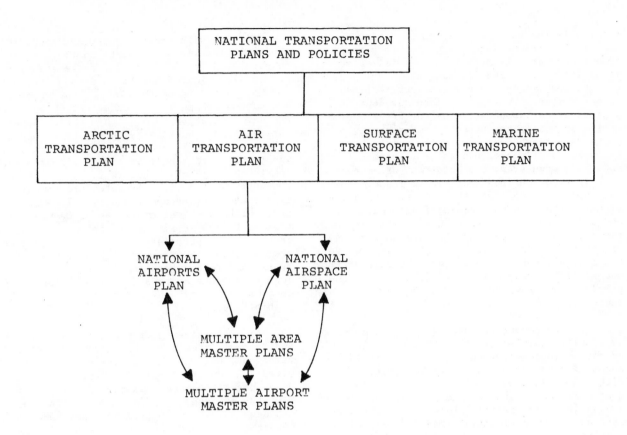

Fig.1. *National transportation system (planning perspective)*

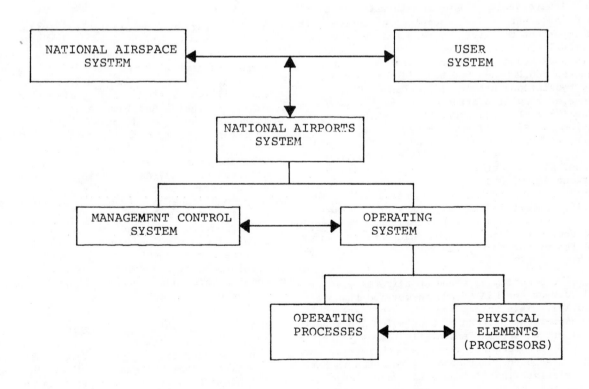

Fig.2. *National airports system components*

previously the various benefits of having an
airport in or immediately adjacent to a population centre greatly outweighed the ill-effects,
it became evident that in many cases this was
changed and, indeed, a complete reversal has
become common. The push of land development
against airport boundaries has occurred over a
series of years; concurrently, many of our airports have reached or passed the point where
expansion of airport boundaries is essential.
When this occurs, land acquisition or expropria-
tion is a contentious and complex issue. This,
cobmined with the inevitable degradation of on-
site areas and in many cases of adjacent land
and water areas, has contributed to the expansion of concern regarding the lives and rights
of citizens. These rights, particularly where
residential, recreational, agricultural, water
and wildlife areas are involved, are often emphasized and exaggerated to the fullest possible
degree.

25. Citizen concern regarding adjacent airports
is usually exploited to the fullest possible
extent by local governments. In fact it is
becoming very common for local authorities to
either disregard our advice regarding development of lands on the periphery of airports or to
demand whole or partial relocation of the airport away from residential areas. Local government desires are, of course, duplicated by other
tiers of government although ensuing proposals
may not necessarily match. In any event, there
are a host of problems and it is now very apparent that the long range future of many of our
airports is questionable and planners must give
full consideration to the full range of social
and political implications.

26. I have dealt at some length with airports
in or adjacent to large population centres. It
is important to note, however, that of the 22
metropolitan areas listed in our 1971 census,
only 3 exceeded 1 million population, 11 range
between 200,000 and 600,000 and the remaining 8
had populations between 105,000 and 200,000.
These metropolitan areas accounted for 11.9 million (55%) of our approximate 21.6 million population in 1971, and only 19 had commercial airports within or immediately adjacent to their
area. Airports within these 19 metropolitan
areas, plus a further 13 airports in cities of
between 60,000 and 105,000 population, have been
subjected, in varying degrees, to questions of
social concern in the last few years. These have
given impetus to a need for environmental, social
and economic impact studies which are an essential feature of our Master Plan development programme.

27. The majority of Canadian airports are located between the USA-Canada border and the 55th
Parallel. This, of course, is coincident with
the historical pattern of population and industrial growth across Canada. In recent years,
however, the need for airports both in size and
number has been questioned, in relation to both
the relatively small land areas where large concentrations of airports occur, and, as to their
appropriateness where other modes may better
serve transportation needs.

28. Coupled with serious questions regarding
the proliferation of airports in the more densely populated areas of Canada, there are many
conversely oriented questions apropos the need
for more airports to the North. Our Provinces
are concentrating increased attention on Northern development in areas within their respective
jurisdictions - generally up to the 60th Parallel. The Federal Government is pursuing a similarly increased course of action with respect to
Arctic developments, that is to say, North of
the 60th Parallel. The related programmes are
aligned to both economic and social perspectives
and, unlike the Southern areas of Canada, air
transportation is either the only possible mode
or the most appropriate mode where other modes
are possible. In these respects transportation
by sea and road, where this can occur, is subject to short seasons and very high costs. The
costs of rail transportation range from high to
prohibitive.

29. As a consequence of increased Provincial
and Federal interest in Northern and Arctic development, new policies and programmes have evolved. Apropos Federal interest, a new Arctic
Development Programme has been developed by the
Ministry of Transport, in consort with programmes developed or installed by other Federal
Departments. Resultant to the surge in Provincial interest during recent years, a variety of
new and extensive programmes and projects for
Northern Provincial areas are installed or are
planned. The demand for air transportation has,
therefore, increased considerably in recent
years. As a natural result, the National Airports System must foster as well as facilitate
social and economic policies, plans and
programmes.

30. The various socio-political influences
which I have highlighted and which affect transportation generally throughout Canada, have
some divergent aims and underlying philosophies.
These are, of course, a natural consequence of
our political system and structure wherein Federal, Provincial and local governments operate.
There are many common issues, however, which
have resulted in increased national interdependency. Many of these issues arise from or equate
with the causes and effects which have resulted
in increased international interdependency
during recent years. I refer here to the many
important concerns such as endeavours towards
social equity, energy conservation, protection
of the environment, and the very lengthy etce-
tera. These require no explanation but they
must be given the utmost consideration in the
development of the total transportation system
towards which our new transportation policy is
emphatically oriented.

NATIONAL TRANSPORTATION PLANS
31. Figure 1 illustrates an outline of the National Transportation System from a planning perspective. The Air Transportation Plan includes
the segments National Airports Plan and National
Airspace Plan, as well as the Area and Airport
Master Plans previously referred to. In an organizational context the two National Plans are

being developed by two separate organizations in our Ottawa CATA Headquarters and the Area and Airport Master Plans are aligned to the responsibilities of our six Regional Administrations. It is important to note, however, that the development process is geared to a universal philosophy wherein:

. we aim to achieve a combination of inputs at and between all components and in correlation with this

. the process is repetitive and continuous.

32. Our National Transportation Plans are essentially intended to guide decision making in the development, installation, renovation and management of transportation programmes. In pursuit of these intentions, we have developed a corresponding set of goals and objectives relative to the development of the National Airports Plan.

THE NATIONAL AIRPORTS PLAN
33. The Plan (when developed) is intended to facilitate the development, management and operation of the National Airports System, the components of which are depicted in Figure 2. Within this broad objective, the following goals have been established:

. to develop a framework of policies and criteria which will ensure the cohesive development of individual components of the National Airports System (by December 1976)

. to identify and establish methodology for assessment of the capacity of the Operating System and to complete an assessment of the capacity of the system (by April 1977)

. to establish methods to monitor and control the performance of the National Airports System and to obtain approval and install a Management Control System to this effect (by October 1977)

. to develop a National Airports Plan relative to Ministry owned airports (by July 1978) and for all airports in the system (by July 1979).

34. It will be observed that the first 3 goals are each relative to development of a system and the final goal is specifically aligned to development of a plan. This is so designed, to ensure progressive understanding and concurrent reorganization of the National Airports system, and to facilitate a progressive and timely combination of inputs between the various organizational components involved.

35. The Management Control System is intended to ultimately provide the ways and means for ensuring that the Operating System is properly

meeting its obligations with an acceptable degree of efficiency and will continue to do so through the foreseeable future. In effect, the Management Control System will provide for the collection, flow and use of information and data throughout the Air Transportation Administration; it is being designed to ensure a common approach and agreement, throughout the organization, regarding programme priorities and related budgets - with performance measurement of the Operating System being a key feature.

36. The Operating System is aligned to requirements for resources (facilities, equipment, manpower and money) to facilitate the operating processes at airports - all being directly relative to the operation and maintenance of airports and the provision of services to airport users.

37. We are confident that our efforts will be successful despite the immensity of information and data which must be assembled and massaged and the host of problematical social, political and technological influences which must be taken into account. I believe we are already launched in the right direction and the considerable joint effort across the entire Air Transportation Administration will ultimately pay off. In summary therefore we are hopeful that by 1980, when the first stage National Airports Plan will be ready for translation into action, Canada should experience the following improvements across the National Airports System:

. The considerable existing network of airports needed to support government programmes will be subjected to a comprehensive and fully participative analysis on a continuing basis.

. A modern National Airports System will ensue; it will be consistent with social, environmental and energy concerns and with the new and evolving political programmes which take these concerns into account.

. The modern National Airports System will provide for air transportation only where the air mode is required on the joint bases - technology, economics and socio-political priorities - and will give way to other transportation modes where necessary.

. The National Airports System will be subjected to a dynamic continuous process, responsive to changing conditions and public perception of need, as well as to the needs of the aviation industry and the travelling public.

. The universal plan should give new health and vigour to the aviation industry, and, should eliminate unnecessary competitiveness in and between the densely populated areas of Canada, particularly between the various transportation modes.

Session II: Discussion

Professor Secor D. BROWNE, Washington DC

I would emphasize strongly - speaking only about the USA - that we are dealing here with a system, consisting of the airport, air traffic control and, most important, air carrying. Such a system in the USA by its nature must be regulated, and the present move towards what was to be called 'regulatory reform' is, in my opinion, a lot of nonsense. At the end of the day we shall wind up with much the same system. Less regulation sounds attractive, but systems mean there must be regulation.

The other question as far as the USA is concerned relates to the necessity of subsidy. Air carriers cannot continue indefinitely to be the filling, however delectable, in the air transport sandwich. The United States air carriers must provide a service from Alaska to Hawaii, and for reasons of advance, communication and the whole economy itself it is my view that all taxpayers should pay for the benefits of all systems. It is politically very attractive, with due respect to Mr Young, to say that users should pay the cost of the service provided; certainly in the USA it is not possible, particularly where there is the ridiculous situation of a subsidized railway service from Chicago to Miami when the taxpayers would be better off to be given free air tickets and $100 to spend in Miami on arrival! When it comes to such discussions I think that the administration and the leaders of Congress are out of their minds!

Mr E. PARKINSON, The Royal Town Planning Institute

People in Britain will be relieved to hear of Lord Boyd-Carpenter's themes of significantly lower aircraft noise level in the years ahead and the feeling that there is no immediate requirement for yet another international airport in the London area.

What I want to emphasize is the sheer uncertainty of the future, for the people involved in all kinds of planning, whether airport planning or town planning. Never have the crystal balls been so clouded. There is a whole range of variables affecting every activity. One particular variable is that a generation is growing up in western society which has not the same values. Most older people have a very common ethic centred on the thrust of economic growth. But as I talk to the next generation, I believe they have another set of values. I suspect it may be in ethical or moral terms a better set of values than sheer economic growth at the centre. If there is a shift in human emphasis from economic expansion and the quantitative growth of consumer durables, to improving quality in an incremental way and bringing back to the centre a debate on the quality of living and human relationships, then that shift in values may profoundly affect the whole of the aircraft planning world.

I detect signs of this. I may be detecting it falsely, but I want to suggest that such a shift of values may profoundly affect all the forecasts being so busily made today.

The CHAIRMAN (Mr Geoffrey Edwards)

I think that if delegates could take from this conference the message that authorities should not deal with planning new airports in the circumstances that existed in the 1960s, because they are no longer here, it would be helpful. My experience is that they do tend rather to do this. Planners would like them to look forward, and to deal with problems in terms of the 1980s,, which will be different.

Lord BOYD-CARPENTER (Paper 2)

May I answer what may be a misunderstanding between Professor Secor Browne and myself on the question of subsidy. I am not a doctrinaire who objects to subsidy in all circumstances, but I do believe that subsidy should be of the kind he was talking about, where the Government decides that a particular thing needs to be done, for reasons of national policy. A classical example of this in this country concerns the Highlands and Islands where my Authority operates eight airports and an air traffic control system. What we have submitted to the Government is that there should be a subsidy for the specific purpose of buying services which are not commercial propositions, but which are necessary to maintain social life in those isolated parts of the country.

What seems to me objectionable is the concealed subsidy, the amount of which is not apparent and no one knows who is getting it, but which distorts economic planning and physical planning by getting the whole business values wrong. Therefore, open, special subsidies for specific purposes, yes; concealed subsidies, no.

As to Mr Parkinson's point, I agree that there is a section of people whom morally one admires up to a point, who regard quality of life as being more important than earning a living. But the trouble with those people is simply that so many of them are not prepared to accept the logical corollary of what they want. If we are to drop our concentration on earning a living, which it seems is a basic necessity of this island, very well. But accept that that may mean a considerable reduction in standards. The trouble it seems to me with so many of the quality of life idealists and the concepts they put about is that they are not prepared to face up to the price of it, which must be diminished economic efficiency, and the price of that must be lower standards of life for all than would otherwise be attainable.

Professor R. DOGANIS, Polytechnic of Central London

Paper 2 left me panting for more. It was interesting and almost philosophical in its approach to airport planning, yet it was talking not of national airport planning, but about capital airport planning. I think the problem in the UK, outside the south-east, and in most European countries, is not that of the absence of airport capacity, but the fact that there is a surfeit of airport capacity. There are too many airports competing for the same traffic. The Civil Aviation Authority commissioned a series of regional airport studies, and then promptly rejected most of the recommendations made by the consultants in those studies.

It would be interesting to find out the current position. If we are entering a third era of airport planning, what does that mean for regional airports? What pattern of regional airports does Lord Boyd-Carpenter envisage for the 1980s and 1990s?

The second question is one related to airport capacity. Dr Treibel and Mr Young described the situation in which a great deal of money is going into airports, and it will be interesting to hear from them the criteria being used to evaluate these investments, particularly the economic criteria.

Finally, I should like to comment on Mr Marking's remarks on Paper 1. He raised a number of controversial issues, but I think there is a significant flaw in the critical comments he made regarding the British Airports Authority. It is true that the British Airports Authority achieves a very high rate of return on its investment. It is equally true that it is unique in the UK in doing this, and that most provincial airports are losing money. What is effectively happening outside the London area is that regional taxpayers are subsidizing British Airways and its passengers, because the losses made by the regional airports which are used by British Airways offset a large part of any profits made by the British Airports Authority from British Airways operations. Presumably what Mr Marking was arguing was not that airports should be run indefinitely at a loss, but that perhaps there should be lower charges at London Airport and significantly higher charges at regional airports to cover very substantial losses.

The point is that throughout the world there is no doubt that certainly outside the USA, airport systems are heavily in deficit, and therefore one should be wary of comments by IATA and airline representatives that they are being too hard hit by airport charges. The airports system, particularly if the costs of the worldwide navigational facilities are included, is making substantially higher losses than the airlines as such. During the next ten years there will be pressure by governments to cut investment in airports and to reduce airport subsidies. Airport planners will face a crucial issue - where to find the substantial investment required for airports, and where to raise revenue to cover the subsidies being incurred at these airports.

Lord BOYD-CARPENTER

I agree with that, except for one thing. I think there was only one consultant's report which the Civil Aviation Authority commissioned with which it openly disagreed. In the other cases the CAA took broadly the report line with perhaps a little different emphasis. That does not matter. The process I think was an intelligent one - to have the facts assembled, in one or two cases by the CAA staff, but in most of the difficult ones by very high level consultants, and then to form a judgment into which we could bring the CAA aviation expertise in order to be able finally to give advice to the government of the day. I obviously cannot summarise this.

I agree with Professor Doganis that Paper 2 was largely based on the London airports because in the UK - not because anyone has planned it - it is to the London area that a large proportion of air travellers wish to go. These are in fact the major international airports. This is where the traffic wants to go, and it is why Heathrow is basically a profitable airport, and carries the other London ones with it.

Professor Doganis asks what about the regional airports? I think that the CAA's advice is fairly clear. We suggest that if by regional airports is meant airports with any substantial scheduled international service, in a small country such as the UK there is room for very few. The CAA suggested specifically that there is such a future, particularly for Manchester, which has actually a larger population catchment area than central London although on the whole standards of income are lower, and to some extent Birmingham. Beyond that, and beyond the other British Airports Authority's airports which are in Scotland, and the special problem of Belfast, one is looking for quite a number of provincial airports for second level services, domestic scheduled services, and a certain amount of holiday charter, such as Luton which municipal endeavour has succeeded in developing.

The documents sound a note of warning that it is unlikely that most of these airports will be profitable, and if local authorities desire to continue to run them, they will have to be subsidized from the rates. I know several authorities are anxious to do so. In fact, Manchester and Luton are profitable in most years and Birmingham has been profitable. On the whole the others tend not to be in the narrow accounting sense, but it is for individual local authorities with whatever the government likes to do from the point of view of regional development, to see whether this should be added to by way of subsidy as part of the general build-up of the areas.

The problems of the UK are special. It is a small country with bad weather, and on the whole very good ground communications. Therefore, I think we are over-ambitious in some ways and in some other ways over-provided.

Professor Dr.Ing. TREIBEL (Paper 3)

I should like to comment on the statement that airports authorities' revenues are not affected to the same extent by a reduction in traffic figures. By way of example I would point out that German airports had losses of more than 50 million DM through the 6 months' go-slow action of ATC personnel in 1973 when traffic volume decreased by some 10%. That illustrates that airports can lose a great deal of revenue by lowering traffic volume.

Another statement of Mr Hammarskjold was that airports have captive customers, and therefore it is relatively easy for them to raise their user charges. Experience in my country shows that airlines can change their tariffs at much shorter intervals than airports - at three or six monthly intervals rather than two years. These examples show that closer co-operation between airlines and airports would be suitable in order to improve mutual understanding of the other's organization.

Mr YOUNG (Paper 4)

Both Professor Doganis and Professor Browne have made reference to the user-pay and other economic aspects underlying the policies applicable to the Canadian airport system. I would like to amplify the Canadian problem. In Canada, 85% of all the commercial traffic volumes is contained by airports which are owned and operated by the Federal government; the capital and operating costs for these airports are far in excess of revenues, and the gap is widening. The deficit has always been borne by the taxpayer and in recent years we have been searching for solutions aimed at alleviating the burden on tax-payers as a whole and providing a more equitable distribution of the cost burden to airport users.

In our search for investment and pricing criteria we have discovered, as inferred by Professor Doganis, that we do indeed have too many airports. Similarly, we have many airports which require upgrading and others which require downgrading, or 'capping' in our terms. Investment decisions are therefore being made with greater confidence but we are a long way from the ultimate - largely because social implications are immense and complicated.

5. Getting the most from existing airports

Sir Peter Masefield, MA, FRAeS, FCInstT, Hon.FAIAA
Director, British Caledonian Airways Ltd

Painful and difficult as the economic recession has been in so many directions during the past two years - not least in air transport - there is one area in which it has offered welcome breathing space. Traffic through the world's major airports has been virtually static during the three years which have passed since the Fourth World Airports Conference in April 1973. As a result, requirements for the building of major new airports during the next decade have disappeared. This Paper examines the background to the development of existing airports to meet the demands of air traffic in the foreseeable future - up to about 1990. It takes as an example the problems of the London area stated in the recent, and excellent, Government consultative document. The conclusion is that, with good planning and vigorous action, London's existing airports ought to be capable of being developed to cope with traffic demands for as far forward as we can see. There is, however, an outstanding need to achieve improved standards of passenger handling at airports throughout the world. New and larger aircraft are, increasingly, making possible the carriage of greater numbers of passengers and more cargo with fewer aircraft movements. In consequence the primary requirement is now for more and better passenger terminals at existing airports. In the London area two essentials to balanced airport amenities are seen as the incorporation of the Perry Oaks site into Heathrow Airport and the provision of a second (primarily landing) runway at Gatwick. The point is stressed that existing airports are now substantial national assets, important both for the development of international and national trade and as centres of stable employment. Airports and national prosperity are closely linked and because of this existing airports, their access and their facilities, should now receive a priority in the planning of national resources.

In a controversial business one of the few subjects upon which there can be no disagreement is that an efficient airport must be a blend of many attributes - in a form and to an extent which will meet the needs of a wide variety of providers and users of services, as well as the interests of those who work there and of those who live round about. Everyone will agree, also, that - to a greater or lesser extent - every airport falls a fair way short of the ideal. It is an uncomfortable fact that the more the traffic - for which every airport exists - the less adequate does it turn out to be.

2. At the same time there is now a general concensus that - after Roissy-en-France (alias Paris-Nord and Charles de Gaulle), after Mirabel (alias Ste Scholastique) for Montreal and after the new Dallas-Fort Worth International Airport, there are few prospects of other major new international airports within the forseeable future.

3. After Aviation's fortunate escape from the potential catastrophe of an airport at Maplin, we have to do the best we can with those airports which do exist - whether around London, New York, Frankfurt or Hong Kong. From both an airline and a customer viewpoint this will be no bad thing - not least in economic terms. It does not mean, however, an acceptance of the deficiencies which exist. There is only one thing in air transport more expensive than a flashy new airport - and that is a thoroughly inadequate old airport.

4. Properly, first things have been put first, and one can record with appreciation that, from an operational viewpoint, the world's major international airports are now better equipped than they have ever been. Standards of safety have been enhanced at all larger airports though some of the smaller fields are less adequately equipped.

5. Safety and operational standards must always come first. Second are the standards of service for those for whom both airlines and airports exist - the passenger and the shippers of goods.

6. As a frequent traveller on both long-haul and short-haul air services over many years, one has to admit that - from a passenger point of view - as the aeroplanes have got better so the airports have got worse. Part of this - but not all - is because the flow of air traffic has increased so much. On the whole, air carriers have done better than have airport administrations in meeting the challenges of growth. I say this with regret as one who has been closely involved in both and in the knowledge of the enormous sums which have been spent. Increased expenditure does not always mean better facilities.

7. Looking back over the years the ground services provided in days gone by and in much less difficult circumstances, at Croydon, at Hythe, Le Bourget, Washington National and at Port Washington in pre-War times, had an informality

and a care-for-the-individual (for both land-plane and flying-boat services) which exists to-day in comparable form only at the better General Aviation terminals at a few, well-conducted airports.

8. Perhaps the peak of good passenger handling in the United Kingdom was attained at Northolt in the early 1950s when it was virtually the private airport of BEA. There, in relation to the traffic the parking was adequate and convenient, the check-in desks were numerous, the walking distances were short and the same standards of individual passenger service were applied on the ground as in the air.

9. We shall never be able to return to the sizes of aircraft which made passenger handling so much easier in those days - the trend is all the other way. Nevertheless because, from a passenger viewpoint, the airport is now the Achilles Heel of the whole air transport system, we can do better - and we ought to plan to do better.

10. Security problems apart, (they represent an unhappy need to reverse the forward trends of 'facilitation'), and taking account of the great-ly increased numbers of people travelling in much larger groups - there is a need for a drive towards better service for passengers at air-ports all over the world. It requires improved design as well as a changed approach to the business.

11. So, in seeking to get the most out of exist-ing airports, high on the list there should come - I suggest - a determination to bring about better standards toward the customer.

12. That brings us to consider what are the essential ingredients of a successful airport in the world of today?

AIRPORT REQUIREMENTS

13. Like the infrastructure of all forms of transport, airports must be designed efficiently to serve its two fundamentals - transport vehi-cles and their users (passengers and goods).

14. For both categories there are, I suggest, five main requirements.

For the vehicles and their operators:

adequate navigational, approach and landing aids and systems;
sufficient runway, and taxiway, numbers and capacity;
enough aircraft stands and aprons;
satisfactory refuelling and servicing facilities;
efficient loading and unloading arrangements.

For passengers and shippers of goods:

good access;
sufficient set-down, pick-up and parking spaces;
satisfactory terminal buildings - including check-in and information arrangements;
minimum walking distances to and from aircraft;
efficient baggage handling.

15. All these ten requirements are important to the smooth working of any airport and they must all be reasonably related to the conditions of peak traffic flows. Though the provision of

facilities fully to meet peaks is always claimed to be uneconomic - and is - one has to remember that today's peaks are tomorrow's normal flows.

16. The real test of an airport - as of an air-line - is not when everything is running to schedule on a fine summer's day but rather when things are all adrift in winter fogs, snow and ice, when all flights are delayed and prospec-tive passengers fill the terminals.

17. On the whole and at present, airports do not do well under these stresses and, somewhat natu-rally, those which do best are those at which traffic is handled in relatively small units. This is where a disparity can increasingly be seen to be arising in administrative and opera-tional planning. Some radically revised think-ing is required.

18. In order best to meet the requirements for the maintenance of the highest standards of technical services together with good surface access it follows that there should be the few-est number of major airports which can serve adequately the traffic demands of any particular catchment area.

19. Such a concentration of facilities must, on the other hand, be provided with such multipli-cations of specialist facilities as is required to achieve both adequate capacity and 'fail-safe' operations when one or more of the main com-ponents are out of action by accident, for main-tenance, for up-dating or for other reasons. Experience has shown that the long-term econom-ics, as well as the safety and convenience of services, fully endorse such a principle.

20. Because means of access, runways and ter-minal buildings are each essential to the main-tenance of continued operations at any airport, clearly the removal from service of any one of those fundamental components should not be allow-ed to result in the closure of the whole of a major airport.

21. Diversions to other, possibly congested, air-ports in such circumstances are no adequate solu-tion even in the short term. They will become even less tolerable as traffic grows.

22. It is axiomatic, therefore, that no major international airport should be wholly dependent upon one single means of access, one single run-way or one single terminal building.

23. There is a further point of importance. Evidence from every form of business, sport and entertainment in which large numbers of people are involved at a time, shows that their hand-ling in very large groups is always unsatisfac-tory and, in times of emergency, can lead to disaster. People react better and can be hand-led more conveniently and efficiently in rela-tively small groups than in very large numbers.

24. At airports all over the world - though it will not be popular to say this - there can be no doubt that the rot set in on the passenger service side when, for what seemed to be sen-sible reasons at the time, decisions were taken to concentrate upon very large multiple-airline passenger-terminals. Today, those who run some of these massive buildings are trying to cope

in them with up to 10 million passengers a year
- which means peak flows of around 4000 passengers an hour, taking arrivals and departures together.

25. The handling of such numbers can be done, but experience shows that tolerable standards of service are then very difficult to achieve. We ought not to accept such an erosion of standards on the ground any more than we would in the air.

26. So I repeat that the solution must lie in a rethinking of the ways in which passengers should be handled, as existing airports are redeveloped to cope with the loads and needs of the future. In the longer term we must plan to handle double the number of passengers per annum - and at peak hours - through existing airports.

27. The inevitable conclusion is that standards of passenger service at airports cannot be improved - and will probably deteriorate in both convenience and in time taken - unless we face up to the problems of providing increased numbers of passenger terminals at all the major airports. Ideally each should be devoted to the services of a relatively few airlines and preferably operated by the airlines themselves, which are the organisations most concerned to achieve high standards of passenger service. Where space is available the best results will certainly be gained from a larger number of smaller terminals rather than from a few terminals of enormous size.

28. And that leads us to the usual '64 million dollar' question. What capacities can we - and should we - plan for? How much airport do we need and how much are we likely to have available?

AIRPORT CAPACITIES

29. Much air has flowed over many wings since the massive Roskill Commission delved into the problems of the London area between June 1968 and January 1971. Much has changed and much is changing still.

30. Over the years possibly more thought and more work has been devoted to the problems of air traffic in the London area and of the airports to serve it there, than has been given to any other area in the world. We now have the Department of Trade's London Area Consultation Document within an 'Airport Strategy for Great Britain' published in November 1975 and prepared by officials of the Departments of Trade and the Environment and of the British Airports Authority and the Civil Aviation Authority. It is, if I may say so, a competent and balanced survey of a most complex and difficult subject.

31. There is, however, one notable gap in the Consultative Document. It does not give sufficient regard to the growing importance of business and corporate aviation - now a permanent feature of British overseas trade and of much domestic business. Nor does it consider fully the development of short-haul cross-Channel services. For both these aspects of the transport scene the future of Southend Airport and, perhaps, of Northolt as well, appear to me to be of significance for the future. Southend now - and

Northolt later - ought to be considered as essential parts of the London airports complex.

32. With reservations, therefore, on that particular subject, let us now consider the problem of the London area as a whole against the background of the new document and the new circumstances which exist today.

33. Like all logical analyses the consultative document starts with a statement of traffic at existing airports, assesses their capacity with and without various developments and then compares those capacities with a series of revised forecasts of demand. In essence, as a result of the present recession, airport capacity in the London area is judged to be adequate at least up to 1981 and probably substantially beyond.

34. That is somewhat of an over-simplification of both the document and the facts but it represents the basis for anyone who may happen to feel tolerably satisfied with the present situation. As I have said, in my view we ought not to be thus satisfied and I am sure that no one who is really involved is other than properly and restlessly dissatisfied.

35. In the old words of aviation planning there are the 'three where' questions - Where have we been?, Where are we now?, Where are we going?

36. The first two can best be answered for airports in the London area in the form of a table of air traffic over the past five years (Table 1).

37. The figures show that, compared with 1972 there has been a general reduction in aircraft movements through the London airports as a whole and that only at Heathrow was there any marginal increase at all, comparing the figures for 1975 with those for 1972. In essence, in terms of aircraft movements there have been three years of breathing space compared with the expected increase of some 15% during that time.

38. Because the average size of aircraft has increased, as well as some load factors, there has been a 5% increase in passengers handled at airports in the London area between 1972 and 1975 - but that compares with the expected 30% increase. The passenger statistics are given in Table 2.

39. These returns show that Heathrow is currently handling some 73% of the passengers on air transport services in the London area - and about 67% of the transport aircraft movements.

40. The potential capacity of Heathrow is, therefore, a key factor in seeking to achieve the best results out of the scarce resources represented by the London area's airports.

41. Many estimates have been made of Heathrow's eventual capacity - the latest in the 'London Area Consultation Document'. It suggests that the capacity of Heathrow's two main runways by 1990 will be 308 000 air transport movements a year used in a form of 'mixed mode' operation described as 'staggered parallel' take-offs and landings. This is a reduction of 30 000 movements a year compared with the estimates in the Maplin review. I hope that when 1990 comes this will turn out to be an underestimate. Let us accept it, however, as a reasonable planning figure for the present.

Table 1. Past and present air traffic : five London airports 1970-1975

AIRCRAFT MOVEMENTS	1970 '000	1971 '000	1972 '000	1973 '000	1974 '000	1975 '000
Heathrow						
Total	270.3	273.5	279.2	294.3	288.2	280.0
Transport a/c	246.4	249.6	256.8	268.2	266.3	257.6
Percentage transport	91.1	91.3	91.9	91.1	92.4	92.0
Gatwick						
Total	92.2	102.6	105.2	112.1	105.3	104.0
Transport a/c	53.6	63.8	75.6	73.1	72.0	72.9
Percentage transport	58.1	62.2	71.9	65.2	68.4	70.1
Stansted						
Total	44.6	41.6	33.9	31.1	32.0	33.0
Transport a/c	6.2	5.7	4.1	3.1	3.3	3.7
Percentage transport	13.9	13.7	12.1	10.0	10.3	11.2
Luton						
Total	52.2	69.6	61.4	61.6	47.2	50.5
Transport a/c	22.3	27.9	31.3	30.7	20.8	19.2
Percentage transport	42.7	40.1	51.0	49.8	44.3	38.0
Southend						
Total	54.0	60.9	60.4	71.0	62.3	61.8
Transport a/c	18.4	21.2	13.7	15.2	15.1	14.8
Percentage transport	34.1	34.8	22.7	21.4	24.2	23.9
Five London airports						
Total	513.3	548.2	540.1	570.1	535.0	528.8
Transport a/c	346.9	368.2	381.5	390.3	377.6	368.2
Percentage transport	67.6	67.2	70.6	68.5	70.6	69.6
Per cent increase or decrease	+5.3%	+6.8%	-1.2%	+5.5%	-6.6%	-1.2%

Table 2. Past and present air traffic : five London airports 1970-1975

Passengers handled	1970 m.	1971 m.	1972 m.	1973 m.	1974 m.	1975 m.
Heathrow	15.6	16.4	18.7	20.7	20.4	21.7
Gatwick	3.7	4.7	5.4	5.8	5.1	5.3
Stansted	0.5	0.5	0.3	0.2	0.2	0.3
Luton	2.0	2.8	3.1	3.2	2.0	1.9
Southend	0.5	0.6	0.3	0.4	0.2	0.2
Total	22.3	25.0	27.8	30.3	27.9	29.4
Percentage increase	+11.3%	+12.1%	+11.2%	+9.0%	-8.1%	+5.3%

Table 3.

	Air Transport Movements	Passengers	Pass per a/c
Peak hour:	42	11 500	274
Peak day:	540	132 000	245
Peak week:	3 500	815 500	233
Peak month:	14 000	3.12 million	223
Annual total	122 000	23.8 million	195

42. Experience of peak traffic distributions at a variety of airports suggests that for an airport with two, parallel, runways a peak hour capacity of about 86 movements ought to be achievable, if not now at least within a few years. On such an assumption, the following related ratios appear likely to result:

Peak hour:	86 aircraft movements (on two runways)
Peak day:	1 100 aircraft movements
Peak week:	7 200 aircraft movements
Peak month:	31 000 aircraft movements
Annual total:	310 000 aircraft movements

Those figures relate closely to Heathrow's potential.

43. When they are translated into numbers of passengers to be handled, experience shows that the ratios are likely to be as follows - on the assumption that by 1990 the average aircraft capacity at a major international airport will be about 300 seats (if it is less the problem will be somewhat easier):

Peak hour:	23 000 passengers (267 pass per a/c)
Peak day:	265 000 passengers (241 pass per a/c)
Peak week:	1.65 million passengers (229 pass per a/c)
Peak month:	6.8 million passengers (219 pass per a/c)
Annual total:	59 million passengers (190 pass per a/c)

The problem thus posed is how such numbers can be handled efficiently at acceptable standards of service in economic conditions?

44. All the evidence from existing airports - where up to 36 million passengers have so far been handled in a year at O'Hare, Chicago - is that tolerable standards will be achieved only if the numbers are divided among a sufficient number of smaller terminals.

45. There is a further point. Although, for economic reasons, the absolute peak hour loads cannot be used to plan the total related capacity of all the units which go to make up an airport, there are also reasonable limits within the ultimate capacity, beyond which no runway and no terminal building should be pressed, taking into account a balance between service and economics and within the bounds of safety.

46. As arbitrary figures within the present and forseeable state of knowledge, I suggest that no runway should be planned to handle more than 42 aircraft movements an hour and that no passenger terminal should be asked to handle more than an absolute maximum of 5000 passengers an hour - even at peaks. Beyond that there are too many people in one building at one time - whatever the floor area.

47. If we take these criteria and apply them to Heathrow's two runway system we arrive at - by about 1990 - a peak hour rate of 84 aircraft movements and a peak hour passenger flow of about 22 500.

48. Thus, Heathrow ought to be provided with not less than six passenger terminals to handle such numbers. Preferably there should be more smaller terminals. In any case the substantial Perry Oaks area between the Western ends of the main parallel runways must be brought into the airport's service area for the construction of at least three - and, much better, five - new unit terminals.

49. If we set Heathrow's acceptable working capacity at about 58 million passengers a year from 300 000 aircraft movements by about 1990 - handled on two main runways and, I hope, through not less than six passenger terminals, what loads must be expected to be carried by the other existing airports in the London area by that date?

50. The latest traffic forecasts from the Department of Trade's Consultative Document wisely suggest a fairly wide bracket of possibilities between 'high' and 'low' figures. For 1990 the suggestions are, in total demand for passenger numbers for the London area.

Year 1990: High forecast	- 106.6 million
Low forecast	- 69 million
Medium line, say	- 88 million

51. If, for this purpose, we leave Southend out of account and accept the Department of Trade's forecasts (which are substantially lower than those prepared at the time of the Maplin review) and assume that Heathrow can be developed to accommodate 58 million passengers a year, then the other three existing airports - Gatwick, Stansted and Luton - must be developed to handle up to say 49 million passengers a year with a more likely figure of about 30 million.

52. Between them these three airports have, at present, three runways which would have, by 1990, a theoretical capacity of about 450 000 aircraft movements which might carry about 85 million passengers.

53. In theory, therefore, there is capacity in hand.

54. In practice the situation is quite different.

55. For instance, in a somewhat arbitary way, the capacity of Gatwick's present single runway has been set at 168 000 air transport movements by 1990 which, in my view is rather high.

56. Experience suggests that the relevant capacity figures for Gatwick by 1990 might be of the order shown in Table 3. The associated requirement would then be for three separate passenger terminals at Gatwick in order to maintain reasonable standards.

57. We might thus expect Heathrow and Gatwick together to have capacities by 1990 for about 420 000 movements and 80 million passengers. On the upper estimate of possible passenger demand that would leave, by 1990, an additional 27 million passengers to be accommodated between Stansted and Luton. On the lower estimate, capacity for an additional eight million passengers might be required in 1990.

58. If the higher potential demand were to be spread equally between Luton and Stansted the requirement would be for about 65 000 movements in 1990 on each of their single runways. Each

Table 4.

1990		Air transport movements	Passengers handled	Passengers per aircraft
Heathrow:	Annual total:	264 000	50 million	190
	Peak hour:	73	19 500	267
Gatwick:	Annual total:	100 000	20 million	200
	Peak hour:	28	7 700	274
Stansted:	Annual total:	38 000	9 million	237
	Peak hour:	11	3 500	320
Luton:	Annual total:	38 000	9 million	237
	Peak hour:	11	3 500	320
Four London airports, 1990	Annual totals	440 000	88 million	200
	Peak hour	123	34 200	278

airport would then have to handle 13.5 million passengers a year through not less than two terminals at each airport.

59. The figures are based on upper level forecasts. Nonetheless they could be handled. If, instead, we look at the more likely middle line between the high and the low forecasts we arrive at the figures given in Table 4 for the year 1990 - remembering still that the traffic during the peak hours in 1990 is likely to be substantially less than the demand during the peak hours of 2000 A.D.

60. These broad approximations do no more than indicate that the four airports are likely to have capacity to handle the prospective traffic up to the early 1990s. They show also that what is required is much more emphasis on three things:

(a) additional terminal buildings,
(b) improved access to all four airports,
(c) a second runway at Gatwick - not on capacity grounds but to ensure safety and reliability of service.

61. Indeed, the loss of the single runway at Gatwick even for a short time from one of many possible causes would not only cost very large and unacceptable sums to all the operators there but also place intolerable loads on the other airports.

62. Additionally, there is a clear and unmistakable requirement for more aircraft stands, more passenger terminals and more loading and unloading gates - together with an additional western access - for Heathrow within the Perry Oaks area. Without it the airport will not be able to cope at any tolerable standard. Action ought to be set in hand at once.

63. To achieve an adequate number of aircraft loading gates with terminal capacity behind them - and to eliminate the unacceptable 'busing' of passengers to and from aircraft - the desirable numbers of terminals and associated 'gates' which require to be planned at each airport work out somewhat thus:

	Passenger terminals	Loading gates
Heathrow	seven	140
Gatwick	three	60
Stansted	two	24
Luton	two	24
Total	14	248

64. So there is a pattern - a requirement for a programme for the building of more, better and, preferably, smaller and better equipped new passenger terminals each closely linked to the aircraft they serve through sufficient loading gates all provided with 'jet-ways' or 'aircraft bridges'.

65. With them must go also the provision of much better information for passengers and their friends about departures and arrivals - still a weak feature of most airports.

NEED FOR BALANCE

66. On the London airports scene a few special points stand out as examples of the need to achieve a balance between the likely traffic demands and the availability of runways, aircraft stands and gates, passenger terminals and access road and rail services.

67. At Heathrow there has been for some time a plan to add to the three passenger terminals in the Central Area a fourth terminal on the south side. Such a new terminal would make possible an increase in the capacity of Heathrow from its present total of about 30 million passengers a year to about 38 million passengers a year - a total which would gradually increase as the average size of aircraft grows.

68. Desirable as is this additional capacity, and relatively economical as it may be to build, in transport terms it is nonetheless very much a 'second best'. It will be remote from the Hatton Cross station on the Piccadilly Tube to which it will have to be linked by a shuttle bus

service. At the same time aircraft isolated on the south side of the two main parallel runways will create a number of problems both for Air Traffic Control and for airline operations. A better solution would have been to create new apron space adjacent to the original BEA maintenance hangars and close to Hatton Cross.

69. The additional South Side terminal at Heathrow will need to be further augmented by the middle 1980s and there can be no doubts that the Perry Oaks area becomes essential to the proper development of the airport.

Perry Oaks

70. The Perry Oaks site between the runways is, at present a reception and processing area for sewage sludge and not a primary sewage treatment works - even so not an ideal companion for Britain's major centre for the reception and processing of passengers. The alternative for the Thames Water Authority would be either to acquire another site at a more convenient place or - preferably - to invest in a more sophisticated disposal system.

71. With good will and a sense of priorities the matter could be resolved relatively easily - though at some substantial 'lead-time' before airport works could begin at Perry Oaks.

72. From a transport viewpoint, the building of a second terminal-focus for Heathrow to the west is clearly sound and right. It would not only add essential capacity at a convenient place but it would also relieve the present excessive concentration in the Central Area. The Piccadilly Line can be extended easily into Perry Oaks - provision has been made to do this - and a planned West Orbital road would give good access.

73. I make a plea for this task now to be tackled urgently in the cause of sound and much needed airport development.

74. At Gatwick the requirement is different - a second runway which remains a high priority to maintain the transport integrity of Britain's second airport as well as to avoid delays in airport movements at peak periods.

75. Gatwick's second runway is needed primarily for landings and, therefore, can be relatively short - around 7500 ft. Economically, and from a broad transport viewpoint, it is now overdue. No other airport in the world is handling international air traffic of Gatwick's volume and importance on a single runway - and Gatwick's traffic will certainly grow substantially.

76. In general, the economics of major airports are likely to improve as traffic begins to grow again and as facilities are provided which can be amortised over many years.

77. May I urge, therefore, that, in the interests of international air trade and a return to national prosperity as well as in the interests of good long-term planning, a determined effort be made to bring existing airports to improved standards for the handling of passengers and goods.

78. In the changed situation of technological development the substantial future increase in number of passengers is likely to be accomplished without a proportional increase in the number of aircraft movements. At the same time the trend of noise is downwards. Airports represent substantial and important national assets and valuable centres of employment. Increases in trade and in employment are now at the top of national priorities.

79. Let us move forward then to achieve the best possible results from existing airports with a determination to achieve higher standards for both the users and providers of services.

6. General aviation facilities

R.A. Smith, OBE
Managing Director, CSE Aviation Ltd, Oxford

The title of this paper has led the writer to spend some time detailing "what is General Aviation today?," as it is fealt that this does need explaining for the benefit, in particular, of those who may be influenced in providing the facilities so badly needed. Additionally it also highlights the problems that this particular sector of aviation has within itself and the inadequate financial return that may accrue from providing such facilities.

INTRODUCTION

WHAT IS GENERAL AVIATION?

1. Before beginning to consider the required facilities of General Aviation everyone should be quite clear what is meant by General Aviation. It is now a much used phrase and very often much misunderstood. It suffers from a number of definitions but until such time as someone comes up with a better one it is intended to use that defined by the United Kingdom's Civil Aviation Authority.

2. General Aviation is:

   (A) All fixed-wing civil flying, except that performed by the major commercial airline operators. This is subject to the constraint that the aircraft concerned have a maximum all up weight of 25,000 lbs. or less, but the definition is extended to cover the special case of executive jet aircraft.

   (B) Civil helicopter operations.

3. From this it can be seen that it covers all private and business aviation, flying schools, flying and gliding club and group activity, and the majority of commercial operations carried out within the weight limitations defined above.

4. Sometimes attempts are made to differentiate firmly between General Aviation and public air transport operations. From the above definition this is certainly not the case as General Aviation does include air transport or public transport in at least two specific areas. These are the third level scheduled services which, in the United Kingdom at the present time, are virtually limited to the Highlands and Islands services in Scotland,

usually carried out in aircraft with a maximum seating capacity of 25; the other being air taxi and charter operations. The latter, by its own definition, being clearly a small aircraft available for hire by the general public on an aircraft rather than a seat basis. These aircraft, being defined as public transport have to be flown by a pilot holding a Professional Licence and must comply with the regulations applicable to both large and small public transport aircraft. There is, however, one difference which may be of interest as this may not apply in other countries. If the air taxi aircraft for example is less than 6,000 lbs. in all up weight it does not, unlike public transport aircraft above that weight, have to operate into licensed aerodromes. It can, therefore, operate into the smallest of landing strips. Within the past ten years or so increasing use has been made of aircraft in this category both single and twin-engined.

5. It follows, therefore, that even the smallest unlicensed aerodrome in the United Kingdom can almost certainly be used for air transport operators to some extent.

6. Reverting to our definition of General Aviation we can identify it further by breaking it down into two general categories:

   (i) Flying for business purposes.

   (ii) Flying for recreational purposes.

7. These in turn can be broken down into corporate and private owners, air taxi and charter companies and third level operators as the "business users" and for the leisure and recreational users the private owners, the flying clubs and groups, gliders and the remainder which generally cover those intrepid aviators such as balloonists, parachutists and the new and rapidly expanding hang-gliding fraternity.

8.   As will be shown later it is clearly apparent from the definitions above that the requirements of all these various users of General Aviation aerodromes are very different. It would be difficult, and indeed it is probably quite a terrifying thought to imagine one single aerodrome catering for all the above diverse activities. However, a mix between these activities is not only possible but works very satisfactorily not only in the United Kingdom but elsewhere. It should also be clearly stated at this stage that many individuals and bodies believe that flying operations carried out for business purposes, and to a limited extent for recreational purposes, can also mix with larger aircraft at the major aerodromes and international airports. This is an aspect which will be dealt with later in this paper.

WHO ARE THE USERS OF GENERAL AVIATION?

9.   Having considered in some detail a definition of General Aviation and the principal sections that comprise it we should now look at the people who make use of General Aviation and who, therefore, require the facilities that we are examining in this paper. As mentioned above it is intended to deal with certain aspects of the requirements of the users of recreation and leisure flying but it should be pointed out that it is not within the scope of this paper to deal with gliding, parachuting, ballooning, etc. Therefore, the paper is confined to the users of powered aircraft only. In considering the users it must not be forgotten that we are considering not only the passengers but also business companies and the pilots and aircrew concerned. Unlike the scheduled and commercial carriers the number of passengers involved in General Aviation is, as we have seen from the definitions and categories, small in number.

10.   Let us firstly consider the users of that category of General Aviation which can be broadly considered to exist primarily for leisure, sporting and recreational purposes. Here the passengers are seldom more than three or four in number per aircraft and in a great majority of cases are not paying for the privilege of flying. One of the exceptions that we should perhaps deal with straight away is the case of the pleasure flying or joy riding passenger. Here we have members of the public who pay for a seat in a light aircraft or a helicopter for the express purpose of being taken on a pleasure flight, usually of short duration, comprising often just one brief circuit of the aerodrome. Although small in percentage these are nonetheless genuine users of General Aviation and the facilities that need to be provided for this minority should not be ignored. It is often by such pleasure flights that many people are introduced to flying as passengers and in some cases as future pilots. It is believed that well over half the population of the United Kingdom and of the United States of America have never flown.

11.   We then have the private pilot either owning his own aircraft or hiring one from his local flying school or club and usually that aircraft will fly passengers, often relations and friends, purely for recreation. This may, of course, vary from a "once round the circuit" initial air experience flight to a touring holiday often involving many thousands of miles of international flying. This latter form of recreational flying has increased considerably in recent years with the introduction of comprehensive radio navigation aids in small private aircraft plus, of course, the comfort now afforded to passengers in such aircraft - very different from the past. A further very important user of General Aviation is the private pilot who may either own or hire an aircraft and use it for business travel purposes, probably in addition to recreation. This category of General Aviation user has increased considerably during the course of the last few years and may be expected to grow further in the future providing the necessary aerodrome and ground facilities are available, enabling him to make use of the national and international airways systems and sophisticated navigation and landing aids which his aircraft will almost certainly be equipped to use. In the United Kingdom there has been a marked increase in the "fly-it-yourself" businessman since the United Kingdom joined the European Economic Community and it is considered that as this country becomes more and more involved in Europe, and markets expand, so further increases may be expected in this category. The great majority of people using General Aviation are members of flying clubs, schools and groups. These will be flying in club aircraft hired for the occasion by a club member. At the present time there are nearly 250 flying clubs and schools in this country and it is interesting that this figure has appeared to have remained almost constant over the last two decades. It is probably true to say that the primary role of the flying clubs in this country is to train people to fly and later to take them on to further more advanced flying qualifications but still generally speaking all related to the Private Pilot's Licence.

12.   In some countries the flying club is rather different to that in the United Kingdom. Here it is generally a small organisation, often a true "members' club" in that it is a non-profit making organisation administered and controlled through a committee of members owning or leasing aircraft for training purposes and also providing aircraft for hire to qualified pilots. Generally it will have an active social membership. Increasingly the social facilities are vitally necessary for economic reasons to maintain the very existence of the club and indeed here may be cited one criticism of this form of flying organisation in that it may be considered to have flying facilities as a secondary rather than a primary function with the flying subsidised by the social activities. Unlike the United Kingdom in many other countries the flying training facilities are provided by specific flying schools which do not generally offer any social facilities and

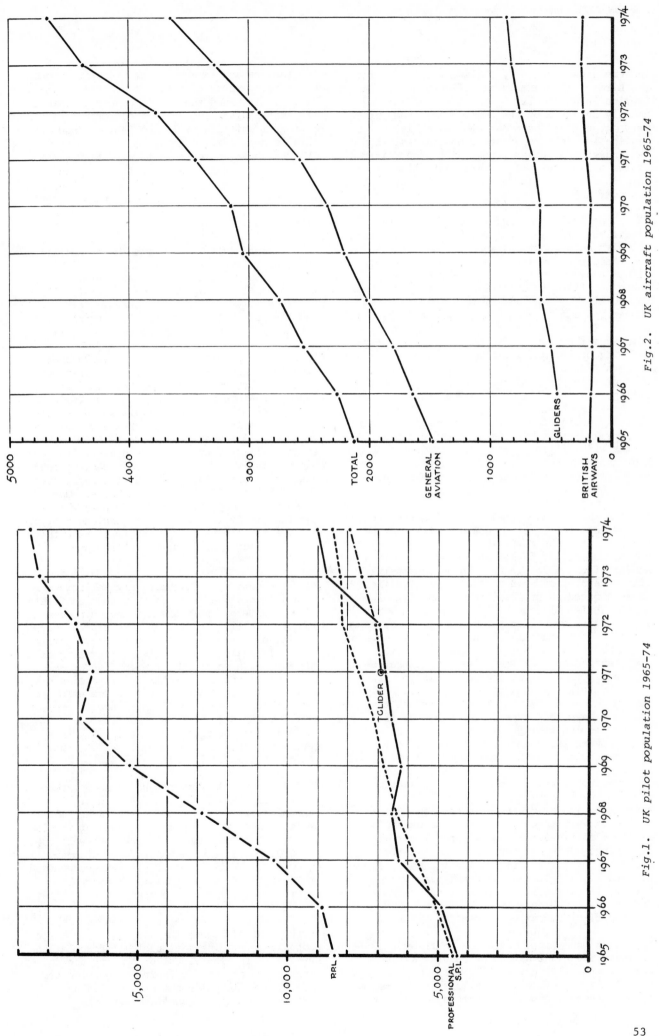

Fig.2. UK aircraft population 1965-74

Fig.1. UK pilot population 1965-74

53

in some cases even only limited facilities for the hire of aircraft by qualified pilots. In America in particular this latter facility is usually provided by the commercially run, often very large fixed-base operator which is a distinctive feature at every General Aviation and indeed many other airfields in the United States of America. There are indications that this is becoming the future trend in the United Kingdom.

13. The flying training sector represents a significant total of the whole General Aviation activity throughout the world. The schools concerned with the training of new professional pilots are, in this country as is generally known, confined to a total of three only. Under United Kingdom regulations this training must be carried out by a specially approved organisation. This is a rare situation. In most countries the regulatory authority may approve a flying training establishment but once its approval has been obtained they can teach for both private and professional licences and ratings.

14. The professional schools certainly in this country generally operate from their own aerodromes with little if any other traffic and in most cases with the school or its parent organisation being responsible for the management of the aerodrome.

15. In the United States of America and indeed other countries it is of course quite common-place to find the flying training school or schools operating from a major airport with student first solos going on simultaneously with scheduled and non-scheduled jet traffic. Those engaged in professional flying training in the United Kingdom believe that such a mix is not to be commended particularly in the early stages of the students' flying training. However, there is certainly merit in student pilots, once they have passed the basic training stage, being introduced on a fairly gradual basis to mixing with the "big boys" at major airfields. Indeed during advanced training it is important that students have this experience, subject, of course, to the use of adequately equipped aircraft having the speed so that they do not create problems in the aerodrome circuit.

16. One would be criticised if this section on recreation, leisure and training flying was concluded without making some mention of the small but very enthusiastic band of General Aviation pilots active in the sporting sphere of flying. This may vary from the relatively new sport of formula air racing in small, often home-built, single seat aircraft over short closed circuits to long distance air rallies and races. Such activities take place from a variety of different categories of airfields.

17. Next one should mention a small but, none-theless, important aspect of General Aviation. Agricultural flying where the users may be con-sidered to be not only the pilots and operators of the aircraft but probably more accurately

the farmers and landowners of the crops, trees, etc., being sprayed, fertilised, dusted, etc., etc. It is hoped that those concerned with this particular, and in some countries, vital sector of aviation, will not feel offended if this is not referred to again in this paper. The reason for this is that apart from a main base with its maintenance facilities, etc., their aerodrome facilities may be considered to be no more than a flat field or stretch of land within which the aircraft can land and take off whilst operating.

18. Having dealt so far with the categories of General Aviation concerned mainly with air-craft at the smaller end of the scale, I would like to deal finally with the corporate or business aircraft owner or operator, air taxis and the private owner using his aircraft primarily for business purposes.

19. The corporate aircraft is clearly one owned by a business company for the transport of the directors, executives and staff and, indeed, customers concerned with the business of that company. Such aircraft would be flown by a professional pilot and crew and could vary in size from a small four/five seat twin piston engined aircraft up to a modern executive jet. Exceptionally corporate aircraft can, of course, even include specially fitted airliners, such as BAC 1-11's, DC 9's and even 707's. One presumes the day will not be far away when an American multi-million dollar conglomerate, or perhaps it will be a pop star, will have the first 747 purely for executive transport purposes.

20. The company, of course, may well own more than just the one aircraft. In America fleets of corporate aircraft are not uncommon, some almost rivalling in size and the general com-plexity of their operation those of the small inter-state airlines. In the United Kingdom and Europe, however, the company owning more than one aircraft is rather the exception but, as an example, in the United Kingdom which is geographically very small there are at present over 200 aircraft used by companies for exclusive business use and the C.A.A., in a recent survey, has predicted over 800 companies owning corporate aircraft by 1985.

21. The Business Aircraft Users Association of the United Kingdom has a membership of 65 companies owning a total fleet of some 110 air-craft. These member companies had, at the last count, a combined annual turnover of well over £25,000,000 and employ a workforce of over 2,000,000. Their fleet of aircraft were based on 35 airfields throughout the country from major airports to small company owned airfields.

22. Parallel to the company owned and self operated aircraft are the air taxi and charter companies providing a valuable transportation service to the individual or company who do not wish to own or operate their own service or, indeed, have insufficient utilisation to justify ownership. Sometimes air taxi

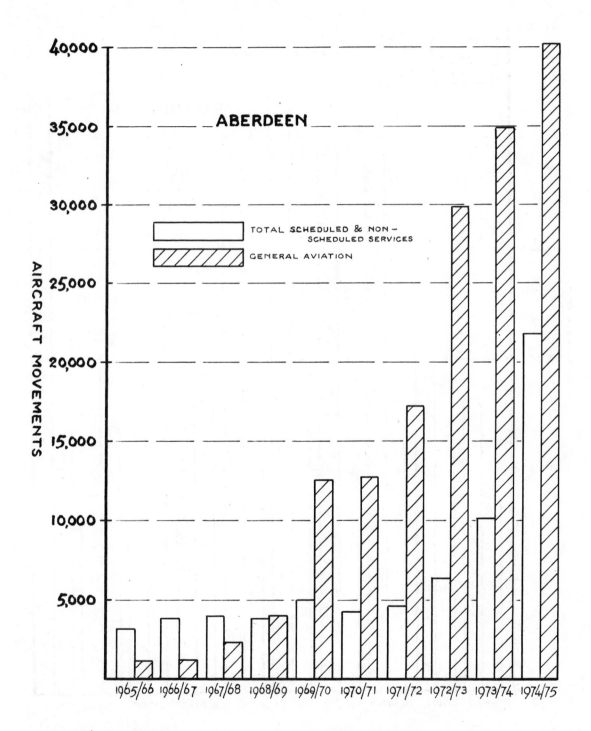

Fig.3.   Aberdeen: general aviation use increase 1973/4-1974/5, 14.7%

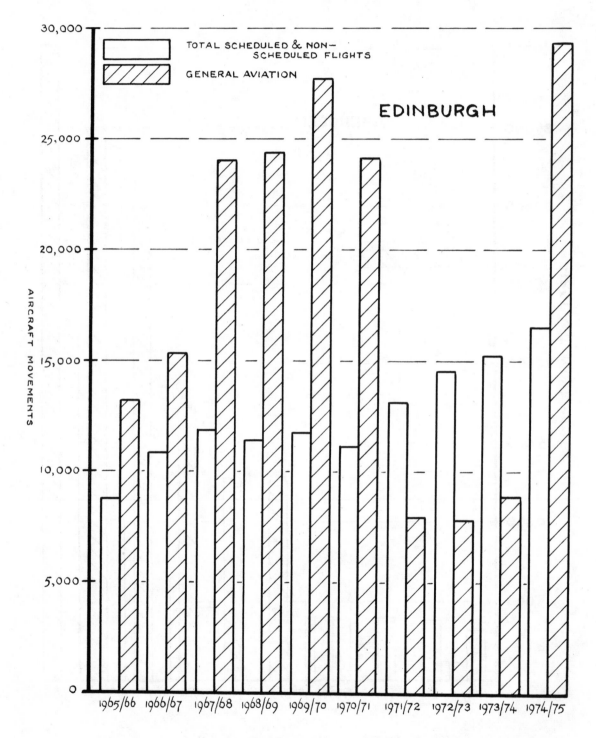

Fig.4. *Edinburgh: gneeral aviation use increase 1973/4-1974/5, 227.2%*

companies provide a pool of aircraft serving several companies who guarantee an adequate annual utilisation to make it attractive to all concerned. These users are in the same category as a corporate aircraft user and demand and expect the same facilities. As with the company owned aircraft the availability of types covers the whole range from small single engine aircraft to the executive jet, the customer from an individual to a multi-national conglomerate.

23. Whilst dealing with the professionally flown aircraft in General Aviation we should mention the third level or commuter airlines. In this country these tend to be forgotten as they exist only to a very limited extent, confined, as mentioned earlier, almost entirely to the Highlands and Island services in Scotland. Since the War many unsuccessful attempts have been made to establish other third level services in the U.K. It is difficult to establish exactly why more of this aspect of air transport has not taken on in the U.K. It may well be due to the comparatively short distances involved and, despite their critics, the good and extensive network of rail services and more recently motorways.

24. So far we have considered the business aircraft as one flown by a professional pilot who, generally, is concerned in that organisation solely as a chauffeur to his passengers besides often running the complete operation, planning the maintenance, etc., etc. We must not, however, forget the genuine business aircraft that is flown, probably just as competently as the professional pilot by an executive member of the company. He is operating on a "fly himself on business" basis in precisely the same way as he might drive himself to and from business appointments and meetings as distinct from his associate in another probably larger company who has a chauffeur driven Rolls Royce. This man is often a highly efficient, well qualified pilot requiring similar aids and aerodrome facilities as a corporate professional pilot.

25. Summing up this particular section, it appears that the many different types of users of General Aviation require different facilities to different scales.

WHAT ARE THE EXISTING AIRFIELD FACILITIES FOR GENERAL AVIATION?

26. Before dealing with the aerodrome facilities which should be provided, we will firstly consider what facilities are available at the present time.

27. It may be helpful if we start by defining, as far as is possible, the different types of aircraft "landing grounds" available.

(A) Airport. This is the term commonly used to describe the main international airports in all the countries of the world and therefore have Customs facilities. However, there are one or two exceptions, certainly in the U.K., where comparatively small General Aviation airfields that have been established for many years, rejoice under the name of airport, even though they may not have full Customs facilities.

(B) Aerodrome. It is proposed to consider an aerodrome as an area of land providing facilities for take off and landing of aircraft, but not including Customs facilities on a regular basis, but with some air traffic control; also facilities for the maintenance and hangarage of aircraft and the home of at least one, but more likely a number of flying schools, clubs and probably small air taxi or charter companies. Aerodromes may vary from a small grass field, capable of use by single and twin engined aircraft, to airfields with hard runways, capable of being used by modern jets.

(C) Airfield. In this case we will consider an airfield as a category of "landing ground" somewhat below that described above as an aerodrome, but above the air-strip mentioned below. Unlike the aerodrome, it is not necessarily, but generally, licensed by the national authority controlling civil aviation and aerodromes.

(D) Airstrip. This is the lowest category of landing ground that we are considering. It would generally be a field of suitable dimensions to enable the operation of one or at the most two or three aircraft, generally belonging to the owner of the land.

28. The airstrip, as defined, may be considered to be virtually the same throughout the world. For many tasks a basic dirt strip is adequate, and has served the needs of many facets of aviation from the flying doctor services, to emergency evacuation and supply work by aircraft of the size of the C130.

29. Although we have talked rightly of the airstrip as being virtually nothing more than a field or a strip of land with a windsock, it is not unknown for some airstrip owners to install fairly sophisticated aids (by airstrip standards) such as an electric lighting system, remotely controlled by radio from the aircraft on its approach.

30. Because airstrips are unlicensed, and there is generally no requirement for "authority" to be advised of their existence it is of course difficult to assess the precise number which may exist not only in this country but in any other. However, it is interesting to note that it was recently estimated that in

the United Kingdom there are now over 170 such strips in use.

31. Many horse race-courses throughout the United Kingdom have established their own air-strips whether in the centre of, or adjacent to, the actual race-course. A number of motor racing circuits in this country have similar facilities. As these have often been construct-ed around disused wartime aerodromes, they can, unlike the horse race-course airstrips, often offer hard surfaced runways.

32. A typical United Kingdom AIRFIELD would probably have an all grass surface, although there are exceptions to this rule, particularly in cases where use is made of part of an abandoned war-time airfield, where, sometimes, sections of the old runways are used. The facilities are minimal, often comprising one or two hangars, plus a clubhouse, used by the resident flying club who are often responsible for the operation and upkeep of the airfield itself. The flying operations carried out on the many airfields of this type that exist all over the United Kingdom may be considered to be real recreational flying, and indeed, are the "grass roots" of this type of aviation. In addition to the flying club aircraft, there are usually a number of privately owned aircraft based on the airfield. As most of these air-fields would be used for training, they would be licensed by the C.A.A. There might well be a ground to air radio service, probably operated from a fairly primitive form of air traffic control tower without full time or licensed air traffic controllers. The flying club would probably also have a small maintenance section to look after not only the club aeroplanes but also those of the private owners based on the airfield.

33. There are seldom the commercial business pressures of the larger airfield, but, probably as a consequence, they are frequently not run as effectively or efficiently as larger airfields. They are invariably operated, and often owned, by private individuals or small companies. These people are very much the benefactors of this sector of General Aviation, and indeed, it is fair to say that without them General Aviation in the United Kingdom would be in a poor state.

34. As we have seen earlier in our definition of "landing grounds", the "AERODROME" comes mid-way between the airfield and the airport. This is probably the most important of all the categories that we are considering, at least as far as General Aviation in the United Kingdom is concerned. This is where it all happens. At the present time, there are only about 118 licensed aerodromes/airfields in the United Kingdom and the majority of these fall into this category. More often than not, they have at least one hard runway, and these aerodromes may be owned and operated by the local authorities, private or public companies, and occasionally even private individuals. Here one would norm-ally expect an air traffic control service, with licensed air traffic control officers, and

possibly with the facilities of a let-down aid of some sort, usually an airfield sited NDB. As with the smaller airfields the operator of the aerodrome is sometimes one of the resident flying clubs, usually the largest, or an air taxi/charter and maintenance organisation. Only in comparatively few cases is there a specialist airfield operating company with no flying interests located on the airfield. On most aerodromes you will find a typical cross section of the General Aviation scene; probably a number of flying clubs, varying considerably in size and number of aircraft operated, a maintenance and service organisation plus at least one company who would be engaged in air-craft sales. Frequently, these companies also operate a maintenance and servicing organisation plus at least one company who would be engaged in aircraft sales. Frequently, these companies also operate a maintenance and servicing organisation and, indeed, the flying club or school as well.

35. Lastly in this section are the AIRPORTS. It is proposed that we should consider in this section airports which not only comply with the definition mentioned earlier, but are also served by one or more scheduled air transport services, either domestic or international. We should start by saying that with one or two notable exceptions, to which reference will be made, the facilities offered by these airports for the General Aviation user particularly in the United Kingdom is, regrettably, minimal. Indeed, it is probably fair to say that the larger the airport the less are the facilities provided for the General Aviation user and it is a pity that the airport management and controlling authority are seldom interested in this category of aviation.

36. At the top of this big league in our land-ing grounds table, London (Heathrow) is obviously number one in the United Kingdom but, compared with America, in 1974 it ranked about number 35 with movements totalling 288,100 with Greater Pittsburgh, P.A., above it with 288,329 movements and Boston, Mass., below with 288,076. As most people will be aware, Heathrow is one of the seven United Kingdom airports controlled and managed by the British Airports Authority, which is a nationalised service enterprise. Those concerned with General Aviation overseas frequently express surprise at the remarkably low percentage of General Aviation in the total Heathrow movements. The latest figures avail-able indicate this is approximately 5.6%.

37. Before concluding this section covering the different types and categories of landing grounds it would be wrong if we did not make mention of the facilities needed for the operation of helicopters. In this country, this particular aspect of General Aviation has grown considerably during the past five or six years. Specialist helicopter landing facilities may be divided into three main categories:-

> Heliports
> Helipads
> Helistops

38. A heliport is generally taken to be a helicopter operating base for one or more operators and, therefore, might include maintenance, servicing and fuelling facilities as well as passenger accommodation and probably some form of air traffic control.

39. A helipad is generally considered to be an area of land approved for use for landing and take-off of helicopters, but unlike the heliport, with the bare minimum of facilities. It would be unlikely to have air traffic control and certainly no maintenance or servicing facilities. It may be staffed on a one man and a boy basis and have little other facilities beyond a telephone and probably some form of small building. Here, it would generally be possible for helicopters to remain, probably not overnight, but certainly whilst awaiting arrival or return of passengers.

40. A helistop is the helicopter equivalent of an airstrip and would virtually be a suitable area of ground for landing and purely as a facility for the dropping and picking up of passengers. Normally a helicopter would not be allowed to remain at a helistop.

41. In summing up it can be seen that, unlike the larger air transport operators, General Aviation can and, indeed, must be able to make use of the whole spectrum of airfields or perhaps more correctly in this context "landing grounds" from the biggest international airport to the farmer's field with a solitary windsock and very little else. Although at opposite ends of the General Aviation scale the user of the corporate million pound plus executive jet has a need for particular facilities just as much as the flying farmer and his Piper Cub operating from a five acre field.

WHAT FACILITIES DOES GENERAL AVIATION REQUIRE FOR THE FUTURE?

42. In the previous three sections of this paper we have endeavoured to answer a number of questions concerned with the General Aviation situation. Firstly what is General Aviation?, secondly who are the users of General Aviation?, and thirdly what facilities exist at the present for this particular sector of aviation?

43. In this, the fourth and final section of the paper, we shall endeavour to look at some of the future requirements for General Aviation.

44. In making plans for the future it is necessary to assess the likely demand. To do this one must have access to reliable past and present statistics and data. In the case of U.K. General Aviation such reliable information is difficult to obtain. With most General Aviation airfields there is no statutory requirement for movement records to be submitted to the C.A.A. The system of record-keeping by individual airfields varies considerably making accurate comparisons difficult.

45. Similarly difficulties exist in obtaining reliable statistics of private pilots' flying hours and the hours flown by their aircraft. Because the U.K., as with other countries, has a five-year licence renewal period it is difficult to get more than an approximation of the number of pilots currently in flying practice at any one time. Of the C.A.A. figures of 20,000 current private pilots it is estimated that only about some 9,000 are active.

46. General Aviation is the predominant force in aviation today. In numbers it has probably ousted military aviation in first place as a result of the reduction in size of most world air forces over the past decade - certainly in the West.

    (A)   In 1974 worldwide General Aviation flew 75.8% of all hours flown.

    (B)   The current world General Aviation fleet is approximately 230,000 aircraft.

    (C)   In the U.S.A. there are approximately 13,000 airports. All but a few are available to General Aviation whereas only 425 are served by the airlines.

47. Despite the problem of obtaining reliable statistics on which to forecast demand, the C.A.A. have produced the first part of a most valuable report on General Aviation; albeit concerning the South East of England only.

48. The conclusion of Part I of this study reveals some interesting figures for the present and estimates for the future. A total of 67 airfields were identified in the study area as being available at present or in the future for General Aviation use. Evidence shows clearly that business, air taxi and charter operations are perhaps not unexpectedly the area of General Aviation likely to grow at a high and sustained rate. As an example there were 157,000 such movements at the airfields being considered during 1973 and these are forecast to increase to 306,000 by 1980 and 493,000 by 1985 - an average of 10% per annum. Recent figures show that in one year members of the U.K's. Air Taxi Operators Association carried 650,000 passengers and 1.5m. kilos of freight. In the mixed business and recreational use the forecast of growth is somewhat less at 7% with anticipated generation of 189,000 movements by 1985 whilst the private, leisure and recreational flying (which includes the flying clubs) has the lowest forecast growth at only 5%.

49. Overall the total volume of General Aviation activity in the South East could grow potentially at just over 5% per annum to 1985. However, it should be pointed out that these figures were based on estimates made during the first half of 1974 before the recent fuel and national economy problems. If, therefore, similar forecasts were to be made now it is reasonable to assume that whilst the growth,

particularly in business aviation, will still continue this crisis has undoubtedly caused a set-back and perhaps the figures forecast for 1985 should now be considered as for 1988 or even 1990.

50. If General Aviation is to survive, expand as forecast and fulfil its role of service to the community, it is absolutely vital that the local authorities responsible for the planning aspects of aerodromes fully understand that they have responsibilities to meet the expected demand. Unfortunately, this is not going to be an easy task although undoubtedly the existence of this joint C.A.A./Standing Conference on London and South East Regional Planning Report, particularly the second part, will help in giving the local authorities the facts behind the case. We live increasingly in an age when protection of the environment is becoming a major factor in the improvement or expansion of almost everything which may be considered to be even in the remotest way environmentally unacceptable. General Aviation is no exception. It is earnestly hoped that planning authorities, who understandably have to respect as far as possible the wishes of environmental pressure groups in their respective areas, will not accede too much to their demands by minimising the provision of local aerodrome facilities.

51. The forecast for General Aviation in the U.K. shows that it will undoubtedly play an increasingly important role in transportation for the industrial and commercial life of the country. Where there is such new development, General Aviation, particularly in the business role, will probably follow. An example of the importance of airfields to industry and the exploitation of national resources is the case of North Sea oil. Before the discovery and exploitation of this the airport of the Scottish town of Aberdeen was virtually dormant. Since the oil boom it has expanded tremendously and at one time 80% of all aircraft movements at Aberdeen were of General Aviation.

52. Throughout the world there is an increasing tendency for industry to disperse. The days are past of one vast monolithic plant engaged in mass production and providing the whole source of employment for one town or city. For work-force and economic reasons, industry now prefers a number of smaller units. This immediately imposes a communication and transport problem. There are already indications that industry will not establish new plants or satellites of others unless there is some conveniently situated airfield for the benefit of the business itself and its customers. This may mean a "field-length" of only, say, 1,000 - 2,000 metres and even sometimes less.

53. Conflicts are bound to arise between different classes of General Aviation user. An example of this occurs between the primarily business aircraft operator flown by professional pilots and the leisure and recreational user including the flying clubs. Should an airfield be developed to cater for one or other of these

two dissimilar groups and not mix them? It is doubtful as far as the U.K. is concerned although desirable in many aspects. There is not at present, nor likely to be in the foreseeable future, sufficient demand for one aerodrome, for example serving London, being devoted exclusively to the business aircraft operator. It is believed that there is going to have to be a mix of interests on most aerodromes although clearly one or other will predominate. As mentioned earlier in this paper mixed-use operations work perfectly satisfactorily in various parts of the world but to be effective careful control in every sense of the word needs to be exercised by the aerodrome operating authority.

54. One of the problems which will always face the General Aviation aerodrome is that of economic viability. It is probably true to say that throughout the world there are relatively few airports or aerodromes, from the largest to the smallest, which are financially self-supporting on flying activities alone. In most cases, and here London (Heathrow) is a good example, any profits made are generally the result of non-aviation activities. Possibly if the duty free shops and other ancillary operations at Heathrow were to disappear overnight then their balance sheet would go from a healthy black to red. A more enlightened attitude in the future by local planning authorities could certainly increase the financial viability of small aerodromes by permitting the development of light industrial sites and encouraging other non-aviation activities. An aerodrome is extremely "land-intensive." If one considers exactly how much of it is actually used for the take-off, landing and taxiing of aircraft the percentage of unused land, apart from growing grass, is very high. This land should be considered very carefully as a potential source of income to the General Aviation aerodrome owner or operator. Replanting of the unused areas could produce income from perhaps hay, silage or even cereals. Besides this there are other potentially profitable operations not affecting aviation safety.

55. Until recently such aerodromes have, broadly speaking, not been too greatly affected by pressure from environmental protection groups. Hitherto, complaints have generally been on an individual basis. However, in the U.K. there are now signs that organised action is being taken rather in the same way as that started some years ago against the large airports. This is a fact which General Aviation must recognise. Without wishing to be too critical of these aerodromes, it is regrettable that in some cases some of this results from the attitude of the owners or operators themselves. There is all too frequently a far too insular attitude taken by them with little attempt being made to keep residents, groups and local councils aware as to what is happening or is going to happen at the local aerodrome. There is sometimes a lack of thoughtfulness resulting in nuisance, much of which could be improved.

56. We should now consider briefly some improvements which need to be made if General

Aviation and in particular the business use sector is to expand and serve industry, commerce and the community as it should.

(A) Major airport authorities throughout the world must accept right-of-access to suitably qualified pilots flying adequately equipped aircraft without the impositions being introduced today and forecast to increase in the future. Apart from any other reasons access is necessary for interlining purposes which form a significant proportion of business flights.

(B) Easily accessible basic accommodation is needed for business aircraft and their users at the major airports, suitably designed to ensure a fast flow of the small number of passengers and crews involved. It should not be necessary every time for expensive and time consuming handling agents to be employed for many flights.

The General Aviation terminal at Gatwick Airport is a good example of what can be done. Unfortunately its days are numbered as the land is required for further expansion for holiday and not business flights. Perhaps a sad commentary on our sense of priorities with, on the one hand, potential thousands of pounds going out of the country and, on the other, a possible multi-million export order coming in.

(C) Some scheme urgently needs to be introduced whereby General Aviation aerodromes can obtain assistance towards the purchase of badly needed landing or approach aids, lighting, etc., to provide better, safer facilities. The cost of providing such facilities in the U.K. is virtually out of the question for most aerodromes. The result is few General Aviation aerodromes available for night and bad weather operations and the dangerous tendency for a few to operate below safe weather limits with inadequate aids. One cannot but contrast the U.K. with the U.S.A. in this respect. In the latter a busy airfield would be eligible for a control tower manned by government personnel and even, if necessary, an I.L.S. in-

stalled and maintained by the F.A.A.

(D) Despite the reduced size of the Royal Air Force there are still a number of excellent military airfields all over the country which could and should be made more freely available to General Aviation. In many cases the amount of flying from these is minimal and represents a valuable wasted national asset which could be further used. Revenue could also result; General Aviation is quite prepared to pay reasonably for normal landing rights.

(E) Perhaps not an improvement but certainly an essential is not to close any more airfields and to accept that light aircraft flying as a sport is a recreation to be encouraged. It is to be regretted that in all its aspects it receives so little national support and encouragement.

(F) In many areas of the world air traffic control aids, procedures and systems leave much to be desired.

Cairo, Tripoli and Lagos seem to attract particular criticism of a below par control system and the airways of South East Italy controlled by Brindisi lacks radar.

Time and money must be spent in putting such areas right if only to save the fuel presently being wasted by unnecessary climb and descent procedures. This seems to be a criticism of both airlines and General Aviation.

(G) Certain airfields still have the land and the requirement to provide either a parallel or STOL runway which could absorb the General Aviation traffic.

(H) A more liberal attitude is necessary by Customs and Immigration to the smaller airfield so that time and money involving dead leg flights are unnecessary for overseas clearances.

57. It is difficult to try and summarise in a few paragraphs the future aerodrome requirements for General Aviation in the U.K. Fundamentally the answer to the question "what is the most important requirement to enable

General Aviation to flourish and expand in the next decade?¦' must be its acceptance and recognition as an essential part of air transportation. The author believes that if the world's business aircraft fleet was grounded we should face the greatest trade recession ever. This recognition must extend not only to central and local government and the C.A.A. but also to the community as a whole. It is a sad reflection of the status of General Aviation that in the original planning of the now abandoned Maplin project no mention appeared to be made of General Aviation. Similarly, and possibly even worse, in a recently published major policy document on Airport Strategy for Great Britain in the first part covering the London area the words General Aviation do not seem to appear even once. Perhaps the Government Department responsible are even unaware of its existence or what it means.

ACKNOWLEDGEMENTS

The writer wishes to acknowledge the assistance he received in compiling this paper from Mr. J. W. Pooley, Airport Director, Biggin Hill Airport. Other information was also provided by the:-

    Aircraft Owners & Pilots Assoc. (of the U.K. & U.S.A.)

    Air Taxi Operators Assoc. Ltd. (U.K.)

    British Helicopter Advisory Board Ltd. (U.K.)

    Business Aircraft Users Assoc. Ltd. (U.K.)

Corrigendum: para. 21 line 6: for '£25,000,000' read '£25,000,000,000'.

7. Airport economics and financing

B.L. Schroder, MA (Oxon), MBA (Harvard)
Director, J.Henry Schroder Wagg & Co. Ltd., London

"A wise man will make more opportunities than he finds" Francis Bacon

OUTLINE

1.　This paper will be divided into 5 parts, (1) the introduction, (2) basic principles of airport finance and the profit objective (3) various methods of financing airport developments including grants, self generated funds and borrowing (5) the conclusion.

INTRODUCTION

2.　During the last two years the majority of airports, and particularly the airlines, have been having a sorrier time than anyone anticipated five years ago.

3.　Airline profits in aggregate have dropped, and well known airlines have been barely making money (and many losing it). (See figure I) In 1975 the U.S. airline industry achieved only 3.6% rate of return on equity. This is not surprising when instead of the 12% per annum growth experienced in the early 70's, world air passenger growth rose, in 1975, by only 3 per cent to reach 529m, according to preliminary estimates prepared by the International Civil Aviation Organisation (ref. I) This led to the present excess capacity, which coupled with fuel price increases, led to unprofitability.

4.　Away however with at least part of the gloom: the International Air Transport Association ("I.A.T.A") reports that its member airlines predict a recovery of growth to 7.7 per cent per annum in 1975-80. This accords also with U.S. Domestic predictions (Ref. 2)

5.　On the other hand airports particularly European ones, did not do well – again due to stagnating traffic. Frankfurt lost in 1974 DM45m ($17.6m) compared with a loss the previous year of DM38m ($14.9m)

6.　Aeroport de Paris, the Paris Airport Authority, also lost Fr.Fr 23m ($5.3m) in 1974 compared with Fr.Fr 18m ($4.0m) in 1973.

7.　In line with Frankfurt, Aeroport de Paris in 1974 only recorded a 1.7 per cent growth in passenger traffic, compared with an average of 13 per cent growth per annum in previous years.

8.　The interesting point made by Aeroport de Paris, was that a fall of 1 per cent in passenger traffic results in a loss of revenue of about Fr.Fr 4m ($900,000) (Ref. 3) This illustrates the point almost everyone

appreciates about both the airport and airline industry: that they are capital intensive with high fixed costs, i.e. if possible an airport should be used to capacity. If only passengers were sardines!

9.　On the other hand, the British Airports Authority ("B.A.A.") managed to make an overall profit on its activities, making an 11.5 per cent return on average net assets for the year ended 31st March 1975, compared with 16.2 per cent the previous year.

10.　The target of return on net assets set by the British Government is for a return on average net assets of 15½ per cent per annum. The rate of return on net assets achieved by the B.A.A. has averaged 14.3 per cent. over the past five years and, combined with the fact that there have been no very major investments (such as for a new airport like Maplin), the B.A.A. have been self-financing from retained earnings for the last six years.

11.　As we look at the overall picture in 1976 therefore, we see airlines generally are having a difficult financial spell at the moment but look forward to better times. Airports have suffered also from the recession. We are reminded that both airlines and airports are in a high fixed cost industry, but can make very good profits when operating at capacity , and when they are not over-invested. Finally B.A.A. demonstrates that good profits allows an airport to be self financing thereby reducing the requirement to borrow.

BASIC PRINCIPLES OF AIRPORT FINANCE

12.　Although airports are faced in the short term with a much slower growth in airline traffic and a somewhat reduced increase in aircraft movements due to the introduction of wider-bodied aircraft, the required investment in airports is still huge. For instance in the U.S.A. it is estimated that $10,600m will be needed 1976-1980, half for existing airports, half for new ones.

Can Airports pay?

13.　With airports now no longer an infant industry,we must once again study the question of whether airports can pay. This is important as it affects the objectives of an airport and the possibilities of self financing its development as well as the possibility of its being able to borrow in the commercial market.

14.   The most interesting studies were done originally in 1967/1968 by the U.S. Senate Aviation sub-committee investigating the advisability of setting up a National Trust Fund to finance U.S. airports. (This work resulted in the passing of the Airport and Airways Development Act of 1970).

15.   The Senate's Aviation Sub Committee at the time calculated that the operating breakeven point for airports in the U.S.A. was approx - imately 70,000 annual enplanements. If depreciation is included, airports would have to enplane over 600,000 passengers annually, before revenue exceeds expense and depreciation (Figure 2).

16.   A later study done by the U.S. Department of Transportation,Federal Aviation Administration in July 1974 showed that the breakeven for airports was at the level of 97,000 annual enplanements. At that level operating revenue equalled operating expenses.

17.   If one added the burden of debt, airports had to have annual enplanements of 275,000 to meet both debt service requirements and operating costs (Ref. 4). The results of this study were in line with the original 1967/1968 U.S. Senate Aviation Sub Committee studies.

The Profit Objective
18.   However, having broadly determined at what point an airport might be expected to pay, we should briefly turn to the determination of the airport authority to make a profit if feasible and possible.

19.   As we have seen in the example of the British Airports Authority, if one does attain a reasonable rate of return on net assets and the dividend payment is small, there are substantial possibilities to self finance an existing airport- preferably a group of airports combined in an Airport/Port Authority. Any losses in one airport or facility might then be balanced by profits in others. A good example is, of course, the Port Authority of New York and New Jersey.

20.   Lastly the profit objective also imposes its own discipline and, as the Edwards Report said in "British Air Transport in the Seventies"

> "We believe that the decision to set
> financial objectives for the (British)
> nationalised industries in 1961 was of
> major importance and has done much to
> ensure financial discipline, which the
> market imposes on the private sector,
> is also effective in the public sector.
> (Ref. 5)

21.   The possible financial objectives of an airport have been argued in greater detail in another paper written by the author for the Third World Airports Conference - The Way Ahead (in 1969). Suffice it to say the conclusion there was that an airport should aim at making a return on the net assets of the airport consistent with its monopoly position and status as a utility, i.e. "A Utility Return".

22.   The utility return allowed could be at the level required to cover the general cost of borrowing in the country concerned, i.e. if the cost of borrowing is, say, 9 per cent, then perhaps 3 per cent above to make a 12% return - having <u>already</u> covered the cost of depreciation on a replacement basis - as otherwise the airport is quietly losing money.

23.   In the U.S. the authorities are currently allowing the utility industry to earn a return on equity of between 11.5% to 12.5%. In 1975 it is projected that the Electric Power Companies will make 12.5% for 1976 (11.8%: 1975)

24.   The Civil Aeronautics Board do allow the airlines a 12% return on investment. However due to the reasons already stated, in 1975, the U.S. airline industry achieved overall only a 3.6% rate of return with Braniff having the highest rate of return at 10.9%.

25.   In summary, therefore, if the airlines are allowed to make a 12% return on assets, I really don't see why airports shouldn't be allowed to do the same.

26.   Landing and enroute charges (only part of which airports levy on airlines), still only represent 8% of operating costs for a short-haul airline compared with 5 per cent for a long-haul operator (Ref. 6)

27.   Assuming 50% of an airport's income comes from landing and ancillary charges, a 1% increase in a long haul operator's costs from 5% to 6%   would give a 10% rise in the income to an airport (1% ÷ 5% = 20% x 50% = 10%). In other words:-

a)   airport charges aren't the most critical expense to an airline

b)   an airport can increase its income substantially and make a decent return at not too great a cost to the airline.

VARIOUS METHODS OF FINANCING AIRPORT DEVELOPMENTS & SOURCES OF REVENUE

28.   There are three main sources of revenue:-

1.   Grants from Central or Local Government

2.   Self-generated funds (from profits)

3.   Borrowed money.

A summary of these sources is set out in Fig. 3.

Grants from Central or Local Goverment
29.   A good part of the original capital for airports came from Central or Local Government, either for military purposes or the development of small civilian airports. Since the War,

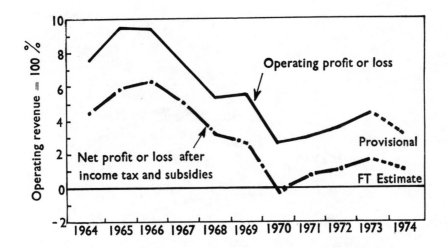

Fig.1. *Airline operating results: operating results and net results of scheduled airlines of the 128 ICAO contracting states (excluding China and USSR) (Source: Financial Times 15.9.1975)*

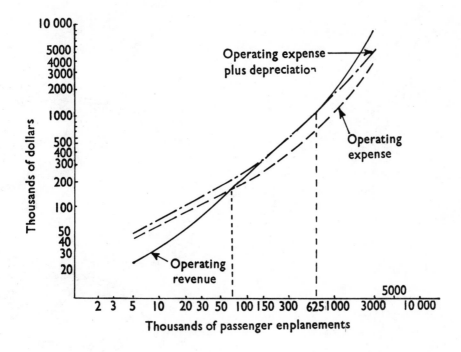

Fig.2. *Relationships of 1966 US airport operating revenue and expense to annual air carrier passenger enplanement level (Source: 1968 Senate Aviation Sub-committee Report)*

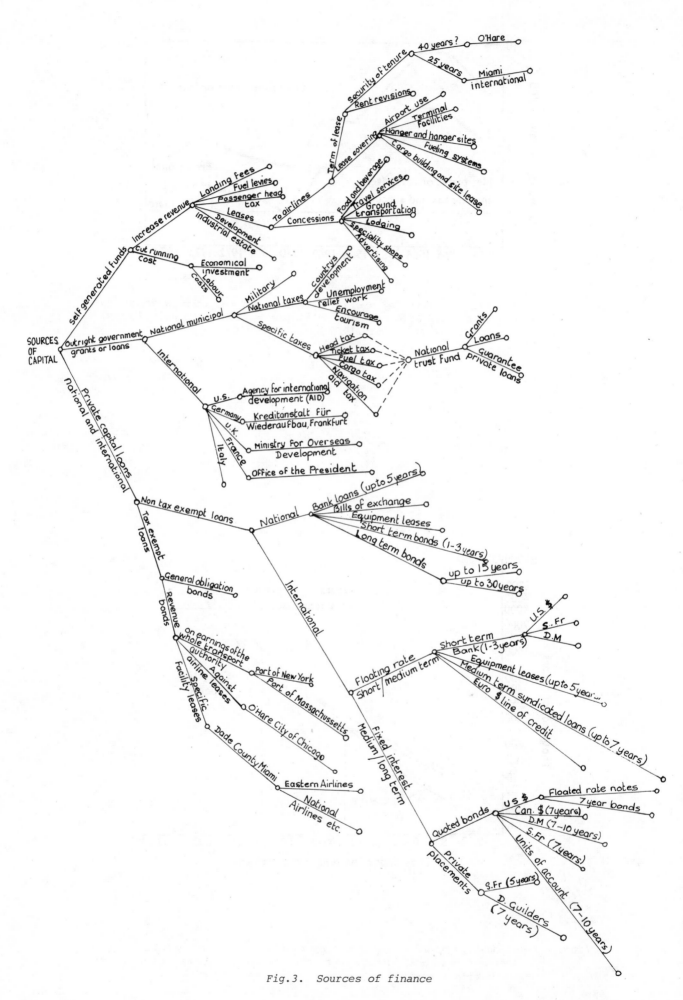

Fig.3. Sources of finance

certain military airfields have been enlarged
for civilian purposes. Due to the fact that
initial costs (runways etc.,) are so high, it
is impossible to make airports pay their way
at the outset and, therefore, grants or the
taxpayer's money had to be provided until the
passenger/cargo throughput was sufficient for
the airport to provide its own positive cash
flow.

30.   Even then, there are often hidden
subsidies. Free Air Traffic Control ("A.T.C")
provided by Central Government is an example.

31.   In the U.S., after World War II, the
federal government, realising that the need
for airports in the U.S.A. was beyond the
ability of the local communities to finance,
established the Federal Aid Airport programme
("F.A.A.P") to provide matching funds for
construction, and for improvements to the
"landing area" (essentially the runways and
taxiways).

32.   From its inception in 1947 to 1970 it
provided a total of U.S.$1.25bn. The Federal
Aviation Administration, which ran the "F.A.A.P",
had to turn down hundreds of requests for help
and had to concentrate on the smaller airports
with the most pressing needs - usually as
might be expected, the smaller airfields without
enough airline business to breakeven on their
own.

33.   The Federal Aviation Administration in
their July 1974 study on "The Airport Passenger
Head Tax" (Ref. 4) gave an excellent breakdown
of all the sources of income, airports of
various sizes would expect to have. These
figures were based on an analysis of the 1973
Financial Reports of 47 air carrier airports.

34.   In examining the table (Fig, 4) one sees
that the smaller airport relies more heavily
on local taxes and "A.D.A.P" funds. Also Bank
loans, being unimportant for larger airports,
produce 15% of all funds for smaller ones.
In three cases, the banks provided unsecured
loans when long term financing was unavailable.
Finally, only the larger airports could get
sufficient airline backing to float Revenue Bonds.

35.   In 1970 the Airport and Airways
Development Act was passed. This Act set up a
special trust fund similar to the U.S. Highway
Trust fund. This was financed by new taxes on
airline passengers, cargo, aviation fuel and
aircraft registrations. Under the Act, a
minimum of $280 million a year from the Trust
Fund was to be used for the Airport Development
Aid Programme ("A.D.A.P") which replaced "F.A.A.P"

36.   The Act proposed that this Fund should
be financed by user taxes which are estimated
to yield for the U.S. National Airport Trust
Fund in 1975:-

		Estimated Revenue for 1975	% of Total Revenue
1.	8% Domestic Passenger Ticket tax	$771.3m	82.1
2.	$3 per head tax on international passengers	$ 51.0	5.4
3.	7 cent tax per gallon on "general aviation" fuel	$ 51.3	5.5
4.	5% way-bill tax on air freight	$ 42.3	4.5
5.	Plane registration and weight fees	$ 23.0	2.4
6.	Tax on aviation tyres & tubes	$ 0.9	0.1
		$939.8m	100.%

By 1980, these taxes are expected to raise
$16,000m for the trust fund, for airport use.

37.   In fact the Aviation Trust Fund has grown
at a more rapid rate than forecast. The forecast
for 1975 was originally thought to promise a
yield of $790m, although it is now estimated to
yield $939.8m (see above).

38.   Like "F.A.A.P", however, "A.D.A.P" provides
proportionately more help for smaller airports
than for major airline centres. In both the
"F.A.A.P" and "A.D.A.P" programmes, the smaller
fields have got about 50% of their financing
from Federal grants, the larger airports roughly
10%. This is due to the fact that "F.A.A.P" and
the new "A.D.A.P" prohibit the use of federal money
for terminal areas. The funds may only be used
for landing area expenses - such as purchase of
land, and paving, lighting and instrumentation
of runways and taxiways. Generally "A.D.A.P"
contributes 50% of allowable costs, but can pay
up to 82% of certain safety equipment.

39.   On June 18th 1973, President Nixon signed
a further Act to help airports - "The Airport
Development Acceleration Act of 1973". This
increased the funds available for A.D.A.P from
$280m to $310 annually and increased the federal
share of approved programmes for all but the 24
largest airports in the U.S.A. from 50% to 75%
and provides for 82% of the cost of airport
certification and security requirements as
mentioned before.

40.   There is a further move among aviation
leaders and members of Congress to allow A.D.A.P
to help with those basic parts of terminal areas
such as lobbies and moving sidewalks etc., which
are incapable of being leased to the airlines
or to concessionaires.

Airport type* / Fund Source	Hub size A	Hub size B	Hub size C	Hub size D	Hub size E
Operating income (less Head Tax)	17.50%	13.04%	9.03%	11.92%	0%
Head Tax	4.28	18.18	7.62	4.71	4.10
Loans	1.92		2.44		15.14
General fund	5.22	6.56	6.64	16.49	23.17
Local taxes	0.77		3.49		1.74
Revenue bond	43.25	29.46	7.08		
General oblig. bond		9.27	30.58	18.77	
State grant-in-aid	0.84	1.16	4.74	5.50	2.26
Federal grant-in-aid (ADAP)	13.99	21.12	25.41	40.18	44.34
Miscellaneous	1.03	0.15	2.14	0.97	0.41
Transfer funds	11.14	1.06	0.80	1.45	8.84

*For purposes of this study, five airport categories are defined

Category	Annual passenger enplanements
Hub size A	500 000 — 2 000 000
Hub size B	250 000 — 500 000
Hub size C	125 000 — 250 000
Hub size D	50 000 — 125 000
Hub size E	Under 50 000

Fig.4.   Sources of funds (Source: Airport financial reports, US Department of Transportation, Federal Aviation Administration, The Airport Passenger Head Tax, July 1974) Shown by percent of total funds

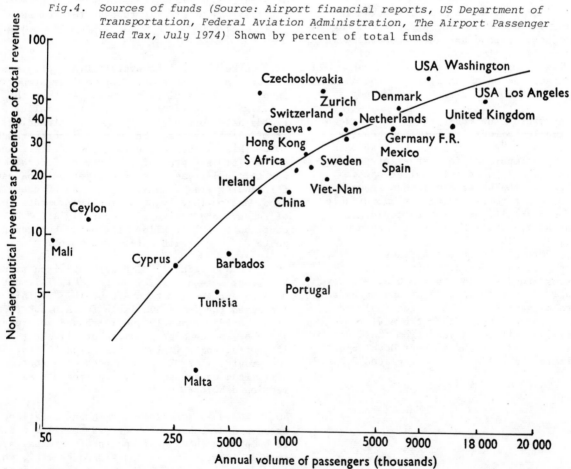

Fig.5.   Non-aeronautical revenues as a percentage of total revenues related to passenger traffic (selected countries) (Source: ICAO Circular 101-AT/22, Montreal, 1970)

41.   A.D.A.P., by virtue of the size of its funds, has been able to provide more help than the original Federal Aid Airports Programme ("F.A.A.P"). As an example of the aid given, A.D.A.P. allocated $50.7m for Dallas/Fort Worth when it was estimated that the total cost of the first stage of Dallas/Fort Worth is $380m. The eventual complex, to be completed some time between 1987 and 2000, will cost $1bn.

42.   The concept of a National Airport Trust Fund could well be applied anywhere in the world. The establishment of such a Trust Fund has certain inherent advantages; it employs the "User pays" principle. All the aviation tax money goes into the Trust Fund for aviation purposes alone and,with anticipated funds, airports can really plan ahead, secure in the knowledge that the funds are growing at a predictable and increasing rate, and are not merely available at the annual whim of the Government or Congress in power at the time.

43.   It would seem a sound idea if all airports, particularly those with limited alternative facilities, were able to draw money for development from a national airport trust fund, either in the form of grants or by having their private sector borrowings guaranteed which would in turn further gear/leverage the original (A.D.A.P) funds. This scheme would provide money, but would not allow the airport to wander from the objective of becoming a viable entity.

44.   To summarise, therefore, Government monies are (usually) the best source of funds after self-generated funds, either because airports can thereby get a free grant or because the interest rates are lower, or because repayment periods are longer - than on monies borrowed from the private sector.

Self Generated funds (from profits)

45.   Perhaps one of the first objectives of any airport management is to try and create a positive cash flow out of profits and properly charged depreciation. This positive cash flow will enable it to meet the cost of at least part of its own further development.

46.   A number of ways of cutting the costs and increasing the income are summarised graphically in figure 4, but most important of all is "the will to make profits". Is the airport management profit-orientated?

47.   To take the various internal sources of self generated revenue - one of the most recent studies of American airports has been done by the Aerospace Corporation (of California). An excellent paper was presented by Mr. Joseph A. Neiss on July 17th 1975 to the 3rd Intersociety Conference on Transportation held in Georgia.

48.   Mr. Neiss, of the Aerospace Corporation in his study, "Terminal Economics & Financing" took the financial results for 1974 of 17 of the largest 25 airports in the U.S.A., together with prior data of 114 other airports, and

produced the following picture of the sources of revenue of U.S. airports enplaning over 2 million passengers in 1974 (Ref. 7)

49.   They were as follows:-

ANALYSIS OF 1974 OPERATING REVENUES. AIRPORTS ENPLANING OVER 2 MILLION PASSENGERS PER ANNUM

Distribution %

	From %	to %	Average %
1) Airfield Area			
a) Landing fees	16.8	61.2	33.3
b) Fuel, oil sales	0.1	11.7	1.1
c) Airline catering	0.2	4.0	1.5
d) Other	0.1	7.6	1.1
Total Airfield	23.7	62.3	37.0
2) Hangar & Building area	2.3	29.6	10.2
3) Systems & Services	0.4	12.7	2.7
4) Terminal Area	11.3	28.7	15.8
5) Concessions			
a) Airport parking	6.3	26.4	15.0
b) Car Parking	2.3	12.1	7.3
c) Restaurant	1.0	10.5	4.0
d) Shops	1.4	10.5	3.6
e) Advertising	0.2	1.2	0.4
f) Ground transportation	0.6	3.6	1.3
g) Flight insurance	0.2	1.7	0.7
h) Other	0.4	17.8	2.0
Total concessions	15.5	47.4	34.3
TOTAL OPERATING REVENUE			100
which in $ per enplaned passenger was	$2.04	$9.44	$3.38

Income is generally used for capital improvements and debt retirement and to establish reserve funds for the retirement of debt in future years.

50.   Taking the British Airports Authority as a possible example of European airports in comparison, this body has followed the trend in its increasing reliance on non-aeronautical income. The mix between aeronautical sources of income and non aeronautical sources has now almost reversed itself in the last 9 years.

	1965-67	1974-75
Aeronautical Sources	63.2%	46.8%
Non Aeronautical Sources	36.8%	53.2%
	100%	100%

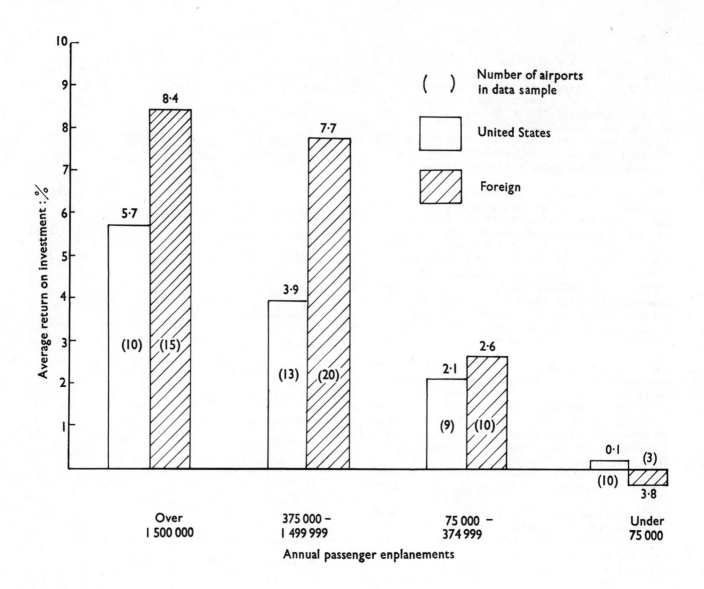

Fig.6. *US vs foreign airports: comparison of rate of return on investment (1970 dollars) (Source: Neiss (ref.8))*

51. Looking at the world picture, ICAO in its circular 101-AT/22, Montreal 1970 on Development of Airport Revenues from Non Aeronautical sources showed that the proportion of total revenue from non-aeronautical resources was:-

	1955	1966-68
In U.S.A.	25 - 40%	Up to 60% (largest U.S. Airports)
In Europe	8 - 9%	30%

(See also fig. 5)

Comparison of U.S. and Foreign airports

52. In an interesting study of both U.S. and non U.S. airports, Mr. Neiss of the Aerospace Corporation did a comparison of their performance. This study showed that the investment in property, plant and equipment was found to be fairly similar for both. However, it was shown that the rate of return (as defined, before interest and depreciation) in foreign airports was substantially higher than in U.S. airports - other than in the group of under 75,000 annual enplanements) (Ref. 8).

53. For the airport group enplaning over 1.5m annual passengers the rate of return is 47% higher. For the group enplaning 375,000 - 1,499,000 the rate of return is 97% higher (see figure 6)

54. This is due to landing and passenger terminal fees being 2 to 3 times higher particularly to international traffic. Concession income is however about the same, though the mix is different. These higher revenues are however offset by the airports often having to cover the costs of air traffic control or meteorological services. The end result however is clear - according to the study, foreign airports generally make a better return on their net assets than those in the U.S.A.

55. In summary when looking at the help provided by self generated funds, the profit motive is essential. If profits can be made, self generated funds is the cheapest form of finance (other than grants from the Government). Non aeronautical or concession income is becoming steadily more important world wide as a proportion of an average airports revenue. However it is interesting to have noted that non U.S. airports, despite having lagged behind U.S. airports in their drive for concession income, have managed to get a better return on their assets (due to heavier landing charges). This has put foreign airports,through profits earned, in a better position to self finance themselves.

Loans from Private Capital Market

56. If the first two sources of funds are insufficient, i.e. self-generated funds and governmental sources, it falls to the private sector to consider the most appropriate methods of raising the required capital in the special circumstances of the airport concerned.

57. Private financing of airports has been most highly developed in the U.S.A. and thus it might be useful to examine how this has been done in past years. Apart from the important source of finance from Federal Aid programmes and grants, airports have also been financed from the private sector through

- city general obligation bonds
- revenue bonds of a port authority or of one particular airport
- special facility revenue bonds.

58. The concept behind bonds is that the borrower pledges, in the case of General Obligation bonds, the full faith, credit and taxing power of the City.

59. In the case of the Revenue Bonds, or specific facility bonds, the borrower pledges that the income of the airport or the specific asset (hangars, terminal buildings) will be sufficient to cover by about 1.2 to 1.4 times the cost of interest and capital repayments over the period of the bond issue.

60. In the U.S.A. between 22% and 56% of the capital of the larger airports (including borrowings) comes from Revenue Bonds of the various kinds. The largest airports have the higher proportion of Revenue Bonds as a percentage of their total capitalisation. In the case of specific facility bond financing, (hangars etc,) the bonds are based on the good faith and credit of the airlines as it is they who will be using that facility. Examples of Revenue Bonds are, of course, O'Hare - and of specific facility bonds, those issued by Dade County for Miami Airport.

61. Recently Blyth Eastman Dillon, the New York Investment Bank, sold $143m of Revenue Bonds for San Francisco. There has been some effect on all tax-exempt issues thanks to the financial problems of New York City, but financings have not apparently been precluded because of that. In essence every financing has been separately analysed on its merits.

62. It has been suggested that a portion of the monies in the U.S. Aviation Trust Fund should be used as security for individual airport Revenue Bonds.

63. This would further leverage/gear the federal funds and make those monies go further, at the same time making it possible for the local municipalities or Airport Authorities to borrow the necessary capital to meet their side of the bargain with the Federal Aviation Authority. If $500m was used out of A.D.A.P. funds, that would support, protect or guarantee local borrowings of up to $5,000m.

64. This idea, of the immediate self-financing of airports against their future profits, through the method of revenue bonds or specific facility revenue bonds, could be applied almost in any

other country as, basically, the bonds are raised against anticipated revenue from air traffic (both passengers and cargo) or against the taxing power of the municipality.

65.   Personally I feel that there is a great opportunity in the future for international airports to be financed through the medium of International Revenue Bonds initially, if necessary, with the guarantee of their respective Governments.

Other Domestic Sources of Finance

66.   Dealing briefly with other domestic sources of finance, they could come, and do come through:-

1. Commercial Banks. These will be mainly short term for working capital purposes or medium term up to 5 years.

2. Bills of Exchange, Acceptance Credits could be employed and could be used to discount the airports' receivables (bills sent to airlines etc. for services rendered).

3. Equipment Leasing - Sale and leaseback of buildings, equipment etc, by the airport. This method can substantially reduce the amount of capital required to be put into ground equipment and buildings, though in comparison domestic leasing (as opposed to export credit) is usually more expensive than short term commercial bank finance.

4. Short Term Bonds (1 to 3 years)

5. Local Long Term Loans from the Government or from private sources such as Insurance Companies, Pension Funds (private placings) and general Bond issues to the general public.

67.   The borrowings could be either secured or unsecured on the assets of the airport, and guaranteed or not guaranteed by the Government or Airport Authority.

68.   Broadly however, airports are wisest to borrow in the long end of the market as essentially their assets are illiquid and in any case new airports need a lot of time before they get a substantial and positive cash inflow in order to repay debt.

International Finance

69   Turning now to the possibilities of international finance, one can repeat the list of sources outlined under domestic finance, i.e. the possibilities of borrowing from foreign banks or through the medium of foreign bonds, etc. But in addition to ordinary foreign banking commercial finance, there are subsidised sources of finance especially tailored for airports in developing countries which will be outlined first.

Subsidised Funds:

a) International & regional Development Agencies

b) Export Credit Agencies.

Trade Funds:

Ordinary customer loans or pre-payment

Commercial Medium & Long Term Funds:

a) Leasing

b) Medium & Long term funds
    i) floating rate
    ii) fixed rate

c) Private Placements.

70. In most projects, one would wish to minimise the use of commercial funds since these, in general, are of the shortest term and at the highest cost, and may demand the greatest security.

Subsidised Funds

71. International & Regional Development Agencies

Since the end of the Second World War, a number of financial institutions providing financial and technical assistance have been established. These are the International Lending Agencies.

72. The World Bank Group (consisting of the International Bank for Re-construction and Development, the International Development Agency and the International Finance Corporation) is by far the largest agency. In 1974/75 alone it approved loans and credits to 72 developing countries, totalling almost £3,000m.

73. Examples of other agencies are the African Development Bank, the Asian Development Bank, the European Investment Bank, the Inter-American Development Bank and the Kuwait Fund for Arab Economic Development. These institutions concentrate on supplying loans and credits or guarantees usually for longer periods and at much lower rates of interest than would be available in the commercial markets.

74. Normally the development agency will make a very detailed study of the project, in order to assess its economic and social benefits. This study and the involvement of the international agency can, itself, be a help in attracting commercial lenders, since the evaluation procedures of these agencies are renowned for their thoroughness.

75. Taking as an example the Agency for International Development "AID". AID did use to provide funds for airports in developing countries, but has not done so recently. However AID will consider financing airport feasibility studies in the U.S. $2m bracket.

INSURANCE / FINANCE

	Agency	Political Cover	Commercial Cover	Eligible Contracts	Performance Recourse to Exporter	Claim Period (Mths.)	Lender	Amount of Finance	Credit Range (Years) *	Lender's Recourse to Exporter	Third Country Allowance **	Effective Interest Cost %pa (excl. insurance premium) ***
AUSTRIA	OKB	100%	100%	No Restriction	100% of claims	Immediate	Commercial Banks	85-90%	5-12	NIL	Small Amount	7½-8
BELGIUM	OND	95%	90-95%	Minimum value of £625,000	Amount required to make good failure	3	Commercial Banks (under auspices of Credit-export)	80-90%	5-10	Part of uninsured%	Small Amount (30-40% EEC allowance)	8-9½
CANADA	EDC	Up to 100%	Up to 100%	Major capital goods exports	100% of claims	4-6	EDC	85-90%	5-10	If applicable Uninsured%	Small Amount	8-10(depending on mix)
FRANCE	COFACE	95%	95%	No Restriction	100% of claims	2-8	Commercial Banks/BFCE	85% (70% in exceptional cases)	5-10	NIL	Small Amount (30-40% EEC allowance)	7½
GERMANY	HERMES	a)90% b)95%	a)85% b)95%	Large projects	100% of claims	a)6 b)3	Commercial Banks/AKA/KfW	80-85%	5-10	a)Up to uninsured% b)NIL	Small Amount (30-40% EEC allowance)	5½-8(depending on nature of credit)
ITALY	INA	Up to 95%	Up to 95%	No Restriction	NIL	3	Special Credit Institutes	80-85%	5-10	NIL	Small Amount (30-40% EEC allowance)	8-10(depending on nature of credit)
JAPAN	MID/MITI	90%	90%	Large Projects (little buyer credit experience)	NIL	2	Export/Import Bank	85-90%	5-10	Up to uninsured%	Small Amount	7½-9(depending on mix)
NETHERLANDS	NCM	a)90% b)95%	a)90% b)95%	Large Projects	100% of claims	6	Commercial Banks/EFM	80-85%	5-10	a)Uninsured% b)NIL	Small Amount (30-40% EEC allowance)	10-11(Market rates)
S. AFRICA	CGIC	100%	100%	Minimum value of £1m.(Major capital goods)	NIL	6	IDC	80-85%	5-10	NIL	Up to 20%	7½-7¾(depending on market)
SWEDEN	EKN	90%	80%	Minimum value of £25,000 (capital goods)	NIL	6	Commercial Banks/Svensk Export Credit	80-85%	5-10	Up to uninsured%	Small Amount	8½-9(Market rates)
U.K.	ECGD	100%	100%	Minimum value of £1m.(Major capital goods)	100% of claims	3	Commercial Banks	80-85%	5-10	NIL	Small Amount (30-40% EEC allowance)	8-9
U.S.A.	EXIMBANK	100%	100%	Minimum value of £3m.(Major capital goods)	NIL	1	Commercial Banks/EXIMBANK	90%	5-12	NIL	Small Amount	7½-9½(depending on mix)

* Depending on nature of contract and whether buyer's country is developed or undeveloped
** Allowance for local costs is the amount of downpayment on exported element
*** These are current rates, which are subject to significant variation

February 1976

Fig.7. Summary of buyer credit schemes in some major capital goods exporting countries (Source: J.Henry Schroder, Wagg & Co Ltd, Project Division)

Broadly AID seems to be no longer considering providing funds itself for airports, but is as an exception currently considering participating in a financing for the construction of an airport in an African country.

Export Credit

76.   Many industrialised countries, in order to encourage the growth of their export business, provide export credit. This is of great relevance to airports as:-

    i)   a great deal of airport equipment is made abroad. Export credit, often at fixed rates of interest, is available for both equipment and associated services.

    ii) credit terms longer than those provided by local banks are often available.

    iii) the interest rates charged are often subsidised.

77.   The principal exporting countries now all have export credit agencies of one form or another. As an example, the proportion of British overseas trade insured by the Export Credit Guarantee Department ("ECGD") has risen from 8% in 1947 to 35% now. A list of various countries principal export credit agencies and a comparison of their terms is attached. (Fig.7)

Trade Funds

78.   These funds should be mentioned even if they are the most obvious. They are ordinary customer loans granted by the supplier of the equipment.

Commercial Medium & Long Term Funds

79.   Leasing
       Apart from very short term funds from international commercial banks, it might be worth mentioning the possibility of leasing. It is possible in a number of countries to get an international lease agreement for equipment for 5 years, but usually at floating interest rates (dependent on the movements of general market rates).

80.   Medium & Long term international funds
       The various international sources of finance fall into two broad categories - floating rate and fixed rate finance. In the case of floating rate finance the amounts raised in a single operation can be considerably increased compared with sums of fixed rate finance, but a borrower will have to face the disadvantages both of being vulnerable to interest rate fluctuations and of being unable to make accurate budget forecasts.

81.   Floating Rate Finance in the international markets.
       First there are Medium term bank credits with maturities ranging mainly from two to seven years.

82.   Most loan facilities are arranged by a syndicate of banks under the leadership of one or more, with one acting as agent for the whole group. Although fixed interest finance for medium term loans is sometimes arranged, the normal procedure is for interest to be adjusted regularly with the interest rate set at a given margin over the cost of time deposits (usually 6 months) in the London inter-bank market at the time the rate is adjusted.

83.   An estimate, based on publicised information, of the funds raised in this manner in recent years runs as follows:-

	$ million
1972	6,857
1973	21,851
1974	29,275
1975	21,046

84.   A major syndicate is normally capable of raising very substantial sums - possibly up to as much as U.S.$500m per loan for a prime borrower.

85.   For example, a syndicate loan for airports was a syndicated five year credit for $100m given to Aeroports do Rio de Janeiro, the Brazilian State Company building the new terminal at Caleao airport in Rio. The cost was understood to be $1\frac{7}{8}$% over London Inter Bank offered rate ("LIBO") (Ref. 9)

86.   There was a further borrowing of $50m by Infraero, the Brazilian National Authority responsible for the country's airport structure. This will be used for the improvement for the 26 major airports which Infraero administers. The 7 year loan was guaranteed by the Brazilian Government and the loan syndicated by a group of four banks led by the Chase Manhattan, and comprising Deutsche Genossenschaftskasse, Westdeutsche Landesbank - Girozentrale and First International Bancshares Ltd., (Ref. 10)

87.   Fixed Rate Finance in the international markets.
       The various international capital markets provide a major source of fixed rate medium to long term finance in a number of currencies.

88.   However a word of warning here; to the extent a foreign currency borrowing is not matched by corresponding currency revenues, the borrower runs an exchange risk. A borrower should always weigh up the interest rate advantages of a borrowing in a "hard" foreign currency such as the Swiss Franc or the Deutsche Mark against the possible capital losses that could be incurred in the event of that foreign currency appreciating in value during the life of the loan against the borrower's domestic currency.

89.   Borrowers in the Eurobond market include international organisations, national and provincial governments and their agencies, and major industrial and commercial companies of international repute. The total nominal value

	U.S. $ millions					
	1973	%	1974	%	1975	%
U.S. Companies	874	20.8	110	5.1	268	3.1
Foreign Companies	1309	31.2	640	30.0	2884	33.6
State Enterprises	947	22.6	542	25.4	3211	37.4
Governments	659	15.7	482	22.6	1625	19.0
International Organisations	404	9.7	360	16.9	592	6.9
TOTAL	4193	100.0	2134	100.0	8580	100.0

Fig.8. Eurobond issues by category of borrower (Source: Morgan Guaranty Trust)

of bonds outstanding in the Eurobond market is now of the order of U.S.$30 billion equivalent.

90. Eurobonds are normally issued as unsecured publically quoted obligations of the borrower. State enterprises and municipalities would require their government's guarantee unless their own financial status were undoubted.

91. Figure 8 shows the approximate amount raised in the Eurobond market over the last 3 years broken down by category of borrower. In 1975 43.5% was borrowed in U.S. dollars, 26% in Deutsche Marks, 8.9% in Dutch guilders, 6.8% in Canadian $ and 4.2% in units of account. Other currencies 10.6%.

92. The "normal" maturity for a Eurobond issue was 15 years, bond maturities have since then tended to be shorter as investors have become more concerned both about inflation and about floating exchange rates. As a result, it is now usual for a new issue to have a final maturity of not more than 6 or 7 years and to have a sinking fund to give an even shorter average life (of less than the seven years).

93. Interest on most Eurobonds is payable annually and both payments of principal and interest are made by the borrower without deduction of withholding or other taxes.

94. In the last five years a number of issues have been made where the coupon is not fixed for the life of the bonds but is adjusted at regular intervals as interest rates change. The normal procedure is for such notes to carry interest at a fixed margin over the London interbank offered (LIBO) rate for six months deposits at the time the coupon is adjusted.

95. It is also at times possible for prime borrowers to raise long term finance on a fixed interest rate basis by way of a private placement of bonds. These are generally placed with a small group of major institutions and for this reason the issuing costs tend to be lower. On the other hand, private placements are not quoted on any stock exchange, are therefore virtually unmarketable and consequently are

normally issued at a higher coupon than would apply to a public issue.

96. The last example of an international airport borrowing direct from the International Bond Market was the Aeroport de Paris when in 2 consecutive years it borrowed first DM65m ($17.9m) in a private placing (15 years) and then again in 1969 when it borrowed on a publically quoted Bond (Luxembourg Stock Exchange $15m @ 9%)

97. In summary, therefore, the following table gives an indication, based on current market conditions, of the approximate terms on which first-class internationally known borrowers could now tap the major sectors of the Eurobond markets.

Currency & Amount	Term of loan	Approximate yield to the investor
US$20 to 75 million	Either 5 years with no sinking fund or 7 to 10 years with a sinking fund to give an average life of between 5 and 7 years.	Depending on maturity & identity of borrower: $8\frac{1}{2}$% - $9\frac{3}{4}$% per annum
DM100m	6 to 7 years with no sinking fund	Around $7\frac{1}{2}$% per annum
Up to D.Fl 75m	7 years with no sinking fund	Around 8% to $8\frac{1}{4}$% per annum.

98. Commissions and expenses payable will very depending on the nature of the issue but would normally fall within a range of 2% to $2\frac{1}{2}$% flat commissions and total printing, legal and other expenses of around $75,000 - 100,000.

99. In summary, if Government loans and grants are not sufficient and self generated funds not large enough, the Development Agencies or the private financial sector can provide funds from a variety of sources. The choice of borrowing instrument

must depend on the availability of the required type of money at the time and the financial circumstances of the particular borrower.

CONCLUSION

100.   Due to the recent economic recession both airlines and, to a degree, airports have suffered financially. However with a forecast turn up in traffic, there is every reason for the larger airports particularly - to again concentrate on achieving a proper ("Utility) rate of return on their net assets.

101.   Apart from government grants (and with money goes power), larger airports should be able to provide out of their profits sufficient cashflow to self finance themselves (unless they are building new airports).

102.   Profits are also important as one measure of efficiency, but also to demonstrate the ability to cover the interest payments on any borrowing.

103.   The concept of a National Airport Trust fund, as started by the U.S. Government and financed through taxes on passengers and airlines is a good one. The idea could be copied elsewhere in the world. Based as it is on the "User pays principle", at the same time it supports the weaker brethren - the smaller airport. If it could also be used to guarantee the loans of airports, this would further leverage/gear the funds and make them even more effective.

104.   The use of revenue bonds, either general or specific facility bonds, either sold locally, nationally or internationally is a concept which could be copied. Probably the first international revenue bonds would have to be guaranteed by the Government concerned until more experience was gained in International Markets with this borrowing instrument.

105.   Regarding international finance, any airport in a developing country should consider enlisting the aid, both technical and financial, of one of the International Development Agencies.

106.   In addition, Export Credit covering the sale of equipment is an indirect source of cheap money lent for longer periods than commercial banks normally do.

107.   Leasing, both domestic or international is another useful method of reducing an airports own capital commitments.

108.   Last, but not least, with suitable Government guarantees, the Commercial Banker stands ready with medium term syndicate credits in international currencies in large amounts.

109.   The international investment banker is able to tailor and package attractive placements or Euro $ Bonds issues, at fixed or floating rates to suit the requirements of the borrower and the market at the same time.

110.   However when all sources of borrowing have been looked at, it still comes back to the question of making a proper profit - to stay free from government, to have money to re-invest and a profit record to persuade the private financial sector to lend to one's airport or airport authority.

Bibliographical References

1.   DONNE M. Financial Times, January 6th 1976.

2.   WILKINSON Dr. K. Flight International, page 235, 31st January, 1976.

3.   Airports International Page 37-39, August/September, 1975.

4.   Federal Aviation Administration "The Airport Passenger Head Tax" paragraph 3.3.2 July 1974.

5.   Report of the Committee of Enquiry into Civil Air Transport "British Air Transport into the Seventies, Chairman, Professor Sir Ronald Edwards, K.B.E., H.M. Stationery Office, London,   May 1969 Cmnd 4018, para 911, page 224.

6.   RAMSDEN J.M. Flight International, 4th September, 1975, page 345.

7.   NEISS J. A. The Aerospace Corporation, "Terminal Economics & Financing" Presented at Third Intersociety Conference on Transportation July 17th, 1975, Atlanta, Georgia, U.S.A.

8.   NEISS J.A. "Economic Viability of Air Carrier and Reliever Airports" presented at 27th Annual Conference of the Airport Operators Council International, October 6th-10th, 1974, San Diego,California.

9.   O'SHAUGHNESSY H. Financial Times, London 19th March, 1976.

10. Airports International, February/March 1976

Session III: Discussion

Sir Peter MASEFIELD (Paper 5)

During the three (quite eventful) years which
have passed since the fourth World Airports Conference in 1973 some thoroughly unexpected things
have happened. In particular, the almost boring-
ly steady growth of air traffic which seemed
likely to go on for ever then, has - temporarily
I think - had a 'hic-up', while, at the same
time, costs have escalated everywhere in a quite
horrifying manner. At major world airports yet
another big change has occurred. The numbers,
and the relative proportion of, movements by
very large, wide-body, aircraft have increased
enormously. So with some notable exceptions airports are currently handling a little less traffic than they did in the peak year of 1973 and
they are doing so with fewer aircraft movements.
Now that the growth of air traffic is beginning
to move up again the trend is certainly moving
in the direction of more passengers and more air
cargo in bigger and fewer and, fortunately,
quieter aircraft.

All these changes have been dramatic and
they have been significant. But they have not
been fundamental. The old problems remain -
though the 'crunch' of some of them has been
postponed. The fundamentals which are still
with us are sufficient airport capacity, and adequate standards. Whatever the changes, I am
sure that we all agree that there can be no com-
placency about either of these fundamentals at
airports everywhere.

Three years ago we were concerned to a
major extent with plans for great new airports.
Two, in Montreal and in Paris, are now in operation - at very substantial costs. The fourth
New York airport and the third London airport
have (I believe fortunately) disappeared. I
believe that we in Britain have had a lucky escape from the potential economic and the operational disasters of Maplin. The fact is that,
for the foreseeable future, we have to do the
best with what we've got.

I want to pay a tribute to the work which
has been done during the past three years by the
major airports administrations, always in difficult and often in frustrating circumstances. In
particular I would like to single out the British Airports Authority who have added the busy
airports of Glasgow and Aberdeen to their responsibilities and are, therefore, now one of the
widest ranging airports authorities in the world,
as well as, I believe, the most profitable.
Aberdeen, with North Sea oil is, incidentally,
one exception to the rule. I see that in the
past year at Aberdeen, aircraft movements have
gone up by about 37% while passenger numbers
have increased by almost 40%. It shows what a
spot of oil can do to the wheels of growth.

It is axiomatic that the more the pressure
on capacity the more the problem to maintain,
and, if possible to enhance, the standards. Because of the let up in traffic growth, and because of the increase in the proportion of very
large aircraft the problem of runway capacity
has, in most places, somewhat eased. In passen-

ger numbers it looks as though, in 1976, at most
major airports the position will be roughly what
it was in 1973, Heathrow excepted, where it
looks that there will be some 10% growth over
the three year stretch. So, if the pressure is,
temporarily, off runway capacity, it is going to
be very much on passenger and cargo handling
facilities during the next few years. And that
means pressure on standards of service.

However difficult the times, there is no
reason to accept lower standards. Major airports administrations and civil aviation authorities' can feel proud of the technical standards
they have set for navigational and landing aids
and systems and for such other essentials as
fire fighting and rescue services; proud but
never complacent. Where, because of pressure of
events, the standards are less satisfactory is,
I believe, in passenger services. I am not
being critical of the immense efforts which have
been made, at great expense, to keep pace with
traffic requirements. What I am saying is that
what is needed is a rethink about some of the
ways and means. In particular, the very large
and impersonal passenger terminal operates, inevitably, at a lower standard of personal service than any other aspect of the air transport
business.

Airports, air transport and the facilities
which they provide, are in the front line of the
battle to promote national and international
trade and prosperity, to counteract inflation,
to create employment and to help to beat the recession. Therefore, the traffic for which airports exist should be helped and encouraged in
every way possible in the widest national interests. National and international trade through
airports are, indeed, top priority. Even curfews are seriously restrictive to trade and to
a return to economic growth and prosperity. So
let us recognize the importance of airports to
national progress and to a climb out of the
present recession.

Existing airports, properly developed, are
the most cost effective (as well as the most
operationally satisfactory) means of providing
for, and developing, air traffic. So, the maximum effort should be put into developing existing airports in the best possible ways. New airports are getting more and more expensive - and
are environmentally out. So, we must get more
out of what we've got, at a satisfactory level
of cost benefit.

Thirdly, in general, although operational
standards at airports are good, and getting better, standards of passenger handling are, relatively speaking, less good - and getting worse.
This is because of congestion, because of the
impersonal remoteness of very large terminals
and because of such unsatisfactory concepts as
very long walking distances and remote car parks.
Furthermore, large airports must think much more
seriously about their responsibilities towards
'general aviation'.

To summarize:

(a) airports are vital to trade and pros-
    perity;

(b) existing airports are now the basis for the future;

(c) recognizing all that's been done, we must have a drive to improve standards, especially standards of passenger handling.

Every form of technological and economic development has always followed a broadly similar pattern: a slow start, an accelerating growth and a steadying up to maturity. It has been the same for the railways, for shipbuilding, for road building, for motor cars - and for aviation. My view is that we are still at the relatively early stage of air transport - that we have to plan for more growth, for 1000 passenger aircraft (perhaps bigger), for hypersonic speeds and, eventually, for much more automation and lower costs. Whichever way it goes existing airports - just as existing main railway stations - have got to bear 'the heat and burden of the day'. My plea is that they should do so at improved standards - especially for passenger handling which, with cargo, is what it's all about. Most of all, that means more and less congested passenger terminals, improved access and enough runways to do the job with a fail safe philosophy.

Mr SCHRODER (Paper 7)

In my Paper, I concentrated on the possibilities of airports making a utility rate of return, which was both a measure of efficiency for larger airports as well as enabling those airports to create part of their own fund requirements from retained profits.

The overall objective of my Paper was to encourage airports to make reasonable profits; these will enable them to become more self sufficient in their funding requirements which, through the growth of air transport, remain substantial. Alternatively, if they have to borrow, profits measure to lenders the airport's capacity to pay.

An important additional point, illustrated by Fig.1, is that there is a substantial multiplier effect on airport earnings provided by a relatively small rise in total airline costs through an increase in landing charges; this on the other hand, has a significant beneficial effect on airport earnings.

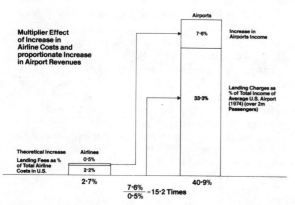

Fig. 1

Professor H. H. HOWELL, Washington University

Having had the privilege of attending most of the past World Airport Conferences, I refreshed my memory of previous events by reviewing the proceedings of the preceding three. So much has happened in the past nine years! Sir Peter Masefield's views have had a remarkable consistency over the years and validity is difficult in an industry that is anything but static.

When one reaches the age where one legally qualifies as a senior citizen there is a tendency to become dogmatic and authoritarian. But reading airport papers from past years gives abundant evidence that dogma can be quite dangerous. For example, the summaries of past conferences say a great deal about a number of terminals. Yet, in one instance a terminal reviewed nine years ago is still, I understand, more than a year from completion. Another appears to have fallen down, yet another has burned down. Most of the remainder have been extensively remodelled. But the ability to remodel indicates a degree of flexibility in original planning - a recognition that forecasts were not precise, that airline practices and procedures change and that the moods of a fickle travelling public vary greatly.

Paper 5 dealt with getting more out of existing airports. Maximum utilization has got to come. Every effort that will increase capacity needs to be explored fully.

In the USA we have approximately 550 airports that receive scheduled airline services. The 23 'large hub' communities generate about 65% of the nation's airline passengers. These 23 large hubs, plus medium hubs, handle more than 90% of the US passengers. Capacity is very much the concern of the large hub airports. It is of increasing concern at medium hubs. Advances in technology and traffic control procedures continue to point to increases in capacity. There is currently much planning for parallel runways and more efficient taxiway systems to enhance increased capacity.

And airports share the concern that more than the landing area requires attention. With US airlines demanding exclusive gates, ramp gate positions are a problem, walking distances longer. Security requirements have presented serious problems at some airports, due to their concept, design and configuration. Federal inspection procedures have been liberalized, but this simplification has not been matched with rearrangement to enhance passenger movements.

Landside capacity also merits attention. Curb frontage, adequate taxi and bus stands, automobile parking and rent-a-car facilities on the airport plus off-airport highway and transit systems need attention to guarantee convenient and adequate access.

Paper 5 touched on these problems. Sir Peter is consistent in continuing to advocate the incorporation of a sewage-plant area into Heathrow Airport. From past papers and some of the remarks today, I have the impression that many Londoners would prefer to see Perry Oaks expand and take over the entire Heathrow complex.

All in all, problems in the US are quite similar to those of the UK.

Paper 6 dealt with general aviation - quite a well-developed industry in the US. Non-airline aircraft account for the bulk of aircraft movements there, based on FAA control tower counts.

There is a substantial part of the total US general aviation activity at the 550 airline airports. O'Hare Field, for example has about 8% of its landings and take-offs made by non-airline aircraft. Most of this is business and executive aircraft activity, with charters and air-taxis. At the smaller airline hubs, general aviation is the primary activity, in terms of aircraft movements. At these smaller airline airports, provision for greater capacity does not mean parallel runways of airline length. Usually, a parallel to the airline runway that will accommodate light twin-engine aircraft is sufficient; sometimes runways long enough for business jets are provided.

Non-airline communities are finding that a good general aviation airport is necessary, if they are to attract business or industrial locations. To this end, the USA has a fairly comprehensive network of local airports for general aviation and, especially, executive flying.

Most of the states now assist local governments in their airport financing, helping them provide the sponsor's share of the Federal Airport Development Aid Program that uses aviation generated trust funds for landing area improvements. Hangars and terminals remain a local responsibility.

The general aviation phase is also the subject of much attention on the part of airport planners. The state of Illinois, for example, has completed a forward-looking plan that has two objectives:

(a) each community of 2500 population should be within half-an-hour's drive of a basic airport for light aircraft;
(b) each community of 10 000 population should be within a 30 min. drive of an airport adequate for business jets.

Illinois has a good history of state financial assistance, with the result that few new airports are required to accomplish these two objectives. But their establishment can well be environmentally difficult.

Capacity is a problem at the strictly general aviation airport, also. The busier ones have parallel, even triple runways or strips. The general aviation airport at Louisville, Kentucky, (Bowman Field), has a proposed plan to provide two widely separated sets of parallel runways in its primary direction, with independent flight pattern capability. These, coupled with triple crosswind runways, sufficiently separated to permit dual flight patterns, provide a theoretical capacity of more than 600 000 annual operations. This plan, however, is generating support for a new airport, away from the city, so that there will be no substantial increase in the current 300 000 annual movements at Bowman Field.

Paper 7 dealt with financing. There is a good system of aviation generated Federal Trust Fund assistance in the USA for local airfield improvements, often with further aid from the state in which the airport is located. Hangars and terminals, however, are not included. The deplorable special requirements of the Federal Program, however, tend to negate some of its effective value.

Local financing, on the parts of the larger airline airports, has become almost exclusively accomplished by revenue bonds. These are backed by airline and concession leases which assure the generation of more than enough revenue for operating costs and debt retirement. Smaller airports can not generate revenues adequate for guaranteed debt requirements. A variety of financing is employed. There is direct taxation in some instances, but voter-approved bond issues are required in most cases. I might add that voter approval of added taxes is increasingly more difficult to obtain. So - the US system has its deficiencies and problems, but our heads are generally above water. In the USA we are planning, we are building and we are now waiting to see what our Congress is going to do with the Trust Fund money that aviation users have generated.

Our airports seek no profit. Fees to airport users are, relatively, quite reasonable. As a civil engineer and an airport consultant, I am happy that our US airport operators do just that and don't compete with me for my daily bread!

So, we are relatively in good shape, pointing with pride but viewing with alarm, and to repeat Mr Hammarskjold's remark facing the future with cautious optimism.

Mr W. A. ALLEN, Bickerdike/Allen/Bramble, London

With regard to Paper 5, one understands a desire to maximize the utilisation of existing facilities but so far as the capacity of the four London airports is concerned almost everything appears to depend upon the ratio between the average number of passengers to be expected per aircraft and the total number of passengers to be carried.

I expect we can agree for the moment that a representative figure for the total in 1990 might be 90 million passengers. When the Government's Maplin review was published it presumed that the average passenger load at that date would be 225. The growth of passenger numbers per aircraft, like the total numbers of passengers, develops exponentially and has done so from the beginning of the industry, positively at first, but negatively later as numbers approach ultimate limits.

The numbers for the London area are all so large that the curves are very steady, and while they do not suggest that a total throughput of 90 million is unrealistic 14 or 15 years from now, they strongly indicate that the average number of passengers per aircraft would be of the order of only 175, and that 225 is most improbable. If the higher figure were, in fact, correct it would imply that by 1995 planes would carry average loads of 325 or 350, and so on.

The figure appears to be crucial, for while the 90 million people would be carried in only about 400 000 movements of aircraft with average loads of 225 people and thus appear to be safely within the presumed capacity of the four airports, they would need about 520 000 movements if the average loads only reach 175 per aircraft; and if one then adds 80 000 to 100 000 cargo movements as does the review, the total capacity of the four airports as presumed in the Maplin review (620 000) would be approached or exceeded.

In this four-airport scenario, Luton and Stansted together are assumed to handle some 120 000 movements, limited by problems of air traffic control, but if Luton were to be closed, apparently Stansted could be allowed 200 000 movements or more and thus provide a way out of that dilemma.

I think the whole situation is more marginal than Paper 5 suggests, and there are many people who see all this as a situation leading back to Stansted as the third London airport.

Sir Peter MASEFIELD (Paper 5)

Obviously no one can tell exactly what will happen, but I think these numbers of passengers per aircraft are growing faster than Mr Allen suggests. Gatwick is now at an average of 74 passengers per aircraft, and going up: at Heathrow it is 86 and going up fast. Wide body aeroplanes are coming in at an increasing rate, and load factors are better. I think that 200 passengers on average by 1990 is not too much to expect. I would be surprised if it is not well above that. Once the growth of traffic starts up again, we shall have our 1000 seaters.

At Seattle Boeing has plans to develop the 747 eventually up to perhaps 1200 passengers. Such a size will bring many airport problems, but a few of such aircraft will help to keep aircraft movements within the numbers which can be coped with - so long as they are not single runway airports.

I am sure that Heathrow, Gatwick, Luton and Stansted can all operate at once to high capacity without interfering with each other; I hope that one day Northolt will be available for general aviation, and that Southend will be in the picture as well. They should be adequate for as far forward as one can see.

Mr G. EDWARDS, GEP

Mr Schroder suggests that airports might be classified as public utilities. I personally think that that is the way in which they should be regarded and financed. I am unhappy, however, that there seems to be a feeling that the great thing to do in running a public utility is to finance its forward expenditure out of current revenue. That is wrong and it is offensive. What it means is that when buying electricity, gas airport charges and tickets, passengers will be asked to pay a cost which reflects the capital expenditure of providing facilities for people who are as yet unborn, in a growth industry affected by inflation. It is reasonable to expect passengers to service the cost of a loan to do that perhaps, but to service the total capital cost seems to me to be economically wrong, and certainly I would have thought, in paying an electricity bill and airport charges, unfair.

Mr SCHRODER (Paper 7)

That is a very interesting philosophical question. The American viewpoint is that their airports, certainly at the moment, do not make such a large rate of return as non-American airports because they finance their future investment through revenue bonds. These require that an airport's income in any year amounts to bet-

ween 125% and 140% of the interest payable on the bonds, added to the required annual repayment of capital.

The British Airports Authority has been given an objective rate of return of 15%. Even though it made only 11.5% last year to 31 March, 1975, it has been able to cover normal development charges out of earnings in 7 out of the previous 9 years. American utilities are currently allowed to make 11.8% on their net assets. This figure is also approximately what the Civil Aeronautical Board allows American airlines to make, which is 12%. If all airports had an objective rate of return of 12%, that would allow them to cover most reinvestment problems, and if less, it would not. Personally I would go for a utility rate of return a couple of percentage points above the long term cost of money to the relevant government of the country: i.e. the cost of long term gilts in the UK at this time is $13\frac{1}{2}$%; plus 2% gives a $15\frac{1}{2}$% objective rate of return, which oddly enough is roughly what the British Airports Authority is expected to earn on its net assets.

Mr EDWARDS

I accept that to maintain the utility in its present form it should be financed out of current revenue. What I cannot accept is that the user in this generation should have to pay a charge which reflects the expansion required in the next generation.

Professor R.DOGANIS, Polytechnic of Central London

I should like to refer to the economic break-even point of airports. The figure mentioned by Mr Schroder was 6000 000 passengers, and he also made the point that a higher rate of return on investment was obtained at foreign airports than at American airports. I do not think that this could possibly be the case in European conditions and in my experience I have found no airports in any developing country which produce any positive rate of return at all. The American authorities who found airports which produce a high rate of return must have looked at a minimal number of airports very selectively.

Central London Polytechnic carried out an analysis of British airports in the 1960s and found the best break-even point in UK conditions for an airport with no major development was about 1 million passengers. For most airports with reasonable development (new terminal buildings, etc.), the break-even point was 3 million passengers.

We are currently examining the situation of British airports for 1974-75 to see whether the position has considerably worsened. There is virtually no airport in the UK making a real profit, even though many are handling more than 1 million passengers. In fact, the curves of airport costs and airport revenues no longer meet. The implication of that is very worrying. It means that the costs of airports have escalated much faster than airport charges, and the two are now moving away from each other to the point where an airport cannot be profitable unless it is in a monopolistic situation.

The figures given in the Paper on the break-

Table 1. United States vs foreign airports

AIRPORT DATA BASE					
United States airports			Foreign airports		
Over 1 500 000 annual passenger enplanements					
Los Angeles	Atlanta	San Francisco	Sydney	Montreal	Toronto
Miami	Wash. National	Denver	Copenhagen	Osaka	Tokyo
Detroit	Philadelphia	St Louis	Amsterdam	Madrid	Palma
Minn. St Paul	Cleveland	Seattle	Zurich	Gatwick	Heathrow
Houston	Kansas City	New Orleans	Le Bourget/Orly	Dusseldorf	Frankfurt
San Diego	Tampa	Baltimore	Hamburg	Munich	
375 000 - 1 499 999 annual passenger enplanements					
Memphis	Cincinnati	Portland	Aeroparque	Ezeiza	Vancouver
Dulles	Indianapolis	Salt Lake City	Bogota	Prague	Cairo
Oakland	Louisville	Milwaukee	Helsinki	Marseilles	Nice
Hartford	San Jose	Ft Lauderdale	Bombay	New Delhi	Djakarta
Dayton	Jacksonville	Nashville	Dublin	Lod	Beirut
Rochester	Omaha	Syracuse	Lisbon	Singapore	Johannesburg
Sacramento	Albuquerque	Tulsa	Gothenburg	Stockholm	Geneva
Birmingham	El Paso	Tucson	Barcelona	Bangkok	Istanbul
Des Moines	Ontario		Glasgow	Luton	Manchester
			Caracas	Christchurch	Saigon
75 000 - 374 999 annual passenger enplanements					
Spokane	Richmond	Greensboro	Perth	Doula	Santiago
Grand Rapids	Shreveport	Jackson	Barranquilla	Accra	Calcutta
Roanoke	Fresno	Moline	Madras	Cork	Shannon
Sioux Falls	Charleston	Boeing Field	Vietiane	Tananarive	Kuala Lumpur
Fort Wayne	Amarillo	Johnson City	Curacao	Auckland	Malmo
Lehigh Valley	Columbus	Tallahassee	Stansted	Prestwick	Ankara
South Bend	Peoria	Lexington			
Youngstown	Palm Springs	Santa Barbara			
Long Beach	Lincoln	Melbourne			
Burlington	Rapid City	Springfield			
Bangor	Elmira				
Under 75 000 annual passenger enplanements					
Tri Cities	Yakima	Battle Creek	Yaounde	Bangui	Fort Lamy
Tacoma	Ventura	Modesto	Libreville	Niamey	Bandaranaike
Pullman - Moscow	Walla Walla	Merced			
Chico	Visalia	Wenatchee			
Mt Vernon	Ephrata	Hoquiam			
Olympia					

even point are therefore misleading so far as the UK and Europe are concerned: they bear no relation to reality.

Mr SCHRODER

Professor Doganis's point on the rate of return figures of US and foreign airports is most interesting. I have amended Fig.6 of my Paper to show (Fig.2 and Table 1):

(a) the method by which the rate of return figures which I used were calculated;
(b) the list of airports forming the sample.

I entirely agree with the point that perhaps too much money was spent on airports originally. In order to make money you have to be very careful how much capital expenditure is put into fixed investments. If that can be reduced, the break-even point comes down.

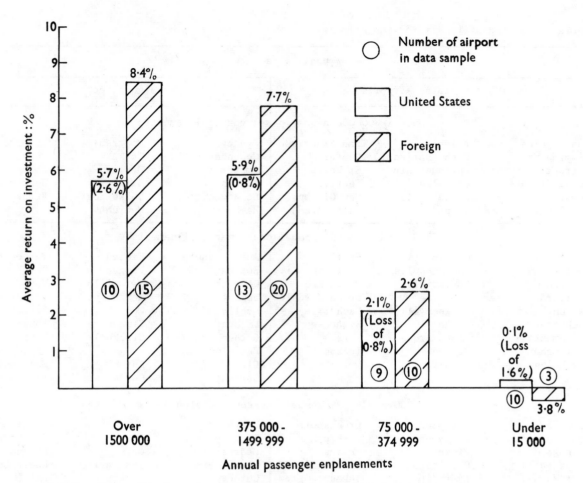

Fig.2. *US vs foreign airports: comparison of rate of return on investment (1970 dollars)*

NOTES

(a) Rate of return figures were computed by dividing operating profit by total investment in plant, property and equipment, less depreciation. In determining operating profit, operating revenues were defined to exclude contributions by local governments or appropriations of tax funds, and operating expenses to exclude depreciation, debt service and capital improvement costs.

(b) Figures for rate of return on investment (in brackets) for US airports are re-calculated to give rate of return on the same bases as (a), but after depreciation and interest costs (see Table 2)

Table 2. Comparison of rate of return figures on the basis of notes (a) and (b) (Fig.2.)

	Annual passenger emplanements			
	Over 1 500 000	375 000- 1 499 999	75 000- 374 999	Under 75 000
Rate of return as defined in note(a) i.e. before depreciation and debt service costs including interest	5.7%	5.9%	2.1%	0.1%
Rate of return as defined in note(b) i.e. after depreciation and debt service costs including interest	2.6%	0.8%	(0.8% Loss)	(1.6% Loss)

The original figures and the corrections were supplied by Mr J.A.Neiss of the Aerospace Corporation, Los Angeles, California

Panel discussion: Sessions II and III

Mr J. R. ADDERLEY, Software Sciences Ltd

We have received such an abundance of opinion and good advice, that I feel I should identify those key aspects which challenge our future, and those opinions which you may subsequently indicate remain a matter of controversy.

Mr Hammarskjold outlined the effect of recent world wide recession on airlines, which have caused them to review their traditional operating philosophies, as a result of progressive declining returns on investment. He suggested that it was relatively easy for airports, and government, to increase the user charges of their 'captive' customers. But I wonder whether you agree? He spoke of the need for co-operation between airports, airlines and government and, whilst acknowledging IATA's contributions in this respect, I question whether the scheduling policy of some airlines at some airports does assist the spreading of peak demands. Finally, I am sure we all welcomed the plea for more flexible planning and responsiveness to unexpected events.

Lord Boyd-Carpenter, the Chairman of the Civil Aviation Authority, treated us to an account of airport planning in the UK in the past, present and future. He identified three eras of aviation, characterised respectively by (a) welcoming, acceptance and accord, which degenerated into (b) noise and excess demands, spawning the search for so-called environmental airports, and (c) a renewed faith in noise technology associated with large aircraft and improved runway movements. This will create capacity which will render Roskill's quest abortive and enable us to use those airports we have enjoyed but under-utilised for many years.

I agree entirely with his identification of the pressures that will be upon airport terminals and groundside access, but I fear that the latter may be compounded by the yet unpublished strategy, for the respective roles of four airports, to serve London.

I only wish that I shared his Lordship's optimism for the effectiveness of quiet noise technology and supporting legislation. Whilst in no way disputing specific decreases in decibels that are attainable with the latest generation of aircraft, I fear that many familiar shapes and sounds will continue, for many years, to inspire us with apathy or hatred as they use international and regional airports.

Professor Treibel gave a lucid explanation of the manner in which German airports function as private companies, with no national airport planning authority, but with the benefit of advice from the German Airports Association.

It is interesting to see that in locations as close as Dusseldorf and Koln/Bonn, only 53 km apart, two airports can successfully compete and hopefully prosper, although I believe that in such circumstances there is some planning undertaken by the State which considers such matters as airspace interactions and inter-airport communications.

Indeed, one might ask what effect has the home base policy of the national carrier, Lufthansa. It has its major facilities concentrated at Frankfurt and operates the majority of its international services from this airport of restricted capacity, whilst other excellent airports remain under-utilised. In other words, does the fact that a major airline operates from a particular airport tend to render it a hub airport at the expense of other equally suitable airports.

Mr Young emphasized the importance of transportation and the role of aviation to serve the vast expanse of Canada. He described the systematic approach with successive hierarchies of transportation and aviation plans including both area and individual master plans. Whilst many subscribe to such systematic planning, further evidence that relates the concept to every day reality and unforeseen contingencies is welcome.

He confirmed that very few airports are, or will be, self-supporting, but as part of Government master plans are being maintained but at low standards of service. Despite all the real estate, it seems that Canada has not escaped the problem of urban versus airport development with its attendant range of social and political implications. This is particularly so in the more densely populated areas immediately to the north of the Great Lakes, with the notable exception of Mirabel and its enviable 17,000 acres. Surely Mirabel is the dynamic proof that, in some locations, environmental airports can and should be built?

Sir Peter Masefield presented an eloquent and reasoned plea for a second runway at Gatwick. The force of argument that justifies the appropriate facilities for an international airport which is forecast by 1990 to receive more passengers than Heathrow did in 1975 is plain. The importance of a runway, available to be used during maintenance or obstruction of the primary runway is unarguable. A few simple calculations will quantify the value, measured in reduced delays and increased safety, if it can be used at peak times or to segregate general aviation. But planners must respect the fears of those more closely involved, who may seek some positive guarantees that their quality of life will not be further prejudiced by still more noise. If Lord Boyd-Carpenter's confident predictions of noise reduction are correct, then surely Sir Peter, and Britain, should have the second runway?

As an international concept, albeit with illustrations related to the national scene, Sir Peter defined the terminal building, passenger handling and groundside access problems, which will dominate airports, as traffic increases. In summary, he advocated the smallest number of airports that can provide capacity to match demand, but an increase in the number of terminals at each airport so that they can provide a safe and adequate service for a manageable flow of passengers.

He also pointed out the need to serve general aviation as more fully described by Mr Smith in Paper 6.

The aspect of most concern to airport planners and operators is the effect of allowing, or encouraging, general aviation or certainly third line feeder services, air taxis, and business/executive aircraft, which have a very real need to use established airports. In general they are fully equipped for IFR flights, with experienced pilots, and with aircraft performance similar to air transport aircraft. They have but a slight affect on runway capacity, although their passenger loads are counted in single figures, rather than in hundreds. Recreational flying comprises such a broad spectrum of capability, skills and performance that its encouragement at an airport may prejudice both capacity and safety, both directly, and because of certain rather unpleasant vorticity characteristics of big brother Boeing and his brethren. Thus, I for one would always advocate segregated minimal facility airfields for recreational flying and adequate facilities at airports for suitably qualified business flights.

Finally Mr Schroder brought us back to our starting point whereby we recognize the domination of the economic situation.

His illustrations of the growth of non-aviation revenue in proportion to aviation revenue is most interesting and will, I feel, find more favour with captive airline friends than his reference to increased landing and en route charges.

Indeed, as mentioned earlier, perhaps airlines could make a more useful contribution to sensible airport utilisation if they co-operated with airports to plan their schedules to avoid excess demands. This could well lead to reductions in delays of which the airlines complain so rightly and so vigorously, and could remove the need for over investment at adequate airports.

In conclusion, we have been presented with a splendid spectrum of facts and opinions, some of which appear to be complete contradictions. But are they? At worst, they may prove that some problems have more than one answer. At best, they indicate that there are different answers when different situations and circumstances affect a particular problem. What is right today may be wrong tomorrow. What is right for Canada may indeed be right for Europe, but it may be wrong.

So consider, plan and quantify your options. Learn from the triumphs and errors of others. But make your own judgment, and retain your own flexibility. I hope that you will take advantage of this opportunity to challenge the future as expressed by our speakers.

Mr B. TUTTY, Director Airports, IATA

The main point that I take from Mr Adderley is that he is concerned at the expenditure forced upon airports as a result of peaking, a notable point and one which airlines would like to respond to. Unfortunately, there are a number of factors which come into this. One is the fact that the passenger is of primary importance, and he likes to travel at a certain time of the day in order to arrive at a convenient time, or for convenience of connexion.

The second point, and I am surprised it has not been raised so far is that of curfews.

Britain probably led the world in the introduction of curfews in the late 1950s and early 1960s, and they have since proliferated. These curfews have forced unnatural peaks on airlines operating round the world services, because if they endeavour to move their schedules out of the peak at one airport somewhere else on their route they will run out of time and have to overnight. In fact at the present moment the situation is so difficult, especially on the Far Eastern route, that if India or Pakistan should decide to introduce curfews, I am afraid that route stops somewhere in the night for most airlines would be inevitable. West European and North American passengers are the most frequent of travellers. Will they give way to the wishes of other countries and travel at less frequent times or in a more infrequent manner?

There is an alternative. It may be that curfews should be reduced. Perhaps the public might accept more noise on the basis that at least 15% of them do travel, and another 15% of the population living around airports, lives off the airport or by the airports. Perhaps more consideration should be given to the generating effect of the airport.

I believe that airlines would like to spread their peaks, but they are in a box, and until the authorities and the communities help a little more, there is not much they can do.

Professor TREIBEL (Paper 3)

Mr Adderley referred to the position of the German airline Lufthansa, and asked why it is that Frankfurt was chosen as the main basis for the network. I must return to the historical background.

After the war, at the beginning in the process of recovery, the Federal Republic of Germany was started following the old Reich. Many infrastructure measures were necessary to rebuild the traffic system. That meant that we prepared the civil airports first for international foreign airlines, beginning in 1947, and with the ADV as an Association for German airports. Until 1955 the Federal Government had no jurisdiction so far as aviation was concerned. On 5 May, 1955, this authority and power was given to the German Federal Government, and from then on it was given authority to allow German airlines to go into business. That was the start of Lufthansa.

In the case of an airline which comes into service in its own country long after some foreign airlines, it is necessary to look carefully at the traffic demand. If you look at Fig. 8 of my Paper you will see that during this time only two airports in Germany collected more than 25% of the total passengers. One was Frankfurt and the other was Berlin. Neither in 1955 nor today could Lufthansa fly into Berlin, so it was logical for Lufthansa to concentrate its international services first at Frankfurt Airport, which was reconstructed very early at the request of the Americans, for military and civil use.

Coming to the question of scheduling, Mr Adderley commented that there is some peaking in traffic, especially in Frankfurt Airport. Two years ago the Minister for Traffic and Transportation authorized an official Federal Coordinator to schedule the airline networks. Since the beginning of 1976 the time-table co-

ordinator is also in charge of all charter
flights, especially those with short announce-
ment. This means that in the case of all airports in Germany at any given moment it is
necessary to go to the scheduling co-ordinator
who can say 'yes' or 'no'. The airline operator
has to ask for permission to fly in and depart
at a specific time. Exceptions are those timetables for scheduled flights of airlines agreed
long in advance.

Experience shows that the pressure in the
peaks diminished in many cases, and we hope that
the apparent success of the German scheduling coordination will stimulate other countries. The
ADV started last November a scheduling seminar
in Frankfurt in connexion with the Western European Airports Association and IATA in order to
produce more aircraft movements per day with
less pressure in the peak hours.

On the question of noise and curfews I may
say that for a long time the German Airports
Association has held the view that aircraft which
follow the Annex 16 or the FAR 36 levels should
be allowed to operate in and outside the airport
despite a curfew. The night flight restrictions
at Munich Airport for example say that 'take-offs
of aircraft in international traffic up to 23.00 h
h local time are excluded from night curfews if
for these flights aircraft are used which do not
exceed the noise levels of Annex 16 to the ICAO
Convention'.

Mr YOUNG (Paper 4)

I had a number of questions put to me, the first
of which was whether systematic planning is working. I hope so, because I feel I was one of
those who introduced it. However, to be quite
honest, it is regionally orientated, and there
are some deficiencies in that respect in that
the interpretation of policies, standards etc
quite often present a problem. In addition,
there was another setback imposed in the last
fiscal year after six month's operation of the
planning system. This took the form of government restraints which cut back the staff resources for this kind of work.

There have also been a number of prediction
failures in terms of forecasting - not significant in relation to aircraft movements and passenger traffic, but lacking in particular for
ground transportation and related systems.
These are being remedied at the moment, and I
hope within a few months that we shall be able
to pick up where we left off previously, hopefully with better techniques.

There have been two other problems, and
these are keyed to the facts we have not yet, in
our terms, a sufficient air carrier or local
government participation. For example, some of
the local governments on the periphery of airports have abdicated their responsibilities by
precipitating private citizens into this participative type of discussion. I think the involvement of private citizens is an idealistic approach, but we are looking for practical solutions; certainly while private citizens must
have access, they must not be given the impression, which they had been, that they are in a
decision making role.

As to the effectiveness of the system,
there were 20 plans completed up to 30 April,
1976. About eight are satisfactory and the other
twelve require varying degrees of modification:
these largely stem from the economic situation
generally but there are some defects arising
from the somewhat erroneous interpretation of
policies I previously mentioned. There are a
further 18 in hand, making a total of 38 which
have been in hand during this two years of the
programme. I am still optimistic that we shall
be able to move ahead. In precise answer to the
question, I personally feel that systematic planning has worked, but effectiveness has been
seriously limited because of the many constraints.

As to the noise problem at airports, and
bearing in mind that we do not have the relatively massive number of movements that there are
particularly at Heathrow, the general public simply will not believe us when we say there may be
or will be quieter aircraft eventually. We can
impose mitigation measures: we are endeavouring
to do this, and the carriers are co-operating
completely. But the general public is generally
sceptical of what is being done now and undoubtedly will be achieved in the future.

Mirabel is decidedly an environmental airport in Lord Boyd-Carpenter's terms. I should
like to say it works, and I should like to say
that it is a financial success. But it is neither. It has many bugs like every other new airport, and from an efficiency perspective, we have
not yet achieved a truly effective method of com-
bining the total flow of passenger processing
within and between the various sub-systems.

In relation to its being a financial success - and perhaps I am speaking out of turn
here - we need to spend more money at Mirabel;
that is to say we are not yet confident of an
adequate return on investment and need to invest
more for more positive returns. This is imperative because in some of the facilities provided
there is considerable over-capacity and in others
under-capacity. Perhaps one of the most important factors is that in designing the traffic
split between the Dorval Airport and the new
Mirabel Airport, we had to depend on our two
major domestic carriers to provide for more domestic traffic than has transpired at Mirabel.
However, with the advent of the Olympics, and
during the two month period of foreign access to
Montreal we shall experience something of the
traffic densities which should occur in about
1980. We feel that we can wipe the bugs out
during and following that period.

I am optimistic that this airport will ultimately be an excellent airport, although it
has a serious built-in problem relating to airport access and particularly to the fact that
there is no rapid transit facility between
Mirabel and the city core which is over 25 miles
away. We have been promised by the provincial
government, which has authority and jurisdiction
over road and local rail transit development,
that up-graded rail access will be provided by
1981, and, while I am fairly confident that they
mean what they say the problem is with us and
will seriously hamper the efficiency of the two-
airport system in immediate future years.

Sir Peter MASEFIELD (Paper 5)

The main point is that we have five depreciated
assets in our old airports, and the challenge is
to make them as good as we can so as to achieve
a satisfactory return and give good service out
of what is there already, rather than building
unnecessarily again in remote places. Therefore,
building on to existing airports is the right
thing, rather than creating new facilities at
this particular time. We have a wonderful past
investment which is worth vastly more than the
amounts at which it stands in the books.

Mr Adderley raised a number of interesting
points, and I will mention two. The first is
where he suggested we might push the passengers
around a bit more so as to avoid peaks. This
horrifies me. The purpose of airports is not to
be an end in themselves, but the means towards
an end - that of carrying traffic. Therefore,
we ought to study the customer more and more and
not push him around. This is the important message of the mid 1970s, that we need to earn our
living, and therefore we have to do everything
possible to give service to the people who are
paying for the business. Most of the revenue
comes from the passengers. Therefore we must
provide service for money from the passenger,
whether he be a businessman on a 747, a member of
the Board travelling in a corporate aeroplane,
or the tourist, who brings volumes of foreign exchange into different counties. So let us study
the passengers more and not push them around.
Transport will always be a peaky business.

The second point is that a second runway at
Gatwick will not add to the noise around Gatwick.
What it will do is to add to the integrity of a
very important investment at Gatwick which can
otherwise be completely shut down for periods by
small mishaps and will be if we do not have a
'fail safe' situation from a second runway when
the first is out of action. A second runway will
not add to capacity so much as to the utilisation - which is the vital factor. It will not
increase environmental noise. It will spread
the same noise if it is used chiefly for landing
in times of no emergency.

A final point in the same sort of sense is
that of maximizing assets. I must stress again
the need for Perry Oaks at Heathrow, because
this is a tremendous asset at Heathrow which can
not be used to the full because of terminal area
restrictions. Let us get the most out of what
we have already, because that is the only way of
making economic sense and developing the business.

Mr SMITH (Paper 6)

I would agree that inexperienced or student pilots should not be involved in international airports. I do have a small fear that many so-
called international airports are inclined to
think that general aviation can take second place.
If this should be so they are losing business
and losing utilization. Gatwick, of course, is
a prime example of where general aviation is welcomed and it became a name throughout Europe.
It is very important, particularly now that
Britain is firmly in the EEC, and we are seeing
more international general aviation traffic here.

Mr SCHRODER (Paper 7)

I would echo what Sir Peter Masefield said, which
was to use what we have, and to earn our living.
In order to do so, I would also add the words 'and
economize'. I think it is really a matter for
debate exactly what is the correct break-even
point for an airport. It so much depends on how
much fixed investment has been put in and the
level of subsequent passenger throughput. As an
investment banker and taxpayer, my constant cry
is to economize. Further, in my view airports
should attempt to make a profit, because that is
a discipline in itself.

Mr H. RICHARDS, Millbank Technical Services

Lord Boyd-Carpenter points out that mistakes
have been made in Britain and in other countries
in the past, and in some cases we have clawed
ourselves back from the brink at the eleventh
hour before making a major mistake. But what
his Paper does not do is to trace the reasons
for the mistakes. I would make a plea for someone to look at why planning mistakes were made,
because it is quite possible that in the future
more mistakes may be made for the same reasons.
I would suggest that one of the reasons could
well be not that planners or engineers have not
the ability to produce the answers to questions,
but that in many instances the wrong questions
are asked.

A classic example of that was the Roskill
Commission. I was a member of that Commission,
and as far as I remember the terms of reference
were:

(a) to site a third London airport, but nobody had determined whether a third London
airport was needed;
(b) site an airport with four parallel runways and capable of handling 100 million
passengers a year, but no one had established that this was the right size;
(c) produce a cost benefit analysis; this
is fine for economists, but if a decision
is made on a cost benefit analysis, it ig-
nores the question of who pays the cost and
who gets the benefit;
(d) establish the timing of the need. But
the terms of reference had already assumed
there was a need.

It became apparent in the first year that there
was no need for a third London airport. The
Commission thought of asking for new terms of
reference. Should they not be establishing an
airports policy for Britain rather than a site
for a third London airport? But by that time
there was so much planning blight across the
country, that someone in Southend, or as far as
Hull, who wanted to move his job and sell his
house, could not because his town had been named
as a possible third London airport. Obviously
the thing to do was to get work over as quickly
as possible and lift the planning blight.

I think even now, not only in the airport
business but in industry in general, the habit
of writing down constraints is still prevalent.
Throughout all industry there is a strong desire
for job definition, which puts a constraint on a
person doing a particular job.

There are in Britain good thinkers, good

engineers and good planners, and the next time there is anything like a commission or a planning committee, its terms of reference should not be written down exactly with an attempt to pre-empt the answer. It would be better if the problem, and what those concerned would like to see achieved were written down. It should then be left to the people who have the job of investigation to come up with any solutions that they find, which may be very different.

A DELEGATE

In the developing world, especially in Africa, there are a number of under-utilised international airports. Indeed, there are no fewer than 50 on the continent of Africa, yet the amount of traffic that these 50 airports handle is less than 10 million passengers. It means that African countries in particular are investing a great deal of money in infrastructures in these international airports, yet the travelling public is limited to a small elite, and there is no return on the investment. I should like to know whether these problems can be solved by governments.

Sir Peter MASEFIELD

The right thing surely is to consolidate on what there is, not to spend more money; but be ready to develop as the traffic grows. I think the African nations as they develop (and of course they will develop because many of them have great natural resources) will find that the traffic over the years will grow to meet their facilities. They will find that they have assets on historical costs which are worth a great deal to them, so they should not be despondent that they have spent money, but they should not be extravagant in what they do from now on. They should economize.

For example, Lagos Airport is stretched to the limit, and that is one example where a bit of development could bring in returns a hundred-fold, because Lagos needs to be connected with more air services, particularly more cargo services. Cairo also, I think, needs some development. Other African airports one can think of have considerable potential beyond their present capacities, but in general, praise the Lord that such as there is is there; make great use of it in years to come, because it will be cheap in 1990 when it is really needed.

Mr SMITH

My own school turns out some 250 professional graduate pilots a year of which about 75% are going to those developing countries; they - the developing countries - need to found and develop airlines. I agree with Sir Peter Masefield that I think this area will generate the traffic in the next few years.

8. A solution to airport noise

K.G. Wilkinson, Hon.DSc, DIC, FCGI, FRAeS, FCIT, FSLAET
Engineering Director, British Airways

I want to deal in this paper with one of the disadvantages which goes with the many benefits that civil aviation brings to human society - a disadvantage which seemed at one time likely to threaten the growth of a still infant industry - I refer to aircraft noise. I put this threat deliberately in the past tense because I believe that we can now see that the trend of airline equipment is leading to a containment of this problem and its reduction to tolerable proportions.

It was, in fact, recognised at a very early date that the noise of aircraft was going to be a contentious issue. In the early days of flying, Winston Churchill proposed and had enacted a law which deprived the private citizen from the right to legal action against aircraft noise, as he was afraid that it would stifle the new born technology. My first figure (1) shows the steadily rising noise level as aircraft were developed but it was the jet age which really alarmed the public at large.

In the wake of this reaction, airports such as London and New York felt obliged to introduce their own noise limits and systems to control maximum noise levels and identify and sometimes penalise offenders. There are now of course a multitude of local airport noise regulations including curfews, and movement restrictions. Finally this led to a concerted effort by Government legislation and Industry to define noise certification procedures which first affected the new widebody aircraft. The knowledge of this impending legislation had a profound impact on the design of engines of high by-pass ratio like the RB.211 intended for these aircraft.

The most eye-catching feature of such engines figure 2 is their diameter and the use of what might be termed a shrouded propeller or fan to provide about 75% of their thrust. In technical jargon we say that such engines have a low specific thrust, i.e. a low number of pounds of thrust per pound of airflow. In turn this implies low exhaust velocities and hence reduced jet noise which was the unacceptable roar associated with the first jet engines. To obtain this low specific thrust we require a high bypass ratio, that is the ratio of airflow which bypasses the core engine to the airflow through it.

Figure 3 shows the effect of this bypass ratio on perceived noise level, pinpointing the various Rolls-Royce engines on the trend of increasing bypass ratio. The 25 PNdB

reduction, from the Avon to the RB.211 is a reduction of almost six times on annoyance and 300 times on sound intensity. But it should be noted that it has required more than just a high bypass ratio to achieve this noise reduction and figure 4 illustrates a number of other design features aimed specifically at noise reduction. Perhaps most noticeable are the acoustic linings on the inner duct surfaces which contribute about 10 PNdB noise reduction and cover around 150 sq.ft of area within the powerplant.

Thus we now have the knowledge, and for some aircraft sizes the hardware, to diminish the aircraft noise problem significantly. However, the normal airline replacement process, made even slower by international economic recession is leading to only a trickle of these new aircraft permeating airline fleets, particularly in Europe on the intra-European networks.

To help explain the ingredients of present day airport noise, we can examine the noise around London's Heathrow airport using data monitored in the Summer of 1974. These data were collected at a monitor station east of the airport during a period of take-offs in this direction during a period of easterly winds, figure 5 illustrates the geography.

Using the NNI or noise and number index as a unit to express annoyance over a day's operation at this location, the variation over eight days is shown on figure 6. Broadly it is around 60 NNI at a position on the fringes of major housing, whereas the Noise Advisory Council has recommended a limit of no more than 50 NNI for such permanent exposure.

Taking one particular day in this period, June 28, we have broken down the total NNI figure into the contributions from aircraft classified in four categories:-

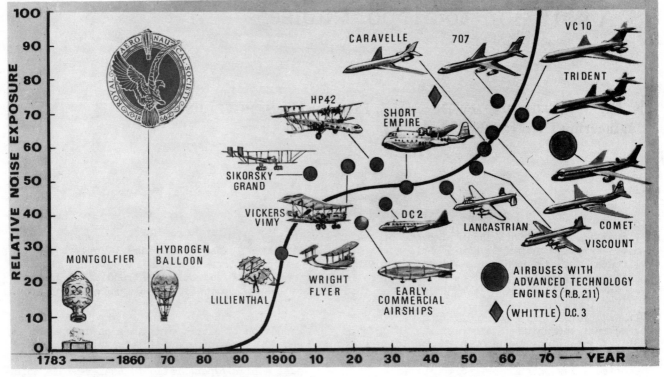

Fig.1. *Historical noise exposure trends.*

Fig.2. *RB 211, showing fan blades and size of engine*

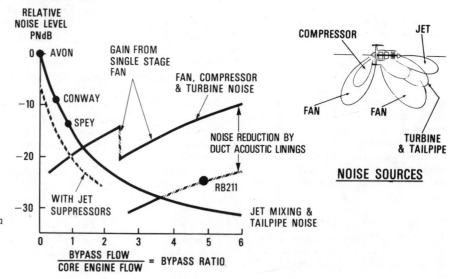

Fig.3. *Noise source variation with bypass ratio*

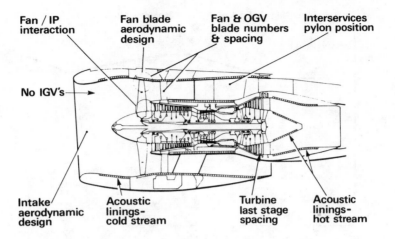

Fan / IP interaction

Fan blade aerodynamic design

Fan & OGV blade numbers & spacing

Interservices pylon position

No IGV's

Intake aerodynamic design

Acoustic linings- cold stream

Turbine last stage spacing

Acoustic linings- hot stream

Fig.4. RB 211-22B noise reduction features

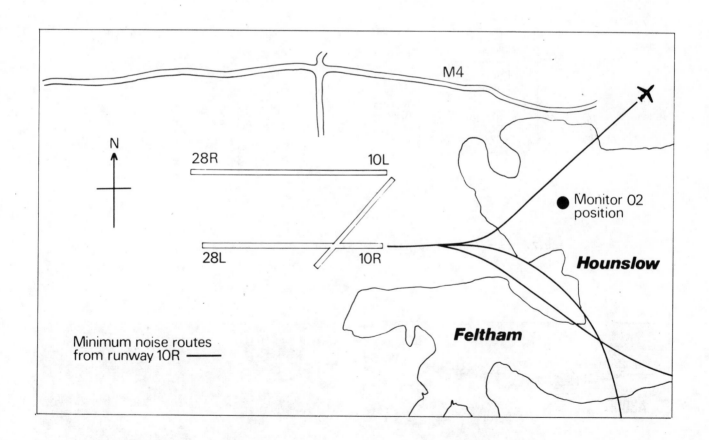

M4

N

28R   10L

28L   10R

Monitor 02 position

Hounslow

Feltham

Minimum noise routes from runway 10R ——

Fig.5. Noise at Heathrow

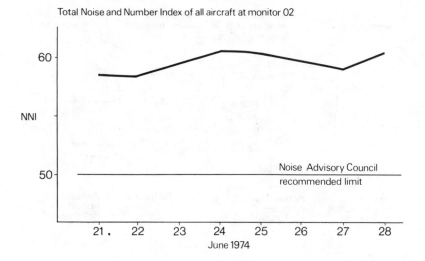

Total Noise and Number Index of all aircraft at monitor 02

Fig.6.   Noise at Heathrow (summer 1974)

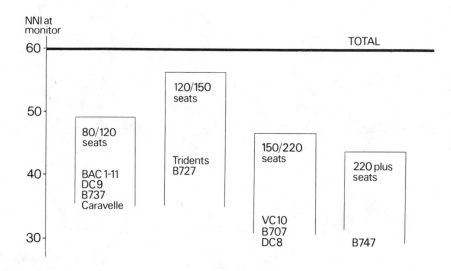

Fig.7.   Contribution to noise by aircraft category (Heathrow, 1974)

Fig.8.   A300B

Fig.9.   DCX 200

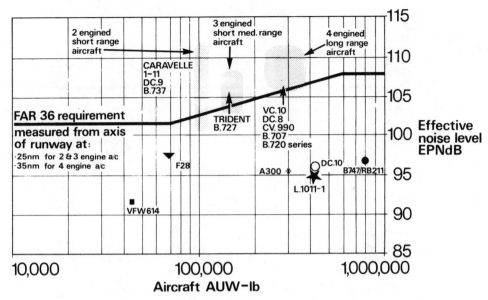

Fig.10. Sideline noise

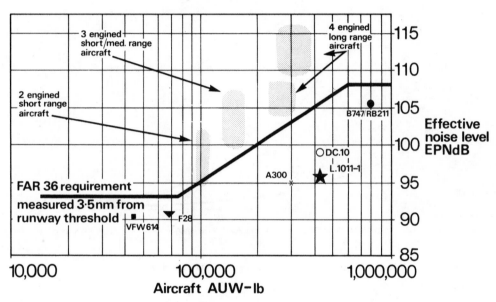

Fig.11. Take off (flyover) noise

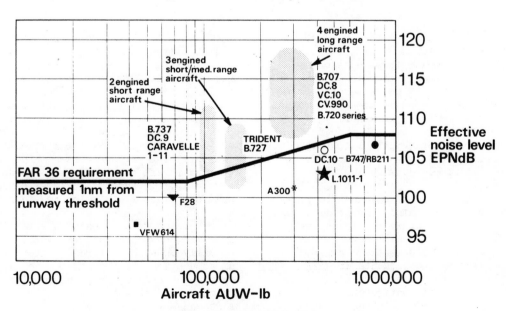

Fig.12. Approach noise

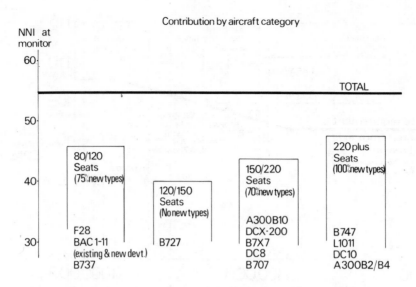

Fig.13. Contribution to noise (1980 levels)

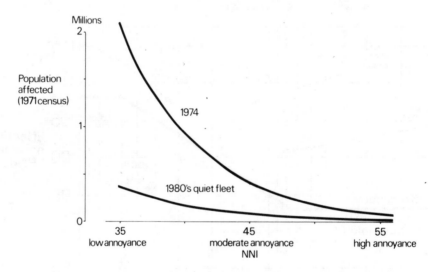

Fig.14. Noise at Heathrow (population statistics)

80 - 120 seats, 120 - 150 seats, 150 - 220 seats and 220 seats upwards. The individual NNI figures for these categories and the number of movements associated with them, (which together with noise level determines NNI) is shown on figure 7. Clearly the 120 - 150 seat category currently dominates, partly due to the high number of movements. The only high bypass ratio engines having any impact are in the 220 plus seat category, in this sample just Boeing 747's.

The dominant category we have identified, 120 - 150 seat aircraft are mainly the Trident and B727 types. As traffic grows we expect that from 1980 onwards airlines will begin to want some aircraft of about 200 seats on routes currently operated by the Tridents or B727's. These could be twin engined aircraft using the RB.211 type of engine in configurations like the A.300B.10, or DCX.200 (figures 8 and 9) a shortened fuselage version of the present

A.300 types. Likewise many more of the B707, DC8, VC10 types in the 150 - 200 seat categories will be replaced by L.1011's, DC.10's and B.747's. The smallest size grouping can expect to use some BAC 1-11 or F28 derivatives for example with smaller engines of increased bypass ratio yielding quiet aircraft. Looked at on the basis of individual aircraft noise certification figures, these various current and possible future aircraft can be compared as shown on figures 10, 11 and 12. Both existing and expected future legislation are identified.

Now reverting to the Heathrow situation, figure 13 shows the NNI breakdown, for say the early 80's, by aircraft category with our assumptions of the mix between old and new types based on our assessment of the maximum rate at which better aircraft could be reasonably introduced.

There will also, of course, be a number of Concorde operations and each individual movement will be at a relatively high noise level compared to the newer engine types. However, with a very few number of movements each day the contribution to NNI is not large, and we calculate this to increase the possible 1980's level by about 1 NNI.

To give a readily appreciated dimension to these results, we need to relate noise produced around the airport to the numbers of people affected by the noise. The figure of around 60 NNI shown in 1974 at our chosen site is in line with the annoyance level given in the final Maplin report (Ref: Maplin, An Airport Survey - 1974), as the 1972 survey values. The report also gives an estimate (illustrated in my Figure 14) of the number of people exposed to various NNI levels around Heathrow in 1972 which I would suggest represents the exposure in 1974 as well. Reducing the level at our site by 6 NNI (i.e. excluding the Concorde effect) is equivalent to one of 1990 scenarios illustrated in the same report and this gives an exposure count shown as the lower line on figure 14. This result is indeed dramatic since almost 2 million people are put below the 35 NNI level which might be said to be a threshold of appreciable exposure.

Now it must be said that my assumption of aircraft types and rate of introduction into service is more rapid than current airline thinking would allow. But bearing in mind that the new aircraft will have improved operating costs, partly from lower fuel consumption, there is incentive to go down this road since compared to earlier engines the RB.211 cycle reduces fuel consumption by up to 25%. We calculate for example that replacing British Airways current European Division fleet with such aircraft would save about 16 million gallons of fuel a year. This represents about 10% of current European Division consumption even though greater capacity is assumed for greater traffic growth.

Clearly there is an opportunity for greatly reducing noise around airports by means which are now well proven, involve no new technology and have the additional merit of paying for much, if not all, the cost over a period of time by saving fuel - i.e. by replacing older fuel inefficient aircraft by newer, quieter and more fuel efficient aircraft.

In my Wilbur Wright Lecture last December, I suggested that reluctance by the Airlines to invest in such aircraft at the present time was due to a combination of factors of which uncertainty of the future and current low profitability were amongst the more important.

I should like to add to this list a further suggestion that it would now be timely for Governments to offer incentives to their Airlines to make this desirable change - both to make life quieter for citizens living near Airports and as a first step in a necessary policy of conserving that irreplaceable natural resource - petroleum.

The incentives could take a variety of forms of which the best may be extension of airport hours for quiet aircraft coupled with reduction of landing fees.

9. Operational techniques for reducing noise

O.B. St John, MA, BSc, FRAeS,
Director of Technical Research and Development, Civil Aviation Authority

This paper reviews various operational techniques for reducing noise nuisance. Of these, some have already been implemented and, where there is no associated penalty in terms of operational safety, further improvement can be confidently expected. In other cases, significant cost is involved and it is necessary to demonstrate conclusively that safety standards will not be impaired. The provision of adequate data to demonstrate the safety of these operations and, in some cases, the development of new equipment, means that such techniques can only be introduced, if ever, on a protracted time-scale. Perhaps the most promising technique, which is applicable even to the latest "quiet" aircraft, involves continuous descent from the stack to touchdown. This is already being adopted by many airlines and, together with the proper management of drag which is closely associated with this procedure, could result in some alleviation in the comparatively near future.

INTRODUCTION

1. Of the available means of alleviating noise on the ground, operational procedures are particularly attractive in that they tend to be both widely applicable and flexible in their implementation. Unlike the development of quieter engines or the use of "hush-kits", operational procedures can be introduced and assessed on a comparatively short time-scale. A number of possible techniques has already been examined which offer hopes of noise alleviation on the ground. Before introduction for general operational use, however, it is essential to demonstrate that such techniques do not themselves have any adverse effect on safety. The collection of adequate evidence tends to be time-consuming and for this reason some of the most promising techniques still await clearance in this respect. Others do not affect safety and in these cases some alleviation has already been achieved.

2. In considering the operational techniques, the benefits on the ground derive from three possibilities:

(i)   A decrease in the noise source by reduction of power: this is often associated with having a cleaner aircraft configuration.

(ii) Increased attenuation as a result of increasing the height of the aircraft over a given point on the approach.

(iii) Changing the plan position of the aircraft so as to redistribute the noise on the ground.

The success of the measures and techniques briefly described below depends on one or more of the above considerations.

3. The ultimate in administrative techniques would be to cause operations to cease by means of a noise curfew. This practice is growing and many airports operate a curfew for night operations, even though the so-called "quiet" aircraft have been introduced. The effects of the curfew result in alterations to schedules rather than to operational practices and therefore these will not be dealt with in this paper.

4. This paper reviews a number of techniques for reducing noise on the ground concentrating on the area in the vicinity of the airport where the noise nuisance is greatest. Techniques applicable to both take-off and approach are dealt with, though the main emphasis tends to be on the latter because of current research and interest in a number of new techniques. For the purpose of this paper, the approach zone is taken as reaching back from touchdown to the stack, ie it includes the intermediate as well as the final approach.

Alleviation of noise on take-off

5. <u>Runway direction.</u> Runways naturally tend to be orientated in accordance with prevailing wind direction, and aircraft handling capability has been improved to the point where there is less operational demand for "crosswind" runways. Of the six runways originally planned for Heathrow, only three are in operation, and the two main, parallel, runways are used for the great majority of the time. At Heathrow, the prevailing wind is westerly but the population density is much lower on the west side than on the east. To reduce the noise nuisance to the population overall in terms of the number of people affected, a runway preferential system is adopted whereby, subject to certain specified conditions, westerly operations are used up to a maximum tailwind component of 5 knots, thus lessening the number of aircraft taking off

over the heavily populated area to the east of
the aerodrome. As a corollary, the population
on the east side is subjected to noise from a
larger number of landings, though of course the
noise level is less than that associated with
take-off.

6. This policy results in about 30% more
westerly operations and this bias could be increased even further if the permissible tailwind component could be increased safely to 10
knots, but consideration would need to be given
not only to the effect of steady tail and cross
winds but also to the associated gust conditions.

7. In certain special cases, where the take-
off lies over the sea or other unpopulated
areas, an extension to this runway preferential
technique could offer important benefits. As
an example, at Los Angeles, using parallel runways, there is pressure to increase operations
over the sea, both landings and take-offs,
over a wider range of what are normally regarded
as adverse wind conditions.

Noise abatement take-offs

8. For many years it has been the practice to
reduce power during the initial climb once a
safe height and speed have been reached. This
technique is related to the positions of the
noise monitors and there has been considerable
discussion as to whether the optimum position
of the monitors has been chosen. It may be
that the optimum position for one type of aircraft is different from that of another but it
would seem that the current positions constitute a reasonable compromise. Noise abatement
take-off procedures are well established and
it is not proposed to deal with them in detail
in this paper.

Minimum noise routes

9. As a result of discussions between the
authorities concerned, routes to be flown have
been evolved to minimise, as far as practical,
the noise nuisance to the population overall.
These have been incorporated in Standard Instrument Departures (SIDs). It must be
accepted, however, that the adoption of minimum
noise routes and a rigid adherence to them must
cause some localised concentration of noise
nuisance. Inevitably a few will suffer for the
benefit of the population at large.

Alleviation of noise under the approach

10. Air traffic control. Because so much has
already been done to reduce the effect of noise
on take-off, and it would not appear that much
more can be achieved by operational procedures,
effort during the past few years has been concentrated on a development of new techniques
and procedures for alleviating noise under the
approach. These measures and operational
procedures are briefly described below:-

(i)   The minimum stack height within the
        London Terminal Area has recently been
        raised from 6000 to 7000 feet. This

not only gives some direct relief to
those under the stack and during the subsequent intermediate approach, but also
provides some alleviation from departing
aircraft which may then be correspondingly
higher.

(ii)   A system known as Runway Alternation
        operates at Heathrow whereby, when
        westerly landings are in force, the
        particular runway to be used for landing
        is alternated, ie if the nominated landing
        runway is 28L in the morning it is
        changed to 28R in the afternoon. This
        sequence is reversed each week so that in
        the above example 28R would be used in
        the morning and 28L in the afternoon in
        the subsequent week. This procedure was
        introduced in 1972 to spread the noise
        from landing aircraft over the heavily
        populated areas as equitably as possible.
        There are environmental and technical
        reasons why this procedure has not been
        extended to easterly operations.

(iii)   A proposal is being discussed whereby the
        airspeed during intermediate approach
        phase, ie from the stack down to final
        approach at 12 miles, will be increased
        initially from 170 to 190 knots. The
        intention is to maintain a cleaner air-
        craft, with less drag, consequently
        requiring less power. Pilots are to be
        advised of their range to the touchdown
        point so that they will be able more
        easily to achieve a smooth and constant
        descent. (see para 12.) A short survey
        in September 1975 during a period of
        2 days showed that 60% of aircraft at
        Heathrow were already achieving a
        measure of continuous descent.

(iv)   The height at which the glidepath is
        joined has been raised to a minimum of
        2500 feet for all normal cases. Wherever
        possible this is further increased to
        3000 feet or more.

11. As these operational procedures can be
implemented within the existing ATC framework,
their impact on safety is minimal and they can
be endorsed without any lengthy trials or
assessment. It must be recognised, however,
that any measures which introduce a more
disciplined stream of aircraft over a greater
range, may result in an increased nuisance
locally, in terms of numbers of movements, in
spite of the overall noise level being diminished.

Continuous descent approaches

12. The possibility of descending steadily from
the stack to touchdown is being examined on the
premise of keeping the aircraft in or above the
notional 3° glidepath plane. This can provide
significant benefit over a range of 8 to 12
miles from touchdown because the aircraft is
higher and the power requirements lower. In
particular, it avoids level flight which is
noisier. The Civil Aviation Authority is in
process of discussing certain aspects of this
technique as stated above, and a series of

operational trials is planned for summer 1976. To derive the maximum benefit, it may be necessary to provide the pilot with instrumental means for achieving the correct rate of descent. There are also likely to be certain constraints on air traffic control in having what is, in effect, an extended final approach. In particular a wide variation of aircraft types, with different performance characteristics, increases the difficulty of achieving an orderly stream of traffic. The UK derives some benefit in this respect by comparison with other countries because General Aviation aircraft are not normally allowed to mix with the main traffic at Heathrow.

4° approach

13. As a natural step from the standard 3° glidepath, a small increase to the glidepath angle is being considered which would produce noise alleviation within the bounds of the current ILS system which can, in principle, be used up to an angle of 4°. This procedure, though technically attractive, suffers from the disadvantage that all aircraft would be constrained to use the steeper glidepath and it is not yet certain that safety margins would not be eroded with certain aircraft types; a protracted programme of certification would be needed. There is an additional potential hazard in that current undercarriages are stressed to allow for the case where the pilot lands from a 3° glidepath without flaring, but not for the rates of descent which would occur from a 4° glidepath.

Two-segment approaches

14. It is possible to achieve a noise benefit by making a final approach in two segments, ie a steep one of about 6° during which the power can be reduced, followed by a standard 3° glidepath. The technique requires accurate knowledge of range so that the standard glidepath can be joined from above at a safe height to allow settling on the final segment. Current thinking is that the height at which the transition must be completed is of the order of 1000 feet so that, theoretically, little or no noise benefit will accrue close to the airfield. Much work has been done in the US and the FAA issued a Notice of Proposed Rule Making (NPRM) in the autumn of 1975 which included the proposed introduction of the practice both as a visual operation and also using the Instrument Landing System for reduced visibility conditions. At the time of writing the formal outcome of these proposals and the reactions of the parties consulted has not been promulgated, but considerable opposition was made to the proposals on the grounds of possible reduced safety and cost. Perhaps the most significant objection was that of inherent risk of operating on the basis of "see and be seen" with mixed two-segment and standard 3° approaches. A General Aviation aircraft on a slow 3° approach would be unable to see a faster airliner on a 6° path above and behind him, and the airliner would possibly be unable to see the smaller aircraft below. Because light

aircraft are rarely accepted at Heathrow this particular problem was not the prime concern of the UK authorities involved.

15. The CAA responded formally to the Notice to the effect that they would wish to have clear evidence that the introduction of such techniques would not result in any degradation of safety, before being able to give the proposals their support. In particular the CAA, with strong support from pilots and others with a concern for aircraft safety, opposed the introduction of two-segment approaches as a visual operation, stressing the need for a single procedure to be used under all conditions. There appeared to be a consensus that further work on two-segment approaches should be aimed at developing procedures for use under all weather conditions which, it was foreseen, would take several years. As a specific outstanding problem, the effect of wake vortices in a mixed situation has still to be resolved.

16. In the UK, there is a continuing programme of research, funded by the Department of Industry, to examine a range of possibilities of using steeper than normal approach paths and the use of two-segment approaches has received particular attention. Flight trials are in progress at the Royal Aircraft Establishment, Bedford using a BAC 1-11 aircraft fitted with an experimental two-segment approach coupler, the initial flight path being defined using DME and barometric height. The system has been designed for use in all weather conditions to current limits, ie it is compatible for use with automatic landing systems. The trial is intended to prove the operational viability of the technique from the aspects of safety and pilot acceptance over the range of weather conditions. Statistics will be derived to demonstrate the level of performance achievable and airworthiness aspects will be investigated. An extract from the comments submitted to the FAA by the Airworthiness Division of CAA is included at Appendix 1.

17. One point of particular interest has arisen from the associated theoretical noise studies. The comparison of noise contour areas, as a measure of alleviation, requires careful interpretation because so much depends on the exact choice of noise level chosen. For example, analysis shows that, typically, beyond a range of about 7 miles from threshold, the noise nuisance at a level of 90 EPNdB can be effectively eliminated by introduction of the two-segment approach technique (fig 1). By contrast, at a level of 85 EPNdB the area on the ground affected may be considerably increased (fig 2). A second point is that the introduction of the quieter wide-bodied aircraft has already reduced the contour areas to the point where any further reduction, as a result of the introduction of two-segment approach techniques, is likely to be relatively small for those types.

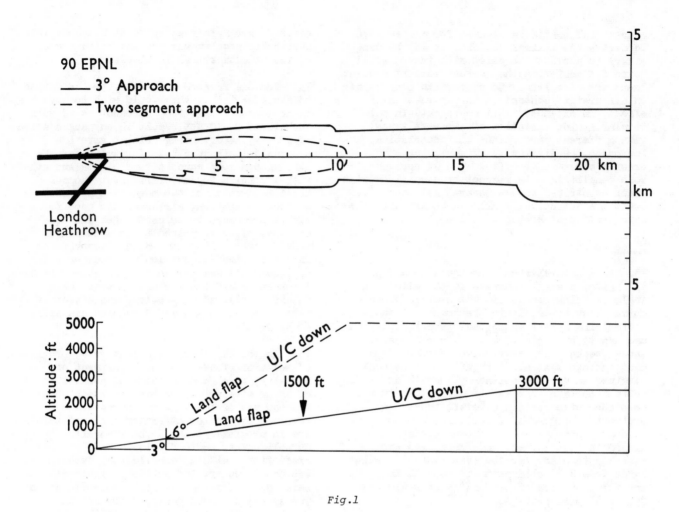

Fig.1

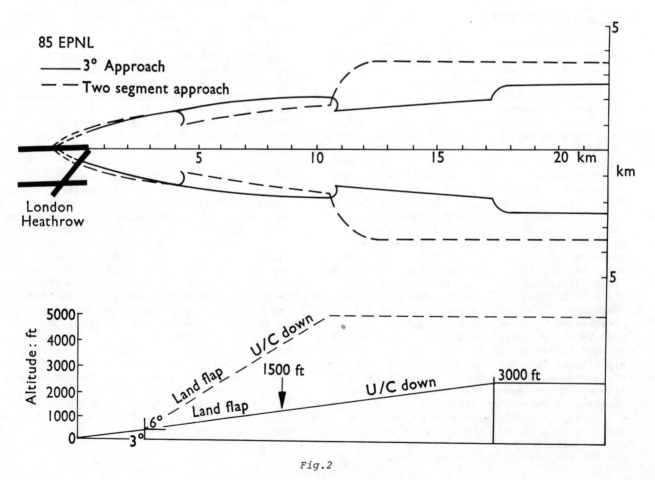

Fig.2

"Managed Drag" approaches

18. During the approach, the noise problem is exacerbated by the increased power required to maintain the flight path when the flaps or other high lift devices and undercarriage are extended. This has been the subject of study by many airlines and, as a result, an IATA recommendation was made to adopt the practice of delaying selection of landing configuration until a height of approximately 1500 feet was reached.

19. This general principle of maintaining a "cleaner" aircraft during the approach is certainly endorsed by CAA. It has already been applied by British and other airlines and it is claimed to result not only in a reduction of noise but also in a saving of fuel and a reduction in engine wear. However, in particular cases, its full implementation is impractical because of incompatibility with the aircraft automatic control system.

20. Lufthansa have given much publicity to their work in this area and an appreciation of the results at Frankfurt over the past years has been undertaken recently by DORA/CAA. There is evidence to show that the introduction of low power and low drag techniques at Frankfurt over a period of some years has resulted in noticeable noise alleviation in a particular centre of population at a range of about 7 to 10 miles from the airfield, under the glidepath. The success of this procedure is attributed to a combination of the effectiveness of the German organisation, the provision of the right ATC environment and good discipline backed by a measure of coercion on the basis of noise monitoring.

20. At Frankfurt, the minimum height by which stabilisation on the glidepath in the final configuration has to be achieved has been 800 feet. CAA are not entirely satisfied that sufficient evidence is available to justify delaying as far as this, and it is believed that Lufthansa intend to raise this minimum to 1000 feet. As to automatic control, no trouble has been experienced in aircraft such as the B-747 and DC-10 which have later generation flight control systems, but with older types such as B-707, B-727 and B-737, approaches tend to be made manually. Because the technique is used with one runway direction only, about half the approaches at Frankfurt are made using "managed drag". In addition, low engine power is not used under icing conditions.

21. As a result of this study at Frankfurt, further consideration is being given to the benefits of introducing these procedures generally at Heathrow. It is doubtful whether comparable benefits could be achieved because conditions, aircraft mix and organisation differ but it is likely that some modest relief to substantial areas under westerly approaches, for example, in the area of Barnes, Putney and Fulham, could be achieved where NNI values are less than 50. Under easterly approaches

and where the NNI value exceeds 50, little benefit would be expected.

APPENDIX 1

EXTRACT FROM COMMENTS MADE BY CAA AIRWORTHINESS DIVISION ON FAA PROPOSALS FOR TWO-SEGMENT APPROACHES.

Flying qualities

1. With initial approach path slopes as high as 6°, certain aeroplane types may have difficulty in closing the approach path from above, following an error or disturbance, due to lack of drag. This problem may be aggravated by aircraft characteristics which result in a reduced maximum descent capability if the target approach speed is exceeded. An additional margin on descent capability to cope with tailwinds will be needed.

2. Poorer thrust response than is the present norm will almost inevitably result from the low rpm associated with the steeper initial approach path. This could have an adverse effect on approach path tracking and speed control both during the initial segment and during the transition to the final segment. On the other hand, with transition heights of the order of 700/1000 feet, height loss in the overshoot due to poor thrust response is less likely to pose any significant safety problems. British requirements for engine acceleration would impose a minimum rpm which might not be low enough to permit a 6° approach to be made with suitable margins.

3. Clearly time is needed to stabilise on the final approach path well before the threshold. Failure to do this will result in unacceptable scatter in speed and height at the runway threshold leading to degradation in landing safety levels.

4. It was not clear whether aeroplanes will be required to perform two-segment approaches with one engine inoperative. Although the steeper initial approach path will have a favourable effect on directional controllability in terms of engine failure, delayed thrust response from the lower rpm's may increase the directional control workload and approach path tracking may suffer as a consequence. The thrust changes to go from 6° to 3° paths may also induce a tracking problem where asymmetry is involved.

5. The higher rates of descent associated with the steeper initial approach path render the aeroplane more sensitive to wind shear.

Aircraft systems and instrumentation

6. It is possible that certain aircraft systems and services (eg pressurisation, de-icing) will be adversely affected by the low engine rpm's associated with the steeper initial approach path.

7. If pilot guidance is based on computed DME and baro height information for the steeper initial approach path and the transition, this information needs to be of adequate integrity. It is understood that DMEs, even when co-located with ILS can still be subject to a significant site error, which would need to be established. The ground facilities would presumably require calibration and their availability and standard promulgated in some manner.

8. In the interests of avoiding a noise "spike" the transition to the normal approach path and associated thrust increase should extend over a reasonable time. A smooth and controlled manoeuvre will demand a high standard of pilot guidance during the transition.

9. Flight instrumentation for the steeper initial approach path and the final approach path must be compatible. Clearly, the reference to different primary information sources at late stages of the approach is undesirable.

Automatic flight control systems

10. An automatic approach coupling system has been developed for two-segment approaches, and the ANPRM states that it is acceptable for use in IFR. The accuracy required of this equipment will need to be defined, taking account of such things as obstacle clearance boundaries, the accuracy of ground derived data, such as DME (see para 7), aircraft characteristics, wind shear etc.

11. Airworthiness Division has no information on the glide path coupling accuracy which an existing autopilot could achieve at low height following a steep approach to 700 feet. However experience in the certification flight trials of Category 2 and autoland systems suggests that autopilots in use at this time would probably not be able to achieve the accuracy

required for Category 2 or automatic landing after such a late coupling manoeuvre. It is therefore possible, or even probable, that the autopilot could not be used below 200 feet on a two-segment approach. The fact that the ANPRM only envisages the use of two-segment approaches in Category 1 conditions seem to support this view.

12. One of the most important consequences of Category 2 and autoland system developments has been to make autopilots generally available which can be used to low height even in Category 1 conditions. This means that in bad weather the aeroplane can remain under stable automatic control coupled to the ILS glide slope for the critical period immediately below the decision height when control by visual reference is inaccurate. As a result a long term improvement in the safety of Category 1 operations was to be expected. If two-segment approaches deny use of the autopilot in this way, an adverse effect on safety level should be expected.

13. It is important that information should be collected on the accuracy of existing autopilots for coupling to 100 feet or autoland in a two-segment approach, to determine whether any further development work would be required to retain the present capability of these systems.

14. The proposal that in Category 2 operations different procedures (one-segment) from the normal (two-segment) would be used, seems to be inherently prejudicial to safety.

15. Assuming that the other issues can be satisfactorily resolved it would seem prudent not to introduce two-segment approach procedures until the automatic flight control systems used can be shown to provide Category 2 capability.

10. Airports and community design considerations for aircraft noise alleviations

J.B. Large

Professor, Institute of Sound and Vibration Research, University of Southampton

Besides the very important problem of noise created by overflying aircraft, there are other noise problems created within the airport and adjacent communities due to aircraft ground operations and other manoeuvres prior to take-off and after touch-down. This paper briefly describes the noise characteristics of aircraft during taxiing and holding; engine ground run-ups; the operation of the A.P.U. and noise before and after lift-off and touch-down. Methods of control are also discussed for all these sources.

INTRODUCTION

1. The problem of aircraft noise has been one of the industries major concerns for nearly forty years (ref.1). But during the past fifteen years aircraft noise has perhaps counteracted, in the public's mind, many of the benefits bestowed by the air transportation industry. The development of the turbo-jet engine and its introduction into commercial service in the late fifties, focused attention on the aircraft noise situation around Idlewild Airport (ref.2), although a significant problem also existed before the introduction of the jet. The well-known Heathrow Noise Survey in 1961 (ref.3) showed a similar problem also existed in London, These situations were to be echoed at all of the major airports of the world.

2. The London noise survey was concerned with the environment produced by overflying aircraft. Relationships were produced which equated percentage of the population highly annoyed, to a noise exposure in terms of an average noise level perceived, and the number of events to which the householder was exposed. This relationship, defined as a noise and number index (NNI), indicated that considerable dissatisfaction existed even at distances many miles from the airport. It has been this aspect of the aircraft noise problem that has received the greatest attention in recent years through engine development, the application of noise abatement take-off and approach procedures and noise monitoring (ref.4). But, although there is no doubt that the aircraft in flight continues to expose a greater number of the population to a disturbance, a problem also exists in communities near the airport boundary and within the airport itself. This is due to aircraft operations on the ground and after take-off and before landing. This paper will discuss some of the adverse noise situations which can occur during manoeuvres in close proximity to the airport boundary.

3. These manoeuvres fall into two main categories: the first arises from ground movements and operations; and the second, during the initial stages of the take-off or the final stages of the approach and landing procedure. Early recognition was given that such problems exist and should be treated in a different manner to those caused by overflights (ref.5). The problems of community noise around U.S. Air Force Bases was investigated in the 1940's and 1950's by collating case history reactions, and relating them to aircraft noise exposure. One of the special problems encountered was the engine ground run-up situation, which usually ran for an extended time period of minutes or hours unlike the 15-30 second overflight duration. It also occurred at unsociable times of day such as the night or evening. These characteristics, together with the usually different noise output than that experienced by overflight, typify the problems of ground operation and the noise near lift-off and touch-down.

4. The features to be discussed are the noise problems arising from ground operation of aircraft, such as taxiing and holding; engine run-ups and auxiliary power unit (A.P.U) operation during cargo and passenger handling. For aircraft on take-off there are problems resulting from maximum thrust procedures prior to take-off roll and loss of ground effects at lift-off. Whilst on approach, there is the special noise problems created due to thrust reversal operation particularly after touch-down, together with the variation in noise levels produced because of changes in thrust levels particularly apparent during an automatic landing.

NOISE SOURCES DUE TO GROUND OPERATIONS

5. <u>Taxiing and Holding</u>: An aircraft, either leaving or returning to an air terminal, must often pass near other terminals inhabited with passengers or airport workers or alongside the airport perimeter with dwellings not too far away. If traffic congestion exists along its

route either during take-off or landing, then the aircraft may be required to hold with the engines operating at a low power setting for several minutes. A continuous flow of ground traffic then could have the effect of producing an almost steady source of noise to those people exposed.

6. Although the thrusts required to move an aircraft are relatively small; for example, an empirical rule of thumb may be taken as:

$$\text{Breakaway Thrust (lbs)} = \frac{(0.04 \times \text{Take-off weight})}{\text{number of engines}}$$

But unfortunately the noise doesn't diminish in direct proportion to the thrust. For an aircraft powered by turbo-jet engines, these are the majority of aircraft in commercial operation, the noise output versus thrust is shown in Fig. 1. It can be seen that the main component of the noise is from the fan although, under certain conditions, the jet exhaust is distinctly audible. The contribution of the fan noise to the total noise level is dependent upon the by-pass ration of the engine. As the bypass ratio increases then the blade passage noise becomes more dominant. The spectrum of the noise output from a low thrust setting perpendicular to the centre line axis of the engine, is illustrated in Figure 2 for distances approximately one thousand feet from the source. At greater distances the higher frequencies will attenuate more rapidly, leaving a spectrum dominated by low frequency noise (ref.6). The composition of the spectra depends upon the angle of radiation, Figure 3, at approximately 70° to either side of the engine axis the noise level is dominated by the noise from the rotating fan and compressor blades. The peak frequencies from this source occur at the blade passage frequency, which is the number of blades times the rotational speeds and its harmonics. The energy in the noise spectrum at frequencies higher than the blade passage frequencies originates from the turbulence associated with the air flow around the blades. The noise generated at frequencies below the blade passage frequency originates from the primary and secondary jet exhausts. During an aircraft overflight, the peak noise level would normally occur immediately after the aircraft has passed overhead, and the duration of the noise would be a function of the distance from the source and the speed of the aircraft. But during a taxiing and holding manoeuvre, it is not unusual for an aircraft to sweep through a 180° arc in order to position itself onto the runway. Therefore the exposure time and the characteristics of the noise during such an operation will consist of a time-varying noise spectra fluctuating between the intensity and frequency envelopes shown in Figure 2.

7. The picture is further complicated because of the placement of the engines gives multiple sources which can be at different heights. For example, the Lockheed L10-11 has the centre engine 35 feet above the ground, whilst the under wing engines are only 8 feet. Shielding of the engine noise by the fuselage, wings, and empennage must be assessed, particularly if the recipients of the noise are not at the same height as the engines above the ground. For example some of the recipients could be inside terminal concourses, in bedrooms, and in upper storey dwellings. Usually in these circumstances, line of sight shielding considerations are adequate, and the aimple logarithmic addition of multiple sources also suffices.

8. Fortunately, it is rarely necessary to take into account the duration of the manoeuvre, unless the frequency of the traffic is such that a severe disturbance to communication exists. This is a situation which can occur within buildings located close to a runway apron route, and these buildings usually house some activity connected with the airport operation. But normally in order to reduce the noise level in areas beyond the airport boundary, it is good enough to estimate the peak intensity. If this type of control is to be effective, then the reduction required in the peak noise level, can be related to its intrusion above the background noise without aircraft interference. The method for such an assessment is still not firmly established but the philosophy expressed in BSI 4142 (Method of rating industrial noise affecting mixed residential and industrial areas) offers a fairly logical guide and indicates that an intrusion should be less than five dB above the background.

9. If an assessment is necessary of taxiing noise from propeller-powered aircraft, then a similar procedure to that described above is applicable, except that the maximum directivity from propeller noise lies nearly in the plane of rotation of the blades. The noise spectrum is entirely dominated by the fundamental blade passage frequency of the propeller and can occur at frequencies of 100 to 200 Hz, a factor of ten lower than the frequencies generated by a turbo-fan compressor.

10. It is normally difficult to obtain noise level information for low engine thrust both for jet and propeller powered aircraft. Manufacturers are naturally concerned with the noise level associated with overflight procedures and rarely present information at a lower performance. It is therefore usually left to the individual who needs this information either to extricate it using the formula given earlier in this paper and extrapolating noise data at higher thrusts through to the lower thrust region, or to find an aircraft of the type needed and attempt the necessary measurements.

11. Engine Ground Run-ups: Another disturbance due to engine noise is that caused by ground running of engines. Although this is a problem which received early recognition as a major source of nuisance in the communities around air bases, it has also produced similar situations at commercial airports. The engine run-ups occur in a variety of situations either after an engine overhaul to test its performance, or as part of a repair or maintenance situation of the total airframe and engine installation. The running period can extend for several hours and the noise levels vary continuously as the engine thrust settings are changed. As in the case of engine

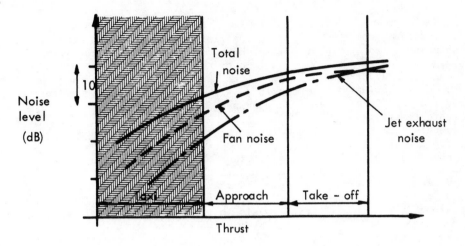

Fig.1. Noise output of turbo-fan engine

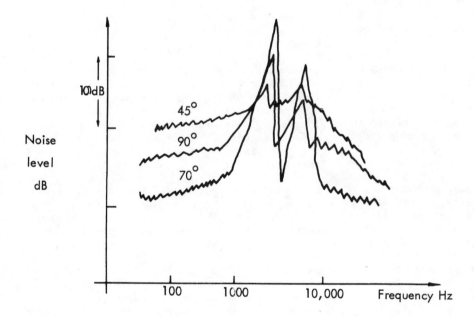

Fig.2. Turbo-fan noise at various angles to engine axis

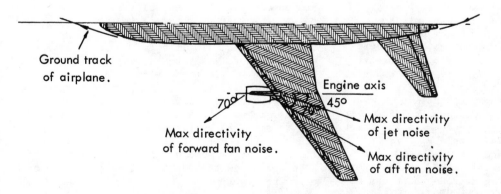

Fig.3. Turbo-fan engine noise directivity

noise produced by a taxiing or holding, the
directivities of the major noise producing components are the same, even for an uninstalled
engine on a test stand, but for the turbo-fan
the noise levels produced will change in spectral
character from high frequency fan noise dominated
at low thrusts to the lower frequency rumble of
the jet exhaust at take-off thrust (Figure 1).
For propeller noise the noise spectra will always peak at the blade passage frequencies, but
the character of the noise may change as thickness noise caused by the blades slicing through
the ambient air at low thrusts gives way to the
noise produced by the aerodynamic pressure
field created by the blades rotating at higher
speeds.   There are a variety of noise control
measures which can be taken to minimise the
impact of this type of operation and these will
be discussed later in this paper.   But to
evaluate the magnitude of the problem the most
satisfactory method is that proposed in ref.7.
Here it is proposed that a 10dB weighting
should be applied to the noise levels in order
to take into account this subjectively less
acceptable operation than over-flight.   The
implication here is that the nuisance arising
from ground run-ups are more easily controlled
than the noise produced from an over-flight or
fly-by.

12. Auxiliary Power Unit Operation: At many
airports auxiliary power unit operation is required either at passenger embarking or loading
ramps or during cargo handling procedures, as
shown in Figure 4.   Not only can the ground
staff be affected, but also passengers or staff
within an acoustically untreated terminal
building.   If the A.P.U. is operated near to
the airport boundary, it can also create a
noise problem in the surrounding community.
The noise hazard inflicted on the ground handling staff must be assessed as an industrial
noise and the workers protected from excessive
exposures (ref.7).   Passengers and the airport
community are usually not at risk, since in the
former case the full outdoor exposure is
normally of a very short duration, and in the
case of the airport community the distances
from the source are large enough to bring them
to a level where an assessment of the problem
should be made in terms of annoyance or perhaps
sleep interference.   A number of organisations
notably ICAO and SAE in the U.S.A. have been
concerned with the prediction of A.P.U. noise
in order to produce a basis for its assessment.
The A.P.U. has essentially the same noise
generation characteristics as an aircraft
engine.   The intake and exhaust will have
compressor and jet noise characteristics
commensurate with its size, blade passage
frequencies and exhaust velocity.   The location and numbers of A.P.U's vary considerably
for different types of aircraft.   For example,
the A.P.U. exhaust on the Boeing 727 is just
above the vertical stairway at the aft.   Many
airlines do not use the A.P.U. during passenger
handling because of the adverse noise situation.
Whereas on the Boeing 747, the A.P.U. is 26
feet above the ground and for the DC-10 over 31
feet.   The location of the A.P.U. is an important factor in determining methods which can be

used to control the noise.   The other important ingredient is the nature of the noise, its
intensity, duration, frequency of occurrence
and the time of day in which the activity occurs.
Therefore, the approach to the assessment has
similarities with the noise produced by engine
ground run-ups.

13. Noise Sources During Take-off and Landing

Take-off Noise: The most common noise problem
associated with the initial stages in a take-off
manoeuvre is the so called "loss of ground
effect".   This is essentially an increase in
noise levels that occur as the airplane leaves
the runway and the excess attenuation of the
ground falls away.   The A21 Committee of the
Society of Automotice Engineers have for many
years considered a transitional loss of ground
attenuation to follow $e^{-\sqrt{\tan 3\Theta}}$ where Θ is the
angle between horizon and the aircraft line of
sight to the ground site.   This relationship
was developed on the presumption that most of
the ground attenuation has disappeared at an
angle of 15°.   Other estimates make the angle
smaller, but there is also some experimental
evidence to show that angles of 40° to 60° may
have to be attained before the influence of the
ground is lost.

14. Another source of disturbance is also present at some airports where pilots are required
to run through the engine thrust cycle before
take-off.   But this procedure is not now
frequently required.   The loss of ground
effect is normally incorporated directly into
the noise exposure models that have become so
common (ref.8).

15. Landing Noise: During the initial stages of
the approach path, it is not uncommon for the
engine thrust to vary due to changes in flap
setting.   This audible thrust change is particularly apparent in aircraft equipped with automatic landing systems.   If this is a significant factor in the calculation of noise exposure,
it can be tackled by dividing individual approach
paths into segments and treating each segment
contribution to the exposure contours.   But a
more important problem which can occur just before landing but principally occurring after
touch down, is the noise produced through the
thrust reverser application.   This sudden
burst of noise of high intensity but short
duration is caused by the sudden reversal of the
exhaust gas flows.   The manner in which this
reversal is carried out varies both by aircraft
and engine types.   The noise is essentially jet
noise generated as the flow is turned by vanes
or louvres.   The direction of the noise as for
other jet streams will have a maximum intensity
at approximately 45° to the exhaust gas stream.
The sudden application no doubt has a potential
to produce startle, or even a certain apprehen-
sion, in addition to the unusual annoyance which
can be linked to the intensity of the noise.
But to date, no satisfactory method of assessment exists other than to treat it as a high
intensity noise source.   In the past, attempts
have been made to add this effect into the noise
exposure contours, but it becomes difficult to

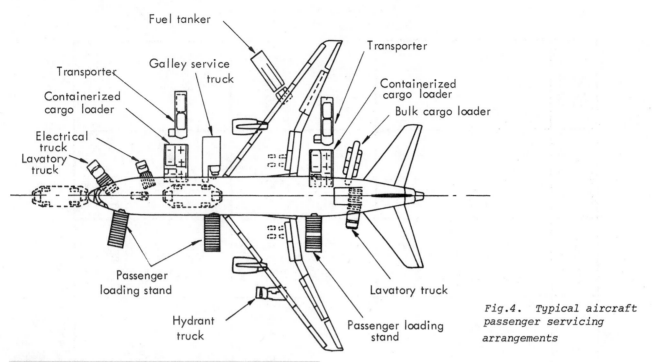

Fuel tanker

Galley service truck

Transporter

Containerized cargo loader

Electrical truck

Lavatory truck

Transporter

Containerized cargo loader

Bulk cargo loader

Passenger loading stand

Hydrant truck

Lavatory truck

Passenger loading stand

Fig.4. Typical aircraft passenger servicing arrangements

Fig.5. Wall at Katsube Toyanaka city to reduce aircraft noise during taxiing

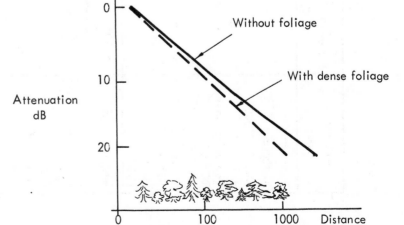

Fig.6. Aircraft noise attenuation over the ground

Without foliage

With dense foliage

Attenuation dB

0

10

20

0   100   1000   Distance

Table 1

Aircraft type	Height centreline Nacelle @ intake ft/in		Height centreline nozzle ft/in		Engine type	Max TOW lbs	Breakaway thrust per engine lbs	Engine setting
2 jet aircraft								
A-300B4	6' 3"		6' 3"		GE CF6-50A	332,700	4,350*	
BAC 1-11 500	9' 0"		9' 0"		RR Spey MK 512DW	99,650	1,993	
B737 200	3' 9"		3' 9"		JT8 D-9	113,000	2,260	
Caravelle super	11' 6"		11' 3"		JT8 D-7	123,460	2,469*	
DC9 40	10' 3"		10' 0"		JT8 D-9, -11	114,000	2,280*	
F28 2000	10' 3"		10' 0"		RR Spey MK555-15	65,000	1,300	
Mercure	4' 9"		4' 9"		JT8 D-11	114,650	3,293	
TU104	-		-		Soloviev D-20P	167,550	3,351	
TU124	-		-		Soloviev D-30	83,775	1,675	
TU134	-		-		-	98,105	1,962	
3 jet aircraft	Centre engine	Outboard engines	Centre engine	Outboard engines				
B727-200	20' 9"	13' 6"	12' 9"	13' 0"	JT8 D	169,000	2,330	
DC-10 30	32' 10"*	8' 6"*	30' 7"*	8' 6"*	GE CF6-50	555,000	7,400	
L1011	32' 6"	8' 0"	20' 0"	8' 0"	RB 211	575,000	5,890*	
Trident 2E	17' 6"	9' 9"	11' 9"	9' 6"	RR Spey RB163-25	144,500	1,926	9500 rpm
Trident 3B	19' 0"	11' 3"	15' 9"	11' 0"	(RR Spey RB163-25MK512-5W) (+ RB162 (tail engine)	150,000	2,000	9500 rpm
TU154	-	-	-	-	Kuznetsov NK-8-2	198,416	2,945	
4 jet aircraft	Inboard engines	Outboard engines	Inboard engines	Outboard engines				
B707 32CC	5' 7"	7' 7"	5' 7"	7' 7"	JT3 D	335,000	3,350	1.25 EPR
B747	8' 6"	11' 0"	8' 0"	10' 6"	P&W JT9D-7W & 3	775,000	7,800*	
Comet IV B	-	-	-	-	R/R Avon RA29 MK 525	158,000	1,580	
Concorde	10' 0"	10' 0"	10' 0"	10' 0"	Olympus 593 MK 601/621	385,000	3,850	
DC8 63	5' 7"	7' 0"	5' 0"	6' 6"	JT3D-3B	355,000	3,400*	
IL 62	-	-	-	-	Kuznetsov NK-8-4	357,000	3.570	
TU144	-	-	-	-	Kuznetsov NK-144	330,000	3,300	
VC-10 super	13' 4"*	13' 5"*	13' 4"*	13' 5"*	R/R Conway RC043	335,000	3,350	

Where several series of a particular aircraft type exist the heavier one has been listed.
* Actual figures from Aircraft Manual.

make such estimates not only because of the different types of thrust reversers in use but also because each type has different noise characteristics and because of the variability in the point of application along the touch-down track.

16. AIRPORT AND COMMUNITY DESIGN CONSIDERATIONS

Taxiing and Holding Noise Control: There are two aspects to the noise problem associated with taxiing and holding: the first is that arising on the 'airside' of the airport and the other which produces landside community disturbance. In the latter case the area to be protected can be a site at a considerable distance from the runway, and the holding areas. This means that the only practicable form of protection will have to be some obstruction between the sources and the site to be protected. Unfortunately, the source heights, that is engine inlet and exhaust heights vary considerably (Table 1. Courtesy of B.A.A). It can be seen that the range is from less than four feet for the Boeing 737 up to nearly 31 feet for the inlet on the DC-10. For most large and medium hub airports, wide-bodied airplanes are now in common usage. It will therefore be the height of these engines that set the standard for the design of an acoustical barrier. The construction of a wall and barrier requires a number of other considerations in its design. The barrier must not transmit the noise through the walls, which means that it must be fairly massive, particularly if the source is close to the barrier. In addition, the wall must be large enough to offer protection along the entire pathway, which exposes the community to noise. All three ingredients of height, mass and length usually leads to substantial and visible structure. The details of construction are very much a function of the above, typical of the wall construction as shown in Figure 5 ref. 9, of a wall 20 feet high and approximately 900 feet long. The second type of barrier is to be seen at the western end of the runway at Gatwick Airport. An earthwork almost 1150 feet in length and 35 feet high designed to protect the village of Charlwood. For heights above 20 feet it would appear that an earth mound is a more practical construction otherwise a wall would require extensive bracing to survive high wind and engine exhaust blasts. The cost of a reinforced wall construction must be compared with the cost of the immense earth volume required for a bank, where the footing will invariably be as wide as the bank's height. Also, from an acoustical point of view, the rounded summit of an earth bank is less sensitive to shadow zone movement caused by changing winds and provides extra surface area to enhance the scattering of the noise as it passes over the barrier.

17. The attenuation of barrier attenuation has received much study in recent years (ref.10), although there are some unusual features associated with aircraft noise. These are the size and number of the individual sources, that is engines, and the possible contribution of each individual source as an airplane manoeuvres, and thus exposes a community to both fan noise from the engine inlets and jet noise together with fan noise as the engines exhaust turn towards the community. Another factor which can also be important, particularly if the area to be protected is several miles away, is the weather. Usually wind and temperature profiles, particularly those associated with temperature inversions, can change the calculated performance based upon standard day conditions.

18. The huge barrier structures usually require some softening of their visual intrusion, which is usually accomplished by tree or shrub planting, either on the earth mound itself or along the foot of the wall. Although it is very doubtful whether foliage provides attenuation of the noise (Figure 6) unless it is of considerable stem and foliage density, but it has a psychological salutory effect of obstructing the view of the noise source from the recipients, and in this way helps to minimise the impact.

19. Most of the airside protection needed during a taxiing manoeuvre will come from having personnel working in buildings adjacent to the runway. Occasionally passengers in terminal buildings are also subject to this type of exposure particularly at some smaller airports and those in warmer climates. In these cases if a reduction is necessary, the control can usually be achieved by using standard sound-proofing techniques such as double wall construction, or thick glass in window areas, or additional mass and stiffness, if necessary on the walls and roofs of the buildings exposed. The amount of the noise reduction required depends upon the proximity of the source to the building surface and the character of the noise. Jet noise, with its lower frequency energy, can provide a more difficult problem than the higher frequency fan and compressor noise source. If soundproofing is impracticable, then a protecting wall or structural screen acting as an acoustical barrier, can be constructed. The amount of attenuation required is dependent on the activities within the building, for a workshop or freight handling area, the interior noise levels can be allowed to be considerably higher than in offices or terminals where flight announcements are necessary. When a new building is to be constructed within an airport complex, then attention must be paid to the aircraft ground traffic patterns. The building then can be designed from the start to be comparable with the external noise environment. This may include the location of rooms in which a quiet ambient is desired away from the major source of aircraft noise.

20. Engine Ground Run-up and A.P.U. Noise Control: The noise problem caused by engine run-ups is now mainly confined to smaller airports and some military bases, where the airport and community population centres are close together. At larger airports, maintenance areas can be located remotely from the community and often curfews are imposed to avoid intrusion during the quieter late evening and night-time rest periods. In the past twenty years a large expenditure of money and design effort has gone

Fig.7. Concorde ground muffler

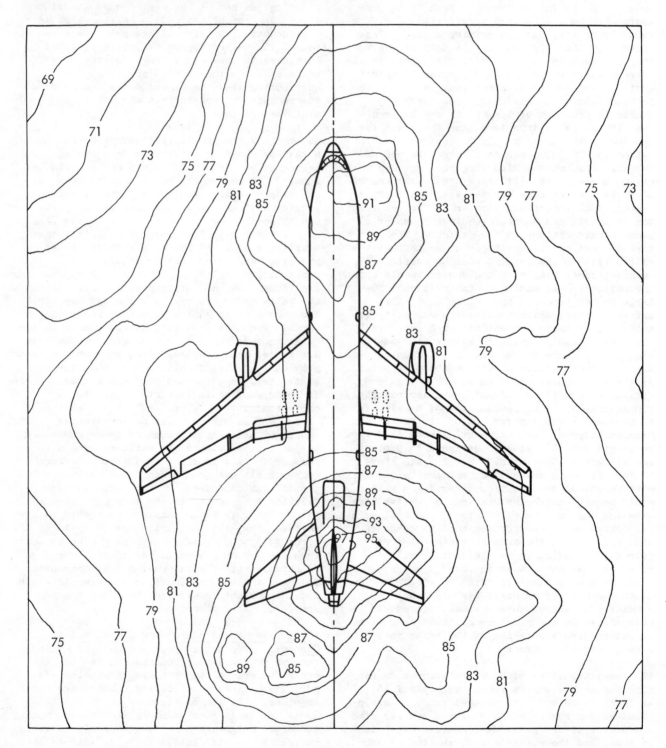

Fig.8. Typical ground noise contures from APU operation

into the development of ground run up mufflers and hush houses. These are devices into which an engine exhaust is directed and a series of chambers suitably baffled to absorb the noise. It is designed to reduce the velocity of the gases to a point where the flow is not a significant generator of noise. Early mufflers essentially just redirected the noise by directing the exhausts upwards, which sometimes, because of topographical and meteorological features of the surrounding areas, produced noise problems in areas remote from the run-up operation. But modern devices can reduce the noise at source to acceptable levels. These devices are naturally massive (Figure 7) because they must be able to match the dimensions of a particular engine-airframe configuration and at the same time, contain the high speed gas flows which exhaust at several hundred pounds a second. Inlet mufflers are also available, these are lined extensively with acoustically absorbent materials to prevent the radiation of the high frequency rotor noise. Dug out areas, louvred blast fences and earth barriers are also used to obstruct the noise emission from the engines, and utilise the same design technique discussed in the previous section.

21. A.P.U. noise has a common factor with that of ground run-ups; that is, the duration of the operation can be measured in terms of minutes or longer, unlike an aircraft fly-by. Protection from the higher frequency A.P.U. noise requires less massive structures than those from engine noise. Barriers must be high enough to cover line of sight exposure from the A.P.U. and the barrier fence must be designed to prevent the transmission of the noise through its walls and so lessen the effectiveness of the obstruction. Similarly, buildings can be designed to minimise A.P.U. operations and, in general, any considerations taken to minimise the noise from aircraft engines will automatically take care of the A.P.U. environment.

22. A far more difficult problem to solve is the protection of ground crew from excessive exposure. It can be seen from comparing the activities shown in Figure 4 with the noise contours of an A.P.U. operation, (Figure 8) that there could exist a potentially hazardous situation if ground crews are exposed for many hours per day over a working life time. To prevent the possibility of occupationally induced hearing loss, care must be taken to see that each worker who is assigned to particularly noisy activities has a work schedule designed to minimise the exposure and that wherever practicable, to use some form of hearing protection. This is a situation not uncommon in industry where workers are exposed to high levels of noise, but because of work pattern, very little noise reduction can be accomplished through structural design. Relief must be obtained through careful work plans.

23. Take Off and Landing Noise Control: Noise at the start of a take-off roll can be reduced in specific areas by means of the techniques discussed before. But thrust reversal noise during landing is not so easily treated because of operational variabilities and the variety of thrust reversers in use giving rise to difference noise emission patterns.

24. Once an airplane is airborne, any possibility of using conventional barriers becomes impracticable, but there have been serious consideration given at various airports, for example, at Los Angeles, to lining approach and take-off paths with specially designed high-rise appartments. The walls and roofs of these structures facing the airport are sound-proofed, the structure profiles then act as barriers to obstruct the paths of noise propagation from the aircraft for both ground operation and at modest altitudes. The use of building to screen highway noise is now commonly considered but as yet no one has implemented any of the designs for aircraft noise. Sound-proofing of individual structures is the usual approach to flyover noise control, while compatible land usage is recommended wherever possible.

24. CONCLUSION

The noise problems produced by aircraft operating within the confines of the airport boundary do not rank in the same order as the noise problems created by overflying aircraft or helicopters. Nevertheless, it can cause severe disturbance to those living within a mile or two of the airport complex, and certain types of noise, such as those generated by taxiing aircraft and A.P.U. operations, can also pose as a hearing hazard to ground staff. Besides the obvious solution of source noise reduction, the usual methods of control are by the use of barriers to obstruct the paths of noise propagation and the sound-proofing of structures to protect those people within their walls. The purpose of this paper is not to give a detailed technical report on the sources of the noise and solutions for their control but to introduce them as an area of noise control which should receive more attention. The problems described in this paper will become more acute in the future, particularly in the United Kingdom where few new airport sites will be developed. Therefore, terminal and apron capacity are expected to control the air traffic capacity at existing airports.

REFERENCES
1. Air Ministry. Report of the Committee on Control of Flying. March 1939. H.M.S.O. London.
2. LARGE J.B. The control of aircraft noise. Aircraft Engineering Volume 47 No.7 July 1975.
3. McKENNELL A.C. Aircraft noise annoyance around London (Heathrow) Airport. Central Office of Information S.S.337. April 1963.
4. LARGE J.B. People, communities and aircraft operations. AGARD Lecture Series 77 on Aircraft noise generation, emission and reduction.
5. Community noise exposure resulting from aircraft operations: Technical review. BB&N Inc. Tech. Report AMRL-TR-73-106. November 1974.
6. LARGE J.B. Aircraft noise and sonic boom. Transportation Noises - A symposium on Acceptability Criteria. University of Washington 1969.

REFERENCES (continued)

7. Code of Practice for reducing the exposure of employed persons to noise. H.M.S.O. 1972.

8. DICKINSON P.J. & LARGE J.B. A mathematical model to determine the economic impact of achieving reduced community noise levels from aircraft. May 1971. For the British Aircraft Corporation and Ministry of Defence.

9. History of Aircraft Nuisance Prevention Association - Japan (Foundation Juridical Person 1975.

10. Proceedings of 'Protection acoustique des zones d'habitation par des écrans' Centre National de la Recherche Scientifique. Marseille 1975.

Session IV: Discussion

Mr O. B. St JOHN (Paper 9)

There has been intense activity in the field of operational techniques for reducing noise during the past few months and there is progress to be reported in two areas.

First, recent discussions both within the UK and informally with the US authorities, have further emphasized the unlikelihood of the introduction of two-segment approaches in the context of current aircraft types or their derivatives. The reasons are simply that the potential benefits to be derived are only comparable with those obtainable by other means which do not incur the technical problems, re-certification programmes and extremely high costs associated with two-segment approaches. On a later time scale one cannot dismiss the possibility of two-segment approaches if one assumes the existence, for example, of a microwave landing system to provide a flexible guidance aid and direct lift control to give better height control on the steeper glide path.

During the summer of 1976 an operational flight programme is planned at Heathrow to encourage all pilots to make continuous descent approaches, in which the aircraft will descend steadily from the stack to touchdown. Air Traffic Control will inform the pilot in the stack how many miles to touchdown are planned so that he can calculate his point of initiation and his optimum rate of descent. This provides a real prospect of significant alleviation and noise measurements will be made throughout the programme to assess the benefit: the expectation overall is to achieve a reduction of about 5 - 6 EPNdB from about 10 miles, increasing slightly with range. At ranges of less than 10 miles there will be some alleviation from the associated effect of improved drag management and this benefit should extend down to a range of about 4 miles.

This exercise has been made possible as a result of the introduction into general operational service, late in 1975, of secondary surveillance radar, mode C, by which height data are automatically provided to ATC so that it is possible to provide an environment in which pilots can make more flexible use of the terminal area.

This technique provides an additional benefit in that it means less fuel consumption for the airline. Typically the potential reduction from stack to touchdown is estimated at 100 kg per approach if one compares a fully developed continuous descent approach with the earlier technique of descending to 3000 ft and joining the glide path at that level.

The hope has already been expressed that this programme should be the forerunner of a progressive movement which might eventually allow continuous descent from cruise altitude with the attractive possibility of reducing or even eliminating (except on rare occasions) the need for holding stack.

Professor J. B. LARGE (Paper 10)

My object is to discuss some of the noise problems caused primarily by ground operation of aircraft, both within the airport and at the airport community interface. The Authors of Papers 8 and 9 discuss comprehensively the current status of community noise alleviation, and I will merely draw attention to reference 1 in my Paper. I would like to highlight some of the other problems of noise control.

As in the case of aircraft flyovers, the noise ingredients are the same, but the quantities are different. During a flyover, which may last up to 30 s, the major components of noise are the forward radiating fan noise, the aft radiating fan noise and jet noise. All are heard, but the peak noise level is set by the source having the shortest path length to the observer. This is usually the aft radiating fan on approach or the jet noise on take-off. In the case of ground manoeuvres in which the velocity of the manoeuvering aircraft is low and the track non-linear, an observer may receive the full intensity of the various individual sources during a pass-by. In addition, the duration of the noise is much longer. The extremes, for example, are a holding operation at take-off, and the gross exposure during engine trim or engine group run-up situations. Because the population requiring protection is relatively close, the source of noise cannot be taken as a point source, which is the case in computing flyover noise exposure. Table 1 in Paper 10 shows how engine heights vary for different airplane designs. Therefore the composition of the noise exposure should include

    (a) the contribution to the spectra of the noise components;

    (b) the duration of the noise;

    (c) the number of sources radiating.

In the case of propeller powered aircraft, the estimation of the noise output is somewhat easier even though protection from this type of noise is more difficult because of the low frequency blade-passage noise which dominates the spectrum. The directivity of the maximum noise intensity lies almost in the plane of the propeller. On the other hand, A P U noise has almost the same characteristic as jet engine noise except that the frequencies in the spectrum are scaled with the engine size and operating conditions. But there are two unusual features: the first is that the inlet and exhausts can be remotely situated from each other; the second that because of their location shielding and non-uniform directivity patterns must invariably be accounted for.

There are three distinct groups of the population that need protection from the source of aircraft noise. The first is the community residing in the proximity of the airport boundary. It would not be appropriate to go into the details of the acoustical measures associated with speech interference, annoyance, loss of sleep, etc., but the method of assessment must be appropriate to the particular community situation.

The airport population, the second group, either terminal passengers or airport employees working inside airport buildings require primarily ease in communication, and in some areas the need for rest and relaxation. In both cases there are prescribed procedures for setting desired criteria. The third group in need of protection is the workers in the proximity of an aircraft or engine during prolonged noisy operations: There are now generally accepted criteria which codify the noise intensity and length of exposure to minimise the prospect of a hearing loss over a working lifetime. A particular sub-problem in this area is the protection of passengers to and from an airplane in an ambient situation.

In order to provide protection in communities adjacent to the airport careful consideration should be given to the layout of taxi-ways, holding areas and cargo bays, and perhaps instructions to pilots not to make undue noise but the most obvious solution is the use of acoustical screens or barriers. Because of the nature of the problem these barriers must necessarily be massive. Because these screens intrude into the normal visual environment their lines are usually softened by vegetation planted near or on the barrier. But perhaps contrary to general expectation, this vegetation does not significantly increase the noise reduction unless it has a high foliage density of the jungle variety. On the contrary, scattering by leaves and branches may increase the noise levels.

Airport terminal and office building designs must be functional in the noise environment to which they are exposed: roofs, walls, windows all require adequate attenuation properties. Flanking paths such as doors, open passages and walkways need screening. Applications to the details of the noise exposure must receive more careful consideration that is included in even the most modern airport design. Protection of airport workers is the most difficult to achieve. Work patterns during servicing and maintenance need careful scrutiny, and the workers exposure must be minimised. If all else fails ear-protectors may be necessary, and mandated in the way that safety helmets, gloves and shoes etc., are used.

So far I have failed to mention the noise problems associated with the take-off and approach procedures, particularly at very low altitudes and on the ground. There are for example, specific problems associated with loss of ground attenuation on take-off, and thrust reverser operations on approach, but there are really no effective measures for protection here. Once the aircraft becomes airborne it becomes impracticable to screen the noise - although a colleague produced a proposal some years ago for a series of high rise appartments on either side of the major approach path into Los Angeles airport. Incidentally, also some years ago now a serious suggestion was made in the early stages of the US/SST program to use rows of water fountains in order to absorb the noise. The massive amount of water needed to produce such an effect would certainly produce more noise than the aircraft.

Finally, I would like to mention another neglected acoustical problem not discussed in the Paper. This is something I call acoustical clutter, particularly inside terminal buildings. The outside noise from airplanes and ground traffic coupled with noise of the interior activities of checking tickets and baggage handling, etc., quite often obscures flight information and other messages broadcast over public address systems. It is also difficult for passengers to find areas for quiet relaxation. Even the most modern airports are not immune from these problems and they vary greatly in the acoustical ambience. For example, the recently enlarged Seattle Airport has remarkable good acoustical qualities. On the other hand the new Charles de Gaulle Airport is somewhat disappointing.

Paper 10 was drafted in the context that in the UK and other western countries much of the future airport developments will be around existing terminal and runway facilities, but also with the thought that the new airports to be built are mostly in parts of the world with warmer climates and where the possibility exists, at least to passengers and airport workers of a greater noise exposure. I hope that in both situations more emphasis will be placed on airport design to alleviate some of the problems I have just discussed.

Mr J. EDWARDS, Plessey Navaids

I should like to put a question to Mr St. John. Superficially it seems that a vast amount of effort and expenditure on two-segment approaches has been wasted. Are there not possible variants in this same area which might show promise? For instance, a slightly steeper approach all the way in is one of the few techniques which might be worth more exploration.

Mr St JOHN (Paper 9)

Some time ago when activity in the USA was at its height, representations were made to Congress quoting very high figures for potential noise alleviation. Naturally there was public reaction in the UK demanding that two-segment approaches be considered for application here. A research programme was subsequently launched by the Department of Industry in close collaboration with the Civil Aviation Authority and the Department of Trade. This covered not only two-segment approaches but also a whole range of possibilities using different glide path angles.

The results of this work have been valuable in several ways. Overall a much better understanding has been gained of the operational and technical problems associated with flying different glide paths. In particular improved methods of predicting noise benefit on the ground have been developed and the pilots' workloads have been studied. This work has certainly not been wasted: it provided a contribution to the UK reaction to the US proposals for the introduction of two-segment approaches in autumn 1975.

The question of slightly steeper approaches than the nominal 3° has been studied in the course of the same flight research programme, backed up by theoretical studies. The main advantage is that it offers some noise alleviation right down to the threshold, but the benefit is comparatively small as it mainly derives from the slight additional height clearance. Typi-

cally for a $3\frac{1}{2}^{\circ}$ glide path there would be an
extra 150 ft clearance at a range of 4 miles.
On the other hand there are a number of operational problems, particularly the recertification
programme which would be necessary. As an example the B747 is currently limited to a glide
path angle of 3.1° and the L1011 to 3.25° in the
context of automatic landing on an ILS glide
path.

Mr T. J. MEYER, Holztwiete, Hamburg, Germany

I should like to give some details of a noise attenuation shelter, consisting of two triangular
roof surfaces inclined towards one another,
braced along a ridge 40 m long and resting on
two base lines each 61 m long. In this way the
aircraft's engines are enclosed in a shell like
structure. The shelter can readily be adapted
both in its direction and in its geometrical
form to suit local conditions. Aircraft can use
the cabin in the 'nose out' or 'nose in' positions. Nose out is preferable for aircraft with
rear engines. The jet efflux escapes through an
aperture measuring roughly 20 m^2 at the rear.
This arrangement for the exhaust gases to escape
freely from the rear of the shelter avoids any
possibility of the enclosure reacting on the engine characteristics or the dynamic stressing of
the airframe. The nose in position ensures better screening in particular for aircraft with
low wing-mounted engines.

The acoustic attenuation levels were measured in the rear half by the Berlin Technical
University Institute of Technical Acoustics.
The shelter reduces noise by 25 to 30 dB(A) within close range (up to 100 m from the exhaust
aperture), the sound level decreases by another
24 dB(A) at a distance of 100 m to 300 m, and
the attenuation rises again by 15 dB(A) between
300 m and 600 m. These figures reveal that the
sound level decreases steadily by roughly 15 dB(A)
each time the distance is doubled.

Dr R. A. HOOD, RTM Planning Partnership

One method of reducing noise which has not been
mentioned, and which is particularly relevant to
certain airports, is that of increasing the
length of the runway. This may seem to be paradoxical, but the major impact of Heathrow for
example is in the area of Hounslow, and if the
runways are extended westward by about a mile,
which I believe is possible, then the position
of the westbound take-off and the threshold for
landing from the eastbound could be reduced by
about a mile further away from Hounslow. Take-
off to and landing from the west could be unchanged.

The impact of the scheme to the west would
be limited to a small increase in ground running
which could be dealt with by various measures.
The improvement to the east could be a decrease
in noise level over Hounslow of about 5 NNI.
The cost of implementing the scheme would be
about £10 million plus £2 million extra in running ground charges.

Is there any serious objection to this type
of solution to control aircraft noise from the
air traffic control operation? In particular,
can the Authors see any difficulties occurring

with the threshold position being half way down
the runway?

Mr St JOHN

This alternative was not mentioned in my Paper
although the possibility of moving the glide
path origin down the runway, though not to the
extent of a whole mile, has been evaluated. An
extra mile of concrete would provide an additional clearance of almost 300 ft which would
certainly give some alleviation to the inhabitants of Cranford and those living near the airport, but this benefit would rapidly decrease
with distance and would scarcely be perceptible
at a range of 4 miles from the airport. To modify one main runway would, of course, only give
this alleviation some 40% of the time, but there
are several reasons, both economic, operational
and technical, why this solution is not favoured.

To lay a further mile of concrete for each
of the two main runways would be costly, but
there are other concomitant costs, both capital
and running, as it would be necessary to replan
the navigation services, airfield lighting etc.,
and the taxiways. To avoid imposing further suffering from aircraft taking off the extended
length of runway would have to be maintained in
full operation, and pilots tend to land on the
first available concrete which might therefore
prevent the realisation of the full potential
benefit.

Dr HOOD

Considering the cost of the various options, this
£10 million for a substantial decrease is quite
a small amount of money for a fairly large decrease in noise.

Mr St JOHN

You are not decreasing noise. You are merely
redistributing it.

Professor Secor D. BROWNE, Washington D.C.

A great deal of what I have heard appears to be
based on the thought that FAR 36 is some sort of
fixed objective. I hope it is clearly understood not to be the case, because the FAA is now
beginning studies on a revised FAR 36. The closer we get to this Nirvana, the more it will
move down the block.

*Mr R. C. MANN, Thompson Berwick Pratt & Partners,
Vancouver*

I understand that the definition of noise is unwanted sound. Could the Authors give me any advice with regard to whether there are parallel
studies on the sociological side being undertaken with the engineering studies? For instance, the dB level experienced by young people
when enjoying contemporary music on records in
some cases exceeds the level of noise which communities object to when they consider unwanted
sound.

Professor LARGE (Paper 10)

There is a great deal of literature on the subject. The more work there is on the effects of

noise on people, the more it becomes apparent that the simple idea of an exposure relationship does not exist. What appears to exist is that for rather specific sorts of sound, such as aircraft of certain varieties, trains or heavy trucks, it is possible to produce what is called a 'central tendency relationship'; as noise increases people's dissatisfaction with it increases, but when all these factors are lumped together, in fact it becomes meaningless. For example, an unpleasant word whispered in one's ear is more distressing than Concorde flying overhead, and it is independent of the sound intensity. What this implies is that when the response of people to noise is examined, the actual physical exposure itself plays relatively little part in individual response. There is a great deal of work going on in this area.

You refer to noise as being unwanted sound. It is a simple definition because it is a varying effect. What is noise to some is sound to others. It has a cultural implication as well. For example, to most Englishmen the sound of sea has a romantic connotation, but to the Jamaican it means a tidal wave is coming, and his reaction to that sound is quite different from that of the Englishman.

Mr F. H. RUSSELL, Sir William Halcrow & Partners

In Paper 8 Dr Wilkinson mentioned that in the 1980s the effect of supersonic transport would perhaps have raised NNI by one. I feel that this pinpoints the fact that NNI is no longer a valid way of measuring the effect of sound on the community. If all other aircraft are in the low noise bracket, then the passage of one Concorde will stand out like a sore thumb and be more stressful than the old type of aircraft in the present pattern. I should add that I am in the pro-Concorde lobby!

Dr WILKINSON (Paper 8)

I do not think this is a statement it is possible to answer. It is a point of view that I

note. I am not sure how one arrives at a conclusion that NNI is not an adequate measure. In any subjective arena of this kind the attempt to attach objective numbers is almost a chimera. But some attempt to measure what happens has to be made. My point in mentioning Concorde was that I believe the row that has been going on publicly about it has got nothing to do with the real inconvenience or irritation of people.

For example, during the 3 months during which the initial Concorde trials were going on, the airport authority received 2500 letters of complaint. During the 3 months' route proving it received 1500 letters of complaint, and during the first 3 months of operational service it received 163. I believe that during the period when the whole business had a high publicity value and was very much in the public's mind, the irritation expressed was out of all proportion to what the average man really thought. I think the real reaction is more accurately expressed by people living round the airport who came on television and said 'What Concorde?'. Now that the Concorde pilots are becoming used to operating techniques, we are finding that the Tridents on the eastbound take-off are making more noise than Concorde.

Professor J. B. LARGE

There are really two levels of response when talking about aircraft noise. It is at the administration level that the NNI comes in. This gives a relatively crude description of annoyance but enables one to make comparisons between different types of aircraft, etc. When talking about individual response, it is necessary to look at rather detailed characteristics, not only of the noise environment to which people are subjected and the details of the noise, but also the social character of the community in which the response is being made.

11. Providing and maintaining visual aids and ground movement guidance and control systems for low visibility operations

G.A. Champniss MBE, FRMetS, MRAeS, MCIT
Inspector of Airside Safety and Operations British Airports Authority

This paper discusses the implications for the airport operator of a decision to provide visual aids for Category III operation. The effect of this decision on the visual aids provided for final approach and landing and ground movement of aircraft. The need for more stringent maintenance standards in order to preserve the integrity of the systems and the methods by which this can be undertaken and the consequential effects.

INTRODUCTION

1.   Low visibility operations by scheduled airlines are no longer a vision but a reality. A number of aircraft types have been, or are likely to be, certificated for operations in Category III, that is to say, with runway visual range (RVR) of 200 metres. Indeed the Civil Aviation Authority (CAA) have authorised operations at Heathrow by Trident aircraft of British Airways European Division with a Decision Height of 12 feet and an RVR of 200 metres.

2.   Operations in low visibilities can only take place when a number of elements comprising the total system are available and proven.

3.   The airline operator is understandably anxious to ensure that the facilities available at the airport permit him to realise the full capability of his aircraft because of the potential commercial benefits. However it is necessary to assess the economic benefits to the airport operator and assess the percentage of an airport's annual traffic which is affected by the various categories of low visibility.

CATEGORISATION OF RUNWAYS

4.   ICAO International Standards and Recommended Practices for Aerodromes (Annex 14) lays down that runways shall be classified according to their availability for low visibility operations. The categories are as follows:-

5.   Precision Approach Runway, Category I provided with visual and non-visual aids is intended for operations down to 60 metres Decision Height and a Runway Visual Range of 800 metres.

6.   Precision Approach Runway, Category II provided with visual and non-visual aids in-

tended for operations down to 30 metres Decision Height and RVR of 400 metres.

7.   Precision Approach Runway, Category III – an instrument runway with visual and non-visual aids intended for operations down to a RVR of –

A – 200 metres: B – 50 metres: C – without reliance on external visual reference.

NON VISUAL AIDS

8.   At airports operated by the British Airports Authority these take the form of VORs, DME and non directional beacons as well as ILS, all of which are provided by the Civil Aviation Authority. A programme of modernisation of the ILS has been undertaken with the result that the categorisation of the ILS systems at the airports is as follows:-

Heathrow	28R	Category II
	10L	Category III
	28L	Category III
	10R	Category III
Gatwick	08	Category II
	26	Category II
Stansted	23	Category I
Prestwick	13	Category I
	31	Category I
Glasgow	06	Category II
	24	Category II
Edinburgh	07	Category II
	25	Category II

(when new runway becomes available)

| Aberdeen | 17 | Category I |

VISUAL AIDS

9. The standards of aerodrome ground lighting to

be met for each runway category are laid down in Annex 14, Part V.

10. <u>Category II Requirements</u>   To operate in Category II conditions Civil Aviation Authority requires, in addition to a suitably categorised ILS and RVR :—

A full Calvert Category I approach lighting system

Supplementary centreline and side row barrettes.

High Intensity runway edge lighting, runway end and threshold lighting and runway centreline lighting.

Runway touch—down zone lighting.

Low Intensity green taxiway centreline lighting.

Short break secondary power supplies.

11. <u>Category III Requirements</u>   To operate in Category III conditions Civil Aviation Authority requires, in addition to facilities listed in the preceding paragraph:

Centreline lighting at not greater than 15 metres spacing.

High Intensity taxiway centreline lighting.

Adjustments to be made to the setting angle of certain runway edge, runway centreline and approach lighting.

Illuminated stopbars at the Category III holding positions protecting the ILS system.

Security measures to ensure that there can be no intrusion into the runway or strip by vehicles or aircraft depending upon the conditions existing at each airport.

12. <u>Availability of Visual Aids at BAA airports</u>

<u>Heathrow</u> – The visual aids associated with the 4 landing directions of runways 28R/10L and 28L/10R meet Category III requirements.

<u>Gatwick</u> – The visual aids serving both directions of Runway 08/26 meet Category III requirements apart from the runway centreline lighting where reduced spacing is required and change in the setting angle of the light fittings.

<u>Stansted</u> – The visual aids serving both directions of Runway 05/23 meet Category I requirements.

<u>Prestwick</u> – The visual aids serving both directions of Runway 13/31 meet Category I requirements.

<u>Glasgow</u> – The visual aids serving Runway 24 meet Category III requirements. Work is proceeding which will result in Runway 06 meeting Category III requirements.

<u>Edinburgh</u> – The visual aids serving both directions of Runway 07/25 will meet Category III requirements apart from the runway centreline lighting where reduced spacing will be required, and change in the setting angle of light fittings.

<u>Aberdeen</u> – The visual aids serving Runway 17 meet Category I requirements.

13. <u>Taxiway Lighting</u>

A specification for a high intensity taxiway light fitting has been developed and fittings produced by two manufacturers which meet this specification. However they are expensive.

A modified low intensity taxiway centreline light fitting has been developed by BAA and a manufacturer. This is in use at Heathrow and goes a long way to meeting the above specification.

This fitting will give adequate guidance in Category III conditions down to a taxiway visibility of about 115 metres (dependent on aircraft type, cockpit cut—off, etc.).

MAINTENANCE OF AERODROME GROUND LIGHTING

14.   Annex 14 requires a programme of preventive maintenance to be employed for all lighting systems and recommends that for Category II systems this programme should meet the objective of 95 per cent serviceability of other lights throughout the approach and runway system.

15.   It is considered that there are some sections of the total approach and runway lighting system which play an essential role in a successful landing in Categories II and III conditions. These may therefore require higher maintenance standards than other sections. The sections in question are those required to enable a pilot to identify his position in relation to the runway and on which he must make his decision either to continue with the landing or overshoot: also a continuing light pattern to provide him with guidance in azimuth during his roll out after landing.

16.   With a RVR of 400 metres and a Decision Height of 30 metres (bottom of Category II) it is likely a pilot will see only the inner 300 metres of the approach lighting system. With RVRs of less than 200 metres (Category IIIB) the effective visual segment will be confined almost exclusively to threshold and runway centreline lighting. Below Category IIIB visual aids will assist only in clearing the runway and taxying.

17.   The essential lighting includes:

the inner 300 metres of the approach lighting system;

ESTIMATED INCIDENCE OF SPECIFIED METEOROLOGICAL CONDITIONS AT BAA AIRPORTS

AIRPORT	CATEGORY II — Base of Lowest Cloud Layer of 5/8 or more ≥30m but <60m and/or Met.Vis ≥225m but <455m (RVR 799–400 metres)		CATEGORY IIIA — Base of Lowest Cloud Layer of 5/8 or more <30m and/or Met. Vis ≥105m but <225m (RVR 399–200 metres)		CATEGORY IIIB — Met. Vis ≥25m but <105m (RVR 199–40 metres)		CATEGORY IIIC — Met. Vis. <25m (RVR <49 metres)		ALL TYPES TOTAL	
	%	Average Hours p.a	%	Average Hours p.a	%	Average Hours p.a	%	Average Hours p.a	%	Average Hours p.a
HEATHROW	0.42	37.0	0.70	61.0	0.69	60.8	0.02	1.4	1.83	160.2
GATWICK	1.40	122.4	2.07	181.8	2.22	195.0	0.05	4.2	5.74	503.4
STANSTED	2.07	181.2	2.68	235.2	1.00	87.6	–	–	5.75	504.0
PRESTWICK	0.17	14.6	0.11	9.8	0.06	5.0	–	–	0.34	29.4
EDINBURGH	0.81	70.8	0.95	83.2	0.73	63.8	0.01	0.8	2.49	218.6
GLASGOW	0.42	37.0	0.44	39.0	0.74	65.2	0.02	1.6	1.63	142.8
ABERDEEN	1.62	141.6	0.77	67.2	0.44	39.0	–	–	2.83	247.8

Fig.1. Meteorological Data: visibility (1969–73)

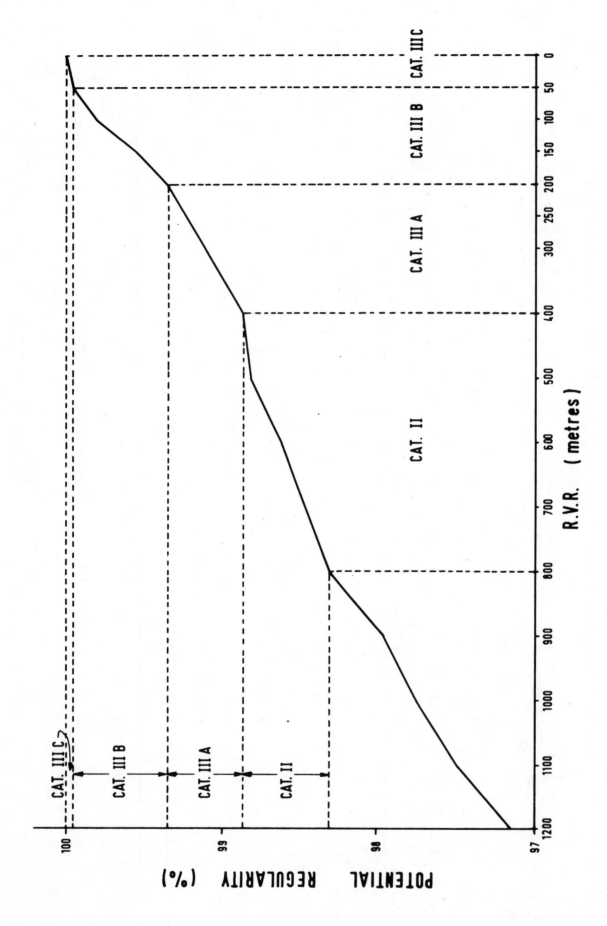

Fig.2. Low visibility movements at Heathrow

the threshold lighting,

the runway centreline lighting throughout the runway with possibly the first 250 metres of the runway edge lights.

18. Annex 14 defines a light failure as occurring when the average intensity determined using the specific angles of elevation, toe in and spread is less than 50 per cent of the specified average intensity of a new light.

19. This reduction can occur for many reasons. The only method of determining the serviceability of a light in situ is to carry out a photometric reading. On many occasions external contamination of the glass lowers the output of runway lighting below the minimum required of a serviceable fitting. In these cases only cleaning may be necessary. If, after cleaning, the light output is still below the specified minimum the fitting has to be changed.

20. At Heathrow and Gatwick frequent light cleaning and photometric measurement has been found necessary to maintain the minimum required serviceability. Heathrow's essential lighting is cleaned twice weekly: at Gatwick a weekly programme has been found to be adequate.

ECONOMIC IMPLICATIONS OF LOW VISIBILITY OPERATIONS

21. The airport must make a very substantial investment if it decides to provide facilities for operations in visibility conditions lower than Category I. This will include:-

Greater ILS reliability and integrity.

Supplementary approach lighting, side-row and centreline barrettes.

Runway centreline and touch-down zone lighting.

Taxiway centreline lighting and at airports with high traffic demand an effective ground movement control system.

An alternative power supply with short break changeover capability.

22. The only additional requirements for Category III operation are reduced spacing of the runway centreline and taxiway lighting. Thus the major capital cost is incurred to meet Category II requirements.

23. Since visibility normally tends to reduce fairly rapidly through Category II to Category III and to increase equally rapidly there appears little justification for meeting Category II requirements unless it is intended also to offer a Category III service.

24. The estimated incidence of specified meteorological conditions at British Airports Authority Airports during the period 1969-1973 is given at Fig.1.

25. At Heathrow the yearly average within Category II is 37 hours and within Category III 123 hours. At Gatwick the figures are 122 hours and 381 hours respectively. At the other extreme at Prestwick the yearly average within both Category II and Category III is 29 hours.

26. There is no justification in providing expensive and sophisticated facilities unless the traffic demand exists to make use of them. Due to the wide variation in meteorological conditions and pattern of traffic demand at airports it is not possible to generalise and therefore separate studies must be undertaken at each airport.

27. For Heathrow it had been suggested that the probability of low RVRs would be greatest at night and during the early morning when traffic demand was low. However examining past data revealed that while this may be true of autumn and spring fog conditions, during winter months there is a considerable probability of low visibility and peak traffic demand overlapping.

28. Analysis of data for a 5 year period at Heathrow showed that regularity increased at a fairly uniform rate to the lower limits of Category IIIB which is the cut off point where visual aids cease to be effective in maintaining traffic. The improvement in regularity in providing facilities for Category IIIC is less than 0.5 per cent. (See Fig.2)

29. At Prestwick Categories II and III conditions occur so infrequently and the probability of these 29 hours coinciding with peak traffic demand is small that there is no justification for providing facilities to permit operations below Category I.

30. At Gatwick because the airline operators have not indicated any intention to provide their aircraft with Category III capability at this point in time there is no economic justification for the airport to provide the additional facilities.

31. Detailed analysis of the meteorological data for Glasgow and Edinburgh has not yet been undertaken, but is likely to be similar to the fog/traffic pattern at Heathrow.

GROUND MOVEMENT GUIDANCE AND CONTROL

32. It is believed that research into the problem of ground movement guidance and control has not kept pace with the development of the visual and non-visual aids to final approach and landing, nor with the requirements of increasing airport capacity. Thus this may prove to be a serious deficiency at some airports in handling safely the aircraft which now, or in the immediate future, will be able to operate in low visibility conditions.

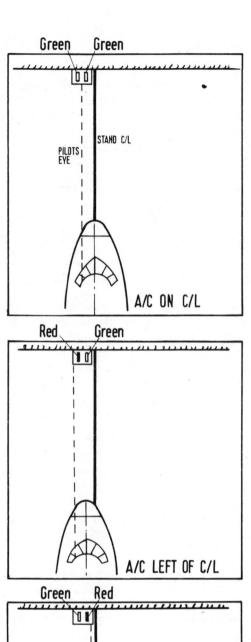

Fig.3. Layout of AGNIS signals

Fig.4. Sidemarker board

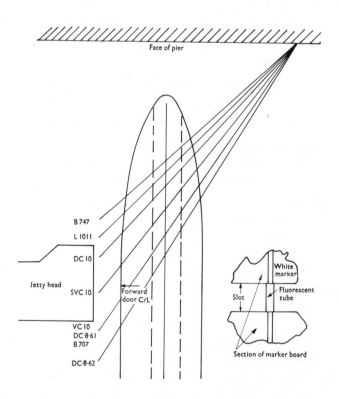

Fig.5. Parallax aircraft parking aid

33. Ground movement guidance and control should provide for the safe and expeditious handling of all aircraft between the runway and the stand. The Operational Requirement (OR) for a system was discussed and agreed at the ICAO 8th Air Navigation Conference held in April/May 1974.

34. The problem which faces airports is what are the minimum conditions at which control and guidance are required? Again this is not a question where one can generalise and the situation at each airport must be examined in depth to determine the extent to which peak traffic demand and conditions of reduced visibility overlap.

35. The ground movement guidance and control system in use at Heathrow goes a long way towards meeting the criteria given in the 8th ANC operational requirement. The system which is based on the selective switching of sections of taxiway lighting has proven successful in visibilities down to the lower end of Category II. Using the modified taxiway light fitting with an appreciably greater output will provide effective guidance in conditions of bright sunlight as well as Category III conditions.

36. It is a financial and economic matter related to traffic demand and any special requirements for low visibility operation to decide how far the system should be developed towards complete automation.

APRON GUIDANCE

37. To enable operations to be undertaken successfully in low visibility it is essential to provide the pilot with information relating to stand identification and guidance before leaving the apron taxiway. The system used must be compatible with the ground movement guidance and control facilities on the taxiway.

38. The requirement has been met at Heathrow by 5 separate indicators,

- Illuminated stand identification numbers
- Stand centreline lighting
- Aircraft Guidance Nose-In System (AGNIS)
- Sidemarker Boards
- Parallax Aircraft Parking Aid (PAPA)

39. Stand Number Indicator This comprises large illuminated numerals either pole-mounted or fixed to the building structure and aligned to the stand centreline marking.

40. AGNIS This consists of a unit fixed with two parallel vertical slots, through which narrow red or green light beams are projected. The unit is mounted on the extended centreline of a stand at a height consistent with the pilot's eye for aircraft likely to use the stand. It is aligned for interpretation by the pilot in the left hand seat.

The system shows a red/green or green/red signal depending upon the position of the aircraft in relation to the centreline, so providing directional guidance for the pilot to correct his course. When the light signals from two parallel vertical slots are green/green the aircraft is on centreline. (See Fig.3)

41. Sidemarker Boards The Sidemarker Board comprises a board 3.6 metres by 1.8 metres, mounted 3 metres above ground level on the nosedock structure. Vertical slats with a black external edge are mounted at specific intervals along the face of the white base board. These slats project 150 millimetres and have coloured sides. The side facing towards the taxiway is green and the side facing towards the pier is red. Each slat is clearly labelled to indicate the aircraft type for which it provides guidance. As the aircraft approaches the correct stopping position the green side of the slat will appear to narrow and exactly on the stop position the black edge only will be visible. (See Fig. 4)

42. Parallax Aircraft Parking Aid Where the jetty arrangements do not conveniently provide a position for the location of a Sidemarker Board PAPA has been provided. PAPA consists of a reference board with a horizontal slot 300 millimetres deep running across its centre. A white fluorescent tube is mounted vertically behind the board which coincides with the appropriate aircraft marking on the reference board when the aircraft has reached the required stopping position. (See Fig. 5)

FLIGHT CHECKING OF VISUAL AIDS

43. An airport operator understandably needs assurance that the visual aids provided are maintained to the highest possible standards. Although much can be achieved by quality control in the engineering workshop and through frequent ground checks, in the final analysis a flight check is the only method of ensuring that the required level of serviceability, setting and output of the light fittings is being achieved.

44. The British Airports Authority undertakes regular flight checks of all runway lighting systems at its airports using an aircraft equipped with a camera so that a visual record of the flight checks is available.

45. This has proved invaluable in achieving and maintaining the required level of efficiency of all the elements of the system of visual aids provided whether for Category I, II or III operation.

CONCLUSIONS

46. This paper assesses the requirements for

low visibility operations and the implications from the point of view of the airport authority. It has examined the steps taken by BAA to meet these requirements at Heathrow and elsewhere. It has examined the maintenance implications of ensuring that airport ground aids for visibility operations are maintained to high standards and the method we have adopted to ensure their continued serviceability.

47. For the future decision will be needed on the extent of developments of GMC and apron guid - ance systems compatible with the requirements of aircraft and the financial outlay involved.

Further funds must be justified by enhanced safety where this may be deficient, or increased capacity in those areas where limitations may be occurring.

48. The British Airports Authority constantly reviews the facilities under its control, making improvements to GMC systems, promoting operational research into new light fittings, using fibre optics for better light output and ease of maintenance, developing apron guidance systems and reviewing our procedures whenever the environment of airport operations indicate such changes may be necessary.

12. Changing passenger needs

G. Pestalozzi, PhD

Chief Planning Engineer, Office of Civil Aviation, Zurich

Passengers' needs, while remaining basically unchanged, have become more varied. The strong growth of the classes of passengers who are more interested in low cost than high standards of service, as well as the general scarcity of capital, demand increased cost consciousness. Airports should concentrate on the basic necessities of time saving and of human environment. Additional comfort and services should be provided only when they do not detract from the necessities, with their cost being charged to those demanding them.

ANALYSIS OF PASSENGER NEEDS

1. The basic needs of air passengers are quite simple and unchanging. What the passenger really wants is this: to drive up to his aircraft five minutes before flight time with the assurance that he will find an acceptable seat in the aircraft, get rid of his luggage, board the plane, and be off. At his destination airport, he wants to leave the aircraft as soon as it comes to a stop, pick up his bags, and drive away to his final destination. This is essentially what he is used to from overland public transport.

2. The foregoing description of passengers' needs oversimplifies matters, of course. At best, it applies to routine travellers, who fly often and are thoroughly familiar with the procedures. They value their time highly, which is probably their reason for choosing air transport. For them, any extra time spent at the airport is a nuisance. However, this kind of travellers constitutes only a part of all passengers, and probably a diminishing one.

3. There is an important segment of the passengers population made up of people who fly only occasionally and possibly for the first time, and who are afraid of it all. Their needs are largely psychological. In addition to being scared of flying, they fear to miss their flight. They will spend extra time at the airport to be sure to get where they are expected to be at the right time. They need the constant reassurance of finding the right place. They may be suspicious of everything, like being misdirected, getting lost, loosing their bags or getting onto the wrong aircraft, plus many other potential mishaps. These passengers need a lot of time and attention at the airport.

4. Finally there are air passengers for whom flying is sheer fun. Their elation starts the moment they leave home for the airport (and possibly long before that). They will want to spend extra time at the airport to bask in its excitement, to highten their elation with ancillary activities, and to communicate their joy to others brought along for the purpose or picked up at random. This kind of traveller could possibly be quite upset by anything that distracts him from his happiness.

5. From the above incomplete list of passengers' needs, one can see the wide spectrum of requirements to be taken into account. This differentiation of needs brought about by the expansion of the air travel market to a wide variety of travellers is probably the main characteristic of the changing picture of to-day's passengers' needs. Add to the different needs typical of the broad categories of travellers described above, the many shades of individual preferences, such as different ideas about comfort and convenience resulting from different means available, special requirements, such as physical handicaps, and many others, and you end up with a staggering range of needs to be provided for.

6. While a major airport, like a large city, has the potential of offering a wide variety of services, there will arise conflicts of objectives and interests. The provisions for one kind of needs may very well be detrimental to others. The airport operator then has to set priorities based on the needs of the market he is called to serve, and also based on the means available to him.

Deficiencies of major airports

7. It can safely be stated that major airports do not satisfy all passenger needs. Some deficiencies, while being very real and annoying, are outside the control of the airport operator. Others are inherent to the size of major airports. Finally there are those resulting from changes in passengers' needs with which airport develop-

ments have not kept up. Deficiencies may concern the basic needs of passengers, since in many cases they result in extra time spent at the airport. Other inadequacies will increase the anguish of inexperienced travellers. Finally, lack of services may diminish the joy and comfort demanded by some passengers.

8. Inadequate land-side access to the airport is an important deficiency which lies largely outside the jurisdiction of the airport operator. However, it has important repercussions on the airport. For one, the access system may in effect limit the capacity of an airport. In any event, inadequacy of airport access will cause departing passengers, and also persons meeting arriving passengers, to go to the airport earlier than would otherwise be necessary. They will add a margin of safety to their access time which, if not actually used, will result in added time at the airport. They may also anticipate access congestion at the peak hours of air traffic and decide to avoid it by coming early. All this results not only in a loss of time, but also in a larger number of persons (and parked cars) being present at the airport, with the consequent need for additional facilities.

9. Airline passenger handling procedures are another source of time loss where the influence of the airport operator is very limited. To the passenger it is not readily apparent why he should check in at the airport between 30 and 90 minutes before flight time, while at a railway station it is sufficient to show up 5 minutes before departure time, or perhaps 15 minutes when border controls are involved. The same criticism applies to governmental control procedures. Again, extra time spent by passengers and their escort at the airport means added space requirements.

10. Much of the discomfort experienced at major airports results from their size, and the amount of traffic handled there. Distances between the different parts of the airport are becoming greater and hence require more time. Facilities are getting huge and cumbersome, thereby increasing the danger of misdirection and the fear of getting lost. Distances have not only become long, but also complicated and often confusing. The sense of direction may be lost completely; it can only imperfectly be regained by directional signs. The large number of people present will inevitably lead to congestion at critical points. It also leads to an impersonal atmosphere, thus increasing the feeling of being alone and the need for reassurance.

11. Most major airports have grown over a long period. They still bear the marks of earlier times, when passenger needs were different and less varied. At least parts of them were built for passengers coming from a select population group: upper echelon business men and well-to-do

travellers. These people demanded high standards of service and were willing to pay for them. While these passengers are still here, they are now a minority. To them have been added those passengers who have switched from other modes of public transport. They fly for the obvious time advantage of air transport, if the price is right. Essentially they do not require better or more costly treatment than they were used to from trains or buses. Finally, there are those passengers who did not travel at all before, or at least not over the distances opened to them by economical air transport. Again, their needs are not so much for high standards of service, but rather for a reasonable price and the assurance of getting to their destination with the least fuss. Major airports have been adapted to these changes to an often insufficient degree, partly because the existing facilities were built for a different purpose and could not be easily adapted to the new requirements, partly because many of the old attitudes persist.

Providing for today's passengers' needs
12. Perhaps the most relevant change in the picture of air transport is the growing importance of cost. Those feeding the air transport industry have become cost conscious. Firstly, there are the passengers. While their needs vary, it may be assumed common to all that they do not want to pay for services which they do not need. The same, of course, holds true for other airport users. A second element is the governments. The financial plight brought on by the current economic recession has led to reconsidering the justification of subsidies to air transport which were current in the past in many different forms and at many levels. The worth of a transport system which is unable to pay its own way is rightly questioned. While help in financing capital investments is still forthcoming there is a marked tendency to recover the cost by charging it to the users. In a similar vein the capital market demands cost consciousness. There will be a tremendous need for capital in the future so that only the most pressing needs can be fulfilled. Passengers' needs at airports will have to be measured against other requirements to determine investment policy. Finally, the new growth picture of air transport requires more careful consideration of cost. In the present climate it can no longer be assumed that rapid growth will permit to cover present excessive costs in the near future.

13. Airports then, have to set priorities in providing for the needs of passengers. It is suggested that they should concentrate on the true necessities first, and relegate improvements of comfort and the fulfilment of wishes and extravagancies to lower priorities. There should be a basic level of service throughout the airport accessible to all, with its cost distributed evenly over all passengers. This level should correspond to some reasonable "least common denominator", subject to the availability of

capital, of course. It will be lower than the level now offered at most airports, in keeping with the needs of the new kinds of passengers. The emphasis would lie on
- short time spent by passengers at the airport;
- simplicity of procedures and facilities;
- congenial atmosphere.
In short, the airport should be less of a perfect machine, but more of a human experience.

14. To concentrate on the necessities does not mean to neglect the amenities; if the capital is available. It does mean, however, that providing for the supplemental needs should not interfere with the necessities. For one, the cost of the additional services should be borne by those demanding them. Also, the additional facilities should not act as impediments to the provision for the necessities. To give an example, additional services require facilities which take up floor space in a terminal building. This increases the size of the building, thereby possibly making the distance to be covered by the passengers longer and more complicated. In keeping with the stated order of priorities, such facilities should be located on the side, e.g., along bypasses which do not affect the primary passenger flow.

15. It has been shown above that passenger needs have become quite differentiated. There are many different kinds of passengers with different needs. It may not be satisfactory to provide one low basic level of service common to all. Particularly at large airports, it may well be possible to separate the passengers according to their needs and to provide different basic levels of service appropriate to the specific groups. A number of airports have found it advantageous to build separate facilities for charter traffic which are normally much simpler than usual terminal buildings. Other special classes of passengers with specific needs are travel groups, "guest workers", passengers without checked baggage, first class and "supersonic" passengers, and others. Of course, it will not be feasible to have separate buildings for all of these groups, but serval classes with similar requirements may be grouped together and provided with a basic service level corresponding to the "least common denominator" of the group. But, here again, care must be taken to allocate costs appropriately.

16. While large airports offer better opportunities to cater to special needs, they create additional needs by the problems specific to them. One area of concern is information and guidance of passengers. As facilities become large spread out and specialised it becomes very important for the well-being of the passenger to provide adequate information. This information should not only tell the passenger what he wants to know, but also be provided when and where he needs it. It must be easy to interpret by the passengers, i.e., be

stated in terms with which he can identify. Also it must be presented in quantities adapted to the time and place where it is given. The larger the amount of information, the more time and effort is required to absorb it. It may be advantageous to develop the information progressively along the path of the passenger, going from general terms to specifics. No information system is complete without the possibility of personal inquiry. Information and guidance systems are the primary means of separating different classes of passengers (and other airport users) and lead them to the facilities provided specifically for them.

17. Another problem area for major airports is land side access. It has already been pointed to the longer stays of passengers at the airport resulting from this, and to the resulting need for additional waiting areas and services to help pass the time agreeably. There is another side to the effect, also. Passengers travelling to a city for business contacs may balk at wasting their precious time there by being held up in traffic from the airport to the city and back. They will wish to conduct their business meetings at, or near the airport. In many instances conference facilities and even hotels have been provided on, or near airports to take care of this need, thereby absorbing valuable space to the detriment of other passengers. It would indeed seem much more effective to improve airport access, since the benefit would be spread to a much larger number of persons. However, the investment required would also be very much larger. This situation is typical for many cases, where alleviating one problem leads to other unwanted problems, since the root cause connot be eliminated.

Concluding remarks
18. An attempt has been made to show why major airports do not reflect very well today's needs of air passengers. This is not so much the result of inadequate development, but rather of changing needs and attitudes. A philosophy has then been developed according to which airport operators might assess the merits of airport improvements to better serve today's passengers' needs. The general idea is to concentrate on the basic necessities of passengers, to provide additional services only if this does not interfere with the basic needs, and to charge the costs to those demanding the services.

19. While these concepts may have some merit in theory, their implementation will encounter considerable practical difficulties. In the recent past, demands for comfort and convenience have probably reached unrealistic levels, spurred on by a long period of economic growth and the faith in an unlimited improvement of the human condition associated with it. In fact, it is difficult to see why air transport should

offer essentially higher standards of service than other forms of public transport. However, it will be quite difficult to convince air passengers, who have become accustomed to these high levels, to accept their lowering, even if new classes of passengers would be quite content with reduced standards in the interest of lower cost.

20. Furthermore, airports are stuck with their existing facilities. They have been designed to past high standards, catering to a class of passengers which may constitute only a minority today. These facilities are here to stay. Their size and layout are fixed and with it the length and complication of connections within the airport. The investments have been made and must be utilized in order to pay for maintenance and debts. To reduce the number or level of services provided could not change these facts.

21. In addition, commercial considerations may have to be taken into account. Many of the extra services are best provided by concessions, since, among other advantages, they offer the best way of charging the cost of the service to the user. However, to make concessions economically viable they have to be able to actively sell their services to as many people as possible, beyond those groups for which the services may be defined as a need. For one, this means that the concessions have to be located near the principal passenger flows, where they almost certainly interfere with the basic requirements of passengers. Also, they will have to attract additional people not only to themselves, but possibly to the airport, thereby adding to congestion. Besides, they will have to be of sizes larger than required for their basic customers, thus adding to the already excessive size of the airport. Quite generally, attractive service at airports, e.g., good access facilities, will bring additional people there, resulting in added size and congestion.

22. Finally, even providing for the basic necessities will probably entail conflicts of interest. Streamlined passenger handling procedures may require a more spread-out building layout, thereby increasing the distance for some passengers and making information more complicated. An effective information system may call for a concentration of the passenger flows, thereby increasing congestion and possibly lengthening distances. The airport operator then has to use his judgement to set priorities among the conflicting necessities, based on the specific conditions at his airport. Perhaps, he may get help from the democratic principle of "the most good for most people", discounting for once the inevitable pressures of special interests.

23. The present phase of the development of air transport, characterized by slow growth and a scarcity of funds available, offers new challenges and opportunities. For one, there is time to think out basic concepts without being pushed into premature action by rapid growth. The thinking can be directed at the real needs again, back from romantic notions of comfort and the fascination of technology. Secondly, increased cost consciousness on all sides forces much more careful consideration of the cost effectiveness of measures taken. It also entails better allocation of costs to those demanding services. Finally, the slow growth of airports will permit gradual spot improvements to better match services with needs, taking into account sound concepts and appropriate costs. In this way it will be possible to transform present airports to conform to new needs and attitudes. Accepting the new challenges and opportunities will make the coming years interesting for airport planners and operators.

Session V: Discussion

Mr CHAMPNISS (Paper 11)

Aircraft may divert for a great many reasons but generally speaking these are

    (a) technical reasons

    (b) company reasons

    (c) weather at destination airport.

Of these weather conditions are the major factor.

If one applies the average incidence of conditions of Categories II and III to the total number of landings it may be thought that this would give an indication of the probable number of diversions 'out'. Taking the figures for Heathrow (1.83% and 137 658 arrivals in 1975) the figure would be 2467. In fact the figure was 383 while for the 11 year period 1965-1975 inclusive the average yearly diversions 'out' was 430. The reason for the difference between the figure obtained by using total arrivals and percentage incidence of meteorological conditions arises from the fact that conditions of low visibility may occur when traffic is very light. This is especially important when examining the economic implications of providing Categories II and III facilities. For example there would be no benefit to either an airline or an airport operator in providing such capability at an airport when analysis of the historical data showed that these conditions occurred at night when the airport was closed. For this reason detailed analysis of the coincidence of conditions of low visibility and traffic offering must be undertaken.

Assessment of the financial implications for the airport of providing facilities for operations in Category II and below is a difficult task since it is not easy to decide the extent of the loss of revenue which will occur. For example the flight might be cancelled or diverted to another airport: alternatively, the aircraft might be held at the point of departure or at an intermediate point. In the last two cases there would not be any loss of revenue. By the same token the passengers who are waiting to join the incoming service may spend more in the restaurant or other concessions as a result of their enforced delay than would otherwise be the case. For the airlines however it is a somewhat different situation, and it is relatively easy to determine the direct operating costs arising from delays, diversions and cancellations.

Diversions must inevitably affect the service given to the passenger. Since the whole purpose of the airline and the airport is to serve the passenger there may be sound reasons for providing facilities for lower visibility operations. These can be summarised as follows:

    (a) the airport operator must ensure that both his visual and non visual navigational facilities are compatible; it is pointless to provide Categories II and III visual aids if the ILS has only Category 1 capability;

    (b) he should assess the potential movements he is likely to gain from operators who will provide the requisite airborne equipment to utilise the better facilities;

    if his operators are not going to go better than Category I there is no point in improving the ground facilities;

    (c) he must take account of the financial outlay, not only in providing the low visibilities facilities but in maintaining them to the required level of operational efficiency; this may require more manpower.

A regular programme of light cleaning will be necessary, and it is necessary to check on the output of the light fittings after cleaning to ensure that they are serviceable.

There is an understandable requirement for control towers to have up to date information on the operational status of navigational aids especially where Category II or III operations are taking place. The present circuit designs provide ATC with visual monitoring of circuit status, but monitoring of individual light serviceability would be an extremely expensive requirement. In a landing situation as the RVR reduces so the effective visual segment of the system is also reduced. Progressively less information is gained from the outer parts of the approach system and in a Category II situation the vital information required to carry out a successful operation is contained within the threshold and the first 1000 m of runway centreline lighting. Within this area a very high standard of light serviceability is required, but outside it random failures of light fittings are of comparatively minor importance. Therefore should monitoring of individual lights be considered it should be confined to this area.

It can be seen that the provision by the airport operator of the visual aids for Categories II and III operations can represent a substantial additional capital expenditure and increased cost of maintenance. Accordingly there may be sound reasons for suggesting that provision of these facilities should entail a surcharge for such operations.

Mr P. R. V. WALMSLEY, British Airways

I should like to take up the challenge that now is the time to rethink the basic concepts for mass air travel. A major hub airport should be able to accommodate 100 million passengers/year, 60 million in and out and 40 million transfer passengers. I would suggest that throughput would need to exist for 20 000 passengers in a normal peak hour, with provision for a rise to 30 000 passengers. This is not unreasonable because it compares with 60 000 passengers at the peak hour at metro stations.

I would assume that 80% of the passengers will wish to use personal transport, and I should like to assume that the distance passengers walk between the kerbside and aircraft seat is the absolute minimum. I should further like to assume that the minimum transfer time between flights is 10 minutes. Then finally I should like to assume that this leads to a minimum distance between connecting aircraft.

At the moment stand time calls for more stands, more gate room, greater distances, loss of control and loss of staff productivity. There is an alternative approach. Imagine a giant carpark straddling a six-lane highway (Fig.1). The aircraft arrives and finishes up on the right

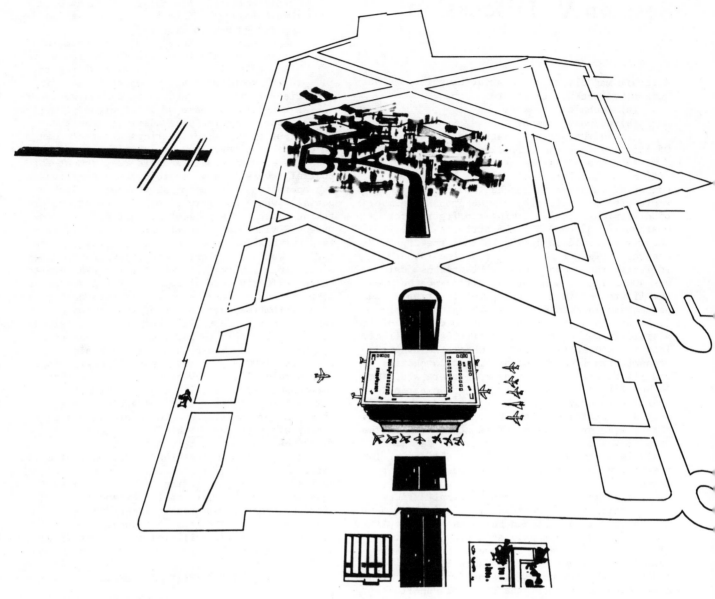

Fig.1

hand side of the terminal. It docks in the area shown, and all the doors open immediately (Fig.2). They are connected by gangways or suspended galleries, and the passengers move through adjustable galleries, either down into the baggage hall or, if they have hand baggage, direct to the terminal at the back. The holds are discharged under cover, and it may be necessary to have larger hold doors to give easier access. In less than five minutes the aircraft is empty and can then be towed off into the marshalling area where it can be inspected.

Looking more closely at the dock area without aircraft and without galleries, into the departure/baggage hall (Fig.3), passengers can descend by lift straight from the carpark above or come from the general terminal area, and can place their baggage into the designated skip. If the departure is some time ahead, they can go back and wait in the general terminal area. On the right hand side there is the same procedure in reverse, where the arriving passenger descends straight into the baggage hall. The skips are basically three trays which lock together to

form a conventional container, and can be handled in many ways, the simplest being by the use of a forklift truck.

The ends of the building can be used for handling conventional aeroplanes, and the building can start with a couple of docks on either side which can be expanded in a modular fashion. A terminal building for 100 million passengers a year would measure 250 m by 1050 m and would need ten docks on each side.

These are some fresh ideas based on the history of transport, and I hope they make a contribution which will enable delegates to think about current problems. I think they meet the criteria of making do with what is already there, because we cannot go on building airports indefinitely.

Sir Peter MASEFIELD

Obviously Peter Walmsley brings great practical experience from the early BEA days to this problem, and it is a very interesting concept.

The idea of having suspended ramps seems to

Fig.2.

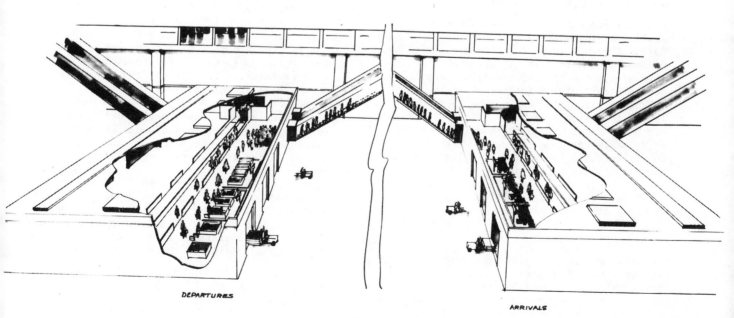

DEPARTURES

ARRIVALS

Fig.3

one to be worthy of exploration. One would be interested in knowing the cost of a building of that type. It might, I suspect, be fairly high. I was intrigued to see that Mr Walmsley showed his building (Fig.1) exactly in the position of Perry Oaks at the west end of two parallel runways at Heathrow. Good for him!

The CHAIRMAN (Mr A. H. Stratford)

There was an interesting discussion on this subject recently at the Royal Aeronautical Society, and the feeling was that mechanical engineers should get to work on the airport situation. Perhaps there is an opportunity for new ideas to be developed.

Mr A. R. WADSWORTH, Van Niekerk Kleyn & Edwards, Pretoria

I should like to take up two points from Dr Pestalozzi's Paper. He mentioned that he thought it was important to reduce the size of airports, and to reduce the number of people present and the time they spent at airports.

A large number of people at airports — and this is particularly true in the case of under-developed countries — are there not to fly but to see people off or to greet people. I feel that in order to maximize the use of existing facilities, we should try and reduce this ratio of passengers to meeters and greeters. After all, airports are concerned with the movement of people by air rather than accommodating a large number of other people.

Dr G. PESTALOZZI (Paper 12)

This goes counter to the basic need of these passengers, which is to combat uncertainty. I believe that these meeters and greeters help passengers to overcome their uncertainties.

Mr G. A. CHAMPNISS (Paper 11)

I am intrigued by Mr Walmsley's concept which would seem to me could give rise to problems so far as flexibility is concerned. It will be necessary to handle at the terminal a multiplicity of types of aircraft ranging from the multideck aircraft of the future, where the sill height of the upper deck may be 35 ft above apron level, to a single deck aircraft. Fin heights may be as great as 125 ft, and I wonder how Mr Walmsley envisages a system which is designed to achieve this level of flexibility. I can see the possibility of a concept designed for one particular type of aircraft, but I think there are some problems if a multiplicity of types of aircraft are to be handled.

Mr WALMSLEY

I should not want to defend the concept as being perfect. I would suggest that if one has galleries which are adjustable then there is no problem. But you may have certain modules for the terminal where you can only handle particular types of aircraft.

Mr D. E. McNAY, Douglas Aircraft Company, California

I see a problem with Mr Walmsley's concept due to the number of services that must be provided to aircraft, such as above deck galleys which need a truck, and cleaners who come with a truck. If all doors are blocked by passenger ingress and egress, the other services must be provided by some other means. It might also be difficult with this system to take care of all the other things that must happen around an aircraft. It is a crowded place from the ground servicing point of view, and the passengers' comfort would suffer if other services were not taken care of.

Mr F. DOVALI, Mexico

In Mexico we should like to have more visitors to the airports. We accept that a certain capacity at the airport is taken up, but they help from the economic point of view. They promote the airports within the community. We would prefer to have more visitors rather than to reduce the number.

Mr J. EDWARDS, Plessey Navaids

I have flown aircraft which have caught fire, and I have been a passenger in an aircraft which has been on fire, so I am not unaware of the hazards of aviation. But I should like to ask Mr Champniss whether airports should buy new fire engines or ILS. Some customers who have limited budgets are faced with the possibility of a choice. Some airlines employ a fire officer, who wants new fire engines. Another part of the airline organization wants ILS. It would be interesting to know whether there is a neutral view on this.

Mr CHAMPNISS

To comment generally, the provision of ILS will improve the regularity of operation, and will permit operations to lower minima than are prescribed for that particular airport with that particular aid. The provision of fire appliances is in the nature of the payment on an insurance premium taken out for something which, sooner or later, will happen through some incident which it is not possible to plan out of the system. It would be a very brave man who would operate an airport without a fire service because of public reaction. BAA has spent many millions on the fire service, and has 394 men employed in the fire service, many of whom will never see what I would term a fire in anger, and long may that continue. But in the final analysis the determination will have to be made by the State certificating the airport. If the State requires a fire service of a certain calibre in order to allow operations to take place, then the airport has no choice in the matter.

Mr EDWARDS

The states I have in mind have one runway, one airport, one authority, and normally three or four people concerned. They have a small amount of money to spend, and the choice is stark though realistic.

13. British concepts

F.A. Sharman, BSc, ACGI, FICE, FRGS, FRSA,
Partner, Sir William Halcrow and Partners

Developing countries need to assess their airport projects on broad economic, political and strategic criteria. Impartial, independent and comprehensive expert advice, such as the British concept of professional service provides, can ensure that studies, designs and construction management are carried out with the client's interests as the paramount consideration. Some examples are quoted. New paving and jointing ideas are described.

1. ECONOMICS
1.1 Benefits
The most difficult but the most essential step in decisions about airports is the estimation of benefit. It will not do nowadays simply to make a forecast of the air traffic that may be expected to use the facility, and to impute benefit to the airport authority on the basis of landing fees, or comparisons with existing airports having similar business. It never was sufficient to do this sort of thing, but in more optimistic days, when growth was considered the inevitable destiny of all activity, it seemed natural enough.

Aviation itself has a poor image when poverty focused aid for developing countries is being applied, and even in the rich but unevenly developed countries, the socially desirable distribution of wealth and conservation of resources is not generally thought to be better served by DC3's and Hercules than by bicycles and carts. So investment in airports has to survive sceptical scrutiny and comparison with the supposed return on various alternative types of spending. Project sponsors, and their consultants and designers, must look very comprehensively at the stream of benefits that may be expected to flow from the work in its life, and compare these with the whole situation arising from a rejection of the project.

A check list for this kind of feasibility or viability study might contain the following:-

Acceptance	Rejection
Improve natural, regional, or local reputation for accessibility in eyes of traders and settlers.	Retain obscurity or reputation for difficult access.
Improve control in emergencies (a) civil strife (b) natural disasters (c) medical service	Lack of control. Absence of medical care.
Attract cosmopolitan influences, technologies, investments.	Retain local loyalties preserve established ways of life.
Attract mass tourism.	Confine tourism to special limited clientele.
Stimulate production of marketable perishable produce.	No stimulus.
Reduce costs of imported goods & delays to supplies.	Reduce investment in transportation.

1.2. The Measurement of Costs and Benefits

1.2.1 It was in Britain that the most elaborate attempt so far made at measuring airport costs and benefits was mounted. The famous Roskill Commission set up a research team which, over a period of two years and at a cost of more than £2m drew up a balance sheet of advantages and disadvantages for four sites (A, B, C, & D) shortlisted as candidates for the third London airport, presumed to be required in the 1980's. The research team and the majority of the Commission were satisfied that the method indicated A: one member of the Commission (Professor Buchanan) said it should be B: the Government chose B but cancelled the whole third airport in July 1974, and there is now a distinct possibility that C will have to be examined. In spite of this discouraging history, the work done on noise and amenity, surface traffic, air traffic, capacity and direct and indirect effect on employment in the area, remains a valuable mine of previously unavailable information. Some of this is relevant to developing countries.

1.2.2 Tangible Factors The most easily acceptable part of the cost/benefit process is the computation of effects that are normally brought in to financial budgets. It might be thought unnecessary to pontificate about this: surely, the reader will say, we all know how to add up the capital and running costs, and how to see whether they can be covered by aviation profits, airports sidelines, and national subsidies? The British precedent of Roskill, not to mention some highly mathematical American exercises, show that it is necessary to plunge quite deeply into fundamental economics and long-range forecasting if even these comparatively elementary sums are going to be right and relevant.

Leaving aside the effects of galloping (or even cantering) inflation, (which in absolute or relative terms is apt to bedevil all investment studies), our knowledge of how transportation efficiency is reflected in the market forces of fares and freight rates is still very sketchy. One is tempted after contemplating the Maplin affair, the Court Line disaster and the irrational decisions being taken all over the world in aviation and airports, to give up balance sheet techniques, and rely on simple opportunism. If somebody can be found ready to pay for an aviation development, don't ask too many questions! If no money is forthcoming, don't waste time looking at the opportunity! To surrender to this is of course an abdication of responsibility by the experts! - la trahison des clercs. The writer makes no apology for thumping a tub against this. If we are not going to press for rationality and breadth of vision against short-sighted expedients and self-interested pressure groups, we are unworthy of any profession and betray any skill we have.

The engineer, the economist, the planner, the architect, the aviation expert, jointly in a team, or severally, all owe to the country they work in, or work for, an honest assessment of the airport as a project in its context. More often than not, they will be prevented from forming or giving their overall, integrated view: "policy" will have been decided by governments, international organizations or commercial empires either before the professionals are consulted, or independently of their work, with unreconciled expert input from in-house professionals in the interested groups. Policy formation, and all decision making, deserves to have the best and most objective technical appreciation as an input. This input must be made more credible, more respectable and more available if it is to make any headway.

Normally, even tangible costs and benefits are not easily brought to a common currency. All the diverse sources of the estimates use their own conventions about discounting and the treatment of tax components. Obviously painstaking and dispassionate integration is essential, and clients who try to get this kind of assessment on the cheap are liable to be misled.

1.2.3. The 'intangibles'. Cost/benefit technique acquired, and still has, a bad reputation mainly because it is popularly supposed to be unperceptive of non-material values. Nothing discredited the Roskill research team in the eyes of the public so much as the use of the insurance value of a Norman church to express the weight which its preservation should have in the balance sheet. Less remarked, but equally unacceptable, was the basing of noise disbenefit value on property cost changes,

rather than on the number of people affected and the intensity of their annoyance or distress. These were real defects, but they are now recognized and can be avoided in future. What remains as permanently valuable is the systematic examination and ranking of non-material or unquantifiable factors, to be put beside the result of the quantifiable part of the balance sheet, so that we can ask the meaningful question - is such and such an expenditure sensible in attaining this and that benefit, with certain stated unavoidable drawbacks?

It is commonly said that the sensitivity to environmental or amenity factors recently developed in the industrialized countries (and which has largely crippled their ability to make provision for future airport needs) has no relevance in developing countries, or in the oil-rich states. This opinion undervalues the ability of developing countries to respond, in their own way, to the opportunity of learning from past mistakes in other places. It may be true that people who are just surviving on incomes around £100 p.a. are in no position to quibble about aircraft noise or the finer points of airport design, but it is brutish to ascribe to their feelings of distress or their opportunities of advancement any less importance than we are learning to attribute to more articulate and economically powerful communities.

1.2.4. <u>Illustrations of Predominant Factors</u>
1.2.4.1. <u>Defence</u> Military requirements are generally beyond the area in which non-political interdisciplinary expert teams can claim decisive knowledge of justification. British consultants and contractors have proved their ability to accept the urgencies and constraints by governments in threatened circumstances, and to achieve strategic and tactical objectives in design and construction at rates of working normally considered impossible or absurdly costly. The construction costs of airports and air bases are generally insignificant compared with those of equipping, deploying and using air and ground forces, so it may make sense to accept a doubling or tripling of the minimum attainable prices in order to make facilities available very quickly. Since competition between contractors often cannot be used in these circumstances, it becomes vital to establish the concept of the totally independent consultant, to whom the client may safely entrust the whole task of reducing waste and extravagances to an absolute minimum, whilst maintaining the over-riding necessity of target dates for operational readiness.

1.2.4.2. <u>Prestige</u> Rulers of many modern states are moved by considerations that have little to do with a precise optimisation of global resources. It is not immoral or unprofessional to accept that the lawful authorities of a country have the right to decide that they want an airport, even if the need is purely political or psychological. One may feel that the money would be better spent on schools and hospitals, where these are lacking, but such opinions must be conveyed through political channels, rather than by professional pressure. The concept of separation between professional advice and political decision-making is just as important as the professional conscience mentioned in section 1.2.2.

1.2.4.3. <u>Stimulus to Economies</u> Ideally, this factor should be capable of inclusion in the cost/benefit balance sheet, but in practice it generally has to be accepted as part of the policy data. If the existence of a new airport can unlock a source of productivitiy which previously remained untapped, the scale of the action so triggered off needs to be conceived in terms of national or regional economics and politics, and translated into terms of possible traffic for the airport, rather than the other way round. There are many tropical and sub-tropical locations where perishable produce could be economically exported to distant markets if an air freight service were sufficiently on the spot and were organized to suit supply and demand. In the long run, the capital cost of the airport with its storage facilities is a small component of the investment, but it has to precede any other action, and its justification is an act of faith.

1.3. <u>The Economics of Selection</u>
1.3.1. <u>Location</u> So far, the discussion has been concerned with factors for or against the airport as such. An integrated "economics" approach is equally necessary when the best of a number of possible locations is sought. Indeed the 'Roskill' approach was conceived simply for this purpose, though its technique inevitably drew in questions of justification and timing. The plainest lesson was that for a large international airport primarily serving passenger needs, surface accessibility in terms of passengers' travel time and running cost of their vehicles, projected over the life of the airport and discounted back as a capital cost, bulks much larger than construction and site cost differentials between one location and another. In developing countries we have nothing like the volume of business and pleasure travel that originates and terminates through London, but when, for instance, the Cairo airport system is studied, likely trends over the next 30 years make the accessibility question much more influential than it seems today. Equally, the residents in Heliopolis may be expected to become less tolerant to airport noise burden than they appear to be at present.

1.3.2. <u>Capacity</u> The cost of delays to aircraft due to runway occupancy and air traffic control, have to be balanced against investment costs for additional runways, taxiways and aprons, and sophisticated landing aids. Fuel cost increases have increased delay costs rather more than construction costs, but the balance has to be calculated up to date for each project.

1.3.3. <u>Life</u> Future technology is impossible to prophesy, and huge, heavy-duty runways may not be needed one day. Must we allow for

writing off the cost of such installations in 15 years? In 30 years? There may be a critical difference between such assumptions. I suggest that steep ascents and descents will always be extravagent in fuel, and as long as flat approaches and take offs are made, our present runway designs will serve a purpose. Thirty years seems a reasonable figure therefore.

1.3.4. <u>Standards</u> Safety is the dominant factor in the selection of standards and appropriate Categories. If the proper facilities cannot be afforded, the whole project must wait until they can. There remain some very difficult judgements on whether infringements of recommended criteria can or cannot be accepted when a runway is licensed. This is a matter for earnest conference between the designer, the licensing authority, the airline operators, and experienced pilots. All should have their say before the authority makes its decision.

1.4. <u>Controls</u>

1.4.1. <u>Feasibility</u> The performance of a full scale feasibility study for any proposed major airport development should be the best means of labelling each sector of the project with its programme of costs, along with the justification of the programme and variations of it linked to alternative indices of growth.

1.4.2. <u>Design</u> The concept of design by consultants, finalized in every detail so that competitive tenders can be compared and contractors can be held to their offer with minimal variation, retains advantages where adequate time exists and where requirements are stable. Often however the client needs to display a guaranteed package, and a turnkey offer is the only way forward. In real emergencies, and where there is confidence in a particular contractor working under the supervision of an independant consultant, a cost plus system will allow complete flexibility so that changes of requirement can be catered for by design changes without disruption, and design can be telescoped into the construction programme. Provided that waste is avoided and motivations are strong, the additional speed so achieved can save as much as the price-cutting of competitive tendering.

1.4.3. <u>Contract Documentation</u> Even if package deal or cost-plus methods are used, it is advisable to maintain interim and final measurements just as if a rate-and-quantity contract existed. Specifications, contract conditions and priced bills of quantity in traditional form, even if they have to be prepared during construction, serve to control and to check the end product, and prevent many potential misunderstandings, disputes, and claims.

1.4.4. <u>Supervision</u> The organization responsible for the design should always be invited to supervise construction, so that modifications can be made when criteria or site conditions change from those originally envisaged, and so that responsibility for the end product is un-

ambiguous. The idea that someone can write a
legalistic contract for the production of a design in such a way that no modification could be
needed, and so that supervision is either not
required, or can be taken on by anybody, is an
illusion.   It is characteristically, though not
of course exclusively, a British concept that a
client authority, having selected its consultants and contractors with great care, will get
the best out of them by recognizing that they
have a strong identification with the client's
interests, rather than by treating them as
potential cheats, liars and incompetents.

2. LOCATION AND LAYOUT

2.1. Physical Constraints Mountains, coastlines
      bogs and shifting dunes seem the obvious
obstacles in the search for the practicable runway. None of these is absolute in preventing
construction: Sharjah (UAE) new runway is on
dune sand (fig. 1), Dubai is built on tooth-
paste-type subkha which, before selected filling
was applied, gave unreliable support to wheeled
vehicles (fig. 2). The tortuous coastline of
Canouan (Windward Islands) did not prevent an
airstrip from being steered across an isthmus
between two hills (fig. 3), and at Bequia
Island the possibility exists of planning off
the top of an unnaturally straight but rugged
ridge to give a hill-top airstrip 60m wide and
630 m long, with completely unobstructed approaches (fig. 4 - the line shows one possible
runway to which the ridge might be carved at
reasonable cost). These are extreme examples:
more generally the precisely optimum line and
level has to be sought among many reasonably
possible alternatives, and the cost/benefit
balance has to be invoked for the small sub-
decision on location, length and obstacle
tolerance just as carefully as the project
feasibility has to be established.

2.2. Runway lengths Typical length criteria for
      short, medium and long-land runways are
2100, 2700 and 3700 metres respectively, but
when minimum-cost emergency or occasional-use
airstrips for very small populations are considered, the 600m airstrip has to be considered.
An illustration of usability against capital
and maintenance costs for a system of 9 airstrips is shown as fig. 5: in this, each
horizontal strip covers the type of aircraft
shown in the vertical columns (only partially
if there are weight or operational restrictions
and the last two columns indicate the range of
maintenance and capital costs respectively needed to bring and retain the facility at the
usability state indicated by the corresponding
strip.   This presentation helps the airstrip
user to select the best combination of investments for the aircraft types and movement
patterns he has in mind.

2.3 Capacity
2.3.1. Runways and taxiways A single runway can
      handle 50 movements per hour if the taxiway
system provides by pass capability at runway
ends along with a minimum number of places
where taxi speed must change. Taxiways with
23m width and stabilised shoulders, and 45m

radius fillets at turns will suffice for all
aircraft.

2.3.2. Terminal facilities In developing coun-
        tries, the adequacy of terminal building
and maintenance facilities often lags behind
need, and the concept of minimising passenger
misery is not sufficiently firmly established
anywhere.   A high proportion of all facilities
is permanently in a temporary condition: consultants, contractors and client authorities
all pay far too little attention to the conditions imposed on travellers and airport workers during the endless periods of construction
and alteration. It is suggested that a named
individual of each relevant organization
should be charged with responsibility for frequent sampling of conditions during design and
construction phases, and for contributing to
the maintenance of reasonable standards.

The following check list of features required in terminal design may seem a restatement of
the obvious, but so many components are so
often neglected, both in temporary and in permanent airports in developing countries (not to
mention places where there is no excuse whatever for deficiencies), that the use of space
in this paper for repetition seems justified.

(a) Sizing of all functional areas should be
based on enplaned passengers, visitor ratios
and aircraft operations forecasts.

(b) Adequate curb space for all automotive
vehicles, for enplaning and arriving passengers
together with parking for rental cars and taxi
queues should be provided.

(c) Adequate convenient parking facilities
close to the terminal area.

(d) A simple, clear and concise sign system to
direct both automotive and pedestrian movements
to, around the vicinity of, and within terminal
areas.

(e) A well-lighted, easily understandable
flight information system providing airline
arrival and departure information at multiple
locations, together with a simple system for
updating such information.

(f) A well-designed public address system, with
good acoustics for passenger paging and other
informational purposes.

(g') Easily determined, fully signed direct
passenger flow routes to permit them to proceed
individually through the terminal to and from
aircraft with minimum changes in levels and
direction.

(h) Secure, rapid and efficient handling procedure facilities for baggage, cargo and mail.
Flow routes for these should not conflict with
passenger flow.

(j) Adequate, properly located concessions for
the convenience of passengers, visitors and
sightseers which do not interfere with passenger flows.

(k) Adequate, properly located airline staff
function areas.

Fig.1. Sand dunes on site of Sharjah new runway

Fig.2. Subkha surface in Dubai giving unreliable support for wheeled vehicles

Fig.3. Runway (left centre), Canouan Island, avoiding topographical constraints

Fig.4. Ridge on Bequia Island, showing possible runway by decapitation

Airfield	Beaver	Skyvan	Caribou	Hercules	Viscount	BAC.1-11	Maintenance (units of currency/year)	Capital (units of currency)
A	////	////	////	////	////		4000 → 16800	8000
	////	////	////	////	////	////	750 → 6000	550000
	////	////	////	////	////	////	500 + 200	350000
B	////	////	////	////	////		4000 + 1000	9000
	////	////	////	////			2500 + 500	22000
C	////	////	////				3000 → 10000	24000
	////	////	////				600	33000
D	////	////	////				3500	6000
	////	////	////				300	45000
E	////	////	////				1500	6000
	////	////	////				750	106000
F	////	////					3500	5000
	////	////	////				600	43000
G	////	////	////				2500	6500
H	////	////	////	////			2500	4500
J	////	////					500	1500

Where squares are incompletely hatched a weight or other limitation applies to that particular type of aircraft

Fig.5. Summary of usability, capital and maintenance expenditure

Fig.6. Concrete runway paving with contraction joint sawn too late

(1) Mechanical equipment, particularly sophisti-cated types affecting airline operations, should not be selected and installed without consulta-tion with the airlines.

(m) Adequate protection of passengers from exposure to weather, blast, noise, fumes and ground service vehicles.

Covered loading bridges providing weather protection and direct passenger enplaning and deplaning to and from aircraft are now generally considered to be a requirement at large and medium hub locations.

3. PAVING
3.1. Novel Solutions Designing from first prin-ciples rather than from tables can solve some tricky problems. At Dubai (see again fig. 2) faith in the possibility of effective fill material control and compaction allowed a run-way to be built up very cheaply to a level where ground water gave no more problems, and where loads were effectively spread before they reach-ed the toothpaste layer beneath. At another and more inaccessible place a runway 4000m long by 50m wide (with adjuncts) containing 120,000 cu. m. of paving quality concrete of 350 to 300 mm thickness was required to be operational 7 months after instruction to start work (design included). Slab or joint reinforcement could hardly have been placed in the time, but crack inducers dividing the paved area into 4.5m squares provided aggregate interlock and pre-vented uncontrolled cracking. The need is well illustrated in fig. 6, where the result of accidental omission of the crack inducers at one location is seen. An attempt was made to saw the joint, but the exact timing needed for this to be a success was missed, and shrinkage prod-uced a through-slab unintended crack.

3.2. Joint Movement It has seemed logical to many designers to take no chances at all with rigid pavement joints, and to provide for temperature movements and long-term shrinkage by carefully designed expansion and contraction joints incorporating sliding steel bars for shear transfer. With large temperature ranges and deliberate avoidance of restraints, very large progressive movements of slabs can build up, with embarrassing conditions round the edges for lighting, drainage and other fixtures. The success of the unreinforced crack-induced system described in section 3.1 above encourages the belief that cheaper concrete pavings with no joint filler problems can be relied upon where rain penetration and local wetting of sub-base or subgrade is not a problem. If each element of the paving is thought of as being anchored to the earth's crust and at its centre, all the size variations of the element can be kept with-in acceptable pore-size limits, and loss of aggregate interlock can be avoided, by choosing the correct size of the element.

3.3. Gravel and Grass Airstrips for remote communities, small islands and flying doc-tors often receive less attention from exper-ienced experts than they should, simply because cheapness is so essential and fees are unavail-able or begrudged. What is at stake is the

safety and feasibility of key activities, the value of which is by no means reflected in the availability of capital for construction. The number of unsurfaced airstrips and potential airstrips in developing countries justifies a small specialist team being ready to integrate itself with the local problem at short notice, offering a world wide experience of grass roots, laterite gradings, ant-hill demolitions, im-provised markings, ad hoc wind observation and all the many other aspects of "intermediate airport technology".

Apart from small aircraft, the following types are some which have successfully operated from "unsurfaced" runways:

Lockheed C130 (Hercules)	DC3
BAC 1-11 / 475 series	Short Skyvan
Boeing 737 (with gravel kit)	Islander
CL 44	Trilander
Vickers Viscount 800 series	Twin Otter
DC6	DH Beaver
Fokker-VFW F.27	Antonov An-22

4. ILLUSTRATIVE CASES.
4.1. Canouan (St. Vincent) The landing strip recently constructed on this small West Indian island (see fig.3) was originally in-tended to cater for HS748 aircraft in phase 1, with 8 to 10 movements per week. A surface dressed crushed rock base was specified for this purpose. Before work started (two years ago) the world recession compelled economies, and provision was reduced to cater for Island-ers. The dimensions of the strip were thus reduced, and the surfacing was changed to a grass-promoting granular grading.

4.2. United Arab Emirates A new runway at Sharjah raised the problem of the possible migration of dune sand into the interstices of coarser sub-base material. Trials were carried out with a recently developed type of fabrics at the interface, and although it was not poss-ible sufficiently to prove the system in time to adopt it on the runway, the road where the trial was performed can be compared with the behaviour of the runway, for which the trad-itional solution of extra sub-base depth was adopted.

4.3. Oman A desert airstrip was proving diffi-cult to maintain under fairly frequent movements by C130's, Viscounts, Skyvans and Beavers. A crash construction programme called for an immediate capacity to receive 30 move-ments/day, of which two thirds would be C130's, CL 44's or DC6's. This was achieved (with an LCN value of 60) by employing 2 large water tankers, 2 or 3 graders, and 2 heavy rollers whenever possession could be granted. While the required result was achieved, it would be more economical to provide a surfaced strip, if the traffic is to persist, rather than to tie up the maintenance plant indefinitely.

4.4. Licata (Sicily). The Mezzogiorno region of Italy, which includes the island of Sicily, has many of the characteristics of a developing country. A report was required on the compatibility of a proposed new airport primarily intended to stimulate tourism, (run-

way length 3000 m) with the extension of industrial development, also planned to assist the
economy of the area.   British consultants were
entrusted with the study, partly because they
were demonstrably detached from any commercial
or political bias towards either form of development.   The report, which examined possible
runway variations, the nature and probable
future of obstacles and intrusion in the flight
paths and horizontal and conical surfaces, smoke
pollution, surface access, navigation aid interference and amenity and urban planning factors,
concluded that the two project programmes could
proceed if certain precautions were observed.
The report was accepted by the Cassa per il
Mezzogiorno.

5.   CONCLUSIONS

5.1.   <u>Policy</u>   Airport policies rest on fragile
and obscure predicitions about need, capacity and benefit many years ahead. Decisions
to build or not to build are nevertheless in-
escapable: it cannot be best to let matters
drift in ignorance of the effects of action
and inaction.

5.2.   <u>Studies</u> Professional, impartial, interdisciplinary study should be applied to
each situation, so that decision makers at
least know, as far as it is possible for anyone
to know, the most probable consequence of the
available options.

5.3.   <u>Feed-back</u> Studies should be commissioned
in an orderly sequence, after the future
dilemmas of decision have been identified. The
teams to be concerned should be offered some

degree of continuity of work, or at least some
probable programme of intermittent activity.
Their professional status should be recognized,
encouraged and respected: they should be protected from pressure groups, and the criteria
assembled by the decision-makers should be fed
back to the team continuously.

5.4.   <u>Location</u> Few places on the earth's surface are incapable of being provided with
aircraft landing facilities.   The cost of
making and maintaining runways is a small
fraction of the total cost of providing an air
service of reasonable frequency.

5.5.   <u>Paving Techniques</u> Important economies in
concrete paving, both in cost and in
construction time, may be possible by the
simplification of jointing systems and the
omission of reinforcement generally.

5.6.   <u>Intermediate Technology</u> Aviation can
play its part in self-help programmes for
developing countries even at early stages of
growth. Remote communities provided with simple
airstrips can be relieved of the most unacceptable kinds of deprivation, and can learn to
combine an unsophisticated life-style or even
a bare subsistence level of existence with increasing contact with the outside world. From
this a controlled advancement of the quality
of life may follow. Tact and foresight in the
planning and execution of airstrip projects in
undeveloped areas is a part of the considered
and integrated approach to airport design and
construction which is advocated in this paper.

14. Airports and tourism on two Pacific islands

L.Fisher
Airport Consultant, California

The author, studying the thesis that there is a beneficial impact from tourism on "developing countries," considers the impact of tourism on the socio-economic character of two Western Pacific islands, namely, Guam, a U.S. Territory, and Saipan, a part of the Trust Territory of the Pacific Islands. Air transportation and airport facilities required to accommodate the tourist traffic are discussed.

INTRODUCTION

1. In September 1975, the Conference Chairman, Mr. Geoffrey Edwards, asked me to contribute a paper dealing with the development of tourism on one of the islands of the Pacific, based on air transport. Instead of emphasizing airport design, with which you all are intimately familiar, this paper considers the socio-economic impact of the tourist boom on Guam, and as it may impact Saipan just 110 miles north.

2. Tourism in the American part of the Pacific is not parallel to tourism in "developing countries." While the islands of the Pacific are "developing" in the technical sense, they do not have the labor-intensive economies which so typically characterize "developing nations" as that term is conventionally used. In the case of the two islands treated here, capital is needed but available, while labor is definitely in short supply.

3. Guam, a U.S. Territory, is the southernmost of the Mariana Islands. Situated in the Western Pacific approximately 3,700 miles from Hawaii and 1,350 miles from Japan, it is the largest and most populated island between Hawaii and the Philippines (see Figure 1). Covering an area of approximately 210 square miles, the island is about 30 miles long, ranging 4 to 8 miles in width. Guam is the gateway to both the Marianas and Micronesia.

4. Saipan, about 110 miles to the north of Guam, is the largest island and center of population, government and business of the Northern Mariana Islands. Its area is only 46 square miles, a fifth of Guam's area. Saipan is the seat of government of what has been, since World War II the Trust Territory of the Pacific Islands, a United Nations Trusteeship. While Guam has been a U.S. territory since 1898, the Northern Marianas were governed by Germany until 1914 and then by the Japanese under a League of Nations mandate until the end of World War II. Both Guam and Saipan are part of Micronesia (see Figure 2).

BRIEF HISTORY OF MARIANA ISLANDS

5. Guam and Saipan have experienced acculturation to Western technology. Contact with the West first began in the Marianas with Magellan's visit to Guam in 1521. By 1688, a Jesuit mission on Guam had begun to spread the Christian religion; the Spaniards always placed great emphasis on the Christianization of the peoples in their colonies. In the Marianas this policy resulted in severe wars which reduced the number of Chamorros from about 50,000 in the 17th century to 4,000 by the early 18th century. Large numbers of settlers and soldiers were brought in from the Philippines and Mexico resulting in the disappearance of much of traditional Chamorro culture. Today the Chamorro language is heavily mixed with Spanish words, and the family has changed from its original matriarchal form to a Spanish style patriarchal form.

6. By the late 19th century, Spain had sovereignty and nominally governed all of what is now the Trust Territory, except for the Marshalls. Guam was ceded by Spain to the United States in 1898 as a result of the Spanish-American War and Spain sold her remaining rights in Micronesia to Germany in 1899.

7. Guam's population grew from 9,676 in 1900 to 85,000 in 1970. It is currently estimated at 100,000. Guamanians account for 56% of the total population; military, 28%; statesiders, 7%; Filipinos, 6%; and the rest consist of Chinese, Japanese, Koreans, and other ethnic groups. Although the Spanish culture has had the most powerful influence on lifestyles, one can witness the "old ways" giving in to styles acquired through constant exposure to the American mode of living.

8. The U.S. military establishment on Guam is by far the single largest economic generator. In fiscal 1974, military expenditures identified with Guam were $183.5 million, 66% ($122.3 million) of which went to salaries of 10,500 military personnel and about 5,286 civilian employees, of which 4,768 were Guamanian. The

total military population on Guam, including dependents, was approximately 24,500. The military is the major landholder on the island. The Navy holds approximately 17% and the Air Force 15% of land on Guam.

9. The Northern Marianas, while of the same Chamorro/Spanish background as Guam, reflect much of the Japanese influence resulting from Japan's occupation from 1914 to 1945. Japan concentrated on rapid development of agriculture and industry on Saipan and in the Northern Marianas. Of a 1940 Japanese population of 84,478 in the entire Trust Territory, 46,000 were on Saipan, Tinian and Rota, dominantly Saipan. In the same year, the indigenous natives numbered less than 5,000 and were employed mostly as manual laborers. This large scale colonization went hand in hand with attempts to turn the indigenous population into Japanese nationals through education and propaganda. To a surprising extent, the success of this effort remains evident today. By 1940, just before the Pacific War, Saipan looked like a Japanese city with restaurants, streets, automobiles, post offices, and many comforts. All were obliterated in the June 1945 landings. The U.S. Navy then counted 2,966 Chamorro, 1,025 Carolinians, and about 15,500 Japanese and Koreans, all of whom were immediately repatriated, ending significant agriculture in the Northern Marianas.

10. Today the Northern Marianas indigenous Chamorro and Carolinian population has increased to about 13,000, of which only about 3,600 are productive, full-time workers, with perhaps another 1,000 part-time and self-employed subsistence workers. Unemployment does not exist. Some 1,000 aliens are also employed on Saipan. The majority of these are skilled and semi-skilled construction labor, with the remainder holding middle and upper level management jobs. The indigenous labor force consists mainly of mid and lower level white collar workers engaged in government and retail services.

11. Saipan, which has over 85% of the Northern Marianas population, at current growth rates is expected to have an indigenous work force of only 5,100 persons by 1993. This work force can be totally absorbed by non-tourist employment already available on island.

12. Guam has an entirely different demographic character, but the labor situation is equally critical -- there is no unemployment.

TOURISM A RECENT DEVELOPMENT ON GUAM
13. Guam was under the direct administration of the U.S. Navy from 1898 to 1950 except for the brief period of Japanese occupation in World Way II. Thus, Guam's people were isolated from the Northern Marianas with their Japanese administration. Travel to Guam, even by a U.S. citizen, required a U.S. Navy security clearance until August 21, 1962 and tourism was unknown. The inauguration of the first direct scheduled flights between Guam and Japan on May 1, 1967 should be considered the beginning of tourism

on Guam. Since then, the principal visitor to Guam, over 85%, has been the tourist from Japan who stays an average of four days. Guam's tourist industry is thus entirely tied to Japan's economy and travel policies.

14. Tourism has grown from 4,500 visitors in 1967 to 260,568 in 1974. The number of direct scheduled airline flights between Guam and Japan increased from two each way per week in 1967 to 20 in 1974. The number of hotel rooms increased from 267 in 1967 to 2,582 in 1974. Prior to mid-1972, growth of tourism was restricted by the availability of hotel rooms, as shown in Table 1. In the last few years, many luxurious hotels developed on Ypao Beach (see Figure 3) can accommodate substantial growth. Between 1967 and 1972, tourist growth was 80% per year, but by 1973, this had declined to 31% and to 8% in 1974, reflecting both the recession in Japan and the competition of Hawaii and other tourist destinations for the Japanese market.

Table 1. Guam Air Traffic and Hotel Rooms 1963-1974.

FISCAL YEAR	AIRLINE DEPARTURES	AIRLINE PASSGRS. DEPLANED	HOTEL ROOMS NUMBER	DEPLANED PASSGRS. PER ROOM
1963	1,651	10,675	NA	NA
1964	1,350	18,371	75	245
1965	1,319	19,715	140	141
1966	1,777	22,265	175	127
1967	2,295	25,435	267	95
1968	2,475	37,978	518	73
1969	2,586	50,566	680	75
1970	3,910	92,475	1,019	91
1971	5,007	136,161	1,235	110
1972	5,672	184,280	2,093	88
1973	7,256	250,854	2,253	111
1974	7,963	303,705	2,582	118

15. Guam and Saipan are the closest warm weather tourist destinations to Japan. The round trip air fare between Guam and Tokyo is only US$217. Until 1973, most Japanese tourists flew as scheduled passengers as part of a tour package. In 1973, the all-inclusive charter business began to generate a substantial business. In both instances the tourist bought the air passage as well as hotel rooms, meals and sightseeing tours as a package.

16. The tourists have changed Guam from a place where the principal restaurants were military clubs to one with a large variety of fine restaurants and clubs, all with Japanese language menus. Commercialization is becoming quite evident in all facets of Guam's private and public sectors. After several years of rapid growth, symptoms of a maturing economy are beginning to surface. Growth in the private sector has outpaced that of the public sector. In the public sector, one now finds a great

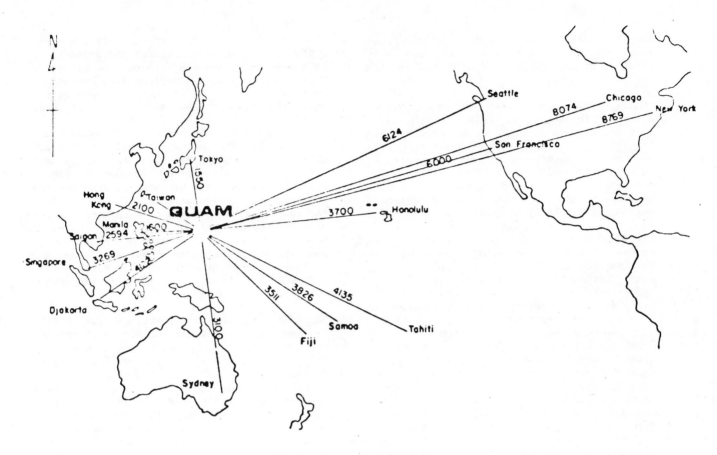

Fig.1. Location of Guam

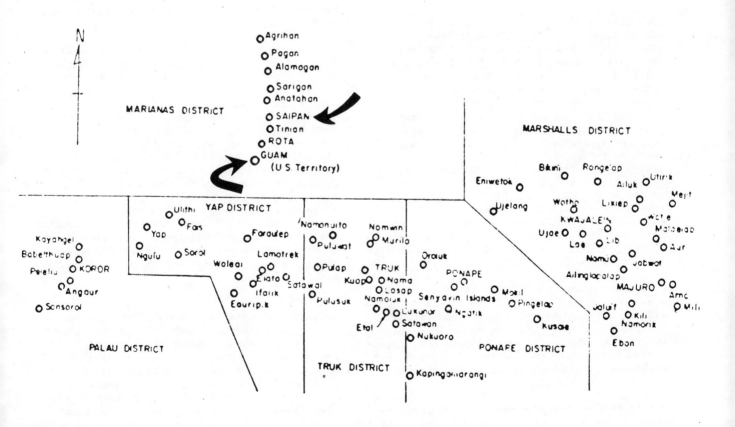

Fig.2. Location of Saipan

many physical as well as socio-economic problems, such as an inadequate road system, a
shortage of skilled labor, and an over-loaded
public utility system.

GUAM'S TERMINAL FACILITIES VERY INADEQUATE
17. Guam is the perfect example of the fact
that the climate and tourist accommodations,
not the airport other than adequate runways,
are the sole factors in attracting tourism.
Guam's 1965 terminal facilities, designed for
one-third or less of the present traffic volume, are so congested, confused and uncomfortable as to regularly be described "a mess."

18. Guam International Airport consists only
of the civil apron and terminal building area
abutting the U.S. Navy's Air Station at Agana,
Guam. Currently it consists of only 24.43
acres -- all that was thought required for
civil use in 1964 when the Navy commissioned
Alfred A. Yee & Associates, Inc., Architects
& Engineers of Honolulu, to design a typhoon
proof civil terminal as part of the reconstruction program after the devastation of
Typhoon Karen in 1962. At that time, Pan American was the only airline serving Guam, with
three flights westbound and three eastbound
each week. The terminal building was then a
decrepit, rusty Quonset (see Figure 4).

19. Alfred A. Yee & Associates designed and
in 1965 the Navy built a Departure Building
and an Arrival Building separated by a covered
open air court used for visitor and passenger
circulation (see Figure 5).

20. Total enclosed space was approximately
22,050 square feet (Departure Building = 11,025
square feet; Arrival Building = 11,025 square
feet) with a covered court of 12,033 square
feet. All structures are of a combination of
poured-in-place, precast and prestressed concrete. According to Yee's report, "The buildings are designed to handle facilities and
traffic for two scheduled airlines on a ten
year projection with a peak of three jet aircraft on the ground at one time." Within 5
years, there were 4 airlines serving Guam and
frequently 5 or 6 jet aircraft were on the
ground at the same time. By 1970, the facilities had been totally outgrown, and temporary
buildings for Continental/Air Micronesia and
Japan Air Lines and a typhoon proof, reinforced
concrete Air Cargo Building had been constructed (see Figure 6). Passenger facilities,
crowded in 1970 with 92,000 passengers, became
unbearably congested in 1975 with over 300,000
passengers, and the two buildings were joined
with an air conditioned holdroom and transit
lounge, a new Duty Free Shop and a long needed
spectators' deck. The arrivals space and associated Immigration and Customs facilities were
doubled and planning for additional terminal
facilities accelerated.

21. A 1970 master plan proposed the acquisition of some 69 acres from the U.S. Navy, 144
acres of Government of Guam land, and 26 acres
of private land, enlarging the civil area to

263 acres. Construction of entirely new aircraft parking aprons, terminal and support
buildings and roads was planned (see Figure 7).
This plan could not be implemented, however,
until formal negotiations with the Navy were
concluded; a lengthy process.

22. In mid-1974, the runways and taxiways of
the Naval Air Station were formally made available for civil joint use under the long sought
Joint Use Agreement between GovGuam and the
U.S. Navy. The Naval Air Station consists of
two parallel runways oriented 60°-240°, with
partial parallel taxiways on each side. Extensive USN operational and support facilities are
located on the southeast side of the runway
complex, and a large Navy housing area and mis-
cellaneous facilities are located along the
northwest side, near the civil aircraft apron
and terminal complex.

23. The principal runway (06L-24R) is 10,015
feet in length and is served with high intensity runway lights, has an approach light system
and both civil and military precision approach
guidance. Visual approach slope indicators are
installed on both ends of the principal runway.
The secondary runway (06R-24L) is 8,000 feet
in length and has medium intensity lighting.
Several non-precision instrument approach procedures are published for the airport.

24. As part of the 1974 Joint Use Agreement,
the Navy agreed to transfer 69 acres contig-
uous to the civil terminal area which prompted
adoption of a construction program to complete
the new terminal complex by 1981 replacing the
current congested facilities.

25. Since development of the 1965 terminal
facilities, Guam has become not only a major
transfer point in Pan American's Western Pacific System with over 120,000 transiting passengers in 1974, but also a turn around station
for Pan American and Japan Air Lines flights
from Japan. A third and minor role is as connection point for Continental/Air Micronesia.
Pan American's transfer function requires as
many as 3 or 4 Pan American jet aircraft on the
ground simultaneously to effect transfers between flights from or to the U.S. and Manila,
Singapore, Hong Kong, Okinawa and Taipai.
Heavy congestion of transit passengers, coupled
with arriving and departing passengers and
Continental/Air Micronesia's connecting passengers, markedly increase public circulation
space requirements.

26. Flights to and from Japan also require
increased circulation space, since Japanese
tour groups tend to "bunch up" and move as a
tightly knit mass. Unless the terminal building is designed specifically to accommodate
such group movements, normally allocated circulation space can be repeatedly plugged up,
causing successive waves of congestion in otherwise adequately designed areas. This group
congestion is particularly evident at concourse
intersections, checkpoints and at curbsides.
Anytime there is a hesitation in the group flow,

Fig.3. *Reef Hotel, one of the several new Japanese owned hotels on Guam's Ypao Beach, less than 2 miles from the Airport.*

Fig.4. *1963 Quonset Hut Terminal – Guam*

Fig.5. *1974 New Terminal – Guam*

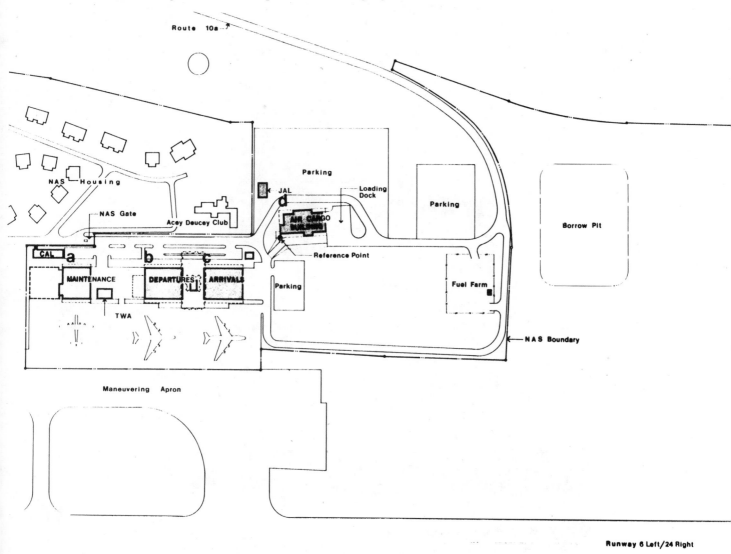

Fig.6. 1974 Terminal Area Site Plan - Guam

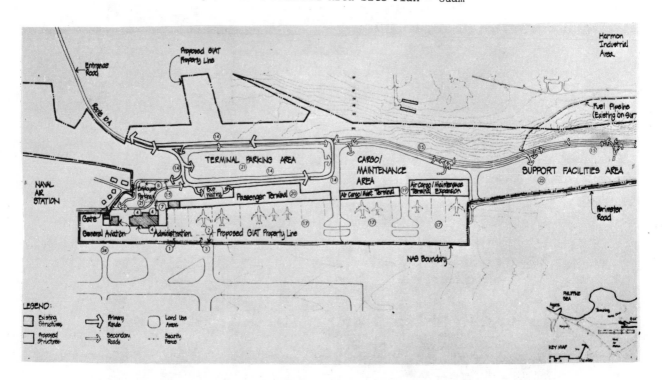

Fig.7. Planned Expansion Terminal Area - Guam

the group masses. This became the key to any design for accommodating Japanese tour groups -- flow them with minimum points of interruption -- and at each point provide space for the massing action.

27. Much of the tourism investment and operations is dominated by the Japanese with heavy ownership of hotels and tourist related businesses. Guam observed that when Japanese financed hotels were constructed, alien labor was used (dominantly Filipino), and many materials were imported from Japan. Much of the food served the tourists is imported from Japan, frequently prepared by Japanese chefs and often served by Japanese waiters and waitresses. Hotels are staffed by Japanese management. Most escorted island tours are by Japanese owned tour companies, travelling in Japanese busses, and with Japanese language tour conductors. When a non-Japanese wants to take a tour, it is rare if he hears the discourse on the tour sights in his own language. A recent phenomenon in Guam, which is now beginning to appear in Saipan, are multilingual signs, menus, brochures and books printed in English and Japanese. In some restaurants catering dominantly to the Japanese, one must ask for an English language menu.

28. Many of the Japanese tourists fly to and from Guam on Japan Air Lines and use a sheaf of coupons for virtually all purchases on Guam and Saipan. These coupons are sold by the Japanese tour operator to the group in Japan and, as a consequence, the tourist introduces little direct money into the local economy. The Australians are said to call the Japanese style of tourism the "boomerang technique" since much of what the tourists spend winds up back in Japan. Many critics claim that all that is generated are Japanese investments with Japanese management utilizing low-skilled indigenous employees. Many alien or immigrant employees are required to supplement the labor shortage on Guam. In 1974, of a total employment of 38,480, almost 40% were immigrants or aliens. In construction trades and services (hotel construction and operation, restaurants and tourist related activities) the percentage of immigrant and alien employment increased to 63%, with two-thirds of these skilled construction workers on temporary off-island hire. It is clear that while many economic benefits spin off to the local economy, the major benefits flow off island and significant changes in life style, religious and family character result.

TOURISM ON SAIPAN IS YET TO BE REALIZED
29. Until July 1962, the U.S. Navy administered Saipan and access was severely restricted. In that year, the Trust Territory Government, administered by the United States Department of Interior for the United Nations Trusteeship Council, moved from rusted Quonset headquarters on Guam to a miniature American suburb on Saipan abandoned by the C.I.A.

30. Amazed officials accustomed to working and living in cramped Quonset huts suddenly found themselves in possession of a two-story concrete office building, 159 first-class housing units, an elaborate social club building and extensive support facilities. Paved streets and broad, neatly trimmed grass lawns gave the place the appearance of an expensive subdivision in the U.S.

31. This complex, which quickly came to be known as "Capitol Hill," became the governmental center for the Trust Territory and the Congress of Micronesia. The existence of this self-contained community on a windswept hilltop with a spectacular marine view on two sides remained unknown to the general public until the island was transferred from the U.S. Navy in 1962.

32. The C.I.A. had developed this complex, with a secured area covering the northern half of Saipan, as the quarters for a U.S. staff to train Nationalist Chinese guerrillas. Strict military control of travel enabled the C.I.A. to run its program on the island with virtually air-tight security. It also killed any possibility of tourism.

33. After the U.S. Department of Interior assumed control over Saipan and the Trust Territory, tourist travel was actively discouraged. Permission to enter, even for U.S. citizens, required a special permit secured in advance. This restriction was only lifted in mid-1970.

34. Air service is the life line of these islands -- inter-island shipping being virtually non-existent for passenger travel except for infrequent service to the outlying islands. Continental Air Lines joined with Micronesian investors to form Air Micronesia and secured operating rights throughout the Trust Territory. They began service in April 1968 with Boeing 727's modified for landings on short coral runways.

35. Prior to 1968, Pan American had provided a contract air service from Guam to Saipan with DC-4 equipment on a limited basis and to Truk and those other islands with landing strips. A Grumman amphibian was used to serve the other islands on a restricted basis.

36. Facts are hard to come by in the Northern Marianas. While patterned after Guam's tourist/visitor statistical reporting procedures (which in turn are based on Hawaii's most successful Tourist Bureau procedures), Saipan's efforts have resulted in partial and frequently conflicting data. Table 2 is the author's best effort at constructing from various sources a reasonable approximation of the air traffic and hotel room count on Saipan since the commencement of Continental/Air Micronesia service in 1968. Note, in 1969, the sudden growth of traffic after the daily 727 flights replaced the infrequent DC-4's.

37. Continental/Air Micronesia currently serve Saipan with 5 flights daily south to Guam. Three of these flights weekly also serve Rota and two

Table 2. Saipan Air Traffic and Hotel Rooms
1968-1974.

CAL. YEAR	AIRLINE DEPARTURES	AIRLINE PASSGRS. DEPLANED	HOTEL ROOMS NUMBER	DEPLANED PASSGRS. PER ROOM
1968	NA	13,205	NA	NA
1969	730	26,346	70	376
1970	1,100*	34,000*	110	309
1971	1,400	37,000	130	285
1972#	1,800	47,000	140	336
1973	2,100	55,000	330	167
1974	2,400	65,000	350	186

*After the Special Entry Permits were no longer required in 1970, Air Pacific, an air taxi service, operated daily flights to and from Guam with intermediate stops at Rota and Tinian.

#1972 and thereafter includes occasional charter flights, dominantly by Japan Air Lines.

flights weekly serve Tinian. From Guam, they operate three flights a week to Honolulu and return via Truk, Ponape, Kwajalein, Majuro and Johnston Island, and also from Guam, three flights a week to Yap and Koror. Daily air taxi flights with DeHavilland Herons are operated by Air Pacific between Guam and Saipan with intermediate stops on some schedules at Rota and Tinian.

38. Guam is western Micronesia's center for shopping, medical services and cultural events. There is a large volume of inter-island traffic, particularly with the Northern Marianas. Of Saipan's air passengers, it was recently estimated that government generated some 11%, local residents 37%, tourists 45%, with the balance of 7% representing off-island business and other travellers.

39. The composition of the tourist market on Saipan to date has been different from that at Guam. In May 1972, Japan and the U.S. negotiated a bilateral treaty granting Japan Air Lines rights to serve Saipan. Japan designated Pan American as the reciprocal carrier subject to U.S. C.A.B. and Presidential approval. After prolonged investigations, hearings and controversy in mid-1975, the C.A.B. recommended to President Ford the award of the route to Continental/Air Micronesia. Japan objected to the introduction of a third U.S. airline into Japan, and President Ford returned the matter to the C.A.B. to obtain further clarification of Japan's position. There the matter rested as of December 1975 when this paper was prepared. Japan Air Lines, although authorized to serve Saipan on a scheduled basis, has not done so, awaiting the U.S.'s award to a U.S. carrier, when, for competitive reasons, Japan Air Lines will commence service.

40. In the past 3½ years, anticipating the major development of Japanese tourist traffic,

Continental/Air Micronesia has built the 184 room beach-front Saipan Continental Hotel. The construction schedule of the adjacent Intercontinental Hotel (PAA) was intentionally stretched out but it now approaches completion. Three other first-class hotels have been constructed or expanded since 1972 in anticipation of a Japanese influx. To the investors in these hotels, restaurants, tour companies and their tourist dependent services, air service to Japan is vital to their success. The weekend visitors from Guam and the few adventuresome Japanese tourists who made the side trip from Guam last year totaled only some 27,000, not enough to even maintain a 50% occupancy of available hotel rooms.

41. The impact on Saipan International Airport has been the same. A new 8,700 foot runway designed for wide body aircraft, a magnificent island terminal capable of accommodating over 500,000 annual enplaning passengers, and the best of roads, auto parking, multilingual signs, and tropical landscaping await the political decision to authorize air service to Japan. Meanwhile, Continental/Air Micronesia and Air Pacific continue their air service to and through Guam while Saipan waits.

42. Air service to Saipan, until December 16, 1975, was accommodated at Kobler Field, which, after Isley Field was de-activated by the U.S. Air Force in 1949, was the only operational airfield on Saipan. Since Kobler Field had been originally designed and built for comparatively light fighter aircraft, after Continental/Air Micronesia began service with 727's, the World War II construction began to deteriorate, and studies indicated total reconstruction of the runways and taxiways was required. When the Japan-Saipan bilateral was signed in 1972, wide body service became a probability and the Trust Territory government decided to keep Kobler Field in operation while reconstructing the abandoned Isley Field. Originally a Japanese military airport and used at the end of World War II as a B-29 bomber field, Isley Field is located 2 miles south of Kobler Field near the southern end of the island. Isley Field's approaches are over water, clear of future obstructions, and free from potential noise-nuisance complaints. Reconstruction has also been undertaken without the problems of maintaining flight operations.

43. The Honolulu office of Ralph M. Parsons Company was retained to design the airfield reconstruction as well as all the buildings and support facilities. The longitudinal gradient of the existing World Way II runways were excessive and a substantial cut, fill and leveling was required which involved the scarification and removal of all the coral base rock material from the former runway, stockpiling and replacement together with new material. The net result was construction of a complete new 8,700 foot by 200 foot runway with shoulder paving and associated facilities such as taxiway, aircraft parking apron, lighting and navigation aids. Many World War II aircraft parking aprons and

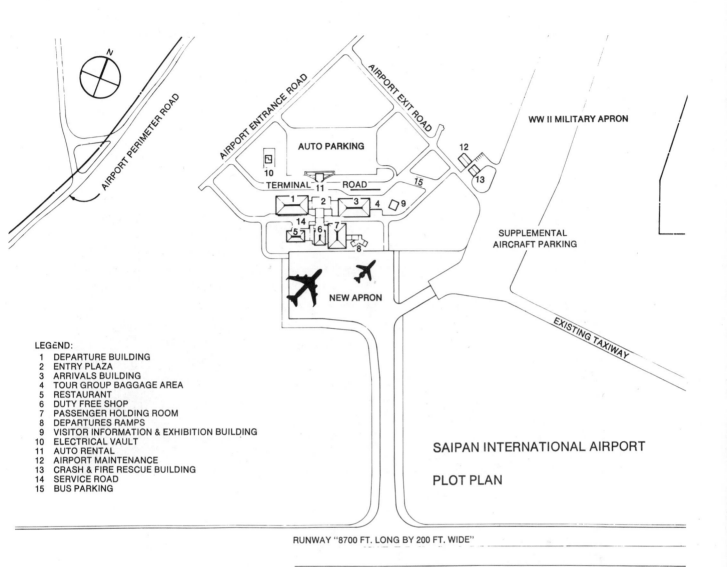

LEGEND:
1 DEPARTURE BUILDING
2 ENTRY PLAZA
3 ARRIVALS BUILDING
4 TOUR GROUP BAGGAGE AREA
5 RESTAURANT
6 DUTY FREE SHOP
7 PASSENGER HOLDING ROOM
8 DEPARTURES RAMPS
9 VISITOR INFORMATION & EXHIBITION BUILDING
10 ELECTRICAL VAULT
11 AUTO RENTAL
12 AIRPORT MAINTENANCE
13 CRASH & FIRE RESCUE BUILDING
14 SERVICE ROAD
15 BUS PARKING

SAIPAN INTERNATIONAL AIRPORT

PLOT PLAN

RUNWAY "8700 FT. LONG BY 200 FT. WIDE"

Fig.8.   Terminal Area Site Plan - Saipan

Fig.9.   Artist's Sketch - Completed Saipan Terminal

Fig.10. Saipan Terminal Construction - December 1975

Fig.11. Saipan Terminal Construction - December 1975

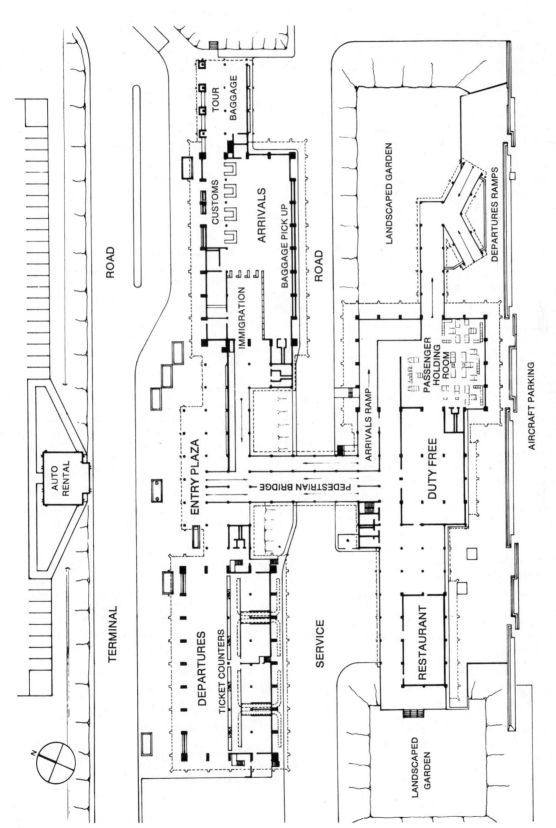

Fig.12. *Terminal Building Floor Plan – Saipan*

taxiways were salvaged and made part of the redeveloped airport. The new access roadway was a
salvaged segment of a World War II taxiway used
for aircraft parking dispersal.

44. In 1973 when the airfield construction was
placed under contract, only some US$500,000 of
the funds accumulated for the entire project
remained for terminal construction. As the
Airport Consultant to GovGuam since 1965 (after
the Navy completed the Guam terminal design and
construction), the author was cognizant of the
substantial airport revenues generated from the
duty free concession there since virtually
every Japanese tourist returned to Japan with
his limit of whiskey and perfume. If Saipan
were to attract the expected volume of Japanese
tourists, duty free concession revenues alone
could fund the terminal facilities that the
airlines, Parsons Company, Trust Territory government and the author felt were required.

45. After confirming that at least three qualified duty free concessionaires would offer
US$1,000,000 or more as prepaid concession fees
for the duty free privileges in the new terminal at Isley Field, special legislation creating the tax exempt concession was passed by the
Congress of Micronesia in February 1974. After
advertising, three bids were received on June
4, 1974 ranging from a low of US$2,570,000 to
a high of US$5,000,000 prepaid concession fees.
The high bid of Duty Free Shoppers Limited of
Hong Kong was accepted, the US$5,000,000 pre-
paid fees deposited to the construction account,
and the new terminal complex placed under construction fully funded.

46. While the financing arrangements were in
process, the Parsons Company, aided by Charles
Wright, staff architect for the Trust Territory,
the airlines and the author developed a design
for the terminal building which achieved an
island feeling, accommodated the unique traffic
characteristics observed at Guam's congested
terminal, and also permitted incremental construction if funding for the whole could not
be generated (see Figure 8).

47. The heart of the design's appropriateness
to Saipan lies in the choice of scale and
materials. Rather than one massive building,
the planners produced 5 separate buildings connected by covered arcades to achieve the open
air feeling characteristic of Pacific island
architecture (see Figure 9). The peaked-roof
structures themselves are not replicas of
buildings indigenous to any one of Micronesia's
districts. Instead, they merely capture the
essence of island architecture through the use
of a series of columns spanned by beams, high
roofs allowing hot air to rise and overhangs
for shade and protection from the rain.

48. The buildings were constructed using a
pre-cast concrete structural system (see Figure
10). Dark volcanic rock from Saipan's Kagman
area are used for wall surface treatment and
also for retaining walls, planters and seats.
Most of the public spaces are naturally venti-
lated, with the exception of shops and restaurant, which are air conditioned.

49. In the tropics, landscaping is an especially important element of the design and has
been extensively used to reinforce the island
setting. Outdoor waiting areas and elevated
observation decks overlooking the apron and
field are prominent features.

50. Charles Wright, then the Trust Territory's
staff architect, said:

"We thought it was very important that people
have a chance to see what's going on, so
that the airport has a friendly feeling.
This is especially necessary in this day
of airport security measures.

"But also, on an island, the airport particularly becomes a gathering place, a focal
point of activity. People just naturally
gravitate toward it. This is true all over
the Pacific."

51. Special consideration was also given to
tour groups which the airport planners estimated may eventually comprise 60% of the traffic. There is a special tour group area in the
arrival building so tours can be pulled away
from other passengers to queue up for busses.
Tour busses have their own service road. De-
paring tour groups have separate check-in
facilities.

52. A pre-World War II concrete structure of
classic Japanese design, used by the Japanese
as an operations building during their period
of administration, is being faithfully restored
for use as a mini-museum of Micronesia and a
visitors' orientation center, appropriately
utilizing this link with Saipan's Japanese past
(see Figures 8 and 11).

53. There is parking for about 228 cars. The
terminal roadway is a snarl-free, one-way loop
that expands from three to five lanes in front
of the arrival building, providing off circulation curbsides at the bag claim area.

54. In the departure building, about 32,000
square feet of space at curbside has been constructed for lease to four airlines for ticket
counters and offices. Additional office space
is available on the mezzanine level.

55. The arrival building across the entrance
court accommodates normal baggage claim, customs and immigration functions. A double-
sided currency exchange counter opens to incoming and outgoing passengers.

56. The departure and arrival buildings are
at roadway level, connected by a 30 foot wide
ramp (pedestrian bridge) to the three two-level
apron-side buildings. This ramp is the backbone of the terminal operation's "flow concept"
and is designed for enplaned traffic volumes
of up to 500,000 annually. Under this ramp,
baggage carts and service vehicles pass freely,
thus facilitating airline operations for baggage, cargo and support services (see Figure
12).

57. The three apron-side buildings consist of the holdroom, the duty free shop, and the restaurant and bar. The duty free shop is at the end of the pedestrian bridge with maximum exposure to the enplaning passengers. At this point, they are turned to the left into a large queuing concourse capable of accommodating tour groups. From this "reservoir" the passengers are processed through security screening into the holdroom and landscaped garden to await boarding. Passengers with more time, as well as visitors and spectators, at the end of the pedestrian bridge, are turned to the right to the restaurant, cocktail lounge and spectators garden. All these activities are on the second level affording a view of the airfield and across the 12 mile channel to the spectacular rocky, wave-lashed north coast of Tinian. The lower level is used for kitchens, duty free storage, airline cargo, operations and ramp crew offices.

58. Isley Field, Saipan International Airport, is a model of an efficient and easily expansible terminal, well suited and sited to serve the transportation and tourist function it was designed for. But even with this splendid facility, all Saipanese are not happy with the thought of the imminent tourist boom when the Saipan-Japan route award is finally made and service inaugurated.

SAIPAN'S CAUTIOUS APPROACH TO TOURISM

59. The Mariana Islands' planner, Thomas Sheehan, recently said, "Tourism, as you know, is a labor intensive industry. We are a labor short area, so tourism is about the worst thing that could happen here." Instead, he opted for improvement of the employment, economic and social conditions of the Mariana Islands' indigenous population by developing the island as a transportation and assembly point where higher levels of skill could be used instead of relegating the indigenes to service industry employment. But he saw little hope -- tourism, he concluded, would grow of its own momentum because of Saipan's tropical climate, beautiful beaches and proximity to Japan. Saipan's proponents of tourism argue that it produces a rapid infusion of money flow into the local economy, thereby improving living standards and social and economic opportunity.

60. If Saipan's tourist growth were allowed to follow the Guam pattern, as tourist activities increase, the demand for labor will increase correspondingly and require more than the available indigenous labor force can supply. Alien labor then would be imported to fill the gap, and the increased population would create demands for public sector as well as commercial services. As alien labor is introduced, the social structure and economic character increasing reflects the alien culture, and the island flavor that attracted tourists in the first place diminishes -- particularly when a starting population base is as small as it is on Saipan.

61. As this pattern progresses, the island economy becomes even more dependent upon the tourist industry which produces only relatively low skilled and low paying jobs. The population, both indigenous and alien, is then tied to the "service industry," basically those hotel, food and recreational activities associated with warm weather resorts. When the warm weather resort attracts its tourists from a broad market, it is a chancy "industry" at best. But when the tourist market is generated from a single source, the island in effect becomes a "commercial colony" of the source of the business.

62. The unpleasant aspects of a significantly alien labor force and the impact of a changing social pattern on a long established community resulting from a tourist boom brought a warning from Saipan Councilman Dino M. Jones who, in October 1975, said, "By 1993 only about 40% of the total population will be indigenous." He added that, if present tourist policies are continued on Saipan, the social problems witnessed on Guam and Hawaii following tourist expansion on those islands would inevitably occur on Saipan with even a more profound effect. In 1993, he continued, according to the present tourist development policies, "About 36,000 will be alien workers and their dependents brought in to fill gaps in the labor market caused by an expansion of the tourist industry on Saipan." Councilman Jones noted that, based upon the Guam experience, the tourist industry creates about 4.5 jobs for every hotel room on the island. Observing that as of 1975 Saipan had issued business licenses for some 6,000 hotel rooms, he concluded, "There may be 4,500 hotel rooms, creating over 20,000 jobs on Saipan, with only 6,000 local workers available by 1993. If this occurs and the Chamorro and Carolinian people do become a minority on Saipan, the cultural dislocations and social problems will be enormous."

63. The die seems cast -- the climate is warm and hospitable, the facilities are in place and the political forces are at work to bring tourism to Saipan soon. Only time will tell whether the Saipanese will be the beneficiaries.

REFERENCES
1. CLYDE, PAUL. Japan's Pacific Mandate. Kennikat Press, Inc., Port Washington, N.Y., 1933.
2. BEARDSLEY, CHARLES. Guam Past and Present. Charles E. Tuttle Company, Tokyo, Japan, 1964.
3. WENKAM, ROBERT. The Great Pacific Rip-Off. Follett Publishing Co., Chicago, Illinois, 1974.
4. GOERNER, FRED. The Search for Amelia Earhart. Doubleday & Company, Inc., Garden City, N.Y., 1966.
5. HEINE, CARL. Micronesia at the Crossroads. University Press of Hawaii, Honolulu, 1974.
6. VINCENT, JAMES M. and VITI, CARLOS. Micronesia's Yesterday. TT Department of Education, Saipan, 1973.
7. DEPARTMENT OF COMMERCE, GOVGUAM. Annual Economic Review, 1974.
8. MARIANAS DISTRICT PLANNING OFFICE. Preliminary Report on the Labor Situation, May 1974, and Preliminary Report on Population, June 1974.

15. New airports for Kenya

D.V. Davies, MSE, DipCE, FIEAust., MRAeS
Chief Aerodromes Engineer, Government of Kenya

A comparison is made of the numbers of international airports in the various regions of ICAO Contracting States and it is suggested that there is considerable scope for aerodrome works in the developing countries. At this time, it appears that over 25 projects for the expansion or development of African Airports which would involve a total expenditure of the order of £1000 million* are either in progress or proposed. Comments are made on problem areas including shortage of finance, over capacity, distance, sophistication and location. Suggestions are made covering several matters which are considered worthy of attention when the planning and design of new airports in developing countries are receiving attention. Details are provided of two major Kenyan airport projects which are nearing completion at a cost of over £45 million. First is the Nairobi Project which is based on a circular departure building facing an aircraft parking apron with a separate arrivals building for passengers and administrative staff. Secondly is the Mombasa project which covers large scale development of the existing airport to international standard to permit direct Boeing 747 flights to Europe to meet the demands of tourist traffic.

INTRODUCTION

1. Although it would be interesting to attempt to present a statement of common views held by the developing countries on the provision, planning and design of new airports, the task would be a formidable one. In the case of Africa, for example, it would be necessary to approach nearly 50 nations which are contained within this vast area of the world's second largest continent.

2. As a result, I have elected to draw on my experience gained in a number of developing countries including the last four years in Kenya, to touch on matters of general concern when the provision of airports is under consideration.

3. The number of international aerodromes in the various regions of ICAO Contracting States are outlined in Table I. This indicates that the majority of these airports is situated in the developing countries but generally they are in the early stages of development and their passenger traffic is low relative to the developed countries. In the case of major African aerodromes, Nairobi has an annual passenger traffic of nearly 1,500,000 as opposed to London (Heathrow) of about 20,000,000.

4. However in the years which lie ahead, with expansion of local industry and manufacturing, rising standard of living and general economic development, the share of traffic associated with the developing areas of the world should increase, and as a result considerable airport construction work is to be expected. Even at this time, there are over 25 major airport projects underway or planned throughout Africa

*£ are £ stg throughout

Table 1 International Aerodromes – December 1974

Region	Internat. Scheduled Air Transport Reg.	Alt.	Internat. Non-Sched. Air Transport Reg.	Alt.	Internat. General Aviation	Total
Africa-Indian Ocean	137	16	2	1	14	170
Caribbean /South American	119	21	0	0	48	188
European	198	22	29	0	129	378
Middle East/ Southeast Asia	119	30	3	0	10	162
North Atlantic/ North American/ Pacific	69	36	0	0	10	115
	642	125	34	1	211	1013

Internat. – International
Reg. – Regular
Alt. – Alternate

which envisage a total capital investment in excess of £1000 million.

5. It is proposed to examine some problems which are encountered by airport authorities, to make several suggestions for consideration when new airports are contemplated and, finally, to report on two major Kenya airport projects which are nearing completion at a cost of over £45 million.

PROBLEMS

6. Finance. When one retraces the steps of time to the end of 1972 before the instability of international monetary exchange rates and the energy crisis, the scale of the unprecedented cost escalation which has since occurred was not generally foreseen. By way of example, some measure of the abnormal cost increases which have been encountered in various parts of the world may be gauged by reference to movements in the civil engineering and building cost indices for Nairobi, as shown in Table 2.

7. Because of the shortage of funds, many airports in developing countries have been financed, and will need to be assisted for the future, by long term loans from international financial institutions or through bi-lateral aid. Although the airport authorities concerned could not have been expected to foresee the effect of the recent world wide inflation, the loan arrangements under which they are operating, have generally required the recipient Governments to meet such cost overruns. Some developing nations who have had major works projects such as airports under construction during recent times are now in a difficult position of having to find considerable amounts to meet these unforeseen costs.

8. Over Capacity. Tourism is a major economic factor in many developing countries. In Kenya's case, currently over 80% of all visitors travel by air and the vast majority are tourists. For these travellers, air travel is in a commanding position relative to other forms of transport because of the long distances from Europe and the wish to minimise travel times and so increase the period available for holidays or business.

Table 2   Civil Engineering and Non-Residential Buildings

Item	Cost Indices	
	December 72	November 75
Civil Engineering (Materials and Labour)	100	176.7
Non-Residential Buildings (Materials and Labour)	100	182

9. The importance of its airports to Kenya can be appreciated when one considers that tourism is now the third largest source of foreign exchange (£34 million during 1975 as opposed to £7.5 million in 1963) after agriculture and manufacturing. Gross receipts now surpass that of any single export commodity and, in due course, tourism is expected to become the largest source of foreign exchange earnings and one of the major avenues for employment.

10. Despite the importance of the tourist industry to the general economy, the benefits are sometimes reduced by the pattern of airline operations. At Nairobi Airport, for instance, air traffic is peaked around 0800 and 2400 hours, as shown in Fig. 1. This is accentuated by the noise abatement procedures in force at some European airports and the desire of operators to depart as late as possible at night before airports are closed in order to make a daytime arrival to facilitate passenger handling. In passing, it is worth mentioning that a ban on operations at certain European aerodromes appears to be applied irrespective of whether 'quiet' or 'noisy' aircraft are involved.

11. In the process, airport facilities are planned for high peak rates which apply for limited periods only and consequently passenger terminals, aprons, car parks, and engineering services are larger and cost more than if the same traffic were spread over a longer time. This situation is worsened by tourist seasonality which leads to further under utilisation of facilities during the off-season periods.

12. Transport. Generally speaking the distances from the supply source for materials and equipment and within developing countries themselves, are much greater than for the developed areas. In kenya's case, imported materials and construction equipment required in Nairobi have to be shipped from Europe, off-loaded in Mombasa and then railed a distance close to 500 km. This distance factor results in added costs, in multiple handling with greater possibility of damage and in additional administrative work in dealing with customs, port and transport authorities.

13. Technology. International airline operations utilising modern high capacity jets, such as the Boeing 747, now span the whole world. Thus sophisticated communication facilities, electronic equipment, operational pavements, approach and runway lighting systems have to be provided and maintained to acceptable standards irrespective of the country concerned. This requires considerable effort by the developing nations where financial and technical resources are usually in short supply and the general trend towards technological advances seems sure to pose even greater demands and problems for these countries.

14. Equipment. With electrical and mechanical items, such as baggage handling equipment, standby generating plant, vehicles and earth moving equipment, while it is easy to decide on the principles of standardisation to reduce stock-

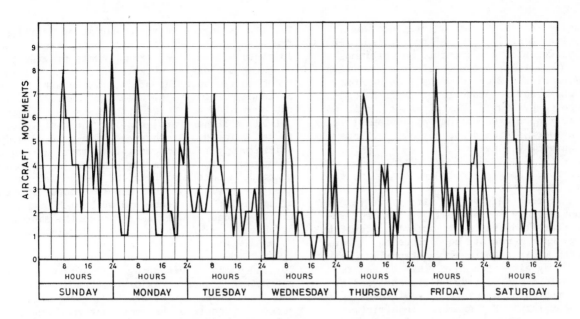

Fig.1. *Nairobi Airport, Kenya: weekly pattern of aircraft movements*

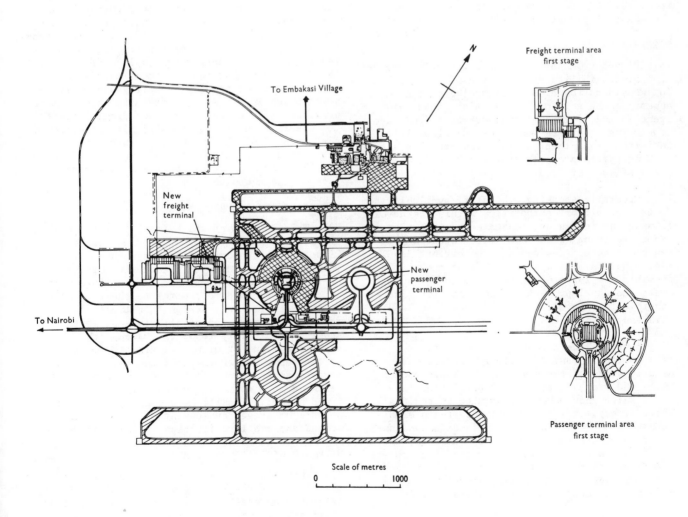

Fig.2. *Nairobi Airport development*

holdings and to assist with maintenance work, this is often a difficult goal to realise. There is a trend for such equipment to be obtained by airport authorities in the developing countries in the form of aid from the developed nations, many of whom require products of their own manufacture to be purchased. As a result, it is not unusual to find a wide variety of equipment at the one airport, which poses obvious problems for the authority concerned.

15. Location. Many airports in developing countries are located in regions where the combination of high temperatures and site elevation require considerably longer runways plus restriction of aircraft operating weights than would be necessary under temperate conditions and lower elevations. This additional construction cost must be met by airport authorities and the reduction in payload due to reduced aircraft performance can represent a severe economic penalty to airline operators. For example, in Africa, there are over 22 airports above 1000m elevation and generally these have relatively high day temperatures. In the case of Nairobi International Airport with an elevation of 1565m and a reference temperature of $23.4^{\circ}C$, the runway length required for maximum permissible weight take-off with Boeing 747 aircraft is approximately 4200m. This represents an additional length of about 900m over the same operation being conducted from, say, London (Heathrow) and there is also the associated payload penalty to be considered.

SUGGESTIONS

16. Planning. Apart from that general recognition of feasibility studies as a starting point for consideration of airport projects, there appears to be a trend by the major financial agencies and bi-lateral aid sources to whom the developing countries must look for financial assistance that their decisions whether to assist with aerodrome projects can best be made on the basis of such studies.

17. Generally speaking, the staff available to Government airport authorities within the developing countries is not adequate in numbers or in expertise to deal with feasibility studies plus the planning and design of large airport development projects. It would neither be economic nor possible for these Governments to employ such staff and developing countries generally find it sensible to engage experienced consultants for this specialised work.

18. However, the technical and operational staff of airports in many developing countries are usually aware of the problems which are encountered and are able to suggest particular features which should be incorporated in the design. While it may, at first sight, appear preferable to have Consultants prepare the design and contract documentation at their headquarters, these are often in areas quite remote from the project itself and this can lead to errors and create problems when local knowledge and close contact between all parties is not possible.

19. It is suggested to Aerodrome Authorities of the developing countries that when Airport Consultants are engaged, arrangements provide for planning and design work to be carried out in the country where the project is located. Experience points to the need for constant contact and communication between the many parties involved in airport projects for the best results to be achieved. At the same time, the main Consultants might be encouraged to form an association with a local firm for preparation of contract documentation, detailed design and subsequent supervision. This has the added advantage of providing experience and work within the country concerned as well as reducing the amount of offshore payments which might otherwise have to be made.

20. Adequacy of Financing. As a result of the recent experience of major cost escalation which can occur over periods of 3 - 4 years which are generally required for construction of major airport works, it is suggested to those authorities providing financial assistance to the developing countries that future loan agreements include adequate allowances to help offset cost increases which can arise because of factors outside the control of any one country.

21. Equipment. Considerable opportunities now exist for developing countries to obtain assistance for the provision of fire fighting, construction, maintenance and airport ground handling equipment. Apart from inviting tenders from suppliers within the donor country, it is suggested that when evaluating proposals, efforts be made to ensure that the equipment manufacturer is able to demonstrate his ability and willingness to supply spare parts at short order. Moreover, as it is essential for aerodromes' staff to be able to carry out repairs, it is desirable that as part of the 'package', training should be provided for the local staff who will be responsible for successful operation and maintenance of the equipment.

AERODROMES DEPARTMENT

22. This Department which forms part of the Ministry of Power and Communications was established by the Government of Kenya in early 1973. This action was taken in recognition of the importance and the specialised nature of airports and it was decided to centralise the responsibility for planning, design, construction, maintenance and operation of all civil airports under one authority to be entrusted with execution of a major programme of airport works within the Republic. Details of the two major airport projects which are now nearing completion in Kenya at a cost of over £45 million are outlined below; in addition, a considerable amount of work on stage development of domestic aerodromes and smaller airstrips is in progress.

NAIROBI INTERNATIONAL AIRPORT

23. This airport was opened 18 years ago in time to serve the first generation of civil jet transport aircraft. Since then, with its first class site on the plains, some 8 miles to the south east of Nairobi, it has coped with traffic

Fig.3. Nairobi Airport: artist's impression

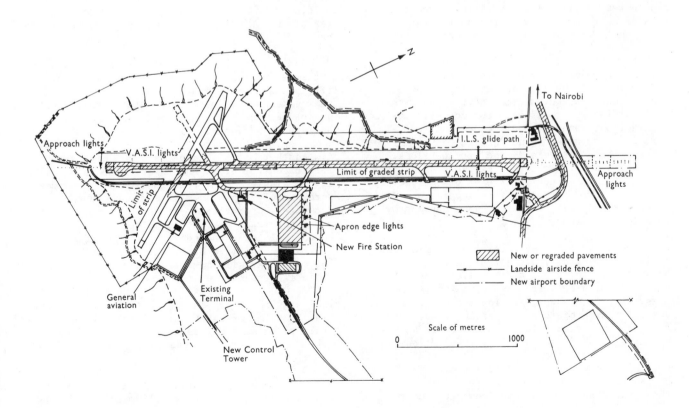

Fig.4. Mombasa Airport development

demands which have increased from 250,000 passengers in 1958 to over 1,380,000 during 1975. Over the same period freight has risen from 6,000 to 30,000 tonnes. In 1961, the runway was extended to 4,120m and it is still one of the longest in Africa.

24. By 1968, the aerodrome had consolidated its position as an international and regional communications centre. Then, with an eye to maintaining its position for the future, the Government commissioned Consulting Engineers, Sir Alexander Gibb and Partners (Africa), to prepare a number of reports on air traffic forecasts, master planning and a feasibility study of the development of the airport. At an early stage, contact was established by the Government with the International Bank for Reconstruction and Development with the aim of eventually enlisting its support for any future project which might emerge. This proved to be very beneficial, and helpful advice and many suggestions were received from specialist IBRD officers over the planning and design phases.

25. Master Plan. The master plan (Fig.2) shows the proposed long term development of the airport. As can be seen, the existing building area is located on the north-west side of the present runway. Thus one of the first decisions was to decide where to reserve space for the eventual development of a parallel runway which forecasts indicate probably will not be required until the early 1990's. In the event, because of future noise disturbance to residential areas, the need for demolition of an existing village, and the adverse operational effect on the nearby general aviation airport (Wilson), it was decided to reserve land for the ultimate construction of a second runway to the south east i.e. more remote from the environs of Nairobi City.

26. For efficient long term development, new terminal complexes for passenger and freight were planned to be located between the parallel runways while a central transport spine with dual carriageway roads will connect with the main Nairobi-Mombasa road; connection to the airport from the extended north east end of the spine will be possible as the city develops. Moreover a new freight road giving a direct connection from the industrial area of the city to the Cargo Terminal will ensure separation of passenger and freight traffic when passing by road to the airport.

27. The concept for each terminal complex consists of a partially decentralised circular departure building and a centralised passenger arrivals building which also contains restaurants, duty-free shops, airline and Government administration offices. Departing passengers approach on a ground level road and are notified by signs, linked to the flight information system, of the unit from which their aircraft is leaving. They will alight from their vehicles at the entrance to the departure concourse or in the carpark adjacent to each departure unit.

28. After check-in, passengers pass immigration and ascend by escalators to the first floor and enter the combined departure and transit lounge and finally embark through airbridges or fixed ramps and aircraft steps.

29. Arriving passengers on the other hand, will disembark through airbridges or aircraft steps and ramps to the departure lounge at first floor level and proceed via the nearest walkway to the arrivals building. There they pass health and immigration and descend to ground level. Information signs will show the flight number and appropriate race-track for baggage collection; then they clear customs and enter the arrival concourse to be met by their friends. A waving base on top of the ring departure building will permit the public to see all aircraft arrivals and departures.

30. The aircraft apron is also circular in shape and provides for power in, push-out operation for various combinations of aircraft of up to 10 Boeing 747s at the one time plus stands for self manoeuvring by smaller aircraft.

31. Provision is available for ultimate development of up to four separate terminal units with a total passenger capacity in excess of 12 million on a yearly basis and for duplication of the freight facilities.

32. Current Contracts. The scope of the present work is shown in Fig. 3. The new passenger terminal building caters for a flow of about 1000 arriving and 1000 departing passengers per hour or of the order of 3 million per year. The ring departure unit will be mainly of one and two storey construction comprising two international and one domestic unit, while the central arrivals building rises to five storeys with a total floor area of approximately 50,000 sq.m for both structures.

33. Apart from the usual internal services such as flight information and public address system, lifts, escalators, baggage conveyors and race tracks, mechanical ventilation to passenger holding lounges and air conditioning of the restaurant are being installed.

34. Another major element is a 50m high air traffic control block and tower. The main building is single storey construction and provides approximately 3,500 sq.m of enclosed space to accommodate operational areas, training rooms and normal services for DCA and meteorological staff. The control tower and cupola are located centrally above the main block and the complete building and tower will be fully air conditioned with a lift connecting the tower and ground level. Other buildings include a new cargo building, of 7,500 sq.m floor area with a cool store of 3,500 sq.m for export of valuable horticultural products, a police station, a staff canteen, a fire and rescue station, a state pavilion and telephone exchange.

35. Civil and other works include the construction of a parallel taxiway, 2100m in length, and aprons serving the new freight and passenger handling facilities. This involves the provision of approximately 300,000 sq.m of aircraft

pavement together with 100,000 sq.m of paved shoulders as well as roadworks and car parks which require 135,000 sq.m of pavement construction.

36. A new airfield and Cat.1 approach lighting system as well as a new remote receiver station, engineering services including electricity, water for domestic and fire fighting purposes, surface water drainage, sewerage and telephone together with no-break and stand-by electrical generators and pumping equipment, as well as a number of sub-stations, are being constructed.

37. In addition to the above work, a dual carriageway road with several grade separated intersections and 15km in length is being provided by the Government, as a separate contract, to provide a high class road transport link to the city.

38. Commercial Accounting System. As part of the overall Nairobi Airport Project, the Government has appointed Accounting Consultants, Touche Ross and Company, to recommend a cost-related user charge system to permit the Aerodromes Department to conduct its affairs on a sound business and financial basis. This work is well advanced and it is due for implementation during the latter part of this year.

MOMBASA INTERNATIONAL AIRPORT

39. The introduction of charter flights and package tours from Germany and Switzerland in 1965 provided a clear indication of the interest of tourists in spending a holiday in the coastal areas of Kenya where it is possible to enjoy the sun and sea and still have access to the game parks and wildlife.

40. Although a rapid increase in the numbers of tourist occurred during the following 4 years, it was apparent that the future potential of the area was restricted by the limitations of the existing airport. As the main runway was less than 2000m in length and not capable of accommodating aircraft larger than DC-9 types, passengers bound for the coast were required to travel by short haul aircraft from Europe making intermediate stops en-route or, alternatively, to first travel to Nairobi and then transfer to DC-9 or F-27 shuttle service to Mombasa. As this shuttle had to be operated at night when domestic aircraft could be released, there was an almost unanimous adverse reaction by European passengers, and tourist operators were becoming reluctant to develop new coastal holidays.

41. Consequently, the Government recognised the need for a full scale investigation including technical and economic study of Mombasa Airport, and Studiengruppe Luftfahrt of West Germany in association with Scott Wilson, Kirkpatrick and Partners of London and Nairobi, were appointed in mid-1970 to prepare a detailed report.

42. The result of the study indicated a favourable outlook for tourism development, provided the airport was developed to international standards capable of catering for high capacity jet

aircraft flying between Europe and Mombasa to meet the needs of tourist, and also local and regional flights.

43. Although the studies indicated that extension of the existing main 09/27 runway was technically feasible and would produce a 'least cost' solution, this would have imposed some noise nuisance on residents and visitors. As a result, a decision was made by the Government, to develop the new runway on a 03/21 alignment in order to prevent future noise disturbance and to protect the environment.

44. Scope of Works. The present development of the airport which is underway is shown in Fig.4. This provides for construction of a new runway 3350m in length, taxiways, aprons, roads, car parks and engineering services. In addition, precision approach, runway, taxiway and apron lighting together with ILS are being provided to permit operations on a 24 hour per day basis.

45. The building under construction include a new passenger terminal capable of handling flow rates of approximately 550 persons per hour, an air traffic control block and tower, a fire and rescue station plus a number of ancillary buildings.

46. The project is costing of the order of £15 million which is being assisted by a long term loan of approximately £6.25 million from the Government of Japan, while the Government of Kenya is providing the remainder of the funds. The prime contractor is the Mitsubishi Corporation of Japan which is utilising local sub contractors for major items of work such as earthworks, pavements and building construction.

47. The project has several features of interest; one was the requirement for aircraft operations to continue unhindered by construction work. Development had to be planned to provide for construction of the new runway in stages and for simultaneous closure of the existing main runway (09/27) and opening of the first 2100m of the new one (03/21). Another has been the need to programme and control the erection of new buildings, including the passenger terminal and ATC block and tower, which are located adjacent to the original main runway, so that work could continue without infringing the transitional surfaces of this runway, pending its eventual closure.

48. Planning and Design. The Aerodromes Department's practice of continuing consultation between all parties concerned - Government departments and control authorities, airline representatives and consultants - was followed. This was arranged through planning meetings to define requirements, to follow progress and to ensure that there was a general understanding and overall agreement as work proceeded. At the detailed design stage, the technical details and production of plans were discussed and agreed at regular intervals between Consultants and Aerodromes Department staff.

49. <u>Passenger Terminal</u>. Considering the passenger terminal, for example, the arrangements for the planning and design phases provided for Messrs. Gollins, Melvin, Ward Partnership of London to provide the expertise but for the contract plans and drawings to be produced jointly by architects (Richard Hughes of Nairobi and Dr. Lippsmeir of West Germany) in conjunction with quantity surveyors (Davson and Ward) and electrical/mechanical engineers (Kennedy and Donkin) who have offices located in Kenya. Not only did this facilitate contact between all parties but it enabled the Government to minimise the extent of offshore payments.

50. It became clear at an early stage that many requirements were of a desirable category rather than being strictly essential, and that without tight control the final cost of the terminal building, would be greatly exceeded. Thus a figure of £1.25 million for the terminal was adopted as a target and as the plan developed, estimates were updated and changes or reductions were made to maintain estimates within the cost-plan.

51. The main factors which were considered to require special attention at the design stage were climate and the form of the building to reflect the spirit of the area instead of, as in so many cases, a structure which has no identification with its surroundings.

52. Following detailed studies of the extent of sun penetration it was decided that particular attention was required in the form of tinted glass on the airside of the building, in the passenger lounges and in the restaurant area to give protection against the low evening sun. To reduce glare and dust during the late afternoon, landscaping and planting, plus retention of high trees such as palms which are growing on the site, was planned.

53. An analysis of air movements showed that by permitting natural airflow through the building, comfortable conditions could be obtained at most times. However in the departure lounge, electrically operated fans were proposed to increase air flow. Although complete details of rainfall intensity in conjunction with the direction and angle of the associated winds were lacking, local knowledge and experience pointed to periods of horizontally blown rain and it was decided to include louvres and covered porches on the land side face of the building.

54. The concept of the building is to provide a large umbrella roof for protection against the sun and rain but with open areas and a minimum of floor to ceiling construction in order to permit maximum cross airflow. At all times, the object of providing a building which would form a pleasant and natural part of Mombasa was always kept in mind. This was accomplished by its open nature, the garden and landscaping around the terminal, the large umbrella roof plus the retention of the existing palms and mango trees which help to blend the terminal with the surrounding landscape. The building, which is being constructed in reinforced concrete, will be painted white in keeping with local practice, and at night the terminal roof and concourse area will be softly illuminated.

55. <u>Progress</u>. Work commenced in June 1974 and it is proceeding to plan. The first stage of the new runway was opened, as planned, on 20 December, 1975, so that aircraft such as the Boeing 707 and DC-8 could commence to fly directly into Mombasa during the peak holiday season. Indications to date are that tourist traffic has increased very considerably and with the completion of the runway and terminal facilities which will enable Boeing 747 aircraft to operate and hence permit lower cost package tours, a considerable stimulus to tourism is anticipated. Completion of the whole project is due by mid 1977.

CONCLUDING REMARKS

56. It is anticipated that considerable airport construction work will be carried out in the developing areas of the world during the years which lie ahead. In the course of the current aerodrome development programme in Kenya, certain experience has been gained which might prove of interest and assistance to some of the other developing countries which are about to embark on similar works. This includes the desirability of a feasibility study as a basis for decision making and to facilitate arrangements for financial assistance, for planning and design work to be carried out locally in co-operation with all the parties involved, for adequate allowances to be made to help offset cost increases which can arise when major works are spread over a period of several years, and for buildings to be designed to form a pleasant and a natural part of the country where they are located.

57. Finally, it is desired to express my appreciation to the Organising Committee for the valuable opportunity provided by this Conference to exchange wide ranging views for the benefit of civil aviation as a whole during this era of great economic demand and changing technology.

Session VI: Discussion

Mr F.DOVALI, Director General of Airports,
Secretary of Public Works, Mexico

Mexico is a country which is developing, and
there is quite a wide range of developments in
that process. It is very difficult to transfer
the experience from one country to another.
Therefore, when one country wishes to develop,
particularly in the field of aviation, the only
way to do it is for it to prepare its own tech-
nicians, naturally using outside technologies,
and then to prepare its own technology and its
own personnel.

Secondly, as we see it, airports in Mexico
are part of the whole infrastructure of transport
in the same way as highways, railroads and ports.
Airports belong to the country, and naturally
have to be developed through the Federal Government's programme and investment in the same way
as other transport systems, the balance depending on which most benefits a particular condition.

Mexico has had a full airport development
programme since 1965, and during this time some
fifty airports, ranging from small airstrips to
the largest airport, Mexico City, have been completed. So with this variety of airport development, I think there are certain points which
should be of interest.

First of all, the view in Mexico is that an
airport is not only a link between two transportation modes, but must be considered also as the
conjunction of systems. The full concept is that
an airport has of necessity to be an amalgamation
of systems in such a way that each could be analysed separately or as a whole. There are five
sections. First there is air space, which in
Mexico is important because there are mountains
all around. Second, there are the runways, taxiways and apron. Third, the terminal area; fourth
access roads and fifth, the fuelling facilities.
All five sections depend on the capacity of the
whole system. Each section is treated separately
in relation to demand and capacity, and they are
then synthesised so that the capacity of the whole
system works together. This is the first concept.

From this the cost of each of the sections
is analysed. For instance, depending on the demand, we do not necessarily build taxi-ways.
There could be only exit taxi-ways for the runways, with parallel taxi-ways for the future, but
not necessarily in that first stage. That could
produce a very big reduction in costs of both
construction and maintenance.

Then in the case of the terminal building,
there is no real connexion in Mexico between the
number of airlines and the number of parking
positions. For instance there could be 1½ million passengers/year, yet a need for only three
positions. So the various components of the
terminal buildings must be separated and analysed to calculate the real capacity. The capacity of each component or sub-system can then be
eventually increased independently of the others.

Naturally there are disadvantages. One is
that continuous co-ordination of the whole programme is required. At present 25 airports are
under consideration. Another disadvantage is

that a full retro-fitting of the original criteria is required to analyse further stages of
construction.

Another experience concerns the financial
considerations. As in Mexico we work under a
Federal programme, it is not necessarily considered that all the airport has to be self-
sufficient. In most cases airports benefit the
country indirectly, so that in the same way that
the construction of highways is subsidised, eventually so is the construction of airports. The
intention is that the airport should be self-
sufficient so far as operational expenses are
concerned, but not necessarily from the point of
view of capital investment.

Another aspect concerns the interpreting of
forecasts. Everybody knows that the forecasts
are guesswork. We cannot see the future beyond
five or six years, so that when analysing some
20 - 50 years ahead, the margin of error is
very large indeed. So it is not the time, but
rather the volume of demand which is taken into
account, the view being that airports should be
designed for a certain volume of demand, but that
it does not matter when this occurs, because it
could depend on political aspects.

Finally, in Mexico we have adopted a different method of studying the effectiveness of
airports from that adopted in studying the feasibility of the third London airport. We did not
follow the lines of cost-benefit analyses, because we thought in some cases one cannot con-
vert all the benefit into costs. When the
airport justifies it, we adopt the full method
of operational research; this was done for
Mexico City, which took some six months of computer work. As a result it appeared that we
could handle 4000 alternative possibilities
concerning the building of a new Mexico City
airport.

Mr B.TUTTY, International Air Transport
Association

In the airport implementation and development
field I spend a great deal of time working with
the governments and airport authorities of developing countries. I was therefore a little disturbed to notice in Paper 13 an oblique reference to airlines in the matter of airport
design and development. I think the words used
were 'aviation expert'. There is also in this
Paper and Paper 14 a complete absence of any
reference to the ICAO's standards and recommended
practices which are mandatory for all airport authorities if they want to develop safe standards
for runways, navigational aids, etc.

Finally, I noticed a reference in these
Papers to the 'client', the client being of
course the airport authority, and in some cases
the government. May I suggest to the Authors that
the client also includes the users of the airport.
In the case of international airports, the airport is usually financed by the government or the
airport authority, but of course the users, the
airlines, have to pay for it in the end.
Surely they should be invited in at an early stage,
and before things begin to get set either on

paper or sometimes as late as in concrete.

In this respect, I notice that Mr Davies referred to 'remote consultant operation'. I would plead with consultants to become involved in the country for which they are designing, because there are all sorts of local circumstances which cannot be picked up from books or reference material. It is essential to see at first hand the problems involved, especially with labour and mechanical plant. It is all very well designing an airport around a sophisticated machine which works in western countries; but if you put it into a developing country and expect it to work the same, this may be a big mistake. It is better sometimes to go back to more elementary systems and elementary machinery and build up experience. Develop airports by stages, and make sure that in developing them the expertise, the spares, and the other supports that are needed are developed too.

Mr Davies again mentioned lending agencies. The world lending agencies sometimes check on local matters, and in other cases they are rather remote about airport developments. I would make a general appeal for lending agencies, whether they be a country or a world agency such as the World Bank, to investigate the particular circumstances in a country before making a loan commitment, in order to ensure that as far as possible their investment will be wisely employed.

The IATA airline involvement in this sort of activity has grown over the last 9 years. Although I would not like to say it is in any way complete, I would suggest to all airport authorities and consultants that where there is a significant amount of international airline operation, they should contact IATA before design or construction, and not merely talk to the local station managers. Many of them are not in a position to give forecasts of requirements; there may be design ideas and forward thinking at headquarters that consultants, designers and architects require, because, after all, they are constructing for five or seven years ahead. IATA will do its best to give realistic examples from experience and its recommendations. These may not always be right, or acceptable, but it will produce a team operation among consultants, designers, airport authorities and airlines.

Mr F. A. SHARMAN (Paper 13)

Mr Tutty implied that somehow we were not seeing eye to eye. While the Paper made only an oblique reference to the client, obviously the airline requirements are an important part of the fitness of the airport for its job. Anybody who does not find out fully what the airlines wants is falling down on his job.

Mr LEIGH FISHER (Paper 14)

I have been in the business of airport consultancy since 1946, and in response to Mr Tutty, it has been normal and customary to the best of my knowledge, without exception, when considering an airport project, to call for the organization of an Airline Technical Committee and an Airline Properties Committee. Their opinion is considered as part of the total overall project.

Mr J.R.HOUGHTON, International Civil Aviation Organization

My job is concerned with technical assistance to developing countries, and for the last five years I have been visiting civil aviation departments in the Middle East, North Africa and Eastern Europe for that purpose. I would emphasize in relation to Papers 2 - 4 that national planning for aviation is not only applicable to countries in Europe and North America. It is essential that developing nations should also prepare national transportation studies, with particular emphasis on aviation. Such studies are just as essential in Africa as they are in Europe.

As regards the funding of those operations, it is within the competence of the United Nations, and I have myself been instrumental in obtaining assistance for departments of civil aviation in the appointment of consultants for national aviation studies. There has normally been no particular difficulty in finding those funds.

ICAO can give some assistance to such development plans and it publishes an Air Navigation Plan every three years which defines ICAO recommended requirements for every international airport in the world. The plan incorporates runway length and navigational aid requirements, and all the basic design features which engineers should use in the airport design.

As part of a national plan for aviation, there should also be a phased programme for the development of the airports. Airports to be given priority in development must be selected on the basis of allocating funds to those projects where they are most needed.

It is also essential to ensure that the preparation of a master plan is the first stage in the development of an airport. In that master plan there must be a phased development programme so that the nation can pursue its development objectives year by year within the funds allocated for national development. It is possible when preparing the master plan to ensure that adequate space is left around terminal buildings, around cargo buildings and at the ends of runways etc for future developments. One need not initially build an airport to achieve the complete master plan.

A simple example occurs in respect of Damascus Airport, where in 1965 a new airport was built at a desert site. It was deemed expedient at that time not to build a terminal building, but to build a cargo building of sufficient size that it would cater, in terms of square feet , for both passenger and cargo requirements. It is only in 1976 that the Syrian authorities propose to build the permanent passenger terminal. That is an instance of an airport being developed over a period of ten years. That is the most economical way of spending when limited funds are available.

In relation to the development and planning of airports, there is the question of air traffic control facilities. This can be expensive in terms of buildings, equipment and training. In the case of many developing countries it is my my view that the volume of air traffic does not justify the initial provision of either air traffic control towers, particularly those associated with terminal buildings, or the manning requirements to provide a fully competent air traffic control system for, say, seven aircraft movements a day. The USA defines that the FAA will not provide air traffic control facilities until the number of movements on an airport reaches 24 000/year. This sounds a large number, but I would seek the experience of our American colleagues as to whether this figure is a fact, and whether they can see any objection in applying that figure to the air traffic control systems in developing countries

Mr FISHER

There is a certain number of aircraft movements at which the Federal Aviation Administration introduces formal air traffic control through a tower. Prior to that there are what are known as Flight Service Stations which are installed at a lower number and provide certain advisory services. Below that there are subsidiary services such as Unicom. In Saipan, for instance,

there is no air traffic control as such because operations do not warrant it. However, in response to the question as to whether 24 000 is a fair number, I should think that it would be necessary just to consider the traffic mix, because for the FAA for example, 24 000 is just a number. But if there were 24 000 air carrier movements at an airport, one would of course want air traffic control. One also has to address oneself to the en route traffic control. In some of these underdeveloped areas there is none, and there are no fundings to enable them. ted with terminal buildings, or the manning requirements to provide a fully competent air traffic control system for, say, seven aircraft movements a day. The USA defines that the FAA will not provide air traffic control facilities until the number of movements on an airport reaches 24 000/year. This sounds a large number, but I would seek the experience of our American colleagues as to whether this figure is a fact, and whether they can see any objection in applying that figure to the air traffic control systems in developing countries.

Panel discussion: Session IV-VI

Mr F.E.DOUWES DEKKER, Schipol Airport Authority

My first comment is addressed to Dr Wilkinson. ICAO is trying to update the Annex 16 requirements. It has been said that these were based on the concept of what was technologically feasible and economically reasonable, and this is the reason why the requirements reflect more or less what can be seen today in the air. However, with the updating of Annex 16 a point is reached at which engineers must ask themselves whether it would not be better to put in the new Annex 16 not what is technologically feasible and economically reasonable, but what is ecologically desirable. Does Dr Wilkinson think it is still possible in Annex 16 to provide for the 1980s a new set of objectives rather than confirmation of technology which is already with us?

All airports are struggling with design standards for planning with respect to noise exposure. There is only the concept of NNI, but the complaints in political situations have usually been a reaction to other effects, and I should like to know whether the noise exposure concept will still be a good one in an era when in effect the noise footprint becomes more dominant than the noise exposure itself.

Mr St John gave us a very interesting reason why perhaps AACC will have to revise its plea with respect to the two-segment approach.

On passenger movements, most people think that that the time necessary for people to move from the kerb to the aircraft is very important, and emphasise the fact that the time should be short and the distance should also be short. I have the impression that it is rather like wanting to overtake another car when you see the red light ahead of you. The process from the kerbside to the aircraft is part of the total transportation process; an experienced traveller can arrive at his aircraft seat from the kerb in about 20 mins, but it takes another 20 mins to get the plane off the ground. Then there is another 40 mins to reach the airport. With flight time added, the whole journey takes about 3 h. Therefore, is this 20 mins in the airport so important? I think one should take into account many factors other than distance and time.

Dr WILKINSON (Paper 8)

On the question of how revised noise requirements should be pitched, I have very little doubt myself that in the end there is no alternative to what amounts to a piece of horse trading between designers and the developers of engines and airframes, and the people who write the legislation and who are holding a balance between what is achievable and what is desirable. The end result is requirements which leave some element of striving to be put forth by designers, and possibly will not give the ecologists everything that they want. I cannot see how it is possible for the target to be set entirely on ecologically desirable grounds, because it would be too easy to end up with something which was not achievable without destruction of a trans-

port system. If that happened, then the rules would be discredited and not observed because they were not attainable.

So far I think there has been a skilfully contrived balance between what is desirable and what is achievable, in that it has not been too easy. It has undoubtedly stimulated designers to put themselves out to make improvement, but targets have not been totally impossible. A classic example perhaps of where the striving for the impossible finally fell by the wayside was the suggestions for retrofit, which were very expensive and which produced little in return, so that in the end interest has been lost. It is almost the essence of wise legislation that it does not attempt to achieve the impossible, but holds a balance, and I hope therefore that the next set of rules will represent another such wise assessment between the desirable and the achievable.

Mr CHAMPNISS (Paper 11)

I agree in principle with the comment relating to retrofit, that any law that is not enforceable is a bad law. On the other hand the problem with retrofit, I suggest, has been influenced by the time factor; the time that has elapsed since the problem and the possible solutions were first aired some 7 years ago. This has inevitably changed the economics and made the proposition less attractive.

Coming to future targets, is it not desirable to indicate to the airframe and aero engine manufacturers a target at which they should be shooting. The next stage of certification, the Annex 16 Mark II, will relate to aircraft entering service in about 1985 and continue in service for 10-15 years thereafter. Thus one will have a completely different situation at that time. I believe it is desirable that targets be set, even if one is unable to see a way to achieve them at the present moment.

Dr WILKINSON

Is not the trouble that any target that is significantly better than the present one from the noise point of view will cost money to achieve, and however good it may be, nobody will spend a great deal of money unless they are obliged to do so. The reason they are obliged to do so at the moment is because there is a law which states that certificates will not be given unless these limits are met.

Idealistic targets, I think, are not worth anything. What has really produced results is funding research which has led to an understanding of what is achievable. What has to be done to produce improvement is follow-up legislation, which requires within a realistic time scale the incorporation of these benefits in new production aircraft. If the requirement was not there, the aircraft would be cheaper, the airlines would pay less for their aeroplanes, and tickets would cost less. So that without the compulsion of legislation, nothing much would happen.

It is also true to say that the design feature which has achieved most current benefits

is the high by-pass feature, which really was
not invented to produce quiet engines but to
save fuel consumption and to produce a more
economical engine. But an expensive piece of
development added to the basic high by-pass
design a number of important features of the
engine including duct treatment and acoustic and
noise making quality of the engine.

Mr LEIGH FISHER (Paper 14)

Is there not also the element that has to be considered at some point, as to the sound levels
which are ecologically acceptable. That to me
relates back into land use zoning and controls
around airports because it depends on who is paying for what. In other words, cost can be reduced for the aircraft by allowing greater noise,
but all that happens is that the cost is transferred over to the airport operator (in noise
suits). If it is a fact that standards are going
to move with technological capability, at what
point should one adopt land use zones controls,
and set up a zone that protects the airport? To
me it is a two-edged sword. Not only the technological but also the environmental costs must
be considered. Unless something is produced
that is ecologically acceptable and can protect
the airport, we shall end up paying multiples of
the cost of technical advances to cure the aircraft noise by paying damages to land owners in
airport environments.

Mr F.E.DOUWES DEKKER

At Schipol we have used so far the concept of
noise and number. Perhaps when we have tackled
the problem so that the really annoying high
noise exposure areas are within the boundaries
of the airport, with a relatively lower noise
exposure outside, we shall come to the point at
which we can discard the number and come back to
the noise. All other noise from highways and so
on will also come within acceptable limits, and
I expect that we can reach the stage in the end
at which the noise produced by aircraft, or
rather the size of its footprint, will be the
only criterion for ecological acceptability.

Dr WILKINSON

I know that the noise and number index has been
under cross-fire, and that there are rival
measures such as equivalent continuous noise
level that have been proposed. However the last
word from the Government on this in the consultative document seemed to indicate that for the
time being, although there were obvious deficiencies in the noise and number index, it felt
this still represented one of the best measures
that had been invented.

Mr SHARMAN (Paper 13)

The consultative document has certainly not been
completely accepted by all interested parties in
this matter, and I anticipate substantial debate
in the consultation phase. The number of exposures to higher noise is not accepted by a
good many commentators as being adequately con-
verted, especially in relation to night noise,
and the question of curfews still has to be de-
bated.

Mr C.J.HOLLAND, R.Travers Morgan andPPartners

While not an expert in the evaluation of noise
annoyance, I was drawn to a remark that results
had been produced by funding of major research.
It is noticeable at this conference that many of
the comments on noise have been from the physical
side, and in the case of Professor Large, from
the physiological side. Little attention is
paid to the research in the field of social
response - the degree of annoyance and to what
characteristics it relates. Examination of the
amount of work done in these fields would probably indicate that the amount spent on the phy-
sics of noise sources far exceeds the amount spent
on examining what the community thinks about it.

If engineers are to reach targets which
will be acceptable, they must do more work on
which characteristics of noise annoy people.
All countries are getting locked in to particular measures which have emerged from past
studies. In Britain this is the NNI index, and
in Australia and the USA the NEF index. There are
are so many entrenched positions to protect,
particularly in countries where there are zoning requirements related to the value of these
indices, that not enough work is being done to
investigate whether there are other measures
which would better reflect what does annoy
people.

Dr WILKINSON

I should just like to reiterate what I said
earlier that research in the past has contributed such a great deal to the quality of aircraft
now coming into service that I think a great
deal of public reaction currently being experienced is really a generation out of date. It
is really irritation at aircraft of the last
generation, which were the major contributors to
airport noise. It is important not to have a
damaging time lag in reacting to public response,
because if it is assumed that further research
and expenditure should be based on what is said
now this will be misguided.

Mr HOLLAND

There may be a tendency for 'quiet' to be something which will be much more sought after, as
nations become economically better off. Therefore, for any given level of noise, greater
annoyance will be caused by it in the future than
has been caused by that same level in the past.
Producing a lower noise climate does not necessarily mean producing less annoyance. There are
indications in the field of road traffic noise,
for example, that annoyance at a given level of
noise is rising. If that is going to be the case
in the air noise issue as well, it is not enough
to show that the last observed levels of annoyance have been met.

Mr O. St. JOHN (Paper 9)

I agree with Mr Holland, I do not think it is
true to say that no work is being done in examining better noise indices, because certainly
some modest work on the social and human aspects
is being done within the Operational Research
Branch of the CAA. But it is not just a question of what constitutes annoyance. There is

the problem of how many people are annoyed. Is it twice as important to avoid annoying two people than annoying one? What seems to be missing is the overall effect, that is, taking into account the population under the source of annoyance.

Mr A.D.TOWNEND, Sir Frederick Snow (International) Ltd

One of the points engineers and planners must remember in connexion with NNI is that it has been stretched to a use beyond its original concept. In the early days when noise became a problem NNI was a brave attempt to start measuring it, but it had two aspects. There was a physical measurement and also a social survey attached to it to determine the response to certain noise levels. Moreover, that response was established for a major international airport in an urban area. Whereas it was a good measure for that situation, it has been stretched to types of airport to which it normally would not apply. For instance, there is a factor in the formula which is governed by the ambient noise level which happens to be one selected for Heathrow. That, surely, is not applicable to all other airports.

The other aspect I should like to mention is that whereas probably it is not a good absolute measure, it is a good comparative measure. In other words, whatever its defects, if one establishes NNI contours for 1975, using the same measurement gives a comparison for, say, 1980. I think it is valuable in that, but it is less valuable as a direct measure.

Sir Peter MASEFIELD, Director, British Caledonian Airways Ltd

What has become apparent is that the bigger aeroplanes, the larger aircraft for major trunk routes, will be much quieter, and are of course becoming much quieter already. This means that the bigger airports, which will have a preponderance of large quiet aeroplanes, will, relatively speaking, get better. The problem arises with the thinner routes. As the old DC 3 was moved down on to secondary and third level services, so aircraft like the BAC 1/11 will gradually be moved out of the major airports, and into regional airports, and of course they are going to remain very noisy for the rest of their lives. Because they are almost written off the books, they will be cheap to operate, and of course difficult to replace. It is always expensive, relatively speaking, to build a new small aeroplane; but it is much cheaper to use an old small aeroplane.

On the social side it is interesting to remark that it is almost impossible to get a house round a major airport. There are on average fewer houses for sale in the region of Heathrow or Gatwick, for example, than there are in SE England as a whole. Social and economic factors come into it: it seems that people are prepared to put up with noise if they are going to be close to their jobs. I should be interested if Dr Wilkinson would comment on whether there might be a quiet small aeroplane in the future.

I wonder if Mr Sharman, who has defended the work of the Roskill Commission, feels that it would be valuable to review its methodology, and see whether it might be streamlined, simplified, and then defined and equated, in case it should ever be used again, though God forbid that it should ever be needed.

Lord Boyd-Carpenter has suggested that the environmental airport should be decisively rejected. I think he is right, but I am not sure that Mr Sharman thinks he is right.

I felt a little depressed that all Mr Leigh Fisher's efforts at Guam and Saipan might not be worthwhile. One can only hope that the tourists may flock there. It is rather like the optimist who feels that everything that happens must be for the best in the best of all possible worlds, compared with the pessimist who fears that that probably is true!

Mr SHARMAN

In fact a review of the Roskill general methodology is being undertaken. As I said in Paper 13, I think that the Commission's report was rather unfairly discredited in the eyes of the general public by one or two clumsy pieces of assessment where, for instance, a Norman church was put into the balance sheet at its insurance value which scandalized ecclesiastics and others; but that should not really have been allowed to discount this huge mass of very valuable and fundamental work. The principle is perfectly sound. If you want to take a sensible decision, you take all the factors and put them into the balance and try to make a rational decision between them. That is all it means. This phrase 'cost-benefit' is nothing more than rationality. The consultative document *Airport Strategy for Great Britain* that is now before the country for comment will, to my certain knowledge, be assessed at least by some authorities on a dusted up Roskill basis, so that the method will come into play again and I hope will be useful.

As to whether I agree with Lord Boyd-Carpenter that the environmental airport is a dead duck, certainly I do not. I believe the word 'environmental' means that the advantage/disadvantage balance sheet must be examined with a sufficient care for the ecology and for the environment as a whole. Opinion swings backwards and forwards whether it can come harmlessly closer to a town or whether it must sensibly be pushed away. I should not be surprised to find that the reassessment which is going on and which will overtake the consultative document, and will bring back a very strenuous attempt to have airports that are not such a problem as those remaining near town airports are bound to be.

Of course, the third London Airport problem has not gone away. The world will not come to an end in 1990, and I do not think that Stansted as an expansion chamber for London can be got away with!

Dr PESTALOZZI (Paper 12)

For the assessment of sites for new airports the cost-benefit technique does not have much application in Continental European countries. In practice, there are no sites for new airports available. We just have to keep the existing ones in operation, almost irrespective of cost. If you consider the alternative of stopping operations, a great amount of cost can be justified to prevent this. There is no need to go into much analysis to realize that.

Dr WILKINSON

Sir Peter is right, of course, that it is always difficult to produce a revised updated version of old types of aeroplanes because it becomes progressively more expensive to do it. There is in the case of the BAC1/11, however, an aeroplane following it up called the F28 which, by virtue of its derivation and development history, will be capable shortly of leading to a 100 seat aeroplane with a version of the Spey engine which is very much quieter than that in the 1/11. It has happened almost coincidentally, but the jet velocity on that version of the engine is considerably less. It responds to duct treatment and silencing, and it looks like being a socially acceptable aeroplane. I think that size of aeroplane will be catered for in the future.

Another possibility is that if the new so-called intermediate sized engines get started in production, it is possible to produce them in a cropped fan cut down version which will again bring the benefits of this stage of engine technology into the small transport aircraft field. So I think there are options which hold benefit, but, as Sir Peter pointed out, that does not alter the fact that the main drift of development and construction work will be to the larger transport aircraft field.

Sir Peter made an interesting point about the saleability of houses around Heathrow. There is another factor that can be added to illustrate the extremely subjective nature of the reaction to noise; there are more complaints made by the residents in Kew and Putney than by the inhabitants of areas directly round the airport. One can think of a number of reasons why this would be so. But the people subjected to the loudest noise do not necessarily make the loudest complaint, and they are prepared to buy houses and go and live in the noise.

Mr F.DOVALI, Director General of Airports, Secretary of Public Works, Mexico

As I mentioned earlier, in Mexico we do not think we can transfer most of the benefits in cost, because many of the benefits are subjective. We have six main factors that we consider as measurments of effectiveness. They are cost, capacity, people displaced by construction, people affected by noise, people affected in the event of an accident, and finally the time of ground transportation. With these measurements of activity we consider an ideal airport as that which gives maximum capacity considering demand, less cost, fewer people affected by noise, fewer people affected by construction work, and fewer people affected by accident, and which is closes to the community. To this ideal airport we give 100% effectiveness, and taking into account various alternatives, not only in location, but in the

operation of various airports in the area, we compare the effectiveness of each solution with the ideal. In that way we arrive at various possibilities. The advantage of this is that eventually when the program is in the computer, anybody can feed into the computer a program given round figures and the importance attaching to each factor. A group of experts can easily analyse the different alternatives and different factors involved. With this in mind, and abandoning the idea of cost, we can evaluate the airport.

Dr WILKINSON

It sounds to me that whether you try cost benefit analysis or any other method of attempted rigorous logic, it is an important alternative to reliance on powerful emotional appeal, which is a notoriously unreliable way of deciding anything.

Mr SHARMAN

This reflects a great deal of what was said to Roskill while he was grappling with the frightful problems of translating varied factors into some sort of common currency. It is a little misleading to call the ultimate Roskill method 'cost-benefit', because it paid tribute to the fact that the most important factors are unquantifiable. But it seeks at least to take those comparative factors which are quantifiable to their logical conclusion, and then ask how much one is prepared to pay for the privilege of avoiding this or that intangible quality, which I agree cannot be expressed except in terms of words and emotions. In the evidence to Roskill there is of course the Lichfield social cost-benefit balance sheet which was a little different from the hard economic cost-benefit analysis that people tend to associate with Roskill. There was a great deal of useful work in those records.

Mr F.H.RUSSELL, Sir William Halcrow & Partners

I was surprised at the suggestion earlier that a developing country might do without an air traffic control system in an airport. An airport in a developing country is almost invariably going to be an international airport, and even if it has only one or two international movements a day, it still needs an air traffic control system. To overcome the problem that was implied, that it is a very costly business to put an ATC tower on a new building, it is now becoming the practice to build a small administrative building with an ATC tower on it, entirely separate from the passenger building, which comes later.

The other aspect of developing countries is that not enough attention, in my opinion, is given to aspects of air cargo. People have in most cases been talking about how to handle passengers and their baggage, but in developing air transport for countries which have very little in the way of transport, air cargo has an increasingly important role to play, either to bring in materials so that they can develop, or to get the products out of that country.

On the importance of passengers at terminal

buildings of airports, one of the things which still defies all the experts is the matter of getting the passenger's baggage back into his hand at the end of the journey. I should like to see some research done on that.

Mr LEIGH FISHER

The question of air traffic control is again a matter of relativity. Take, for instance, the island of Pa Pau. It is a few hundred miles from anywhere else, off the airways yet has a schedule every other day. It would certainly not be sensible to propose an air traffic control en route system and an ATC tower in that case. The air carrier itself provides en route and airport air traffic control through its company radio system. The answer depends on what is meant by 'developing'. Developing can be from a population of 500 upwards. In the outback of Australia, there are many places without ATC which have scheduled services. They get en route traffic control through radio communications. I am no expert in air traffic control, but I must repeat that traffic control is relative to the region, the amount of traffic, the character of the traffic and the character of the airport.

Mr DAVIES (Paper 15)

On the subject of air traffic control, whilst making no claims to being an expert I do have some practical knowledge as I was trained as a commercial pilot in Australia and I have managed to keep a current licence. I took the view that Mr Houghton was making a case for not providing air traffic control facilities regardless of the number of aircraft movements. In the case of Kenya, there are air traffic control services at five airports comprising two international and three domestic fields. Apart from these aerodromes there are close to 150 smaller airfields which serve game parks, border posts, tourist resorts etc., and obviously it would not be practical for each of these airstrips to have air traffic control facilities. However at the other end of the scale the general aviation airport of Wilson, which is located close to the approaches to the main runway at Nairobi International Airport, has some 15 000 movements/month comprising a large proportion of the test and training category. This aerodrome has air traffic control and, based on my experience while operating from Wilson, these services are essential; due to the combination of an adjacent military airfield and an international airport, together with the high level of movements at Wilson, without air traffic control operations would be hazardous. However between these two extremes there has to be a cut-off point when ATC is not considered to be justified.

As to the need for greater recognition by developing countries of the importance of air cargo, that point is valid. There is some acceptance of the need for special consideration of air cargo in Kenya because, as part of the work which is in hand at Nairobi Airport, a new freight building designed to handle up to about 90 000 t/year is in the course of construction. This building is designed to cope with a wide range of horticultural and dairy products, including cut flowers, high quality fruits, meat and general cargo. So there is some sign of appreciation of the important role of air freight by at least one developing country.

16. Rail access to major airports
with special reference to Heathrow, Gatwick and Birmingham

W.W. Maxwell MA, FIMechE, FIEE, FCIT

E.L. Rockwell Dipl-Ing., MIngF, MCIT
London Transport Executive

Dealing solely with passenger traffic, railway or railway-type transport to airports is analysed and certain systems are described in detail.

A.   GENERAL

INTRODUCTION

1. When we were asked by the Organising Committee to present a paper at the 5th World Airports Conference on 'Rail access to major airports, with special reference to Heathrow, Gatwick and Birmingham', we were also given the following guidelines:

'One of the most difficult problems faced by major airports in the future is likely to be the provision of adequate surface access and the interface with other transport systems.   The paper examines the probable need to turn increasingly to public transport to meet the requirements of surface transport to airports in the future, and shows that rail links have both attractions and drawbacks.   The paper uses the London Underground extension as an illustration of the general worldwide aspects of the surface transport problem.'

On behalf of London Transport we were pleased to accept this remit as it agrees completely with our understanding of the problem and our approach to it.

2. We have interpreted the subject as relating to passenger traffic only.   The handling of railway freight at airports is an altogether different problem;   moreover, despite the great increase in air cargo traffic over the years the transfer of goods between air and rail does not appear to have assumed major significance.

3. Rail access to airports has been the subject of some - though not many - earlier publications. One of the most helpful papers on this topic within the last five years or so has been the report on 'Airport to city communications' presented at the Rome Congress of the Inter-national Union of Public Transport (UITP) in 1971 by Dr. W. J. Ronan, then Chairman of the New York City Transit Authority (now Chairman of the Port Authority of New York and New Jersey). His report was mainly based on a questionnaire sent out by the UITP, and the assistance received from public transport representatives in London, Paris and Rome was kindly acknowledged.   More recently, a similar topic 'The customer and the surface phase of air transport' has been the theme of a Convention called by the Royal Aeronautical Society in

London in May 1975.

4. We propose to deal with the subject, first of all, in general terms by reviewing the kind of passengers who might be expected to use a railway to or from an airport, and discussing the types of railways which might perform this function.   This should enable us to compare the merits of private and public transport and, as far as the latter is concerned, the res-pective merits of buses and railways for airport purposes.   We then intend to give brief descriptions of the present and proposed rail access conditions at Birmingham and Gatwick, before turning to Heathrow, where the construction of the Underground extension has been preceded by particularly thorough investigations which may be of interest to other planners concerned with ground problems at airports elsewhere in the world.

TYPES OF POTENTIAL RAIL PASSENGERS AT AIRPORTS

1. In connection with rail access to airports, it would be quite wrong to consider the interests of airline passengers only.   At some of the major airports, many thousands of people are employed - there are over 50,000 at Heathrow! - so that the airports may be regarded as towns in their own right which require adequate ground transport facilities even apart from airline passengers.   Other categories of would-be rail passengers include air passengers' escorts, sightseers and other visitors, and possibly, in some cases, also some ordinary urban commuters.   This must be kept in mind when considering the merits and otherwise of rail access to airports.

2. But let us, nevertheless, first consider the air passenger.   He, too, is by no means a homogeneous creature, capable of being adequately represented by some standardised Mr. or Mrs. or Miss Average.   The genus comprises a wide range of species, from the package tour party for a chartered flight, arriving at and departing from the airport in coach loads, to the business executive travelling first class and taken to and from the airport by a company limousine.   In between these extremes is a vast range of ordinary tourist class passengers - families going on holiday, businessmen travelling with light luggage to a one-day conference in some other town,

globetrotters making trips for a great variety of purposes.   We have no reliable information about the composition of that body of people collectively known as air passengers, but we understand that there has been, in recent years, a significant shift - percentagewise - towards the brief-air-trip passenger travelling with light luggage.   If this is confirmed, it is bound to have a bearing on the merits of rail access.

3.   Closely related to this heterogeneity of air passengers is the question of passengers' escorts, i.e. the movements of other people in connection with an air passenger's trip.   Where a passenger is taken to the airport or collected in the car of a friend or a member of the family, or in a chauffeur-driven company car, every departure or arrival of the air passenger will involve a second car trip without him. If he comes by taxi, this second trip would of course be avoided if the taxi can find a return fare.   Similarly, there are no second trips if the air passenger arrives in his own car, parking it at the airport; but this obviously makes a claim on parking accommodation which may be difficult and expensive to provide.   But even apart from the friend acting as a driver, an air passenger leaving or arriving by air, and arriving or leaving by any ground transport mode, is often also escorted by other people - parents seeing their children off, people meeting some friends, relatives or business contacts, etc. - and all those people must, on each occasion, make a return trip to the airport, i.e. make two single trips where the air passenger makes only one.

4.   Depending on the size and importance of the airport, the number of air passengers and their escorts likely to use a rail link to and from the airport may well be considerably boosted by that generally more land-bound category of people, the airport staff.   For them (with the possible exception of air crews on long-distance flights, staying away for a number of days), the trip is in the nature of an ordinary daily commuter journey from home to work and back, though with a greater incidence of shift work than in the case of the ordinary 9-to-5 commuter.   If the number of staff employed is significant, the very fact of their daily movements (as opposed to the occasional trips of air passengers and their escorts) makes this category a potentially very important component of would-be passengers for a rail link.

5.   There are, however, also other categories of casual visitors who will have to be taken into account.   Among them are the spectators who may be attracted by the comings and goings at a large international airport.   Their number will of course vary, not only with the inherent attraction of the airport, but also very much with the season, with the school holidays and with the weather, but the number can reach quite high figures and, as the maximum attendance is likely to coincide with the main travel season during the summer

school holidays, may well add to the peak demands on ground transport facilities at the airport.   Amongst other visitors will be business and trade representatives dealing with the often great number of shops within the airport precincts, though most of these, especially if they have to carry samples, would presumably always prefer to use their private car.

6.   Finally, depending on the geographical position of the airport in relation to the town, a rail link between airport and town may also have the incidental function of carrying ordinary urban commuters who happen to live in the vicinity of the airport and find the rail link a convenient means of going to and from work.   When considering the traffic likely to use a proposed rail link to the airport, it is therefore necessary to take a wide range of potential users into account.

TYPES OF (EXISTING OR PROPOSED) RAIL SERVICES TO AIRPORTS

1.   Now, what kind of rail services are available to carry these passengers?   In principle, a distinction might be made between three different types of rail access to airports by passenger trains, viz:

(a) a line or service specifically designed to link the airport with the centre of the town, generally leading to some sort of in-town air terminal, without intermediate stops;

(b) a service associated with ordinary (stopping) suburban services of the main lines; and

(c) a service associated with ordinary (stopping) services of a metropolitan railway of the 'Underground' type.

In actual practice, there may of course be some intermediate variants of rail facilities which do not strictly conform to this simplified classification.   Each of these types will bestow different degrees of benefits to different categories of rail passengers. Without claiming to present anything like a comprehensive survey, we should like briefly to enlarge on the three main types by reference to some actual examples.

2.   An early example of a specialised airport service - type (a) above - has been in existence for many years in Brussels where the airport is linked by a special railcar shuttle service of the Belgian National Railway Company (SNCB) with an in-town air terminal incorporated in the 'Halte Centrale' of the Brussels Junction Railway and run by Sabena, the Belgian airline. Another example of an airport directly served by a main line railway is Gatwick, to which we shall revert later.   And if the term railway is taken to include railway-like facilities of a non-conventional type, the Hitachi-Alweg Monorail between Haneda Airport and Tokyo must

be mentioned. These rail facilities are open
to the general public, though there are certain
air terminal facilities at the in-town end.
Even so, all these specialised railways are
mainly designed for rapid connection between
town and airport, suitable for airline
passengers with in-town origin or destination
rather than airport staff, visitors, etc.

3. Railway services of type (b) normally take
the form of ordinary suburban railway facilities
mostly electric and running at frequent and
regular intervals, which in addition to serving
a chain of suburban stations also call at a
station closely linked with the airport. A
recent example is that of the Rhein-Main
Airport at Frankfurt where a specially built
railway station is served by a branch of the
electrified suburban railway system ('S-Bahn').
Another 'S-Bahn' branch to the airport has just
been opened in Dusseldorf. The Swiss Federal
Railways have begun the construction of a 6½km
long loop line to serve Kloton Airport, Zurich.
A similar facility is planned by the Netherlands
Railways for a connection between Schiphol
Airport and Amsterdam. In a sense, the future
plans for Birmingham Airport (to which we shall
revert later) may also be said to come under
this heading though, in this case, the emphasis
is on intercity rather than suburban railway
services. Railway services of type (b) cannot
offer the speed of a specialised rail service,
but are of potential benefit to a greater variety
of passengers.

4. With railway services of type (c), finally,
the airport becomes just one of many traffic
objectives served by an urban-type rapid transit
line which might similarly serve the main line
railway terminals and provide a more ubiquitous
network with frequent services - often so
frequent as to obviate the need for published
timetables. As a rule, such railways cannot,
because of their 'universal' nature, provide
special facilities for airline passengers; on
the other hand, their very universality will
tend to offer valuable facilities for all
categories of passengers at the airport, not
least for airport employees. Among existing
examples are Cleveland, where the airport is
served by a recent extension of the Cleveland
Transit System, and Boston and Berlin
(Tempelhof) where the rapid transit stations
are, however, not directly incorporated with
the airport so that passengers still have to
walk or take a short bus ride. In future, one
of the most prominent examples will be provided
by the Piccadilly Line extension to Heathrow
Airport, which we shall discuss in some detail
later on.

COMPARING THE MERITS OF GROUND TRANSPORT
MODES AT AIRPORTS

1. Having briefly reviewed the categories of
potential passengers and potential services for
rail facilities at airports, we can now try to
compare the merits of the different ground
transport modes with each other. If we again
confine ourselves to basic principles, such

comparisons can be conveniently reduced to two:
a comparison between private and public
transport and, within the latter, a comparison
between railways and buses. However, even an
academic appraisal cannot be carried out in a
vacuum. Among the local factors having a
bearing on the modal choice will be the quality
of road access to the airport, the ground
origins and destinations of airline passengers
and other potential railway users, and the
existence and functions of an in-town air
terminal.

2. It is perhaps especially the last-named
feature which is likely to have a bearing on
the 'modal split' at least of the airline
passengers component of airport ground traffic.
If there is an attractive, well-situated in-
town air terminal available, where airline
passengers can entrust themselves and,
particularly, their luggage to the airline or
airport organisation, this will no doubt
attract a greater proportion of airline
passengers to public transport - especially if
this is provided in the form of a fast rail
link. We do, however, understand that - if
only for economic reasons - the general trend
of the policies pursued by the airline
companies is away from in-town air terminals
with check-in facilities, and towards a greater
emphasis on passenger handling at the airport
itself. ** If that is so, the incentive for
airline passengers to use public rather than
private transport will, to some degree, be
lessened.

3. However that may be, there will of course
always be a high proportion of airline
passengers who will prefer to travel by private
ground transport almost irrespective of the
quality of public transport service on offer,
for the obvious reason that the private car
generally offers a higher degree of mobility
and comfort, not confined to a public network
or to timetables, and makes it much easier to
convey baggage. On the other hand, the use of
the car always requires either the assistance
of a driver or the parking of the car at the
airport during the absence of the owner. Moreover, with the increasing congestion on the
roads, which tends to slow down road access to
the airport and - worse still - to make the
road journey time unpredictable so that
departing air passengers must allow a much
greater time margin if they do not wish to miss
their flight, there is bound to be a shift of
emphasis towards greater use of rail access
where this can be provided.

** cf. "Report of a study of Rail Links with
Heathrow Airport", part II, 1970. para.7.5.5
". . . the assumption that town check-in
facilities were an unmixed blessing and that
their capacity would grow with the growth of
air travel has been widely questioned, not
least by the airlines."

4. In comparing buses with railways, it goes without saying that for most airports, for economic and/or geographical reasons, a choice between these two modes of public transport will not arise, and coaches on specialised services and/or buses on normal routes will continue to be the only form of public transport (apart from taxis). But where such a choice does arise, the slowness and unpredictability of road journeys again militates against the use of buses as compared with rail access. A relevant example has been provided by the coach service between the West London Air Terminal and Heathrow Airport, where departing airline passengers no longer have the guarantee of connecting with their flight, and must therefore allow considerably more 'contingency' time, in addition to the slower journey as compared with a railway - an advantage of the railway which represents an important off-set against the much higher capital cost of a rail link.

5. If the railway already has important advantages to airline passengers, the case for rail access to the airport is greatly strengthened if all the other categories of potential rail passengers - and especially airport staff - are also taken into account. We are therefore convinced that rail access to airports will come to play an increasingly important part in the future; it is, in fact, surprising that this process has been rather slow in starting. In accordance with our remit, we shall now turn to the specific cases of Birmingham, Gatwick and Heathrow.

B. BIRMINGHAM AND GATWICK

BIRMINGHAM

1. Birmingham Airport is situated about 7 miles from the centre of Birmingham alongside the Birmingham-Coventry trunk road and a short distance away from the Birmingham-London railway. The airport is now under the control of the West Midlands County Council and handles a total passenger traffic of about 1.1 million passengers per annum, including about 40,000 in transit, i.e. not requiring ground transport.

2. Up to the time of writing (December 1975), the airport has had virtually no rail access as there has been no station on the adjacent main line railway within convenient reach of the airport. By the time this paper is due to be presented, however, 'Birmingham International' station will have been opened about a mile away, mainly to serve the National Exhibition Centre which will have been opened shortly afterwards. The new station, designed on a generous scale, will be served by a fair number of local and Inter-City trains at frequent and regular intervals. And as the station will be linked with the airport by fairly frequent local buses, covering the distance in a few minutes, rail access to Birmingham Airport is expected to account for a significant share of the total ground traffic within a short time.

3. In the longer term, an ambitious plan for erecting a new airport terminal building adjacent to the new railway station is designed to make the railway the principal mode of access to the airport as well as to link the airport directly with Europe's largest exhibition site on the other side of the railway station. But the plan calls for major works, including the diversion of a major road, the levelling of large areas of ground, and the construction of vast concrete aprons so that its realisation is bound to take some time.

GATWICK

1. Birmingham Airport will then have the benefit of rail access facilities similar to those enjoyed by Gatwick, London's second airport, for many years already. At present, out of a total annual traffic of the order of 5 million air passengers, rail access at Gatwick accounts for about 2½ million and this figure is expected to rise to some 9 million out of 16 million by the 1990s.

2. British Rail are about to start work on a major improvement scheme which will involve a remodelling of the entire station layout, the widening of the platform, and the construction of a new station concourse on the same level as the airport terminal. In addition, there are plans for increasing the train frequency to and from Victoria to eight trains per hour. At least half of these trains will have detachable portions for airport passengers.

C. HEATHROW

Heathrow Airport data

1. Before discussing the schemes for rail access to Heathrow Airport, it would seem useful to recall some of its vital statistics. Although the total air passenger traffic at Heathrow lags well behind some of the American airports, especially O'Hare Airport in Chicago, Heathrow has by far the greatest number of passengers on international flights, requiring a much more extensive system of customs and immigration facilities. This is also one of the reasons for the great number of staff employed at the airport, amounting at present to over 50,000 although, because of rest-day rotas, the number of staff working on any one day is about 35,000 "only".

2. In 1974, Heathrow handled a total of almost 21 million air passengers, including nearly 400,000 transit passengers requiring no land-side transport. Earlier surveys suggest that about half of all air passengers requiring land-side transport arrived or departed by car or taxi; most of the remainder came or left by airline coaches, and a relatively small number by bus, including a London Transport expresss bus connecting the airport with Hounslow West station, the former terminal of London Transport's Piccadilly Line. Present forecasts envisage that the total annual air traffic will reach the ceiling of 30 million passengers, set by the existing three passenger

terminals, during the 1980s, by which time a
fourth terminal on the south side of the airport
may have to be in operation.

History of the rail link to Heathrow

1. The idea of a rail link with Heathrow
Airport was first mooted in 1956. At that
time, however, the prospective growth of air
traffic was under-estimated, and it was thought
that the pending construction of the M4 motorway, with its spur to the airport, would take
care of the traffic growth then expected.
Then, as air traffic shot up rapidly in the
meantime, the question of a rail link was again
taken up in 1966, this time by the 'Transport
Co-ordinating Council for London'. This body,
having looked at various options, including
non-conventional railway-like modus, and short-
listed two schemes based on conventional rail
links, came out in 1967 with a majority
recommendation favouring a British Rail link
with Victoria to replace the present coach
services.

2. Subsequently, however, there were important
changes in circumstances. The airlines were,
at that time, not prepared to abandon their
coach services in favour of a rail-only link as
originally envisaged by British Railways;
there were also clear signs of the general trend,
already referred to, away from check-in
facilities at comprehensive in-town terminals
and towards a greater concentration of handling
facilities at the airport. Finally, it proved
difficult to find, even after prolonged
examination, a reliable yet of necessity
sophisticated baggage handling system for
airline passengers using the British Rail link.

3. For all these reasons, it obviously became
necessary to re-examine the problem. So, in
September 1969, the President of the Board of
Trade and the Minister of Transport (as they
then were) asked the interested bodies to look
into the matter again. As a result, a
'Heathrow Link Steering Group' was set up to do
this under the chairmanship of the Ministry of
Transport, with representatives of that
Ministry, of the Board of Trade, the Greater
London Council, the Westminster City Council,
the British Airports Authority, the then BEA
and BOAC, British Rail and London Transport.

4. The Steering Group published a short summary
report in May 1970 and a more detailed report in
August of that year. They came to the
conclusion that, in all the (changed) circumstances, the best solution would now be to build
the Piccadilly Line extension, yet to continue
the operation of the coaches. London Transport
promptly submitted the scheme to the Greater
London Council, who adopted it in July 1970,
promising to pay 25% of the infra-structure cost
on the understanding that 75% of that cost was
to be met by the Government. In the event, the
Government first refused to make any contribution at all but later consented to pay 25% so
that London Transport still has to find 50% of
the cost which was then expected to amount to

about £15 million, including land and rolling
stock, but excluding the cost of the connections
between the Underground terminal and the three
airport terminals. Mainly because of
inflation, the cost has now risen to about
£27 million. However, unlike most other
schemes for the construction of new urban railways, the Heathrow extension of the Piccadilly
Line was expected to be self-financing, even
including the servicing of the full capital
cost of construction.

Description of the Piccadilly Line extension

1. The Piccadilly Line extension links up with
the existing line at a point just east of the
former terminal, Hounslow West, where the line
has been diverted to new platforms, linked to
the existing booking hall. The extension has
a length of about 3½ miles, including 2 miles
built partly by 'cut-and-cover' methods and
partly on the surface, the remainder being in
tube tunnels, mainly below the airport runways.
There is one intermediate station at Hatton
Cross in the south-east corner of the airport,
on the main Great South West Road and near the
principal airport engineering and maintenance
areas; this station was opened in July 1975.
The terminal station, Heathrow Central, due to
be opened in 1977, is being built in the centre
of the airport near the control tower and will
be connected to all the three existing air
terminals by means of pedestrian subways
equipped with moving walkways. The station
will be in the form of an island platform with
two tracks which will be used alternately by
reversing trains but could be extended westwards
if and when it is desired to extend the line,
e.g. to another air terminal at Perry Oaks.

2. As the Piccadilly Line extension is part of
an 'ordinary' urban railway, the train service
will be largely governed by the requirements of
commuter traffic. During commuter peak hours,
Heathrow Central will be served by trains every
4 minutes. The off-peak services, though less
frequent, will be strengthened compared with
the present services by extending to Heathrow
certain trains at present turning at stations
nearer town so that the train services will
range from 8 to 12 trains per hour outside the
commuter peak periods. In spite - or because -
of its character as an urban railway, the
Piccadilly Line is well suited to serve the
airport. Firstly, because the service is not
only frequent but also relatively fast, with
trains normally running non-stop over the 2¾
mile section between Acton Town and Hammersmith.
Secondly, the Piccadilly Line directly serves
the most important tourist and hotel areas in
Inner London (including Kensington, Piccadilly
and Bloomsbury). Thirdly, the Piccadilly Line
has interchange facilities with all other lines
of the Underground system, including a
convenient cross-platform interchange facility
with the District Line at Hammersmith, so that
it provides, directly or with but one change,
convenient connections to most parts of London
and to most of the main line terminals.

Potential shortcomings of the Piccadilly Line extension

1. However, the utilisation of an urban-type railway for rail access to an airport also has certain potential drawbacks which must be taken into account when new facilities of this kind are being planned. These potential drawbacks have certainly been the subject of thorough discussions in the case of the Heathrow link, especially in relation to the alternative scheme for a non-stop service of British Railways' trains to Victoria. They can be conveniently discussed under four headings, viz.

   - journey time from and to town
   - congestion during commuter peak hours
   - the luggage problem, and
   - the service gap at night.

2. There is, first of all, the question of a longer journey time by ordinary tube train for airline passengers travelling all the way between the airport and central London. In fact, the actual train journey from Heathrow Central to the fringe of the central area at Hyde Park Corner will take about 35 minutes, compared with a non-stop run to Victoria, which would have taken about 23 minutes. However, from a passengers' point of view, this differential would be reduced in the first place by the longer average waiting time for the necessarily less frequent BR service where the headways might have been 10 or 15 minutes, compared with 4 or 5 minutes during the day on the Piccadilly Line extension.

3. But perhaps even more important is the fact that the destination of the great majority of (say) incoming airline passengers is not Victoria but anywhere in Greater London with a preponderance of central London in general and the hotel areas in particular. Nearly all the airline passengers would therefore have to continue their journey from Victoria by taxi, car, bus or Underground and, by the time they have done that, they might as well have taken the Piccadilly train all the way which, rather than depositing them at a single fringe point with heavy traffic concentration, enables them to go anywhere in town as far as the ubiquitous Underground system will carry them. The advantages of the Piccadilly Line link are of course particularly obvious for airline passengers with West London destinations and for most of the airport staff for whom a non-stop link with central London would be useless.

4. The next obvious potential objection is the possible non-compatibility of airport traffic and urban commuter traffic. In the case of the Piccadilly Line extension, this question was thoroughly investigated, not only by London Transport but also by the impartial Steering Group. Fortunately, the air traffic peak does not normally coincide with the much heavier commuter peak. Moreover, the peak of airline traffic occurs during the summer holiday period when the volume of commuter traffic is markedly lower. Furthermore, commuter traffic on the Hounslow branch of the Piccadilly Line had shown, at least up to about 5 years ago, a steady decline over the years (no doubt partly due to the counter-attraction of the airport as a large-scale workplace) and was expected to decline still further, leaving relatively more space for airport passengers.

5. The latter would in any case have virtually no difficulties at any time during off-peak and in the counter-flow direction of the commuter peak; even in the direction of the main commuter flow, incoming airline passengers would always find a seat at Heathrow Central where the trains start empty. The only potential difficulties of any significance could occur if a heavy outgoing airline traffic should coincide with the evening peak hour of home-going commuters, which may happen, e.g. on a Friday evening in the summer. Altogether, however, it was worked out that no more than one-eightieth of the total time spent by all the airline passengers using the Piccadilly Line would be spent standing. The latest estimates indicate that, overall, some 20% of all outgoing air passengers will be unable to get a seat immediately but even they will, as a result of the continual turnover of Underground passengers, have the opportunity of obtaining seats after a few stations.

6. Closely associated with the question of peak-hour travel is the question of airline passengers' luggage. Here, it is first of all relevant to recall that (in contrast to the alternative British Railways scheme) the scheme for the Piccadilly Line extension was intended to go forward while the airport coach services from and to the in-town air terminals with check-in facilities would still remain available. It is true that the check-in facilities at West London Air Terminal have meanwhile been abandoned but the coaches still take luggage and it seems reasonable to assume that air passengers with particularly heavy luggage will always prefer to go to or from the airport by coach, taxi or private car.

7. On the other hand, perhaps partly due to the greater incidence of trips by businessmen travelling with light luggage, the average weight of luggage per person is declining, so that a greater proportion of air passengers would have no difficulties in handling their luggage during an Underground journey. The problem will therefore be much less of a worry than the time-honoured practice of main line railway passengers using the Underground for trips to or from (say) Victoria, King's Cross, Liverpool Street or Waterloo, i.e. at more critical points of the network, at more awkward times of the day and generally with heavier luggage. However, despite these favourable portents, the new trains which have just been introduced on the Piccadilly Line in fact provide better luggage accommodation as they have larger vestibules.

8. Lastly, another potential problem arises because tube railways run in narrow, single-bore tunnels so that maintenance work can only be carried out while train services are suspended. This must be done for an adequate period once every 24 hours, and is most conveniently done during the small hours of the night. This need does not arise with the surface line trains of British Railways, where maintenance work can be carried out between trains. However, the airline traffic during the night hours is very light and can easily be carried by the airport coaches which would, in any case, continue to operate, if only in order to cater for the special requirements of air passengers carrying heavy luggage.

9. To judge by the example of the Piccadilly Line extension to Heathrow Airport, we therefore feel entitled to state that all the potential drawbacks of an airport being served by an urban type railway can either be avoided or sufficiently mitigated. Let us therefore, in conclusion, recall the merits of that rail link.

Conclusion

1. After a construction time of six years - unfortunately prolonged by industrial disputes - and for a capital investment which, because of inflation, is likely to rise from the original estimate of £15m. at 1970 price levels to over £30m. by the time the line is opened in 1977, the Piccadilly Line extension should have a drastic effect on the facilities at Heathrow Airport.

2. Connecting the world's busiest international airport with one of the world's busiest rapid transit systems, the Piccadilly Line extension is expected to handle, at Heathrow Central station, fairly soon after opening, a traffic of nearly 11m. passengers per annum, including 7.5m. air passengers, 1.8m. journeys by airport staff, and 1.6m. other journeys (air passengers' escorts, sightseers, etc.). Passengers will have a frequent and direct service, unencumbered by traffic congestion on the roads, to the main tourist and hotel areas in central London as well as large residential areas in West London, with easy interchange connections to and from other points of Greater London and many main line terminals.

3. As the Piccadilly Line extension is short compared with the rest of the line, and as the line near its suburban end is by far not used to capacity, the airport traffic can be carried at no more than marginal costs, which is also reflected in the fact that the number of trains required for service on the Piccadilly Line, at present nearly 80, will only need to be increased by two. The investment therefore results in a more economic use of existing assets and resources.

4. On a wider scale, the scheme will also give rise to other important social benefits, reflected, e.g. in the fact that road congestion and the need for new road works will be reduced and that planning developments along the line will be encouraged - a process that has already begun in anticipation of the opening of the extension.

5. To the extent to which the Piccadilly Line extension to Heathrow Airport can be regarded as typical, it should encourage the pursuit of similar schemes for rail access to major airports throughout the world.

17. Access to Los Angeles International Airport: landside restraints

C.A. Moore
General Manager, City of Los Angeles Dept of Airports

In examining the problems of access to Los Angeles International Airport, it was necessary to evaluate the freeway system as it exists today and the patterns that it will take in the future. Studies were made as to the total number of passengers that could gain access to the airport via the existing street system. It was determined that the figure of 24 million could be increased to 33 million by increasing surface connections from the north, south and west. Utilizing the figure of 33 million passengers, estimates were made as to how this figure might be increased by the completion of the freeway system to a total capacity of 56 million annual passengers.

1. A projection made in 1967 concluded that the capability of access to Los Angeles International Airport on existing external freeways and surface streets was approximately 24 million annual passengers. It was further concluded that by the year 1975, with proposed freeway and road systems expansion programs, 40 million passengers could be reached and that with additional work sometime in the late 1900's, a capacity of some 50 million passengers could be handled in terms of access limitations.

2. West access: The first option for increasing access capability to Los Angeles International was considered to be a new road approaching from the west; thus adding one million annual passengers to the surface access traffic volume.

3. South access: The second option was a tunnel connection leading from Imperial Highway on the south side of LAX, directly north to the proposed new west terminal, adding another one million passengers to the system.

4. North access: The third option was a tunnel from the north connecting Manchester and Lincoln Boulevards via a route under the northerly pairs of runways to the proposed new west terminal, adding some seven million passengers to the total.

These new access route systems gave a base passenger figure of an annual passenger capacity of 33 million. To reach the 40 million capacity, which was the first milestone to be achieved in 1975, based on the 1967 study, we depended upon the further development of the freeway system surrounding Los Angeles International Airport. We expected to have Freeway Route 42 along the south side of the airport, connecting to the Imperial tunnel, which would provide capacity for an additional seven million annual

passengers.

6. The ultimate passenger capacity in terms of route access as conceived in the 1967 study depended on an extension of the freeway on the south to the west, connecting to a freeway extending to the north, parallel to the western boundary of the airport, which again connected to Route 170, running easterly and parallel to the north boundary, connecting finally with the Santa Monica and San Diego Freeway systems.

7. This ultimate freeway system could add capacity for 32 million annual passengers to the base figure of 24 million passengers, giving us a total capacity of 56 million annual passengers.

8. All of these projections for access capacities and growth were based on a situation which existed in Southern California and Los Angeles at that time. The annual passenger growth rate was rather dramatic, running at approximately 15 percent, while at the same time we had an ambitious and well-financed highway program under the State of California developing the new freeway system and spending literally billions of dollars of combined State and Federal funds in its achievement.

9. About 1972, like the rest of the world, we suddenly encountered the first strong effects of the environmental movement.

10. The most immediate effect of the environmental movement was to cause a complete slowdown in the freeway and highway development program. The political struggle which developed within our state legislature for the determination of the extent to which funds would be used for construction of freeways or diverted into mass transportation systems, either buses or rail systems, reached major proportions.

11. Suffice it to say, for purposes of this comparison that; one, traffic did not generate and continue to develop at the rate indicated in the 60's; Los Angeles International is at approximately 24 million passengers in 1975 when, back at that time, it was projected that we would have a total of 40 million annual passengers in 1975. The west terminal which was intended to be constructed by 1975 and other terminals in the program were not constructed. The highways and freeway, as contemplated at that time, were never built; instead, more than $100 million had to be diverted to the acquisition of land for airport use and environmental reasons, and alternative programs of remote parking had to be adopted.

12. Los Angeles International today is a regional service facility, providing the major airline/airport service for the five-county area around Los Angeles. Access to the airport is predominantly by private vehicles. The airport is serving slightly less than 24 million annual passengers as well as charters, charter activity, general aviation, etc. This level of activity causes particularly high level of usage of street and freeway system in the area. Most of the street systems are improved to reasonably current standards. The volumes exceed 129,000 vehicle trips per day in the airport area, with over 75,000 in the central terminal area alone. Those trips are spread rather generally and rather evenly over the entire area with no main sector of the area accounting for more than 12 percent. The average trip length for passengers arriving at the airport is 20 miles. I have attached copies of the directional distribution. Over 50 percent of the airport-area employees reside near the airport with an employee average trip length of nine miles.

13. Airport-area traffic accounts for 17 percent of the total vehicle miles on the San Diego Freeway and 34 percent of the street travel miles within the area. Roughly 25 percent of the total daily vehicle miles travelled in the street and freeway system is due to Los Angeles International Airport. The airport-related traffic accounts for 1.7 million vehicle miles of travel in the area served by LAX, or approximately 530 million annual vehicle miles. Each originating passenger generates .56 entering vehicles, or 1.1 vehicle trips per day. Ground traffic volumes vary seasonally or monthly and by day of the week.

14. The highest and most sustained demands on the system occur on Fridays in the summer months. A peak Friday in July represented conditions exceeding 95 percent of the daily traffic volume throughout the year. Friday had the longest sustained peak travel period and was most critical to the elements of the internal ground transportation system. Therefore, Friday has been used as the design day for these analyses. The traffic volume entering and leaving the central terminal area on

this peak day in 1972 was estimated at 92,000 vehicles as compared with an average of approximately 75,000 vehicles per day. The peak hour on the design summer Friday was at 8:00 p.m., with an hourly entering volume of 3200 vehicles. This peak does not conflict with normal highway peak, which is 4:00 - 6:00 p.m. The peak hour entering volume on the design day was 7 percent of the daily entering volume. It is interesting to note that on peak air passenger activity days, traffic volumes exceed available roadway capacities by as much as 30 percent. During these times Century Boulevard, which is the main entrance roadway, has been congested heavily as far east as the San Diego Freeway, about 1-1/2 miles from the terminal. This condition is related to lack of adequate parking capacity at locations of high parking demand as illustrated by congested curb loading space in the central terminal area and lack of street capacity to accommodate these volumes within and adjacent to the core area. One of the corollary problems on peak days, in fact the principle problem, is congestion which develops internally within the central terminal area itself, causing further congestion to develop outside of the airport.

15. In order to attack the traffic management problem due to the high ratio of vehicle trip per passenger at Los Angeles Airport and due to the curtailment of the highway construction program, a change in direction has been indicated which leads to the development of better traffic management; for example, widening of the central terminal area roadway, which is currently underway, the installation and development of an airport radio system at 530 hertz on the dial of the car radio transmitting information to the passenger once he leaves the freeway as to parking and traffic conditions in the terminal. More sophisticated signing systems are also being studied using changeable message signing for use by cars in the area on the surface streets. The main thrust, however, is to prevent the car or entice the car not to make the trip to the airport or, if they still insist on doing so, to make it more attractive to them not to enter the central terminal area. The original development in this area was the so-called VSP parking facility located at about two miles from the central terminal area; VSP being an acronym for Very Simple Parking for Very Smart People at Very Special Prices. By offering a free ride from those areas as it is done in many airports in the world at a sufficiently low price, many of the long-term parkers were induced to use that facility which has now been increased to 4,000 spaces with an ultimate capacity of 6500. A new remote parking area closer to the terminal area on the north side at an intermediate parking rate has been opened just recently. It has an initial capacity of 6,000 cars with expansion ultimately to over 9000 spaces. This area will be the first one served, hopefully, by a grade-separated transportation system, so that

people parking in that lot will be delivered directly to the front of the terminal on a grade-separated access system which initially will probably consist of an elevated busway, but one which has been designed so that when volumes warrant a shift to mechanical transportation can be readily made.

16. In addition to that and not satisfied with the results being achieved by the domestic bus or limousine operators serving the airport, we have initiated our own bus system from the principal traffic generating point in terms of automobiles -- that is, the San Fernando Valley, located some 20 plus miles from the airport. Traditionally, bus services to the airport have centered around hotels and hotel/office building complexes and catered to the business traveller who may not wish to avail himself to the use of a private automobile. Our new bus system, which is called the FlyAway system, is operated at our Van Nuys Airport property from a small terminal facility and is aimed at enticing the residentially oriented originating passenger not to drive his car all the way to the airport but rather to park there at a very nominal rate and to ride the so-called FlyAway bus, a service into Los Angeles International. This service is operated at the present time on a 30-minute headway from 5:30 in the morning until 1:00 a.m., with 45-minute service between 1:00 and 5:30 a.m. To give you some idea of how this is working, even though its existence has been very short, the average passenger load prior to our operating this system from Van Nuys Airport was about 80 per day combined round trip passengers. Now we are running an average in excess of 500 with peaks of close to 900 a day and the volume is gradually climbing. I think it is fair to state that it is not a profitable operation at the present time. The private operators, of course, must view profit as one of their prime considerations, as we indeed must, in the long term. However, other mitigating factors enable us to subsidize it for some considerable period of time in the hopes that the volumes will build up to the

level of profitability. It is estimated at the present time that 700 a day average passengers on the route will provide a profit-making situation. But, it is very clear that at the moment the parking lot at that location has already had as many as 1,683 cars stored in it and that there are at least 700-1000 vehicle trips a day that have been removed from the terminal area from this one operation alone.

17. It is a small start but, hopefully, an indication that with some hard work, new marketing techniques, new image making and attractive economics, we may find another way to reduce our peak problems at Los Angeles International. I have mentioned earlier in my paper that provisions were being developed for grade-separated connection from a remote parking area, northeast of the airport to the central terminal area in order to attract more cars to that as a more viable alternative. You should note that the system to be used there, ultimately mechanical in nature, will be developed so as to be compatible with the area-wide transit system that is expected to be developed throughout the metropolitan area and that, ultimately will be connected so that at a future time, it will be possible to get an airport-bound vehicle, designed with the airport passenger and his luggage in mind and give him access from a great many areas of the Los Angeles basin directly to Los Angeles International Airport and its terminals.

REFERENCES

Olson Laboratories, Inc., Anaheim, Calif. Urban development and transportation studies, Volume Four - Los Angeles International Airport Draft Environmental Impact Report, July 1975.

Wilbur Smith and Associates, Inc. Study of external roadway system serving the Los Angeles International Airport, 1967.

Office of Facilities Planning, Department of Airports. Airport Access Evaluation - LAX, December 4, 1975.

18. Passenger buildings

B.J. Mayes, ARIBA

Gollins Melvin Ward Partnership, London

After an era of expansion economic restraints are leading planners to consider flexibility and economy in the design of passenger terminals but the paper examines the basic requirements and how these have been and are being met.

In probing future ways that the design of passenger buildings may develop, one is immediately faced with the fact that there is no clear-cut consensus of opinion as to the best solution for the resolution of the present problems facing the designer of these buildings. Airport authorities, airlines, passengers, concession-aires, State authorities all lay down require-ments which are in themselves schizoid or in relation to the other users, incompatible. To synthesize all these demands into an inspired space programme which will both meet present demands and yet be flexible enough to take con-siderable stretching and alteration before the need to rebuild, is a most difficult task. The alternative of a super-compromise solution seems to lead inevitably to buildings where nobody gets anything they want. Other examples by people with large "bees-in-their-bonnets" about theoretical solutions to the problems lead one to be wary of extreme experiment when considering buildings of this sort. Perhaps it is a healthy sign that passenger buildings have not yet been refined to norms which can be simply stated and that there is still room for develop-ment and imaginative thought in their planning.

On the matter of flexibility, some reality has to be incorporated in the requirements so that all-embracing statements as "the design should be such that it can be readily expanded, both vertically and horizontally, in all directions without impairment of critical operating areas and equipment" (Ref.1) are really meaningless. There must be much more reality in the exact limitations of what has, and has not, got to be flexible if the solutions are not to be hopelessly uneconomic. Yet the only really new situation to face our industry since the 4th World Airports Conference held in London in 1973, must be the fact that economy as a paramount element in the equation has been forced on us by the economic recession in many of the countries represented at this conference. This has had a world-wide effect on the growth of the airline industry and national and private expenditure in building hardware. That this great interest in "cost effectiveness" has resulted in the reappraisal of

what seemed established practice is only to the good. That it might lead to the mediocre or lowest common denominator will need careful watching. Of course, what we must be planning for is a new boom - hopefully not too far off - where large increases in passenger throughput can be easily dealt with without drastic alterations or large capital expenditure. Here we return to properly planned flexibility.

It is not possible in a paper of this size to cover all the possible permutations and theories which might usefully be pursued when consider-ing our future passenger facilities as there are so many basic forms these can take, ranging from large international or domestic terminals serving nations or major conurbations through their smaller brethren to terminals for the executive or general aviation. Therefore, this paper will deal mainly with the larger passenger buildings (of international or domestic type) with a short review of a terminal in a developing country, because it reflects how in particular locations not necessarily repeatable in others it is possible to design facilities capable of handling large volumes of people at a compara-tively low capital cost.

The fact that the slow erosion of the excitement and glamour from Aviation has resulted in a much more commercial and pragmatic approach is a change that will continue - possibly in a way experienced with rail transport. Is it true that the greater the passenger throughput, the more impersonal the service? If so, must we plan for what is no more than a mass transportation system? The further down this road one goes, the more it would appear that the individual passengers comfort and convenience will be sacrificed to the needs of economy and efficiency when handling a large volume of passengers. But, presuming the passenger has a choice, will he prefer to sacrifice personal service for an ultimate improvement in the speed and price of travel?

It would no doubt be useful here to re-state the principles that have guided us up to now in the design of passenger buildings, and which form the basis on which the future will develop.

1. Minimising passengers travel distance in walking between main elements and up and down travel.

2. Close coupling of car parking facilities and other mass transit systems to the terminal functions.

3. Clear and simple direction, flight information and general information sign systems. An audible PA system.

4. Curb set-down and pick-up that will provide adequate space for private, public, interline and other vehicles.

5. A quick check-in, rapid and safe baggage handling system for both outbound and inbound services and the minimum delay in immigration customs and security clearances.

6. As much concession space as is feasible without interfering with the proper function of the terminal buildings.

7. Where economic, passengers should have all-weather protection from when they arrive by car or transport system to the boarding of the aircraft.

8. Flexibility at gates to cater for all types of aircraft.

9. An attractive building structure - flexible in form but built of permanent hard-wearing materials with highly sophisticated electronic and environmental services.

10. A reduction in the personnel necessary to run and maintain the facilities to a minimum. Fail-safe alternatives to avoid strike paralysis where possible.

1. PASSENGER TRAVEL DISTANCE
Here we have the Holy Grail of all terminal planners. Immense research has gone into the various solutions which have been built in the last decade in order to reduce the distance walked to an absolute minimum. Two main streams of airport development have appeared which have had their impact on terminal design and passenger movement.

A. The first continues the time-honoured principle of parking the aircraft against the terminal building with some mechanical connection between aircraft and building or a short walk across the apron to the aircraft.

B. The second separates the aircraft function from the building, the interconnection being made by mobile vehicles. In this system the aircraft can be parked some distance from the buildings and only requires ramp service buildings to be adjacent.

Type A These fall into two main categories - linear and decentralised in plan, or centralised with satellites. The largest and most typical of the linear type is probably Dallas/Fort Worth (Fig.1.) described in the last World Conference. Here the loops maximise the interface area between aircraft and building while providing a modular building form which gives flexibility for future expansion. Each module can be self-supporting in dealing with individual airline requirements and caters for both inbound and outbound passengers at the same level. Unfortunately, as the road system has to be split onto two levels this requires passengers to make a vertical movement which is not ideal. Because of the linear nature of the plan, the concept requires a transit system of some sophistication and at the present time this is not functioning and perhaps exhibits the Achilles heel of this solution. No doubt the defects will be resolved, but the second most difficult problem relates to interline operations and parking. The ideal situation of parking opposite one's module which reduces walking distance to a minimum, is only available on busy gates for a short period - if you catch a mid-morning flight it can mean quite a walk. Similarly, a return to another gate creates the same problem. Thirdly, it is imperative to warn passengers of their gate before arriving at the terminals requiring a most comprehensive sign system at the road entry. A similar layout is employed at Kansas City airport where passenger walking distance is claimed to be as little as 75'0" and there are numerous other examples. (Fig.2)
The second variant of Type A is illustrated in the layout employed at Tampa, Florida. Here, the central terminal is connected to remote satellites by a horizontal "people mover", similar in function to an elevator or lift. This airport has been in operation for 4 years and has now proved the system to be efficient and workable. Because of the high percentage of aged and infirm in the area who use the terminal walking distances are most critical and these have been reduced to a minimum. However, due to the layout, it has still been necessary to create a multi-level central terminal with the consequent need for passenger vertical movement. Airports employing this transit system are Seattle-Tacoma and Miami International. Other airports such as Newark, Paris and Munich are actively considering its implementations.

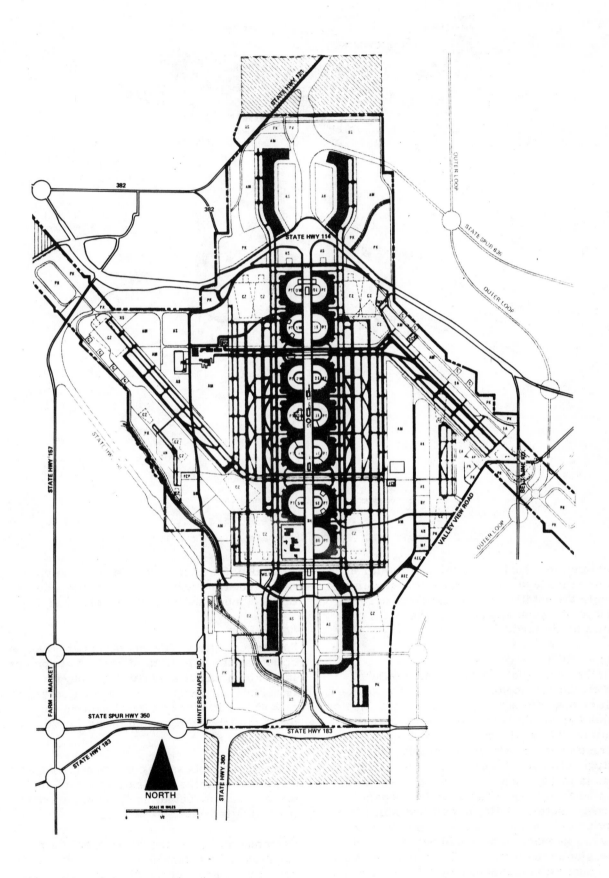

Fig.1. Dallas, Fort Worth (Airport Planning and Development, Publication No. 673B)

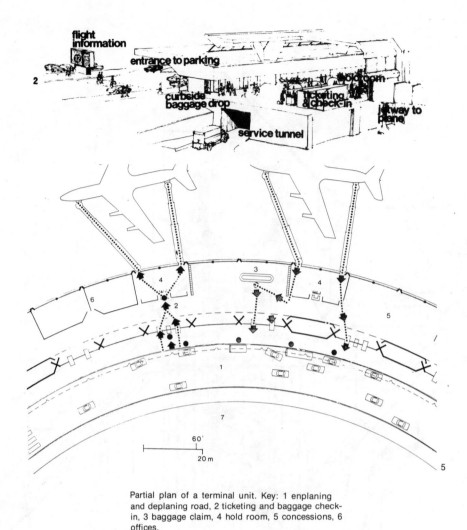

Partial plan of a terminal unit. Key: 1 enplaning and deplaning road, 2 ticketing and baggage check-in, 3 baggage claim, 4 hold room, 5 concessions, 6 offices.

Fig.2.   Kansas City (Edward G. Blankenship, 'The Airport')

There are many similar examples of the linear and satellite layout and it appears that with new airports the satellite system is likely to be employed for international, and the linear system for domestic operations.

Type B   (Fig.3.)

With the opening of the new Toronto Mirabel Airport (the first major airport to be planned and built as a remote gate concept since Washington Dulles Airport) there will be a valuable opportunity to observe the operation of this most interesting and controversial layout. The connection between the central terminal and remote gates is by Passenger Transfer Vehicles which are similar to those which have been operating for many years at Dulles Airport and which are reported to have an acceptable service record. They are intended to carry 150 passengers at speeds of up to 20 m.p.h. There is a maximum passenger walking distance of 280 ft. although this can be doubled on an interline flight. The great advantage of the layout is its compactness and the fact that it can operate both inbound and outbound passengers on a single level, thus avoiding vertical movement and allowing greater

flexibility for future alterations. It is probably worth repeating here the passenger sequence of both outbound and inbound travel. (Ref.2.)

"Outbound

Passengers arriving by bus or by car driven by someone else will descend at the main processing curb and enter the boarding lobby immediately. Those driving by themselves will park in the attached tri-level parking garage and reach the lobby via moving ramps from the lower parking curbs.

Signs at the processing curbs and the parking curbs will give the precise location of each airline, thereby obviating cross-flow traffic inside the terminal.

Passengers pass by the ticket check/baggage counters and are issued a boarding pass indicating the number of the PTV boarding sector in the security area. These counters are located at right angles to the flow of traffic, whereas the airline reservation and information counters face the processing curb.

Passengers proceed to the unified outbound security area that serves in place of separate departure lounges. This is one common room that extends the length of the enplaning section.

Boarding the PTV's is via one of 18 loading docks equally divided among three boarding sectors on the airside of the building.

The aircraft are parked around three servicing positions each capable of handling six aircraft. The servicing positions are not assigned to specific airlines.

Inbound
The deplaning sequence at Mirabel is as follows:

Arriving passengers enter the mobile lounges and are driven to the arrival section of the terminal, to one of 18 arrival gates.

Passengers disembark and follow linear flow-lines through customs inspection and passport control to the baggage claim area. Each of the six baggage claim areas is capable of taking all the baggage of a Boeing 747-sized aircraft. The sequence is designed to take 30 min. from aircraft chocks-on to exit of the passenger from the terminal.

Passengers connecting from domestic to international flights will go from the aeroquay - the four nose-in parking positions physically attached to the terminal to handle such flights - underground to the terminal's outbound security area. Transit passengers will be transported to the terminal if the stopover time is in excess of one hour."

An additional advantage of the remote gate concept is that it allows the aircraft to self-manoeuvre on and off the parking stands and is flexible enough to accommodate and service all types and sizes of aircraft. It is perhaps worth noting that even here it has been found necessary to make provision for 4 nose-in stands against a building (called an Aeroquay) for inter-connecting domestic and international passengers. Nevertheless, the main functional layout relies on the Passenger Transfer Vehicle.

What are we to learn from these differing concepts in order to plan our future airports and terminals? There is no argument among the experts that the remote gate (Type B) layout shows economies in building size and aircraft servicing facilities although there is less agreement about a similar reduction in passenger walking distance. In a feasibility study Studiengruppe Luftfahrt carried out for the new Munich Airport in 1970 concepts of Types A and B were produced based on similar criteria to

compare their respective merits. These showed interesting results. (Fig.4.)
(This information is only included in this paper to illustrate the comparisons where the basic information is common to both concepts, and does not in any way illustrate the present proposals for the Munich II Airport.)

Other claims for Remote Concepts are that the terminal building can be planned to suit the needs of the operators and passengers without the necessity to take into account the aircraft as a module of the building plan. Four mobile lounges each on a 4 metre module could service a Boeing 747. Thus a module of 16 metres along the perimeter would be required compared with 70 metres needed for a 747 in nose-in configuration. Aircraft types may change, movements increase, and schedules instantly alter without compromising future expansion in that the parking apron and buildings are not interrelated. Parking stand utilisation is improved by reason of the open apron. The buildings can be sited further away from the noise and interference of aircraft operations, while ground access roads are unimpeded. Also aircraft ground time may be reduced by the avoidance of the necessity of taxiing to the terminal. The proponents of Type A (and these include the airline operators) argue that Type B, while sharing some advantages in economy and flexibility has considerable disadvantages. They point out the obvious necessity for close-out time being advanced by as much as 20 minutes and that this, especially on shorthaul services, must be regarded as a reduction of passenger standards. They point out the difficulty of transit and transfer passengers who, unless they have separate transport, have to cover the distance from apron to terminal and back to their next aircraft to make their connection. Walking distances may be reduced but the new decentralised facilities in Type A are not very different. The mobile lounge itself can be a considerable obstruction on the parking apron and can be affected by weather and road conditions. Additional personnel would be required due to the separated functions (although this may be equally true of the decentralised modular terminal). Passenger comfort is reduced, apart from the advancing of departure times, due to the necessity when unloading to delay the lounge for the last passenger to be loaded (also true of busing operations and very frustrating to those passengers with short connection times). There is a limitation on VIP and first class service - unless a separate vehicle is provided. Lastly, the economic and capital cost savings are not as great as may at first be assumed.

There seems to be no absolute way of reconciling these two sets of arguments other than by a

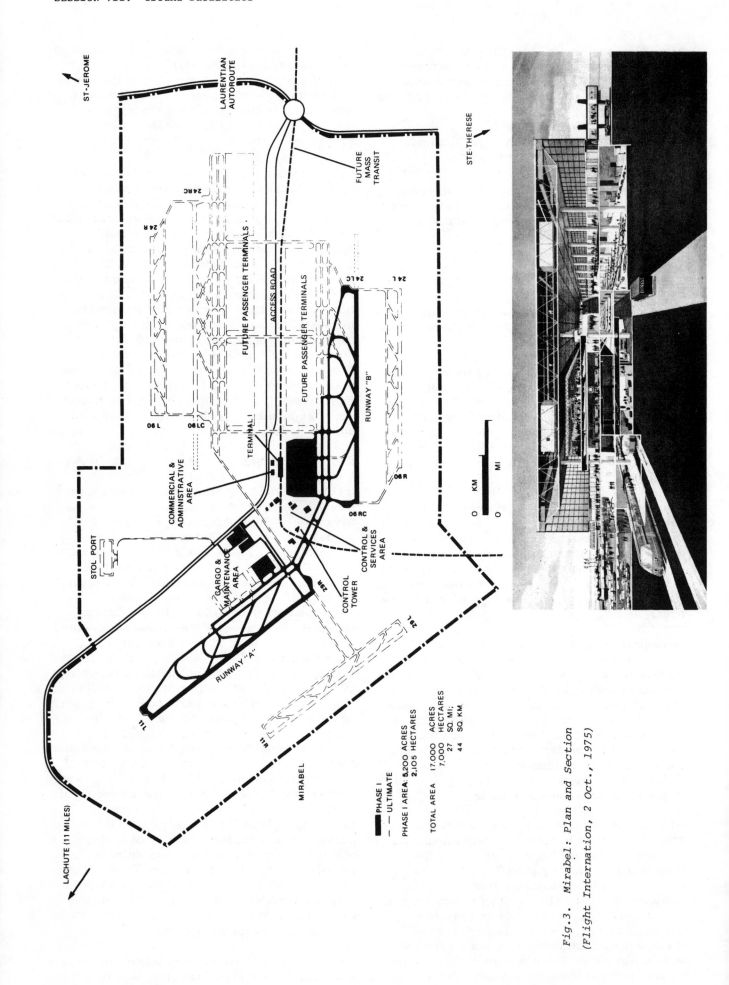

Fig.3. Mirabel: Plan and Section

(Flight Internation, 2 Oct., 1975)

hybrid solution of fixed and remote gates. The fixed gates would handle all shorthaul and much of the main volume. Remote gates would handle longhaul, charter and peak overload traffic. A Systems Analysis or Cost-Benefit Study would be useful here. This should be investigated, but before doing so perhaps we should again look at the importance of passenger walking distance. While the British Airports Authority recent passenger survey highlights the importance of this factor, do passengers appreciate the benefit of, say a saving of a total of 50-100 paces which may well be critical when choosing a concept.

2. PARKING AND TRANSIT SYSTEMS

Almost as many variations on the theme of parking the motor car exist as for the passenger areas. Parking can be over gates (Boston); over the central terminal building (Toronto Dorval, Charles de Gaulle Paris, Houston); open parking in the centre of terminal loops (Dallas Fort Worth, Kansas City); separate multi-storey structures linked to terminals (Mirabel, London Airport Heathrow); or below the main terminal (scheme for Greater Pittsburgh). The quest has been not only to place the bulk of garaging as close to the terminal as possible but also to try and site the parking adjacent to the actual aircraft gates. While these criteria can be met, especially where the design is based on parking above the terminal areas, (an expensive solution with limited possibilities for expansion)multi-storey solutions have to be employed if walking distances are not to become extreme in those airports where the automobile is the principal means of transport. Surface parking can only be provided by the extravagant use of land and this inevitably leads again to problems of walking distance - especially if it is not possible to park near to departure or arrival gates.

Sophisticated people-mover systems have been employed to link parking areas to passenger terminals, for example the Braniff link at Dallas/ Fort Worth, but these again add considerable cost to car parking both in capital terms and future maintenance. Other alternatives such as off airport parking with mass transit links have been put forward but these require the passenger to make a further interchange, possibly with his baggage, and would probably be no less expensive.

The linking of passenger buildings to high speed, high capacity ground transport systems linking direct to city centres or to stations on rail and underground networks are now planned into new terminals, usually at a level below the main passenger floors. A typical example is incorporated and illustrated at Toronto/Mirabel. (Fig.3.)

Without doubt, this link can be most important but in any dispersed layout of passenger buildings a secondary distribution system may be required of the Dallas/Fort Worth type to avoid multiple stops on the high speed system and this itself may erode away all the time gained in having a high speed link.

There is, at the present moment, a noticeable reaction against the automobile in some Western countries, especially in the U.K. and this may well indicate that the future fears of larger and larger demand for parking areas in scale with increases in passenger traffic will not be realised, especially if an attractive public transport alternative is available. This is the argument always put forward by those who advocate the use of mass transport instead of the automobile, but so far there are few examples to provide evidence, although some successful results have been obtained.

3. INFORMATION AND DIRECTION SIGNS FOR PASSENGERS

Slowly, an acceptable International standard for sign symbols has developed although this is still far from universally adopted. The colourful and varied interpretations of the male and female figure are a case in point.

Designers and airport managers have come to realise that the minimum of simple but explicit signs is the ideal solution. Only this can avoid the confusion at many road intersections where not only is it impossible to take in all the information presented at a glance, but the absorption of this information itself can slow down traffic flow. As mentioned previously, some large terminal complexes rely heavily on passengers being presented with gate information before arriving at parking areas, and here is perhaps the most difficult of all the problems facing the designers if the passenger is to absorb the necessary detail in a very short space of time. There is obviously a good case for the specialist designers of information presentation to be on the design team from the inception of the project - as for the modernisation of Orlando Airport, Florida - if passenger streaming and movements are to be properly controlled.

4. CURB SPACE

It is possible to fairly accurately predict the peak requirements for curb space by Systems Analysis. These can vary considerably in relation to the speed of passenger flow through the building and are intimately linked to the method of loading and unloading passengers to and from the aircraft. It may not be possible or economic to plan for theoretical peak conditions as curbside congestion may not be experienced due to other factors such as road-access, parking facilities and so on.

DESCRIPTION	AREA IN M^2	COST IN DM
CONCEPT A		
1. Two main runways, lighting VASI, taxiways, aprons for passenger terminal, freight, maintenance & general aviation.	2,809,560	252,106,719
2. Vehicle Circulation Areas All roads, parking, railways, bridges, tunnels etc.	514,845	106,150,234
3. Infrastructure Water supply, drainage, electricity, gas, sewage disposal, landscaping and enclosures.	2,734,111	250,153,661
4. Superstructure All airport buildings including terminal, central tower, multi-storey car parks, admin building, etc.	441.700	1,004,235,600
CONCEPT B		
1. Two main runways, lighting VASI, taxiways, aprons for passenger terminal, freight maintenance & general aviation, aircraft parking stands & lighting.	2,216,410	217,291,044
2. Vehicle Circulation Areas All roads, parking, railways, bridges, tunnels, PTV roads and bridges.	938,058	111,543,018
3. Infrastructure Water supply, drainage, electricity, gas, sewage disposal, landscaping and enclosures.	2,123,833	166,839,083
4. Superstructure All airport buildings, including terminal, central tower, multi-storey car parks, admin building, mobile lounges & associated parking facilities.	357,700	810,075,600

SUMMARY

CONCEPT A

	COST
Engineering works and sub level construction	608,410,614
Superstructure	1,004,235,600
Total DM	1,612,646,214

CONCEPT B

	COST
Engineering works and sub level construction	495,673,145
Superstructure	810,075,600
Total DM	1,305,748,745

Fig.4.   Munich II, charts showing comparative size and cost: base criteria (approximate costs, 1971 rates; costs refer to first phase of airport) (Studiengruppe Luftfahrt)

5. CHECK-IN, INSPECTIONS AND BAGGAGE HANDLING

There seems no reason other than bureaucracy why these formalities should not have been simplified long ago. To quote Mr. Kurt Hammarskjold: (Ref.3.)

"Air travel in 1980 will be more commonplace than it is today and customers will be more critical about the quality of the air-transport product. Elimination of governmental barriers to travel and the introduction of a "passport card" (similar to a credit card) would allow easier handling by airlines, travel agents and immigration controls alike. Standardised baggage clearance, the elimination of unnecessary queuing and form-filling (embarkation, currency declaration and hotel registration, for example), and simpler airline procedures will be demanded. In short, the traveller will expect a highly efficient, faster and more comfortable air-transport system."

The modernisation of baggage handling has had a chequered history. In some cases highly automated systems have been found to be unreliable and have been taken out and replaced by more orthodox systems, while in others persistence has proved that these problems are not insurmountable. (Frankfurt/Main A.G. is a good example of what can be done to make a complex and large-capacity system operate well.)

Security systems must now be included as part of the initial design brief. It is hoped that their necessity will diminish with time but this seems unlikely at present and therefore this requirement must be built into the system of passenger processing. Another paper will deal with this subject in more detail.

6. CONCESSIONS

A greater emphasis on concession areas as revenue in the cost-effectiveness of passenger buildings has brought into highlight the need for their proper integration into the terminal plan. An example of the way this can be done is illustrated at terminal 1 of Charles de Gaulle Airport, Paris, where the second, transfer level, (Fig.5.) is designed to contain the shopping area, with restaurants, bars, post office, medical services and so on. Not only is this important element given a prominent position in the passenger route but it is separated from the busy arrival and departure areas and thus does not interfere with them.

7. ALL WEATHER PROTECTION

Naturally, this is a matter of both economy and climate. A minimum of covered way on the land side between buildings is required for rain and sun protection and too often this is not provided. It is a serious criticism of the open parking concept that walking distances to a covered area can be excessive in inclement weather. On the airside it is also a matter of economy and climate plus safety and avoidance of delay to passengers walking on an active apron.

8. FLEXIBILITY OF AIRCRAFT GATES

This is a desirable requirement but difficult to achieve if air bridges and fixed ramp services are provided. Here is a situation where the limits of flexibility required should be carefully examined if uneconomic and complicated solutions are to be avoided.

9. & 10. ARCHITECTURAL BUILDING FORM AND STRUCTURE MAINTENANCE

Although it is expected by national and local communities that their terminal buildings should be of outstanding architectural design, it is important that this should not be confused with the requirement to create an architectural monument. (Ref.4.) As Congressman Dale Milford of the American House of Representatives Aviation Committee has put it in the context of Government funding of general aviation terminals: "....I'm for it, provided rather tight strings are placed on it so no Taj Mahals are built with Federal money." In the oil-rich states of the Middle-East, and in certain terminal buildings built for airlines, it has been thought necessary to create buildings of a distinctive or national style but the future trend seems toward a plainer and more functional modular building providing large uninterrupted spaces for maximum flexibility. These do not have to be uninteresting and very often gain by the exciting use of large span structures of functional form. In the quest for flexibility and open space, risks of fire or explosion must not be overlooked. The mechanical and electrical services in these buildings must also be of modular form for flexibility and should incorporate all the latest energy-saving and technological ideas.

NEW AIRPORT TERMINAL FOR MOMBASA, KENYA

This is an example of an airport terminal to handle quite large numbers of passengers - mainly charter - at peaks experienced in the mainly holiday character of the area. It is now under construction and was designed by Studiengruppe Luftfahrt as part of the general improvements to the airport and will replace the existing terminal buildings. The first report on the concept was submitted in 1971.

General

The concept provides a multi-flexible series of spaces to accommodate current and future needs beneath a canopy roof. Primarily, protection has been provided from the sun and from the rain to give shade and shelter. Beneath this umbrella the terminal functions are arranged. In the first phase facilities are provided to process 500 arriving or departing passengers in a peak hour. Passenger peaks occur at weekends only – mainly charter flights direct from Europe – the remaining traffic being of a local nature from Nairobi, Malindi, Kilimanjaro, etc. Concept design, therefore, anticipated large spaces for passenger peaks, with the inevitable under-utilisation of the terminal for the remainder of the time.

The natural landscape forms part of this 'garden' terminal. Passenger functions are located under cover in garden courts as an extension of surrounding vegetation and landscape. The building is open on all four sides and enclosures are only provided where required for security, protection from noise and privacy.

The terminal consists of two levels of accommodation. Main passenger handling activities are planned at the ground level, with public areas and administrative offices on the first floor.

Short term expansion may be obtained by expanding the passenger handling accommodation on both sides of the terminal; the building is planned in the future so that a complete two-level terminal operation may be achieved, with departing passengers on the upper level and arriving passengers on the lower.

Departures
A large porte cochere extends from the terminal over the set-down road (Fig.6.) protecting passengers from sun and rain. Check-in counters are designed to process four passengers simultaneously, with a straight flow line to passport and immigration controls. Within the Departure lounge, snack bar, bar and restaurant facilities are available before entering the hold areas prior to flight departure. A small VIP suite is provided adjacent to the hold areas.

Arrivals
Passengers arrive at the terminal by bus and are immediately processed by health and immigration controls. There is a direct link for transit passengers to the departure lounge. Two race track baggage claim devices are located in the baggage hall prior to customs checks. A similar porte cochere to departures has been provided for waiting passengers to be protected from sun and rain outside the terminal and up to the terminal road.

Upper Level
This contains restaurant facilities for both the general public and 'bonded' departure passengers. Viewing decks are also located at this level. The remaining space is occupied by airport management and airline offices, and separated physically from public access.

Concessions
These are provided on both levels. It is proposed that banks, a post office and hotel reservations facilities will be located in the main concourse at ground floor level. (Fig.6.)

Microclimatic Report
A complete study was carried out to examine in detail the following:
1. Sun and light, Solar and Heat Radiation, Sun Protection.
2. Glare and Visibility.
3. Temperature.
4. Rainfall and Winds.
5. Humidity and Comfort Requirements.

1. Sun and Light
Mombasa's situation $4^{\circ}02'$ South, $39^{\circ}37'$ East, is specified as Savanna Zone influenced by the Monsoon; especially by its close position to the Indian Ocean the Solar radiation is quite moderate to high, with relative high absorption and a high heating effect. As the night temperature falls to about 10° to 15° centigrade, no heat storage by the building material is wanted. Reflecting effect (without glare) by white or light coloured paint is necessary and is provided, which allows at the same time, lighting in deep rooms. The heating effect in a warm climate with warm night temperatures makes sun protection necessary in certain areas.

With the help of Solar Charts and Shadow Angle Protractors the periods of possible Sun Penetration and the necessity for sun protection was determined.

2. Glare and Visibility
To reduce glare to passengers, visitors and staff from the effect of the concrete apron during the evening hours, this will be achieved by two kinds of planting: flat horizontal creepers and high trees such as palms.

Some operational offices on the airside need a clear view to the service road and parking apron. Where the open view might be disturbed by vertical sunbreakers, the offices will be provided with special protective glass.

Planting will be required, and it is proposed that the area on the terminal airside will be landscaped for anti-glare and anti-dust.

3. Temperature
The mean maximum temperatures vary between 28°C and 33°C, and the mean minimum temperatures between 21°C and 24°C. No precaution against cold is necessary (extreme minimum temperature 15°C), and flexible ventilation openings against extreme cooling effect by wind are provided.

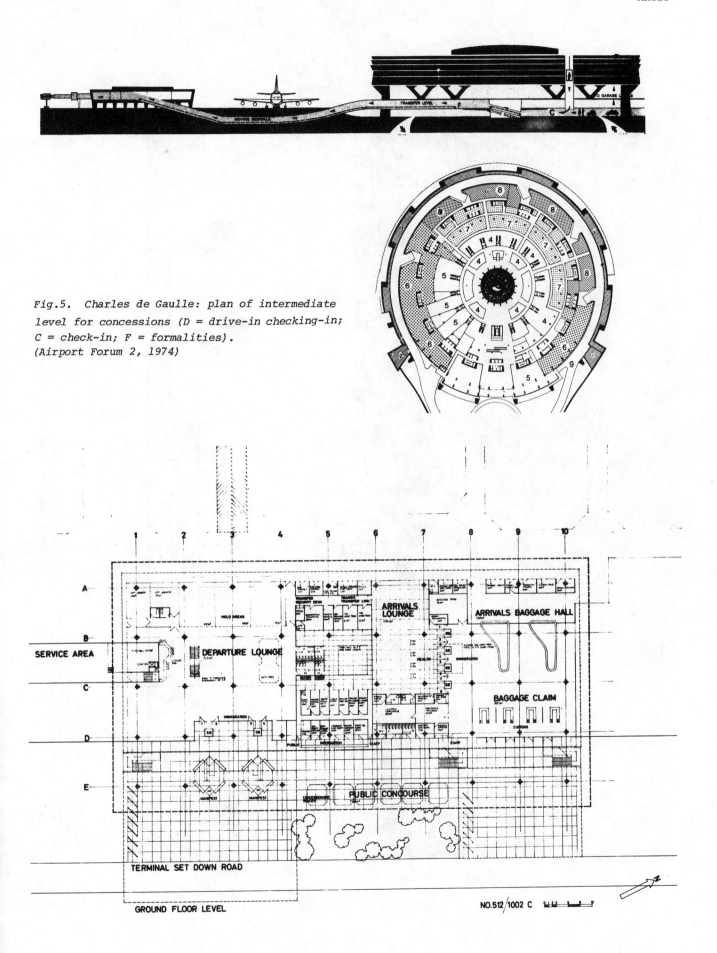

Fig.5. Charles de Gaulle: plan of intermediate
level for concessions (D = drive-in checking-in;
C = check-in; F = formalities).
(Airport Forum 2, 1974)

Fig.6(a) Mombasa: diagrammatic plan

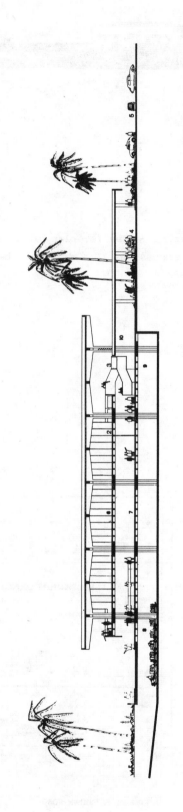

Section
1. Terrace 2. Staff canteen 3. Public access 4. Terminal set
down road 5. Public car park 6. Restaurant 7. Departure lounge
8. Tunnel 9. Departure baggage hall 10. Public concourse

Fig.6 (b) Mombasa: perspective and section

Where sun protection is necessary, care has been taken to separate the construction from covering material to prevent additional tension between cold and hot units. Expansion is minimised by sun penetration effect (direct sun radiation).

4. Rainfall and Wind
The strongest rain falls in April and May and is combined with intensive winds up to 20 knots from the south. The passengers on their way from bus, taxi or car to the building and the check-in counters require protection against rain. Rain breakers in the upper part of the airside facade and the porte cochere roof of adequate width and length will provide the main protection. The movement of the air does not reach a velocity which requires special wind protection apart from the above-mentioned rain protection.

5. Humidity and Comfort Requirements
Major efforts have been made to create the maximum comfort for the users of the New Terminal Building, especially within closed rooms, by using the factors of the climate: air temperature, humidity and movement of air. The high humidity during early morning hours is mainly due to the maritime influence. By heating up during the morning hours in general, an average humidity of 66% is available: but the comfort climate depends further more on the velocity of air movement. The wind, its direction and speed allows comfortable conditions at 46% (or 56% of the time per year if SW and SE are included), and the layout permits a gentle air movement. This wind from the south is generally cool; in April and May wet, but comfortable. December and January are the driest but not completely dry months. At this time more breeze is required, and we have attempted to open the east side as much as possible for wind access.

By increasing the possibility of horizontal air movement the skin temperature can be reduced. However, the mean maximum temperature in the afternoon may reach 32°C. If it remains higher than 30°C, human resistance and efficiency may begin to fall markedly. The velocity of air should be 1.0 to 1.2 m/sec at that temperature; if the room temperature falls to 28°C, speed may be reduced to 0.5 m/sec. As the available wind speed is normally higher, it is only a question of opening and regulating to adapt to the velocity of air movement to the relevant temperature. Nevertheless, it was felt advisable to install mechanical air fans, especially in those rooms where the airflow is blocked by building functions.

SUMMARY
While the past and present can be the basis for predictions for the future we will not be able to find the answers without posing questions for research and study. In an economic climate which cannot be accurately predicted many of these questions may well prove hypothetical. The hiatus in the galloping expansion of a few years ago has now provided a period for sonsolidation and observation. The effect on passenger building design is already with us and the uncertainties of the future have led planners to conceive much more flexible and economic solutions. It is now possible to make computer models of almost all concepts and configurations for analysis and certainly this is a tool that will be used more and more both in terms of planning efficiency and cost-effectiveness. A secondary but important study should relate to the personnel necessary to operate and maintain the buildings. Very often schemes of great merit for improving passenger facilities require additional staff to operate them and this is true of decentralised layouts. Is it possible for the passenger to carry out more of the processing system himself than is now permitted? When one considers the millions of wasted man-hours observable in any airport terminal there must be some way that this large labour force can be utilised in some way to help itself. Or, perhaps the problem lies in the view that passengers in the mass are really mindless, helpless zombies who cannot be permitted to carry out even the simplest operations themselves. Maybe the more automated systems of check-in baggage handling, federal inspections etc. forecast for the 80's may bring the answer.

ACKNOWLEDGEMENTS
The author is most grateful to Mr. Vaughan Davies, Chief Aerodrome Engineer, Aerodromes Department of the Kenyan Government and the Terminal Planning Committee for permission to reproduce the information on the Mombasa Terminal.

The Airport - Edward G. Blankenship
Mobile Lounge or Fixed Gate - Hans-Henning Kuckuck. Airport Forum 1/1975.
A Plea for the Mobile Gate - Earl E. Bomberger. Airport Forum 3/1975.
Segregating the Aircraft - B. Mayes. Flight International 15th June 1972.
Computer Analysis of Airfield Operations - Robert Horonjeff, Donald Maddison Airport Forum 2/1974.
The Passenger Terminal - A Systems Analysis Approach - Paul Baron, Dirk Henning, Airport Forum 2/1974.
Cost/Benefit Analysis in Terminal Planning - Peter Wolf. Airport Forum 3/1975.
Studiengruppe Luftfahrt - Anglo-German Aviation Consultants. The author's firm are the design architects.

REFERENCES
1. R.J. Sutherland, American Airlines - "Airport Planning - An Airline View" Interavia 6/1972.
2. "Mirabel Airport" - Aviation Week & Space Technology - November 17th 1975.
3. "The 1980 Passenger" - Kurt Hammarskjold. Flight International - 20th November 1975.
4. "Reporting Points" - Flying. December 1975.

19. Security problems at airports

R.Farmery
Security Adviser, Department of Trade

The paper considers the effects and needs of security to combat aviation terrorism. The nature of
the threat either of sabotage or hijacking is analysed and a brief history of moves to define and
combat such threats is given. The UK position is set out in detail. The separate roles of airport
security staff and police are outlined, and practical measures for achieving security are described.
The need for future airports to be planned with security in mind from the outset, and the need for
security awareness throughout the industry are stressed.

In 1937 newspaper headlines in England were
devoted, for some weeks, to a case of robbery
with violence which was called the 'Mayfair Men
Case'. Four men had arranged for a jeweller's
representative to call at the Hyde Park Hotel
with a case containing some £25,000 worth of
jewellery; they had hit him on the head with a
small stool and almost - but not quite - killed
him; had decamped with the jewellery and were
caught at Oxford Airport with the loot whilst
trying to hire an aircraft to the continent.
For this they were given prison sentences
ranging from 5-15 years (with penal servitude)
and floggings ranging from 6 to 12 strokes with
the cat-o-nine-tails. The headlines were one
inch high and they occupied the newspapers weeks
when the offence was committed and for further
weeks during the trial. It was a wonder for
far more than nine days.

It is perhaps, worth a few moments of thoughtful
comparison with attitudes in the present day -
1976. £25,000 is pin money; robbery with
violence is an everyday occurrence; crimes of
violence have increased to the stage where the
terms 'doubled' and 'trebled' are meaningless;
in scope and in range and on a world wide basis,
violence of every sort is escalating and,
regrettably, people - Governments, industry, the
public generally - are coming to accept it as a
facet of everyday life. No longer does one
see the staring headlines unless the particular
catastrophe - be it robbery, bomb explosion,
shoot up - results in large scale death and
destruction or is in an emotive element, and it
seems that the element which is more emotive
than most is that of aviation. International
wars are a commonplace - the media are sated
with Vietnam, Middle East, Congo, Angola, even
Ireland - but given an aircraft crash or an
airport explosion, then everybody starts to take
notice; perhaps only for a few days, but long
enough to affect the industry adversely. And
so, we have been driven - and I say driven
advisedly, for although the policy of Government
is to take all practical initiatives against

terrorism there are other spheres where a more
complacent attitude persists - to apply the term
'Security' to aviation, to airlines, to airports.

So, how do we define security? It is a poor
word, for its meaning is diverse and embraces so
many spheres. The baby in its mother's arms,
we are told is getting security of a mental,
psychological, environmental nature; the
householder locking his front door is getting
security; the policeman on the beat is giving
security; the soldier in Northern Ireland is on
security duties; so is the airline officer
investigating ticket frauds and thefts; so, in
fact, is the man who goes round and closes the
windows - he is stopping heat loss and heat is
money. We may define security then as that
process which prevents the erosion of assets and
these assets are very wide indeed and may include,
not only the more tangible things such as
material and profits, but those which are more
difficult to define, such as staff loyalty,
technical know-how and business secrets, and
commercial goodwill. However, for the purpose
of this paper, we shall consider that security
which arises from the need to combat terrorism
on whatever scale it affects us. Once again,
we are faced with definition problems. What is
terrorism? How does it differ from crime? It
is certainly right to say that terrorism is a
crime - both national and international - but
the converse is by no means the case. Perhaps
it is as good a definition as any to define
terrorism as an act of extreme violence committed
by one party against a second perhaps with the
intention of influencing a third party or public
opinion generally; a form of blackmail by
violence or threat of repetitious violence.

It is the purpose, then, of this paper to
consider the effects and needs of that security
required to combat aviation terrorism on the
airport environment.

The first step in this process is the consideration of the term 'Threat'. This factor cannot
be over emphasised. More misdirection of

effort in the security field arises from a lack of appreciation of the threat than from any other single cause. If the threat is wrongly assessed, then the remedies to meet it must, of necessity, be haphazard and only coincidentally correct. Over-reaction will mean wasted resources and under-reaction will mean, often enough, tragedy.

It can be stated, in broad principle, that the terrorist threat to aviation consists of sabotage - either to aircraft or airport installation - and hijacking of aircraft. This said, one can then start to break the threat down into more detail. From whom does the threat arise? It may be from the organised terrorist groups of International standing, predominantly of Middle East origin, though to an extent of Far East origin and also of local origin in so many countries. They are a world wide phenomenon and we can all call to mind our home bred variety. Their motivation is political and their planning, training and execution is likely to be of a high order and does not exclude the ability to mount complementary operations in two or more places at once. The perpetrators are likely to be determined, intelligent, and of high morale. On the other hand, it may be from groups of petty criminals, activated by motives of person gain and quite local in origin. Their operational skill will, probably, be of a lower order and their determination and morale more suspect. It may be the single terrorist, motivated by spite or real or imagined grievance; perhaps of unsound mentality. There may well be backing, openly, from well organised political forces and, less openly, from governments.

To whom may the threat be directed? To any person, airline or airport which may be considered open to pressure by reason of its nationality, the type of passenger it is carrying, the destination to which flights take place, its national sympathies, its relationship with others, perhaps simply its open-ness and vulnerability, and which has neglected to take effective security measures.

The assessment of threat in detail is a matter for a skilled agency, with all the necessary resources for the collection and collation of intelligence; its assessment in the light of national and local circumstances; and the formulation of an authoritative statement of threat, constantly updated and re-appraised in the light of fresh information. Such an agency exists in the great majority of countries and its statements must be regarded as authoritative. The threat is so widespread and the intelligence gathering and collating resources of the aviation industry so small, whilst its sphere of influence is large, that the task could not be taken on internally. The temptation to make up one's own 'threat' - which an be strong at times - must, at all costs, be resisted. In this particular sphere, as in most others, the person acting in isolation just lacks the resources and the basic information.

It is perhaps, correct to say that the first aspect of terrorism to make its impact upon the aviation world was the hijack. The first recorded hijack took place as long ago as 1930 in Peru (and it is interesting that the same pilot was again hijacked in 1968 - perhaps lightning does strike twice). The second hijacking did not occur until 1947 and its incidence was slight and irregular until the late 1960s. Then, in 1968, there were 35 hijacked incidents, of which 30 were successful; in 1969, 87 incidents, 70 successful; in 1970, 82 incidents, 56 successful; in 1971, 59 incidents, 23 successful; in 1972, 60 incidents, 30 successful; in 1973, 22 incidents, 11 successful; in 1974, 26 incidents, 8 successful; and in 1975, there were 20 incidents of which 5 were successful.

The incidence of sabotage is less spectacular but none the less deadly. Between 1946 and 1955 there were 6 acts of aviation sabotage; between 1956 and 1965, 9 incidents; between 1966 and 1972, 20 incidents; in 1973, 25 incidents; in 1974, 36 incidents; and in 1975, 14 incidents. In both hijackings and sabotage incidents, upwards of 1000 people have lost their lives.

It is a sorry picture and, regrettably, such is the climate of world opinion that, as with other crimes of violence, the sense of outrage is tending to lessen with each tragedy, despite the impact of such incidents as the La Guardia explosion of 29th December last.

There is no sign at all that the present violent trends will abate in the foreseeable future - in fact, very much the opposite is the case and those who rely on the philosophy of 'It could not happen here' or 'It will not happen to me' risk an extremely rude awakening. We must accept the fact that violence of every sort is going to be an increasing factor in local, national and international life. This said, measures must be taken to combat the violence; to thwart the terrorist or, at best, to deter him; to protect the aviation industry generally from the effects of this violence.

As early as 1963, the International Civil Aviation Organisation had become seized of the problems of violence, lawbreaking and unlawful seizure in respect of aircraft and had promulgated the Convention on offences and certain other acts committed on board aircraft - better known, perhaps, as the Tokyo Convention - in an attempt to formalise international attitudes. The convention applies only to aircraft in International flight and, for the most part, concerns itself with those offences which are already part of the criminal law of the majority of civilised countries. It devotes but two short paragraphs to the problems of hijacking, confining itself to the recommendations that states shall take all appropriate measures to restore the command of the aircraft to its lawful commander; to enable the passengers and crew to resume their journey and to restore the aircraft to its lawful owners. In the two years prior to 1970, there were 122 hijackings and in 1970, ICAO promulgated a further convention, this time directed specifically at the suppression of unlawful seizure of aircraft, and generally known as the Hague Convention. This convention is by no means exhaustive, but it does perform the important function of defining the offence of hijacking - "Any person who, on board an aircraft in flight, unlawfully or by force or threat thereof, or by any other form of intimidation, seizes or exercises control of that aircraft or attempts to perform such an act - or is an accomplice of such a person - commits the offence of hijacking". It is worth noting that the aircraft must be in flight and the person hijacking it must be on board it and that, additionally, the offence can only be committed - by this convention - when the aircraft has either departed from or landed in a country other than that of regis- tration. In other words, this convention does not admit of hijacking an aircraft which does not leave its own country. Hijacking did not abate in 1971 and, in that year, there was yet another convention and, this time, its provisions were much wider. Known as the Montreal Convention, it is directed at the Suppression of Unlawful Acts against the Safety of Civil Aviation. The first article of this convention contains five suggested offences which may endanger an aircraft in flight or in service: first, performing an act of violence; second, destroying an aircraft or damaging it; thirdly, placing any substance or device which is likely to destroy or damage aircraft; fourthly, destroying, damaging , or interfering with any air navigation facility; fifthly, communicating false information. It further constitutes the offences of attempting or being an accomplice.

The noteworthy point in this convention is that, for the first time, we see the term 'in service' being used. Whereas 'in flight' generally embraces 'doors shut' to 'doors open', this new term 'in service' is defined as from the beginning of the pre-flight preparation of an aircraft by ground personnel or by the crew until 24 hours after any landing - and that landing must be one where the competent authorities take responsibility for the aircraft, not one made under duress.

The value, of course, of international con- ventions, lies in the steps taken by various states to ratify them and give them the power of law within that state and it will come as no surprise to any of you to know that there are still a number of countries which have not ratified all the ICAO conventions and some which have not ratified any of them. The numbers of abstainers are, however, dwindling and there is an increasing degree of ratifica- tion, particularly amongst the Arab States.

The United Kingdom has ratified all the conven- tions with, successively, the Tokyo Convention Act of 1967; the Hijacking Act of 1971; and the Protection of Aircraft Act of 1973. The first and second of these Acts had less impact tham we would have wished upon the general atmosphere of lawlessness which persisted, for they depended, for their effectiveness, largely upon international co-operation and, regrettably, hijackers were able to pick out, without any great bother, those countries which were not renowned for co-operation - certainly with the Western nations. The Hijacking Act has, as its main point of interest, that it establishes, in British Law, the crime of hijacking as defined in the Hague Convention. Nothing, however, in the first two Acts makes any provision for the defence of airports or airlines of this country against aviation violence. The Protection of Aircraft Act, on the other hand, not only establishes in Part I the various offences outlined in the Montreal Convention and deals with their punishment and the various aspects of International Law which arise from their commission but in Part II continues with measures which are designed to protect aircraft and persons and property on board them; aerodromes; and air navigation installations. It empowers the Secretary of State to require information from airlines and airports as to the measures they are taking to protect and secure their aircraft, passengers and property; it empowers him to direct operators to search passengers and aircraft; to modify aircraft; to instal special equipment in aircraft - and the power applies not only to UK registered aircraft, but to any others which operate in the United Kingdom. It empowers the Secretary of State to direct airport management to search aerodromes, aircraft, and persons and property which may be in the aerodrome; to direct operators and airport management to guard aircraft and aerodromes by such means as may be defined; to specify the minimum number of persons used for searches and guarding, their qualifications, the equipment they shall use and the manner in which their duty shall be carried out; to construct, alter or demolish buildings and works - and this without liability for breach of contract. It constitutes the offence of having an offensive article - or anything which appears to be offensive in a UK registered aircraft, or any other aircraft in the United Kingdom, or in an aerodrome or navigation installation. Furthermore, it gives the Secretary of State power to authorise 'inspectors' who can inspect and enter any aircraft or aerodrome or installation within the United Kingdom and require operators and airport management to give him any information he needs and, if necessary for his purposes, can actually detain an aircraft.

Part III of the Act is that which defines the powers of constables, the punishments for committing offences and failure to comply, the methods of administering the Act, various other definitions and - perhaps most important in the eyes of operators and airport management - permits the Secretary of State to make reimbursement for the costs of the measures recommended by his inspectors and the needs of security.

This Act is certainly the most important to be passed in the field of aviation security. Many Acts make offences and define punishment - very few state so clearly what measures can be directed by Government to combat the offences. It is a considerable step when Government not only decides that the flying public and the aircraft in which they fly shall be protected in this country, but also indicates how that protection shall be achieved and accepts, in principle, the responsibility for the financial outlay for that protection.

There is not time to delve into the methods employed in countries other than the United Kingdom to protect the industry from acts of violence and it would be presumptuous of me to endeavour to do so.

It is, perhaps, sufficient for me to say that the United Kingdom has taken a lead in the European Civil Aviation Conference (ECAC) to press for the adoption of standardized and consistent methods of ensuring aircraft security throughout Europe with marked success and it is hoped that this initiative will lead to emulation by countries outside the European sphere.

Within the United Kingdom, the present machinery, both at Government and local levels, to combat aviation violence and terrorism has resulted from the ICAO recommendations. The Department of Trade is responsible for the National Aviation Security Committee, and recommends the establishment of security committees at the airports in receipt of its aviation security advice.

The National Aviation Security Committee (NASC) was set up in 1971 with the following terms of reference:

"To advise HM Government and the civil aviation industry, including the airport authorities, regarding security measures to meet threats of violence to civil aviation; to recommend appropriate security measures; and to keep such measures and their effectiveness under review".

The Committee comprises representatives of Government Departments, the Civil Aviation Authority, the police, airlines, airport authorities and trade unions. It is chaired by a senior official of the Department of Trade, which also provides the Secretariat. The Committee meets at least quarterly, and more often as required. A note of its discussions is sent to those airlines and airport authorities in regular receipt of security advice from the Department of Trade who are not themselves members of the Committee.

The NASC and the Department of Trade recommend parallel security committees at airports. The terms of reference should be adapted from those of the NASC in accordance with local conditions and should provide for consideration by the airport authority, airlines, handling agents and other interested parties of the advice on the current threat and on recommended counter-

measures received from the NASC and the Department of Trade; discussion of methods of practical implementation of recommended measures at the airport; review of the effectiveness of recommended measures and the need for additional measures; and reference to the Department of Trade and the NASC any problem which cannot be solved at local level. Within this framework the Committee should keep under review the need for supplementary security surveys of the airport or any part of it; the need for security education and training at the airport; and provision for security measures in airport development programmes.

Airport Security Committees should in normal circumstances be chaired by the Airport Director and the membership should include the airport security officer and representatives of the police; Immigration; Customs and Excise; Air Traffic Control; other officers in charge of tele-communications; medical, firefighting and other rescue services; British and overseas airlines using the airport; aircraft handling agencies; organisations providing major and critical services such as fuel suppliers, and trade unionists employed at the airport. It is recommended that there be some cross-membership between the Airport Security Committee and the Airport Facilitation Committee so that each can take account of the problems of the other.

It may now be valuable to look at the matter from a more practical viewpoint. We have all seen, within this country, the effects of security - the searching of passengers, erection of fences, closure of doors and denial of access, wearing of Identity cards, protection of vital installations. How is it all done? In the first instance - always define your threat. This aspect cannot be over emphasised and, by those who are laymen, it is almost always overlooked. If we are to achieve any real security, then we must know the nature of the threat, its seriousness, whence it comes - as much about it as possible. Only thus will it be possible to make our security measures practicable and practical. The next step is to survey the object of security. It is usually thought that surveys apply only to airports but this is not so. An aircraft, an airline's operations, an outlying navigation installation - all are susceptible to survey. The aim of a survey is to establish those measures which can be practically applied to the object to improve its security to a point where it becomes a hard enough target to deter or frustrate the attacker - and, in this respect, it may not be just a physical attacker - it may be the attacker who is seeking information, the attacker who is seeking the subversion of staff, the attacker who is seeking to destroy credibility. In practice, in the realm of terrorism and the airport it is usually the physical attacker we are seeking to frustrate though it may well be that plans and instructions will have to be made known on a restricted basis to ensure confidentiality of valuable information. The surveyor must commence by deciding what must be protected and what can be ignored and in this endeavour one must be ruthless - to protect that which is unnecessary is to waste resources which may be better employed elsewhere. For example, complete fencing is not a panacea for preventing unauthorised access. The fence is not, of itself, a sufficiently positive security measure. It is but a deterrent to the intruder who is not very determined. Its value lies in the fact that its defining line has to be overcome and this involves delay and makes the intruder obvious to the watcher. But to watch continuously an entire airport perimeter fence is extremely expensive in manpower and time. Careful surveying should be directed to determining those areas which are most vulnerable and giving them that fencing which will enhance security, provide a definitive line for both the security guard and the intruder and act as an initial deterrent.

The surveyor must also be aware of the needs of, in particular, facilitation. Security must be geared to the flow of passengers and the pursuit of business interests. Without doubt, there are some areas where security will intrude but these must be kept to a minimum and their necessity carefully explained. The views of others must be considered and there must be full consultation in the course of the survey. So it is from the survey - the visit by the 'Inspector' mentioned in the Protection of Aircraft Act - that airport security measures stem. The careful definition and protection of the Airside/landside line; the guarding of gates and buildings; fencing and protection of windows; the examination of vehicles and of pedestrians' identity cards; the protection of sources of power supply. These measures are designed, in short, to see that only the right people and things get to the places where they need to go. The extraneous, the casual, the trespasser, the terrorist, are excluded.

The searching of passengers and their baggage in varying degrees is the result of a different type of survey - perhaps not so obvious or so conscious; the survey of an airline's operations and how best to secure them. The best way of preventing hijacking is, of course, to stop carrying passengers or, since aircrew have been know to hijack their own aircraft, to stop flying altogether. It sounds, I know, ridiculous but, in fact, one Government, under threat of hijacking recently, did just this. They locked an aircraft, surrounded it with armed guards, refused to allow the crew access and cancelled the flight. It seems a strange way to run an airline!

So, we have the contentious subject of passenger searching which is now almost universal in its application to airline operations to a greater or lesser extent. Thus far, we have considered the measures that can be taken and the legislation and theory which generates and supports them. It might now be worth while considering what is being done, by whom and how within the industry to ensure a reasonable level of security.

Within the United Kingdom, Government has sought to achieve a level of security for the flying public, whether of this country or visiting or transitting nationals of other countries, by adopting a policy of co-operation between the various interests concerned - by means of NASC - and by making available to the aviation industry advice, assistance and financial reimbursement both to airports and airlines. At the same time, Government has maintained that implementation of security of airports and airlines, is a management responsibility. Government, therefore, has provided the means of surveying airports and airline operations and thus ensured a common standard of threat assessment and of recommended measures to combat the threat, and has issued advice and recommendations on the measures and manpower needed. Management has been left to get on with the implementation of the recommendations and the employment of the manpower, following which Government has reimbursed cost. The result is a largely voluntary system of security though, as has been seen, the Government has the power to issue its own directives and to enforce them if it is felt that prudent measures are being ignored. There are, of course, other approaches to the problem. Some Governments have taken the line that security is something to be imposed by a direct involvement, usually by the use of military, para-military or police personnel or by the enactment of regulations backed by financial penalties and administered by specially constituted enforcement agencies. The aim remains the same.

Within the United Kingdom, therefore, the security of the various airports is the responsibility of the airport management, assisted in its policies and methods by Government advice and using its own security staff; the security of aircraft and the flying passengers, again, is the responsibility of airline management, with Government advice and, usually, using hired security staff. Only where there is some specially high level of threat, either to airport or to airline, are police directly involved in the basic security problem. To many, particularly those from other countries, this will seem paradoxical, but it stems from the form of police in this country. Contrary to most worldwide practice, the British police are not a Government controlled agency; their powers are not delegated but arise from each individual constable's authority under the law. Hence, the police are not numerous and are not at the beck and call of central government. They tend to be a select body, highly trained in the prevention of law breaking, the detection of the law breaker and the preservation of the public peace and their role is exercised more especially when law is broken and the peace is actively breached. To employ police in a largely static role - for example, gate guarding - and in a largely passive preventive role - for example, passenger searching - appears to be to waste the selective training they have been given. In other words, in terms of threat, to squander all too valuable resources.

The role of the police, in aviation security, is two fold. First, and most important, is their inevitable involvement in the committed act of sabotage or hijacking. These are crimes and it is for Police to contain them, terminate them and investigate them. Police will therefore be involved in security at all airports to the extent that they must be ready to act when sabotage has been committed or when a hijacked aircraft arrives at an airport in their area of responsibility. To this end, then it is essential that airport management co-operates fully with police in preparing contingency plans to deal with these particular crimes. To wait until they occur is too late. Plans must be made and plans must be exercised. Aviation is an esoteric business and police are not generally familiar with it. Only by co-operation can the best plans be achieved.

The other involvement of Police is seen to be that when the threat of a particular act of violence is so high as to indicate that violence may, at any time, be imminent. It may be that an airport has such prestige that it is a continuing target for violence; that a certain flight by reason of ethnic origin of its passengers or by its destination or by national affiliation may be a target of continuing high threat. Then the presence of police at the airport or at the point of passenger search or at the aircraft becomes one, not of providing a basic security, but of preventing an imminent crime or breakdown of law and order. The Policing of Airports Act, by which local police forces have been given statutory responsibilities at a number of airports - particularly the larger ones - will come to mind but it must be remembered that this Act does not given Police any overall responsibility for airport security. It merely ensures that the larger airports are given the benefit, in these disturbed times, of policing, in the widest sense of the word, by modern, well found and well supported police forces, equipped to combat crime and preserve public order. That there will be, of course, a tangential security benefit to any airport with such a force, goes without saying. It does not follow, however, that every airport needs the presence of Police to achieve security. Every airport does need a security force, which should not be confused with a police force.

The security of aircraft is usually attained by searching in varying degrees of depth according to the threat envisaged at a particular time. In general, the threat is held to be one of hijacking and the search, usually of passengers and their hand baggage, is designed to discover weapons which may be used to perpetrate the crime. If there would seem to be a threat of sabotage, then the degree of search can be intensified to include, for example, a search of the aircraft followed by close guarding; search of technical equipment as it goes on board; search of flight stores; search of technical personnel and/or of flight crew, search of passengers hold baggage. But of all the security measures taken at airports, passenger searching is probably the most contentious for

it has an immediate effect upon facilitation. It interferes with the efficient flow of passengers and their baggage; it delays them; it forces upon airlines earlier call forward times; it occupies valuable space; it is, to a greater or lesser extent, socially unacceptable though most people seem not to resent this search but to positively welcome it. There would seem to be no other method of preventing the carriage of weapons and other offensive articles on board aircraft. How best then to do it? All other factors being equal, it can be said that the nearer to the aircraft passengers are searched the better, assuming that the aircraft itself can be accepted as 'clean'. Within practical limits, this would seem to mean searching at the gate giving access to the aircraft. If there is a gate lounge, into which passengers can be fed following search of themselves and their baggage, so much the better. But this method has the disadvantage that it requires a diversity of search areas and a multiplicity of searching teams, with the associated impedimenta, machines, tables and so on. Additionally, it involves calling forward the passenger early enough to permit the searching of 150 to 350 people.

It is possible to minimize the number of sites and the number of searchers by carrying out the search operation at the head of the appropriate pier or walkway. This method, however, implies that the pier itself is sterile from a security aspect and this is frequently difficult to ensure for, in the majority of cases, the arriving passenger uses the same pier as the departing passenger and may well have come from an insecure airport. Additionally, the problem of early call forward still exists, though perhaps not to so serious a degree as in the gate search system.

By taking yet another step backwards, so to speak, away from the aircraft, it is possible to search passengers, almost simultaneously with initial check in, at the departure concourse. Obviously, this involves the security of the concourse. Given that it probably contains a duty free shop, toilets, bars and refreshment areas, it is not an easy task nor one that lends itself to absolute security and, in most cases, after leaving the concourse, the departing passenger again mingles with the arriving passenger.

The decision as to where to interrupt the passenger flow to make the necessary search is one that must rest with individual airport managements in consultation with their user airlines. The factors of space, time, convenience and cost will all have to be balanced against the level of security to be achieved.

Next, how to search? The better question might be "What to look for?" The one is dependent upon the other. Obviously, searching for a 9mm automatic is a different technique from searching for a small electric detonator; searching for a swordstick different from a piece of plastic explosive. Fortunately, as practised in the main at present, searching is confined to looking for objects which might be used to hijack an aircraft - the pistol, explosive, dagger or other sharp or offensive object. Thus the search can be carried out with comparative speed, in the knowledge that the present threat does not postulate anything which is so small as to lend itself to secretion in body cavities, or very sophisticated hiding places. This is not to say that such things do not happen; they are the extreme and call for extreme measures which need not be discussed here.

Basically, any search depends upon visual observation, combined with a knowledge of the items and persons undergoing search and of the hiding places which might be adopted. This, when combined with a systematic plan of search and an alert mind should produce a satisfactory, if not very speedy search. Speed of search can be engendered by the discriminating use of various aids. That which is most common is the metal detector, either of the hand held or the detector gate variety. These have the ability to indicate the presence of metal in reasonably small quantities - certainly small enough to give ample indication of a pistol or grenade. They are in common use and are of considerable value, for the detector gate, in particular, when correctly used, can greatly ease the process of search. The other technical aid which is most commonly seen is the X-ray machine or fluoroscope. At many airports, there is an implicit dependence upon the X-ray and baggage can be seen going through X-ray on conveyor belts, the picture being scanned by security guards, and never a single piece being given any sort of examination. It may well be that every piece of baggage so scanned can be positively identified as having nothing offensive in it but one must doubt it. The real value of the X-ray may be said to lie in its ability to examine that which it is difficult - or perhaps anti-social - to open, in that it can offer a picture to check that the contents of a stated piece of goods are what they might be expected to be. It seems to be frequently unappreciated that the X-ray is an aid to the security guard, not a security barrier of its own accord. There is, of course, cosmetic and deterrent value, but the real security value of searching to prevent hijacking must surely lie in the capability of the man - assisted by various technical aids such as detector gates and X-rays. There are, of course, a vast variety of security aids. They must not be allowed to obscure the fact that the eventual security lies in the ability of the security officer to make conscious decisions using the necessary aids and his own skill and experience.

The present state of the art has been touched upon fairly generally in the foregoing, but there must be concern for the future. The writer does not know of one airport where security has been taken into account as an operating factor in the design stages. The reason the design of an airport of any size is a very long term project and any airport already in existence - even the most recent - must have been in the planning stage long before the present wave of national and international violence was clearly perceived. But there are no indications at all, at present, that violence is receding or even likely to recede in the foreseeable future. The social climate is such that minority groups are being encouraged to make themselves heard and terrorism on a larger or smaller scale seems to be one of the ultimate methods of propagating the minority message. As long as this remains the case, there will be violence and we shall have to take measures to combat and prevent it. These measures will become more and more a part of our daily life. The ready acceptance of searching by the airline passenger is something that would have been almost unthinkable even ten years ago.

Future airports, therefore, must be planned with security in mind from the very outset. At every stage, security must form a part of the planning concept. Long before the architect starts to put lines on paper, the security problems of the country, of the user airlines, of the very locality must be assessed and the current and developing threat adduced. At the design stage there must be recognition of the needs of security; the siting of entrances, exits, gates and lounges; the minimizing of access points to airside; the methods of restricting unnecessary movement and access the possible segregation of the departing and arriving passenger; the very space for the mundane aspects of security searching and guarding and the staffs necessary to do these routine tasks; accommodation for the more specialised areas of incident control rooms and emergency communications - these must no longer be the afterthoughts of threat induced compromise planning; security surveying must start with the first stages of construction so that possible security weaknesses can be seen at the earliest stages. And following construction, airport authorities must be seized of the necessity to employ trained professional security officers at management level to ensure that security remains involved in every aspect of the airport's existence.

If there is not to be a continuing recurrence of terrorist acts directed against the aviation industry - all of them costing money and good-will - then there must be a security awareness and a security involvement throughout the industry as a whole.

20. Changing cargo needs

S. Köhler

General Manager, Cargo and Airmail, Lufthansa German Airlines

Speed of loading/unloading is vital for economic air freight management. The paper describes recent developments to achieve this.

Development of Air Cargo Traffic

1. The changing needs of cargo ground facilities have to be seen in the context of the tremendous growth of air freight market.

To start with, let me give you, therefore, some highlights of the enormous expansion in terms of quantities and technology in this field:

- Within the last 30 years the world air cargo traffic has developed from

    appr. 100 Mio. tkm in 1945   to

    appr. 22 Bio. tkm in 1975

- i.e. Air Cargo increases at an average rate of 20-25% per year, it doubles every 4 - 5 years.

- This development - at a reduced rate though - is still continuing inspite of recessions and degressive economical trends.
  Lufthansa prognosis for 1980 is appr. 38 Bio. tkm.

One has to realize the phantastic changes in technology that were necessary to make such a growth possible. It cannot be explained by just one phenomenon alone, but only by accumulation and multiplication of a whole set of various tendencies, such as

- Development of higher speed aircraft, resulting in reduced transport time

- Extension of route network - more airports being served

- Size of aircraft fleet and better use of every single aircraft

- Higher aircraft capacities in terms of volume and payload

- Introduction of wide-body and all-cargo aircraft and so on.

All these tendencies developed separately but simultaneously and altogether had a multiplying effect, which made it possible, to ship today the volume of air freight that is demanded by world trade.

Ground Facilities

2. However, in face of these spectacular achievements, one is easily inclined to forget about the efforts that have taken place "behind the lines" and, that were necessary or even prerequisite to keep the sophisticated aircraft technology operable and that no less called for rapid changes and advanced technology for itself.

I am talking about the wide field of air cargo ground handling, about the operational methods involved and about the ground handling facilities and their changing needs.

The fundamental service advantage of air freight is speed of transport but much of it is being lost on the ground. Today the average transport time of air cargo shipment is appr. 6 days. Only about 8% of this time the shipment is actually being moved in the aircraft. The rest of the time is needed for the handling of shipments on ground for storage, ground transportation, waiting, delays, etc.

This shows that the solution for further improvements is to be sought on the ground.

2.1 Ground Handling. In the beginning the ground handling of the air cargo shipments, i.e. loading and unloading of the aircraft and the transportation at the airport - was done almost exclusively by hand.

1950, for example, the unloading of a DC-4 with an average load of 4 - 5 tons of cargo took about 1 1/2 to 2 hours and involved normally 4 - 6 persons.

It would be quite a simple calculation to find out how long it would take today to unload, for instance our B-747 F all-cargo jumbo jet, with a payload of possibly 100 tons, if we still tried to use the same methods in handling the cargo.

However, today we need only about 45 minutes to get this job done.

Of course. this was not achieved in one day but rather by a long chain of improvements characterized by ground handling being the bottleneck of air freight.

Until comparatively recently, the commonly used method of handling cargo was to haul it from the terminal in trucks and to load it into the aircraft manually piece by piece. Particularly heavy or out-sized pieces posed problems but, by and large, the handling systems in use, though they could have improved upon, were more or less adequate for the job to be done.
Gradually, however, fork-lifts and other equipment for raising cargo to the level of the aircraft came into more general use as the volume of cargo grew and handling methods improved.

In the 50s Lufthansa tried to cope with the extreme increase of air shipments by improved methods in handling the cargo. Simple facilities were used, lift trucks, conveyor belts, etc. Storage and transit areas were enlarged in accordance with growing demand. Planning was done, however, on a rather short term basis, measurements and building projects were rather adjustments to momentary situations and were outgrown as soon as finished. Mechanized equipment was installed to put in order the increasing amount of consignments, facilities that could sort about 3000 pcs/h.

This is just to give a short view of the long history, consisting of several phases, of our "Frachthof I" in Frankfurt.

2.2 Unitization. The needs of the ground handling facilities changed, however, considerably with the growing use of aircraft containers and pallets.

Before, a large proportion of air cargo was made up of package type consignments, where the handling problems were basically the enormous quantities and the sorting. In order to reduce the number of handlings and thus keep the handling cost low and time short, carriers were concentrating more and more on unitization. This means more extensive use of containers and pallets and mechanized methods of handling these "unitized" loads in the cargo terminals, on the ramp and for loading and unloading of aircraft.

Lufthansa purchased her own pallets and containers. The units were loaded before arrival of the aircraft so that upon arrival only the complete units had to be changed. By eliminating the handling of each package the ground handling time could be reduced considerably.

The costs, however, could only be reduced substantially once one was able to make shippers and their agents build up one large consignment out of many small shipments. This was promoted by the introduction of special rates that gave sufficient incentives for the use of containers.

Containerization started in 1963 and since then has become more perfect and standardized.

At present, the IATA airlines offer two programs as far as containers and pallets are concerned:

First, the so-called Standard-resp. Shipper's Containers (11 of them IATA registered), which can be bought by shippers. They are fitted with fork-lift pallets and can thus be picked up by trucks at the shipper's premises and transported to the airport without the need of any additional loading equipment. By means of these units the loading and unloading times of an aircraft can be reduced considerably.

The second program, which started mainly as a reaction to the development in the field of sea container transport, is the FAK-program, applicable anywhere from a 20-foot to the LD-containers.

Although this FAK-program is a step towards a true door-to-door service it is not fully comparable to surface container transport. This is mainly due to the fact that these units are integrated parts of the aircraft: consequently, the trucks that take them on, have to be equipped with the same roller beds as the aircraft - a costly investment still abhorred by many forwarders.

But air cargo must offer intermodal containers which can be exchanged between all means of transportation. In size they must be able to compete with those of surface carriers.

Lufthansa made the first step towards intermodal units by operating the 10-foot "Bungalow" container.

The 747 F has demonstrated the practicability of operations with 8 x 8 ft quasi intermodal load units, the first of which was the Lufthansa "bungalow" consisting of a 96 x 125 inch pallet with a rectangular fiberglass body. The latter is fixed to the pallet by metal locks and a net. It has a quadripartite folding door on the front side which allows customs sealing.

For surface transport the bungalow container can be placed on and firmly locked to a transport pallet equipped with roller tracks. This pallet has fork lift tine slots and ISO/SAE corner fittings. It can be locked on a truck and lifted by crane in the same manner as a true 10-foot-ISO container.

After two years of use we found only one drawback with the bungalow unit: the body of polyester has not been strong enough to absorb all the shocks and cresting occurring during the ground handling resp. the loading and unloading of the aircraft.

We therefore decided to replace the complete load unit by structural 10-foot metal aircraft containers which will be the main container in use for the next years of 747 F operation.

The combination of oversize load-unit capability and large containers has resulted in a significant increment of new air freight business.

When looking into the future, the first problem we envisage is the simplification of container ground handling in order to upkeep a successful operation. Although I shall deal with this aspect a little later on, let me just give you some information in advance:

Our first step was the introduction of our fully automated terminal in New York with nose dock facilities for the 747 F; a similar yet considerably larger terminal will now be built at Frankfurt Airport.

Secondly, there has to be an exact plan on which containers should be used in the future. We think one can safely say that the main share will be igloo operations, especially considering interline traffic. As for the lower deck, we shall continue to use the LD-7- and the LD-3-containers, which, however, shall carry only a small share of the combined traffic between them.

The larger part will focus on the use of our 10-foot bungalow in combination with the platform. In order to satisfy certain market demands and to contribute more intensely to intermodal traffic, we have introduced a 20-foot metal container with ISO measurements and ISO corner fittings. We believe this container to be a further incentive towards a profitable way of shipping goods by air.

Air Cargo Terminals
3. With increasing operation of all-cargo aircraft requirements as to ground handling shifted somewhat.

The fact that all-cargo aircraft can operate independently from passenger terminals opened new possibilities for reduced handling.

In addition to the development of the specialized handling equipment, a related development became the planning of integrated handling and warehousing systems where aircraft can dock directly at these facilities.

The basic principles and requirements for proper cargo handling under these conditions and the respective cargo flow patterns have been a matter of close studies. The overall concept of integrated systems have become more and more important with the need for increasing size and investment of these projects.
Capability of expansion, location, access and accommodation for special cargo have to be considered and fit into the concepts as well as the anticipation of changing requirements in the future.

The warehousing systems are planned to be as mechanized and as automated as possible in order to reduce labour.

Apart from the necessary capabilities of handling the more traditional package type of shipments, emphasis is put on handling, transport and processing of unit load devices, which makes up for almost 20% of total volume at Frankfurt Airport.

3.1 The New York Cargo Terminal. For over almost 3 years now, the B-747 F has been off- and on-loaded at Lufthansa's US$ 16.2 million cargo terminal at Kennedy International Airport.

The terminal embodies the latest in cargo handling technology, and as to the layout of its automated systems, it is the most advanced air cargo terminal in the world. It is a facility which comes closest to the concept of a building functioning as a machine.

The terminal was planned with the emphasis on maximum utilization, flexibility and expansion capacity. It will have the capability of handling up to 260,000 tons of cargo per year by 1985.

The terminal's warehouse building covers 97,000 square feet of ground space and reaches a height of 56 feet in the high bay area. Interior spacing, size and arrangement of storage media and warehouse operations are compatible with anticipated as well as present needs.

The terminal's nose dock mates with the 747 F's main deck. The aircraft's own internally-powered conveyor system moves the cargo pallets and containers in and out of the jumbo's nose section over the powered roller surface of the nose dock which is part of the terminal's weatherproof container storage system. All level, roll and pitch movements of the aircraft are instantly and automatically evened out by the nose dock itself.

A large elevating transfer vehicle (ETV), directed by a supervisory computer, moves the containers to and from the nose dock, to and from pre-determined storage decks. There are 225 structural steel decks in four levels in the storage area which can accommodate all kinds of aircraft pallets and containers up to 20 feet in length.

The ETV, a combination of conveyor and stacker crane technology, can handle two ten-foot containers or one 20-foot container at one time. It can transfer the main deck's complete load of 28 inbound and 28 outbound containers and pallets between the nose dock and the storage decks in as little as 43 minutes. Lower deck cargo will move into and out of the system with mobile equipment via air side transfer stations.

Cargo that does not move out of the terminal immediately is stored in carts in a ten-level, 1,300-bin towcart stacker. The stacker's storing and retrieving cranes are also directed by the supervisory computer.

Since the beginning of its operation, the system has worked to our full satisfaction. Perhaps at some time in the future a second nose dock, capable of servicing even the next generation of freighter aircraft, may be necessary.

On the other side of the Atlantic, at Frankfurt airport, we have had very good results with our stationary 747 F loader from which, in the case of unloading, the load units are transferred onto a transporter and then onto dollies stationed around the aircraft. This transfer, however, represents a minor bottleneck timewise which will be eliminated when our new cargo terminal becomes operational.

3.2 The Frankfurt Cargo Terminal. This terminal which has been operating since May 1971 covers a ground space of 39.500 square meters.

The Frankfurt terminal presently handles some 267.300 tons of cargo per year. Daily turnover is about 735 tons, rising up to 900 on the busier days. In 1974, 10.3 million single packages moved through the terminal at the rate of about 28.200 per day. The terminal processes cargo for some 150 incoming and 150 outgoing passenger and freighter flights each day, and serves 15 other airline customers in addition to Lufthansa. On the terminal's "land" side, there are 50 truck docks for customer pick up and delivery of cargo. The terminal's high degree of flexibility is necessitated above all by the fact that 80 percent of the cargo handled here is in transit.

Shipments bound for Frankfurt itself are assigned to a separate section of the terminal to be customs cleared and dispersed by a separate handling company. Unit loads in direct transit (15.900 in 1974), for example a through-pallet originating in London and destined for Hong Kong, bypass the terminal altogether. The rest, in fact most, of the cargo arriving in Frankfurt is processed by the terminal's semi-automated cargo distribution system, which comprises 14 input conveyor belts and 48 output belts.

224 trolleys circulate continuously on a loop-shaped track to connect the input and output belts. The 48 destination belts receive cargo assigned to the more than 100 destination Lufthansa serves. Cargo is taken from the belts and stored in adjacent racks until made ready for shipment. Cargo, the dimensions or weight of which are not acceptable to the distributor, are stored either on warehouse trailers or, if they are particularly large or heavy, in the heavy goods section. There are also special places for perishables, live animals, valuable goods, radioactive goods and human remains. The whole terminal is supervised by closed-circuit TV (10 cameras and 17 monitors).

Although the Frankfurt terminal has achieved a very high rate of reliability in its automated sorting system (and thus a high overall degree of cargo handling efficiency), it has reached

the point where in the very near future it will almost have reached its capacity. Lufthansa will have to move out then as the terminal will not be able to handle the increasing volume of cargo efficiently and economically.

The answer is a new computer-controlled cargo facility to be built near the present one.

3.3 The Frankfurt Cargo Terminal of the Future.
Although the new terminal will be slightly smaller than the old one (38.500 square meters), its initial handling capacity will be 50% higher (530.000 tons versus max. 360.000 t p.a.). It has a projected end capacity of 1.5 million tons a year but will be built in stages according to demand. Lufthansa planners have made it clear that they will not switch over to highly mechanized and computerized cargo handling too fast, and so the introduction of sophisticated computer systems to run the terminal will be a step-by-step process with plenty of staff training and equipment "familiarization" in advance. Another important factor is that the design provides for considerable expansion in the terminal's size and systems according to demand with no interruption to the cargo flow during construction stages.

The terminal will have five major components:

- A radial pallet distributor centre with stationary aircraft docks (between 3 and 5 of them in the first stage) for direct pallet/container transfer to/from the freighter aircraft;

- A five-level pallet stacker with 700 storage positions for pallets and containers up to 20 feet long;

- A separate pallet stacker system for cargo transported on passenger aircraft;

- A central terminal for build-up and break-down of pallets. This also comprises a nine-level "box" stacker with some 4000 storage positions;

- Office building with areas for administration, documentation, pick-up and delivery of consignments and customs clearance.

A special feature of the terminal is the independent storage system for containerized and bulk cargo assigned to passenger aircraft. Aircraft containers and bulk cargo stored in ground transport units are delivered to this position by conveyor from the central terminal. When the flight is ready, the units are transported on dollies to the passenger terminal where their contents are loaded into the aircraft bellies.

Necessitating this particular development is the already large (and increasing) amount of cargo transported in the belly compartments of the jets in the Lufthansa fleet. At present, 30 to 35 percent of all Lufthansa cargo ex Frankfurt is carried this way, and by 1978, it will increase to 45 - 50 percent.

Future Developments

4. Further developments are still a matter of debate among forecasting experts. Whereas some advocate the growing importance of all-cargo aircraft in the future, it becomes apparent, that there are tendencies towards a reverse trend making more use of wide-body capacities for cargo transportation.
This seems to be more advantageous in several respects, i.e.

splitting the risk of too big capacities,

more favorable cost situation, etc.

One thing, however, is for sure, further rationalization cannot be sought in sophisticated facilities alone. Even though the technical progress in building and equipment was a prerequisite to keep up with the phantastic growth of air cargo, it has to be realized that enormous investments by the airlines were necessary to achieve what we have today. There is no question that further investments will be necessary in the future - and they will be made - but we will also have to think about other - more efficient - ways to improve ground handling.

4.1 One possibility of making air cargo handling more economical which definitely has not been fully used yet, is the facilitation of procedures and operational methods and the application of data processing.

Though various projects are in process there is still a wide field for action to be taken.

One example that demonstrates the possibilities is London Heathrow.

What differentiates the London terminal from its "brother" terminals in Frankfurt and New York is the unique computerized customs clearance system, know as LACES (London Airport Cargo E.D.P. Scheme). This is a system whereby the airline, agents and customs inspectors are linked together by computer for the purpose of speeding up the clearance of cargo through customs. The parties through Visual Display Units (VDUs) are linked to the central computer which governs the whole system and takes the major decisions on how a particular piece of cargo is to be customs cleared. The VDUs resemble TV sets and typewriters combined.

Information about a consignment is filed with the computer through a VDU, and almost immediately the computer advises which of three standard procedures is to be applied to the clearance of that consignment along with a calculation of duties, taxes or other charges payable. There are three clearance methods known as "channels".

Channel 1 enables customs officers to release a consignment subject only to a scrutiny of its documents. When satisfied, the officer presses a key on his VDU which causes a release note to be printed out in the Lufthansa terminal.

This authorizes Lufthansa to hand over the shipment. About 15 percent of all consignments are cleared through channel 1.

Channel 2 clearance means the consignment has to be physically examined, and about 20 percent of all consignments are cleared in this manner. The remaining 65 percent are cleared through channel 3 which gives automatic clearance subject to an hour's delay so that customs men have the opportunity to intervene should they become suspicious about a particular consignment.

The real advantage of LACES is that it replaces sluggish paperwork with computer electronics and is helping make the speed of cargo on the ground more commensurate with the speed of the jet freighters that carry it through the air. One good example: prior to the advent of LACES, the average storage time for a piece or cargo at Heathrow was 72 hours. The computer has, on average, reduced this to 22 hours, while Lufthansa's best clearance time for a consignment so far is 11 minutes.

Lufthansa plugged into the LACES computer in September 1971 after a lot of preparation, study and training, and is now one of the system's most active supporters. Recently, it introduced yet another technique - built around LACES - to speed up cargo clearance even further. The technique is simple, effective and indicative of Lufthansa's innovative approach to cargo handling.

Consignments from a passenger flight arrive outside the warehouse in their transfer box. The unloading officer reads the relevant information from the packages into his small radio, the signals from which are picked up inside the terminal by the VDU operator who punches the information immediately into the computer. This enables the clearance procedure to start practically before the cargo has reached its storage racks. It has eliminated the need to build a conveyor in order to bring the inbound cargo to the VDU operator for processing, and has thus saved valuable warehouse space. A similar technique is also being used for the off-loading of freighter igloos.

The LACES-Lufthansa partnership will continue to bring more customer benefits as improvements and refinements unfold in the future. At present, LACES is confined to import and transit freight, but it's due to incorporate export cargo inventory control and accounting during 1974. And if Lufthansa cargo specialists in London have their way, it won't be too long before the LACES central computer is linked with the Lufthansa computer in Frankfurt, thus enabling cargo bound for London to be customs cleared even before it arrives.

Ladies and Gentlemen, let me finish with a short summary of what has been said:

The current trends in cargo terminals and ground development are strongly influenced by the operation of all-cargo aircraft and there especially by the B 747 F with which a whole new generation of new equipment came into use. In the future, however, we feel that further improvement - especially ground handling economy will have to take place in the area of operational methods and mainly EDP.

Session VII: Discussion

Mr ROCKWELL (Paper 16)

Since our paper was prepared, British Railways
have suggested a slight change of emphasis and
some additional information in our remarks about
Brimingham and Gatwick.

In the case of Birmingham, we would now prefer the end of the second paragraph to read '...
rail access to Birmingham Airport is expected to
influence a change in the pre-existing pattern
of surface access', and the first part of the
third paragraph to read 'In the longer term, an
ambitious plan for erecting a new airport terminal building adjacent to the new railway station is expected to account for a significant
share of the total ground traffic in the future
and is designed to link the airport ...'.

In the case of Gatwick, we should have pointed out that the first airport station dates
back to 1935 and can be regarded as the pioneer
of all air/rail interchange stations. The station was redeveloped in 1958 but is now undergoing another major reconstruction, with three
out of six platforms signalled for two-way movements and with an additional footbridge serving
as an entry concourse for air-to-rail passengers.
At the same time, the special train service to
Victoria will be increased to four trains per
hour (Sundays up to 8), corresponding to an annual capacity of 10 million passengers, which
leaves an ample margin over and above the air/
rail traffic of 7.2 million expected in 1985.

Mr R. A. HUBBARD, Wilbur Smith and Associates, USA

I wish to limit my remarks on ground access to
the major airports in the United States.

Mr Moore has outlined the problems relative
to the Los Angeles Airport which is one of the
USA's largest airports.

Through the historic development of urban
centres America has experienced a much more diverse land use pattern and, consequently, has
found it more difficult to select concentrated
corridors for the specific treatment of fixed
guideways for airport access. The predominance
of the motor car and motor bus has led to the
airport access being principally by motorway or
high-grade, controlled access facility. Sometimes (e.g. Dulles Airport, Washington) the
motorway had no access provisions and nothing
moves on it except traffic to and from the airport itself.

An airport access project in the United
States generally takes in three key elements:
  (a) the central terminal area, (CTA), the
  circulating roadways and parking facilities;
  (b) the linkage between that and the regional road system;
  (c) the road system to serve the region itself.
The regional road system airport demand, even
measured in terms of vehicles or persons, whether
passengers or staff or service facilities, comprises only 1% or so of the total movement. The
airport corridor itself ranges from 50-95%. The
length and scale of the airport roadway access
varies greatly, from something just over 200 ft

at Lindberg Field in San Diego, to 6½ miles in
the Dulles area. Each of these has to be treated quite differently in assessing its problems.

There has been mention of a number of cities
in the USA which are planning rail links. At
the moment Cleveland, Ohio, is the only one that
has a fixed facility in operation. Oakland,
California, and Boston, Massachusets, each has
a rail service that is within reasonable proximity of the airport, through a bus interchange.
But other cities are planning these. For example, Washington DC, through the Washington
National Terminal, will have rail access, due
largely to the extension of the Metro. The
Metro there was opened in its first section in
March 1976 and is expected to be completed to
the airport within another year. However,
Washington National Airport is geographically
constrained. The maximum size of aircraft that
can land there at present are the 727s. These
have a reasonably good range, and journeys from
places like Houston, Miami, Boston and Chicago
can be handled by the 727. The trans-continental
flights which use the wide-bodied ships, the 747
and others, cannot move in; instead they go to
Dulles. The journey downtown is then 10 mins by
cab or limousine. It is quicker by Metro, but
the one to Dulles is a long way away in terms of
implementation.

Less than 20% of any of the airport patrons
come from any one central area. There is a diffused pattern at Kennedy Airport; passengers
from Long Island, Winchester County, Connecticut
and the downtown Manhattan area are only 20% of
the total. Any rail link must have, for the
sake of economic feasibility, a use for other
types of movement.

The economic requirement for such a rail
link at Kennedy will be about US$450 million.
In terms of self-liquidation or of meeting up to
the average on other rail services, this is not
possible. However, when one considers that the
entire capacity of the airport itself to expand
is totally dependent upon ground access in such
a case, it could be economically viable, not as
a facility in itself but to make the airport
function properly.

These are some of the main criteria; the
predominance of the freeway systems and the
heavy investment mean, for the most part, ground
access in the USA will be predominantly by motor
vehicle. The intention now is to divert people
from the private car into some form of upgraded
public transport, including the mini-bus, the
para-transit - all the catch words that one can
put to this type of operating vehicle, which
basically say 'do all you can to get door-to-
door service'.

Flight times have diminished; ground times
have increased. It takes the same amount of
time to travel from New York to Chicago today as
it did in 1950, because of increased ground time.
The heavy constraints on limited ground access
in airport developments are very serious. Some
programmes indicate that airport facilities will
be virtually controlled to what they are today.

Mr Moore referred to 40 million passengers

213

Table 1. Heathrow: access analysis

1975 Three terminals				
Annual passengers: 21 million			Airport workers: 51 600	
Vehicle journeys: 000s/day			**Daily highway loadings: %**	
Air passengers: cars/taxis		30 000	M4	(28 560)	28
Airport workers: private vehicles		52 000	A4	(28 560)	28
Freight, business, spectator vehicles		16 000	A30	(32 640)	32
Bus, coach and other vehicles		4 000	A3044	(12 240)	12
		102 000			100

1985 Four terminals				
Annual passengers: 38 million			Airport workers: 55 000	
Vehicle journeys: 000s/day			**Daily highway loadings: %**	
Air passengers: cars/taxis		40 000	M4	(35 750)	25
Airport workers: private vehicles		64 000	A4	(35 750)	25
Freight, business, spectator vehicles		36 000	A30	(57 200)	40
Bus, coach and other vehicles		3 000	A3044	(14 300)	10
		143 000			100

Piccadilly Line daily passenger journeys: 45 000

1990 Five terminals				
Annual passengers: 55 million			Airport workers: 64 000	
Vehicle journeys: 000s/day			**Daily highway loadings: %**	
Air passengers: cars/taxis		55 000	M4	(36 600)	20
Airport workers: private vehicles		69 000	A4	(36 600)	20
Freight, business, spectator vehicles		55 000	A30	(51 240)	28
Bus, coach and other vehicles		4 000	A3044/ M25	(58 560)	32
		183 000			100

Piccadilly Line daily passenger journeys: 70 000

per year at Los Angeles as opposed to an uncontrolled growth of up to 80 million. Much of
this is due to limitations of ground access.

A system of regional and reliever airports,
very heavily orientated to charter and general
aviation, is now being devised in order to produce a more scattered pattern of those activities requiring runway demand and also to reduce
the ground access requirements.

Dr G. PESTALOZZI, Amt fur Luftverkehr, Zurich,
Switzerland

Paper 16 has very aptly divided the types of
rail access to airports into three categories.
I suggest there is a fourth category of some importance - which is realised at Zurich Airport.
This is a tie-in to the main line, inter-city
network of the railway, as distinct from a tie-
in to a suburban type of rail link. This is
particularly important where there is a pattern
of decentralised population centres, as we have
in Switzerland, and also of touristic areas,
some distance from the airports.

Originally, a three-tier system of public
access to Zurich Airport was planned:

(a) buses for the area immediately surrounding the airport;
(b) an underground railway for the metropolitan area of Zurich;
(c) the federal railways for connexions to
more distant points.

Unfortunately, the intermediate level, the underground railway, will not be constructed for
quite a number of years and this function has to
be shared between the other two.

The rail link now under construction ties
into the inter-city network; the first stop
after leaving the airport will be Zurich main
station. In this sense we have a direct link.
It is almost a specialized airport-to-city
centre connexion. But, without changing trains,
it can go on to more distant cities like Berne,
Interlaken and Lucerne - the idea being that
trains run through the airport on the main E-W
connexion through the country, so no change of
train at Zurich would be involved. At a later
stage trains will stop at the airport, go to
Zurich centre and then to other cities. At a
later stage it is contemplated that there will
be one train every hour in each major direction
from the airport.

This is a fourth category of rail access
which is quite important.

Mr M. G. HUDSON, GLC, Department of Planning and
Transportation

Taking a slightly wider view of the London scene
might be of some interest and serve as a warning
to those who have problems of expanding airports.

In the Greater London Council, our consideration of the London Airport situation endorses
the theme of Paper 16, that ground access is the
greatest of the problems posed by growth of air
traffic at the London airports. Unfortunately,
I cannot share the Author's optimism about the
amount of traffic that the underground extension
to Heathrow will attract.

A survey carried out in 1975 by the Airport
Authority indicated that at Heathrow, which has
a working population of 51 600, about 37 500

people are at work on an average day, and that
about 26 600 cars are brought in by these workers. These form the greatest volume of vehicular journeys to the airport. If anything can be
done to get them out of their cars it would contribute materially to solving the traffic problems there. Relatively few of them live near
the airport and only 1% (about 500) use the
Underground station at Hatton Cross, which serves
the No.1 Maintenance Area, which has 10 000 working in it.

In the long term the line may open up a new
catchment area to the east of the airport for
workers who can currently get to the airport
conveniently by public transport.

If the line is to make a significant contribution to getting people out of their vehicles,
to relieve the already congested approach roads,
the Underground must be made more attractive to
encumbered or handicapped passengers by the provision of a lift at Heathrow and facilities such
as porters, taxi ranks and easier platform access at stations serving hotel areas. Otherwise
coach services are likely to increase.

The possibility of commuters being attracted
to using the line has been suggested. Experience in other countries - Cleveland in the United
States is a good example - indicates that the
newly-attracted commuters could well outnumber
the airport passengers, and create problems with
their demands for out-of-town parking space. If
the peaks overlap, there may be capacity problems. The vehicular journeys concerned with
air cargo at Heathrow are only a small proportion; they form about three per cent. We have
not concerned ourselves with those.

Table 1 shows an analysis of the access problem at Heathrow. The figures at the top are
taken from a 1975 British Airports Authority survey. The predictions for 1985 are mine. It is
assumed that a fourth terminal has been constructed on the south side of the airport, which
it is not possible to link into the Underground
service. It shows 38 million passengers being
handled each year. In 1990, if Sir Peter
Masefield has achieved his ambition and there is
a fifth terminal at Perry Oaks, it will be handling 53 million passengers a year. The predictions for the Piccadilly Line underground traffic are taken from Paper 16.

There is a rough break-down on the left-
hand side of the various vehicular journeys between users, showing a considerable increase between 1975 and 1990. Because of the congestion
prevalent at the moment the British Airports
Authority have already proposed to turn the approach spur road to the airport into a toll road,
as a traffic restraint measure.

Figure 1 illustrates the effect of traffic
predictions. The A30 on the east side of the
airport is expected to be dualled, so that there
will be dual three lanes in each direction, before 1980, and with a provision for grade separation for the Terminal 4 area. This should cope
with the traffic demands in 1990. On the west
side of the airport the local road, the A3044,
will be able to cope with the traffic up to 1985,
with that from Terminal 4 and the air cargo terminal. But if there is a fifth passenger terminal in the Perry Oaks area, with an additional
15 million passengers/year, it would be essen-

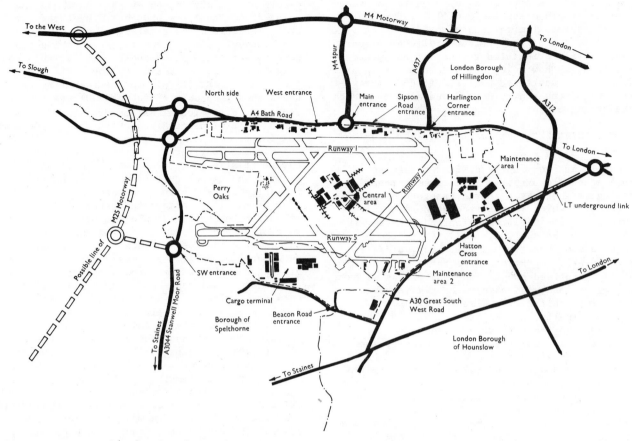

Fig.1. Heathrow airport, London: general layout and access roads

tial to have the M25, between its junction with
the M3 and M4, completed throughout its whole
length, because the local road will not be able
to cope with the traffic. The real problem
comes on the M4.

The tunnel to the central area terminals is
near capacity at times. Before 1990, the airport spur road and the elevated section of the
M4 will be grossly overloaded and quite unable
to cope with the traffic generated. Some radical solution has to be found before that time.

It is essential that all possible measures
to attract workers and passengers to use the
Piccadilly Line are pursued and a further rail
link may need to be provided, possibly from
Paddington to the north of the airport.

The inevitable transfer of air traffic from
Heathrow to Gatwick and the growth at all the
London area airports including Luton and Stanstead
is likely to generate new demands for inter-
airport transport and high quality road links.
The M25 ring around London could provide the
basis for a good road network, but it is not
programmed for completion before 1990. It should
be given high priority treatment.

There is therefore a need for an urgent and
detailed study of all aspects of access to the
four London area airports, followed by a programme of quick action by all the authorities
concerned.

Mr J. K. WILLIAMS, West Midlands County Council

There are two schools of thought in the West
Midlands regarding the location of the new terminal at Birmingham Airport. The older one says

it should be located next door to the National
Exhibition Centre (NEC) and the railway station
and the second, now growing because of the high
cost of the first location, that it should be on
lower ground further away from the station and
nearer to the cross runway, losing the physical
connexion to the station.

The second case is strengthened by the passenger survey carried out in 1975 which suggested that only 15% of total air passengers would
use rail. Passengers at Birmingham come from a
great diversity of origins and are largely home-
based with their cars available for use. In
addition the airport is located very close to a
principal hub of the national motorway network.

The present modal split is over 70% by private car and less than 10% by public transport.

Considering the railway, my opinion is that
the only justification for the construction of
the new railway station (Birmingham International) was the NEC, as its location is beyond the
suburban development of Birmingham. However, it
can now help the suburban service on the line by
enabling trains to be turned round there for return to central Birmingham instead of having to
go through Coventry.

Mr N. SEYMER, W. S. Atkins Group

Luggage is fundamental to the whole question of
rail links and how to use them. It seems to me
that British Rail have made a mistake at Gatwick
in planning only staircases and escalators. If
people are carrying luggage, neither is a good
way to move up and down levels. At the next station up the line for the fast trains, East
Croydon, there are ramps down to the platforms.

I do not know why they have not got them at Gatwick. Better still would be inclined moving footways.

Taking the wider theme of luggage, the Piccadilly line extension to Heathrow is fine for the 'briefcase brigade'; but the so-called 'luggage vestibules' on the new rolling stock are no wider than the vestibules on nearly all rapid transit stock, except in London, and they are not much use for large luggage.

The proposed British Rail link from Victoria to Heathrow was planned on the basis that passengers would check in their luggage at the in-town terminal (on which I worked for a year). This was to have the biggest handling system ever built, which was to transfer luggage from all check-in desks to containers for particular flights. However, the shape and size of the containers was never agreed. British Rail wanted them tall and thin, and the airline people said that such containers would be blown over if there was a high wind on the apron. At that time the 747s were coming into service with their containerized baggage. It seemed to me that the containers loaded at the in-town terminal should have been the ones that went straight through to New York. Nobody seemed to have thought of that at that time.

Perhaps it is as well the BR link did not get built. People coming into London would have had to reclaim luggage at the airport, go through Customs, and then check it in again for the rail trip to Victoria. Thus incoming luggage would have been un-bulked at the airport, and then re-bulked for the trip into town. It seems to me that if there is to be an in-town terminal handling luggage, there must be Customs facilities there, so that 'through containerization' is possible. If the Customs people decline at first to operate such a system - well, there is always someone (perhaps the Prime Minister) who can oblige them to cooperate.

Mr ROCKWELL (Paper 16)*

I was particularly intrigued by Dr Pestalozzi's comparison of the three airports in England with Kloten in Zurich. The best comparison is with Birmingham, where the rail connexions are also more 'inter-city' than suburban, but new links at Kloten will link the airport to Zurich-Schafhausen and other major suburban centres in the area.

In response to Mr Williams' comments on Birmingham Airport, I understand that the railway share of the city centre/airport traffic will not be very substantial. I know of no alternative plans but I consider that the design of the station might serve as a transportation centre between the airport terminal, the inter-city station and the Exhibition Centre.

I am generally in agreement with Mr Hudson, but in the past there have been various revisions of the traffic estimates, especially in 1969 at the time of the Heathrow Link Steering Group. Efforts were also then made to establish a modal

*Editor's note: We record with regret that Mr Rockwell died during the preparation of the conference proceedings for publication. This reply and the one given later in the session have been prepared by his co-author, Mr Maxwell, from the transcript of Mr Rockwell's replies at the conference

split in traffic to and from the airport on generalized cost estimates, which were published by the then Ministry of Transport. It is true to say that the Piccadilly Line link is designed for present traffic but in 1985 the total traffic on the Heathrow extension is expected to be of the order of 11 million, $7\frac{1}{2}$ million being air passengers and the remainder mainly staff and partly spectators and commuters, especially at Hatton Cross where traffic up to now has been low. However, the station has only been open a few months and it has been learned from experience on the Victoria Line that the build-up of traffic on a new line is fairly slow. Also at Heathrow there is a 25%/year rate of turnover in staff employed at the airport, so it would seem that once facilities are provided a large proportion of those working at the airport will eventually come from the west London suburbs, which will have the underground service provided by the Piccadilly Line. This has been taken into account in these calculations.

The estimates prepared so far were based on the assumption of a free choice for the passenger but if, as Mr Hudson mentioned, there is to be some measure of restraint upon the private car, these assumptions will have to be drastically revised. The line may then have to carry far more traffic than predicted, although commuter peaks and air passenger peaks do not coincide as the number of commuters is 10% lower than normal during the summer months when the number of air passengers is at its peak.

The Heathrow plans provide for an extension from the Central station to any fourth or fifth air terminal at Perry Oaks. But Mr Hudson was quite correct in saying that if there should be any more than the 50 or 55 million passengers expected, there will need to be a further rail link. Instead of the original idea of a link with Feltham on the Southern Region, a link from the north from the Western Region into Paddington will probably be preferable as it is less crowded and encumbered with fewer flat junctions and has no road level crossings such as at Barnes and Mortlake.

In the more distant future the construction of a cross rail link, as embodied in the London Rail Study, would create the lines linking the terminals on the fringe of central London radiating from a common point, perhaps near Covent Garden. Of these, the Paddington link would be on the weakest link in terms of traffic and easily able to accommodate extra traffic from the airport.

In reply to Mr Seymer, among the findings of the 1969 Steering Group and other surveys, there was the scheme that envisaged a direct British Rail non-stop link from Heathrow to Victoria, which was rejected partly because it was not possible to find a suitable, foolproof luggage handling system which would enable luggage to be sorted at the in-town terminal at Victoria and safely delivered to the aircraft for which it was destined. Other reasons for the rejection were that it did not cater for airport staff, who were not interested in a direct central London link, preferring to commute to and from suburbs.

Mr R. A. HUBBARD (for Mr Moore, Paper 17)

Findings from studies in the USA coincide closely with those of Mr Williams, of 70% by private
automobile. Even in New York City - quite dense
compared to other cities - the public transport
and limousine mode counts for less than 25%,
which is slightly more than the national average.

Another point is air cargo and its increase.
A doubling of air cargo demand in the USA between 1975 and 1985 has been predicted. One of
the shortcomings of airport access planning and
accommodation has been in relation to goods movements. These cannot be accommodated in the commuter corridors. Industries and industrial
sites are distributed throughout most metropolitan centres and these will provide further road
space demands. Even with rail links we do not
see in America any decrease in road space requirements.

Mr E. E. WARBURG, International Aeradio Ltd.

Mr Mayes has emphasised considerably the passenger flow requirements of airports. I was delighted to see that, at one airport at any rate,
there is a distance between the car and the aircraft of only 75 ft. This has never happened to
me.

He comments that architects and designers
are becoming more conscious of the requirements
of economy in the design of airports and terminals. This reminded me of Mr Hammarskjold's address at the last IATA General Meeting in Oslo,
where he commented that 'consultants have a ves-
ted interest in making the project on as large a
scale as possible'. He went on:

'Not only do consultants' fees normally relate in direct proportion to the total cost
of the project but also, in many cases, the
consultants are an arm for the export of
airport technology and material from their
base country. Containing consultants' ambi-
tions and rationalising their recommendations is therefore becoming a key part of
our overall programme for containing airport costs.'

This comment is perhaps even more relevant here.
The second point which is very close to the
heart of operators of airports is the requirement of architects and designers to consult the
specialist when preparing designs. Operators,
are often asked, even in this day and age, to
operate futuristic air traffic control towers
which, from a technical point of view, are quite
inoperable. There may be trouble getting on to
the roof and installing radio antennae, which
are more than necessary!

The other specialist area sometimes forgotten by the designers of airports concerns
local conditions. At one airport in the Far
East, designed by Western consultants, the Customs formalities area was placed next to the
airline ticket counter, as the ones in North
America, where Customs formalities are of the
briefest. In the Far Eastern territory concerned, however, a very thorough Customs examination was carried out, which meant that the queue
of people awaiting Customs clearance extended
outside the building so that no-one was able to
reach the airline ticket counter.

Mr Farmery emphasised that the security

engineering aspect has been completely forgotten
and is omitted far too often. I was impressed
by his heterogeneous collection of rules and
regulations on an international level, and I was,
at the same time, more than depressed by the
number of hi-jacking incidents which are continuing. One is also depressed, in the security
business, by the lack of a sense of urgency in
the implementation of security systems.

Together with British Airways, my organization has implemented security systems at airports in the UK and abroad. It is only when a
hi-jack occurs that suddenly there is a flurry
of activity and we get one step nearer to a complete revision of the necessary security systems.
I hope a greater sense of urgency will infil-
trate into the appropriate department, so that
some of these problems will be sorted out more
quickly than in the past.

Mr Kühler told us that cargo is doubling
every 4 or 5 years and there will obviously have
to be some radical re-thinking as to how this
should be handled. I was depressed to hear the
time which it takes to clear cargo through the
present computer system at London Airport.
Mr Kühler estimated a time of 22 h as an average
and this compares very poorly with the passenger
reservation systems at present in general use
which give a response time of $2\frac{1}{2}$ s! The two may
not be quite comparable, but the cargo situation
will have to be cleared up very soon. It is
sometimes said that the problem is one of industrial relations, and if this is so, the sooner
it is overcome, the better.

I would congratulate Lufthansa on their in-
genuity in their method for collection of cargo
which they have introduced at London Airport to
overcome these problems.

Mr R. C. MANN, Thompson Berwick Pratt & Partners,
Vancouver, Canada

Whereas the public seem to be insisting that:
      (a) investment in airports be reduced; or
      (b) benefits to traveller and non-traveller
      alike be increased,
there seem to be options with regard to either
reducing the costs of plant or increasing the
utilisation of plant through more intensive or
extensive use.

What are the prospects for sharing facilities, and the responsibilities and opportunities
involved therein. In the case of western Canada
I would assume the Coastguard, Air-Sea Rescue,
the RCMP, or the Civil Defence might be involved.

Is there any possibility of coordinating
budgets with military airports. I am also
curious to know whether there has been any experience in turn-key construction of facilities -
facilities built by entrepreneur developers,
turned over to the federal authority and leased
back.

Mr B. MAYES (Paper 18)

The possibility of sharing facilities has been
examined, but only vaguely. It is necessary to
define the scale; what type of airport or airport
building is to be considered. A small airport
serving a small community may have very close
sharing relationships. I do not think they have
been explored, but there is a potential. I find

it slightly difficult to envisage Hounslow sharing London Airport!

There is too a very serious security problem. This makes sharing anything which is in international use almost impossible.

I am not competent to deal with military matters.

.

Mr H. YOUNG, Canadian Air Transportation Administration, Ottawa, Canada

In relation to military airport installations in Canada, the military budget has been reduced so extensively that many of the airports they owned and operated have been - and undoubtedly more will be - turned over to Transport Canada. For instance, there were two in 1975. There are seven combined military and civil airports in Canada; additionally (and this may also relate to the rest of the world), military airports are always designated as an alternate for emergencies.

In the recent past air carriers and private entrepreneurs have constructed facilities on our airports. These have ranged from cargo buildings to air terminal buildings. CATA is looking at this aspect with some reserve, qualified only by the fact that CATA simply has not the budgets to expand facilities. There are some $6 billion needed for expansion of facilities between now and 1985. This figure is founded on previous methods of assessment of facilities and we are trying to reduce this by the systems approach, which should reduce both the number of airports and the expense of facilities needed at others. Anyone can build facilities on CATA airports, providing we realize enough revenue.

Mr Mann is particularly interested in Vancouver. There the problem is runways, although by about 1980 additional cargo facilities and certainly new air terminal buildings will be needed. There is no way to allow private entrepreneurs on the airport but the carriers may be allowed to build, particularly insofar as cargo and maintenance facilities are concerned.

Mr G. GILL, International Aeradio Ltd.

Mr Farmery's excellent paper highlighted the disturbing number of hi-jacking incidents, defined as 'successful' or 'unsuccessful'. Is it not a fact that, irrespective of whether or not a hi-jacked aircraft becomes airborne, if a captain has unlawfully been relieved of his command, then the ground security defences have been defeated and the incident therefore must be regarded as successful?

Mr R. FARMERY (Paper 19)

The short answer is 'no'. This is a very knotty problem, because captains of aircraft are always very loath to admit that they have lost command of the situation. In fact, as soon as any duress is applied to an aircraft captain which causes him to do anything out of the routine, in other words, to change his standard flight plan, then he is no longer in command of that aircraft; the hi-jacker is. That does not mean to say that a hi-jacking has been successful.

If somebody steals your wallet, they have committed a crime (in exactly the same way that

if people apply duress to the captain of an aircraft they have committed a crime). If the thief is caught stealing your wallet, then that crime has been unsuccessful. If the hi-jacking is eventually resolved, then we can say that that hi-jacking has been unsuccessful. That is not to say that it has not occurred. The difference here is between the actual commission of a crime and whether that crime is successfully dealt with, or becomes more serious. I do not think that the ground defences have been defeated because it is possible to hi-jack an aircraft.

The security defences are not a single line aimed in one particular direction. They are in depth. The aim of the security is not only to prevent hi-jacking but also, if it does occur, to contain it. If it is contained and resolved without loss of life, loss of aircraft, etc. it may be an awkward, difficult incident, but it is unsuccessful.

The Balcombe Street siege in London is a recent example. Four men took over a flat and its occupants and were there for some days. A crime was committed; they are currently on trial. The crime, I suggest was not a successful one.

Mr J. DRURY

I want to raise the question of airport planning and the intrusion of the increasing amounts of cargo on to passenger aprons.

It is undoubtedly true that cargo will increase in volume soon and increasing amounts will be carried in the bellies of wide-bodied aircraft on both short haul and long haul routes. This takes the form of cargo in containers and pallets. There is a great amount of congestion on some aprons, because the inherent turn-around of the aircraft, both in terms of the service vehicles and, soon, in terms of the cargo vehicles that serve them.

What can be done to cut this?

I would suggest that any airport with a predominance of linear planning in aircraft stands will be faced with the problem of congestion. Airports like Schiphol which have a finger with an angled parking policy would escape it. Added to the problem is a new generation of combination aircraft carrying cargo pallets and passengers in alternative arrangements on the main deck. A 747 turn-around I experienced recently involved twelve pallets coming off, as well as 250 passengers.

The turn-around times of the A300B airbus, because they are all on short haul routes, are quite quick. They can take up to four pallets and a number of containers as well as baggage. The passenger baggage has to come off first, and the cargo goes on first on the return journey.

If, as is often the case, the cargo terminals are anything up to 4 kms away from the passenger terminals, it means there is either a large number of vehicles shuttling on already congested perimeter roads or an increase in vehicles waiting on the apron to put in and receive cargo. It will not be possible at some airports, I suggest, to use the same vehicles to go that distance to the cargo centre.

With combination aircraft in peaks, there would be such a bulk of cargo and vehicles on the apron that, unless the spacing of the aircraft on the stands is considered in planning these modern facilities, it could lengthen the turn-around times on the aircraft.

Has anybody done any more thinking about this? Is there a possibility of building satellites for cargo in passenger areas? Is there a possibility of rapid transit of some kind, or special routes from the cargo centre and passenger area?

Mr S. KÖHLER (Paper 20)

It is certainly true when with belly-loaded cargo in an aircraft exclusively, and many more such aircraft coming to one airport at the same time, that within one peak to change cargo from one aircraft to another presents a difficulty. In most cases this cargo will be delayed, because it will be taken to a cargo shed, sorted to the various aircraft, and re-loaded, perhaps in the next peak. Time is lost.

A change to containers means it is possible to unload an aircraft faster and even to shorten the turnround time.

The Frankfurt system is that there will be a satellite for a container to be loaded and unloaded within the same peak. That will be for 'final destination loaded containers', i.e. throughgoing containers. The rest of it will have to go to the cargo terminal, undergo the difficult and cumbersome procedure of sorting and there be passed into new containers. These will again be loaded in the passenger area. There is somewhat of a mixture.

I can only support what has been said in the question. It is true that there are difficulties with tarmac space on passenger aircraft. It will be extremely difficult when one aircraft is lined up next to another and there is no space in between, especially when it is a 747 side cargo door aircraft which, on the main deck, loads up to 40t of cargo, in addition to 200 passengers, and which also carries the usual load of containers in the belly.

Cargo traffic between the passenger terminal and the cargo area over an ever-increasing distance may call for modern high-speed equipment to carry a higher number of containers, and perhaps not over the tarmac but over separate cargo roads.

Mr G. ASENDORF, Frankfurt Airport

First of all, I wish to congratulate you on your Heathrow Piccadilly Line extension: 7½ million travellers per year were mentioned. This is less than 40% of your total passengers, I suppose.

Mr E. L. ROCKWELL: About 30%.

Mr G. ASENDORF

I think it will be a lot more than that. Our experience at Frankfurt was 30% after six months and it is now 41% and our line is not as attractive as yours will be. Trains start every 20 min from Frankfurt main station for a 10 min. ride.

Our railway station is two levels below street level and three levels below departure level. It is not very convenient to get from the station to the departure level. But, in our experience, passengers still prefer it to high parking fees and traffic congestion on the autobahn - although there is a very fine road connexion to the airport.

On the other hand, I think there will be fewer employees than you expect. At Frankfurt Airport there are 27 000 employees at present, and less than 10% use the train. The reason is a simple one: the average travel time from their housing areas on private transport to the airport is about 20 min. Add 10 min. for train connecting time, and it will easily run into 30 min. This is too inconvenient for most of the employees. It will take a couple of years to improve this.

We also have the problem of taking baggage up and down escalators and, because of this, we developed the so-called 'escar', an escalator baggage cart. It has been in use for two years, and it is relatively safe. There have been some accidents but they are decreasing. Due to their construction, the carts are fairly heavy and expensive to handle. It is a second-best solution; the ramp solution is still a better one, finally.

I would like to encourage all my colleagues all over the world to start to think about baggage again. There have been several major drawbacks with baggage sorting systems around the world, I know. Our system, however, is now in operation and works very well indeed.

Let's face it: as long as the number of passengers per movement increases, we will have transfer problems. Airports like Heathrow, expecting more than 60 million passengers a year, will have a great number of transfer passengers and it is the baggage which will create the problem.

The sorting system at Frankfurt is very specifically designed to meet our needs and it simply cannot be adjusted to other airports, but it proves that a large systems is able to work.

Heathrow Airport handled 21 million passengers or 400 000 tons of baggage last year. This is not much less than what was handled in cargo. But who talks about baggage? Remember: baggage is as sensitive as passengers and as helpless as cargo!

Mr ROCKWELL

Let me refer back to the traffic estimates for the Heathrow extension. By 1985 11 million passengers/year will use Heathrow Central station, 7½ million of whom would be air passengers, corresponding to about 30% of the total ground airline traffic, with the exception of transfer passengers who do not in any case leave the airport. The British Airports Authority say that the level of staff due to rationalisation will not rise as a proportion of the traffic they handle and so their estimate here must be accepted.

It is difficult to say whether there will be more traffic on the extension than is forecast, as it may well also depend on whether there will be any measures of restraint on motor vehicles which would artificially increase the traffic to be handled.

Many origin and destination surveys have been carried out among passengers using Heathrow Airport and there were various estimates of how many will travel by Underground and how many will still use private cars and the airport coaches. The comparison here with Frankfurt was interesting as coaches do not compete with the S-bahn rail link which is half-way between a metropolitan railway and a fast direct rail link. The dispersal problems also differ between there and Heathrow.

The CHAIRMAN, Mr D. ALLFORD

As a consumer I have rarely had to present baggage tags. I used to think that was marvellous until, two weeks ago, arriving at Lagos, I picked up my bag - which is quite distinctive - to find that somebody else had one exactly the same and had taken mine away. My bag was missing for three days. Had there been a baggage tag check, which is statutory but hardly ever used, I would not have suffered. I suppose the answer is: travel light and take bags on the aircraft. But this was a serious setback.

Mr E. REY, IBERIA Airlines, Heathrow Airport

The luggage tag is an identification tag. IATA states that the baggage is delivered to the passenger and from the passenger to the airline. The weight of the luggage and number of pieces are clearly specified on the ticket upon check-in. The tag is merely for identification. A long time ago the airlines decided they had to risk the occasional mix up in which the passenger picks up somebody else's baggage, but it gives a tremendous speed in the delivery of the baggage to the passengers. If we had to put additional staff on the carousels to identify individual luggage it would delay the handling of the luggage to the passengers.

The transfer of baggage at Heathrow has been, and still is, the main headache of the airlines operating into Heathrow. Heathrow is the No.1 transit airport in the world and will lose many passengers to the benefit of other airports because of the appalling conditions of transfer. Only Terminal 3 has recently completed a certain sorting area for the transfer baggage. Terminal 2 has nothing whatever. The development is being studied. Terminal 1 is operated only by British airlines and Aer Lingus and has better facilities.

I have in mind a sentence from Arthur Haley's novel *Airport* which said: 'Heathrow is the kind of madness that only the British mentality can create'. I do not see Heathrow working in the future with the 55 million passengers forecast, unless something dramatic is done about those aspects which have been mentioned.

Sir Peter Masefield mentioned a fifth terminal three years ago. It should already be built. If it is not I hope I shall not be in Heathrow in ten years' time!

Mr W. THOMPSON, General Manager, London Stations, British Airways European Division

On the question of transfer of passengers, there have been arguments for years with the airlines about what they do and do not want. There is at last a transfer facility for Terminal 3. If the airlines can be persuaded to start using it, I do not doubt that it will be very effective, but so far they very rarely do.

On the question of putting in wider subways between the terminal buildings, I do not believe a passenger who wants to transfer from Terminal 3 to Terminal 1 wants the pleasure of walking when he can go round by a bus that operates on a 10 min. service. Nor is there any problem of staying within the 40 min. transfer time, and certainly within a 90 min. transfer time.

No 100% reliable mechanical handling belt to cover that sort of distance has yet been devised. At some time or other it will break down. What is to be done with a belt that is three-quarters of a mile long and where, somewhere in the middle of it, is a bag that someone needs for despatch but which somebody at the other end does not know they are due to receive, and the belt breaks down? It will take a long time to find out that the bag is there at all and to recover it. By that time, the passenger ought to be well on his way to somewhere else in Europe.

The idea was turned down partly on the grounds of cost, but also because it would not satisfy the function that was required of it. A frequent bus service or vehicle service between terminals is a much better way of doing it. The last survey showed that no transfer bags sat on the deck for more than 10 min. before being collected by a vehicle.

The problem does not lie so much with the facility, as with the organization that is needed, first to make sure the transfer bags come off the aircraft first and, secondly, that when they get to the other end, they are picked up quickly and taken to the aircraft that requires them, and not mixed in with all the other bags from the terminal building and re-sorted again somewhere further down the line.

21. Fire-fighting and rescue techniques and equipment.

P.Nash, BSc, FIFreE
Head of Extinguishing Materials and Equipment Section, Fire Research Station, UK

J.E.Lodge, Chief Fire Service Officer, Civil Aviation Authority. UK

Part I of the paper deals primarily with the development of fire extinguishing materials to deal with the high potential fire risks presented by modern aircraft. The aim is to achieve major control of the fire within a very short time in order to effect rescue. The advantages and disadvantages of water-based foams, dry powders, inhibiting liquids or gases and water sprays are discussed. In Part II the practical aspects are dealt with, particularly in relation to the recommendations of the International Civil Aviation Organization. Both parts of the paper emphasise that speed and efficient deployment of staff and equipment are essential, and that airports must have emergency plans for instant implementation.

I. RESEARCH AND DEVELOPMENT ON THE EXTINCTION OF AIRCRAFT CRASH FIRES

1. INTRODUCTION

The modern aircraft presents an extreme problem in fire-safety under major crash fire conditions. With a high potential risk to life and property – some 400 lives and many £M per aircraft – it suffers from the fact that its resistance to fire penetration is minimal, and the likelihood of a major fuel spillage and ignition (despite the use of the higher flash-point hydrocarbon fuels) is still relatively high. The larger the aircraft, the greater the risk to each passenger of death and injury in crash conditions. Even though the use of jet engines and jet fuels has reduced the general level of risk, there have been retrograde steps, such as the introduction of integral tankage in lieu of bag tanks, which have offset to some extent the advances gained. The large aircraft of today is a highly stressed structure capable of resisting adequately its designed loads, but fragile when subjected to the unusual loads imposed by a major crash.

There are three main avenues to a remedy to this situation:

a) to increase the impact-resistance of the aircraft structure and its resistance to fire penetration

b) to contain the fuel, or better still, to develop a truly safe fuel which does not give rise to a highly dangerous fuel mist or spill fire capable of enveloping the aircraft

c) to improve the airfield fire-fighting facilities to make them capable of dealing with the most severe aircraft fire wherever it may occur.

None of these remedies is likely to be the complete answer to the problem, which requires a combination of all three.

The first is the province of the aircraft designer and while, no doubt, some advantage could be gained in making an aircraft which could crash, as well as fly, more safely, it is likely that the weight penalty involved in all but relatively minor improvements would be totally unacceptable in a competitive aircraft. It may therefore be concluded that the present resistance to penetration by a major fire of some 1 to 3 minutes is not likely to be improved by more than a further 2 minutes at most. The advent of improved fuel containment and of truly safe fuels is a much more promising proposition, although even this has its weight penalty. It tackles the problem at source by preventing the intense fire situation developing. The possibility of improvement in aircraft crash fire-fighting is the remedy with which this paper, and the following one by Mr John Lodge, seek to deal. Its general thesis and conclusions will apply even though the first two remedies are sought, since it is only by a three-pronged attack that a problem of this magnitude can be resolved.

2. THE TIME/RESPONSE PROBLEM FOR AIRCRAFT CRASH FIRES

The salient feature of a major aircraft crash is the lack of time available to carry out fire control and rescue operations. In the worst case such a fire can grow to its full magnitude in some 1 to 2 minutes, and the low resistance of the fuselage to fire penetration of, say, 1 to 3 minutes at maximum intensity means that any passengers capable of being rescued after the initial impact will have a survival time of some 2 to 5 minutes. Of course, not all crashes take fire, or take fire immediately. Even when they do they may not be the subject of the maximum rate of fire growth, or the fire may not involve the fuselage. To this extent, the advent of the higher fire point fuels, eg kerosines, and the random chances of the crash,

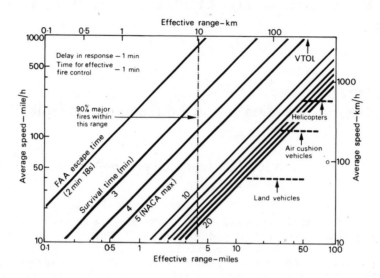

Fig.1. Effective range of various appliances

ccme to the aid cf the fire-fighter. It is shown, however, in Fig.1, that even in a less than maximum case the task of the fire-fighter in reaching and controlling the fire is a singularly difficult one. If the call is given immediately the crash occurs and the brigade responds in one minute, and is also capable of controlling the fire in 1 minute, the effective range cf a land-based appliance capable of an average point-to-point speed of 40 miles per hour is but 0.2 miles under extreme growth conditions (survival time 2 minutes) and 4 miles where the survival time is extended to 8 minutes. Four miles is the distance from appliance base within which 90 per cent of crashes occur. This means in effect, that land-based appliances are really only effective on or immediately adjacent to the airfield. Off the airfield, a major crash is likely to be far less survivable, and it could be argued that the problem, involving but 10 per cent of the crashes, need not be considered in the same way as adjacent to the airfield.

If the areas between airfields are to be covered at all adequately, an airborne appliance is essential. Thus a helicopter crash tender with a point-to-point speed of 250 mph could be effective up to a range of 4 miles for a survival time of 2 minutes, and up to 30 miles for a survival time of 8 minutes.

The above performances show the extreme nature of the problem, the urgent need for a really safe fuel and fuel containment, and for 21st century fire-fighting - preferably airborne.

3. THE RELATIVE IMPORTANCE OF FIRE CONTROL, FIRE EXTINCTION AND THE PREVENTION OF FIRE RECURRENCE

Paradoxically, the Fire Commander arriving at the scene of a crash dces not have as his immediate priority, the rescue of life. He has first to 'extend the time scale of his operation' by gaining a rapid control of the fire so that it no longer menaces the lives of the cccupants and of his fire-fighters. Once major fire control has been achieved and the fire situation made safe for rescue to proceed, he will divide his forces, some to rescue and some to extinguishing the residual fire and preventing recurrence. This principle was often expounded by the late Mr J A Brooker, a previous Chief Fire Services Officer of the Ministry of Civil Aviation.

Fire control is the first priority in all cases, and it is convenient to describe it in the terms used at the Fire Research Station and other laboratories, where a reduction of 90 per cent in the radiant intensity of the fire is described as '9/10 control'. It is the aim to achieve this in about 1 minute if life is to be saved. The concept of 'cutting a path through the flames' to enable rescue to proceed is rarely, if ever, possible except for aircraft containing only 1 or 2 occupants. Calculation shows that to reduce the heat radiation to tolerable levels, the flames would need to be pushed back well clear of the aircraft - to the extent that '9/10 control' would automatically be achieved. The value of ultimate extinction at this stage will depend upon the likelihcod of a reflash over the fire area - and with all agents but foam this is an ever-present possibility.

The fire area needs to be secured for a period long enough for rescue to be completed - a time which may vary from a few minutes to several hours dependent upon the number of persons to be saved, the degree cf entanglement within the wreck etc. It follows that the main agent must give either complete fire extinction or a long-term security to the area, which means also that '9/10 control' will be followed as soon as reasonably possible by complete extinction.

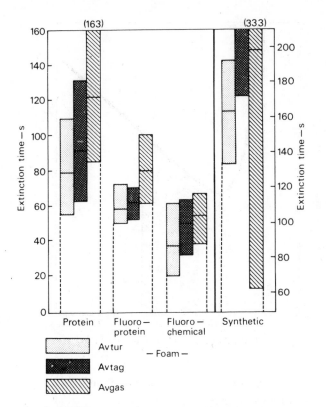

Fig.2. *Fire control times of various foams*

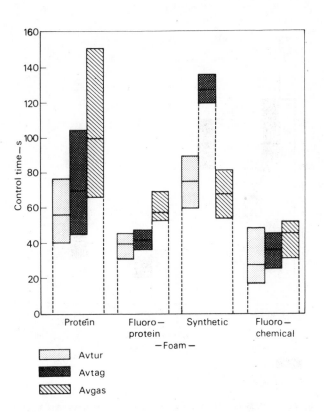

Fig.3. *Fire extinction times of various foams*

The relative importance of fire control, fire extinction and security of the fire area will therefore depend largely upon the type of aircraft, the life-risk and the agent used. Fire control is always of paramount importance, fire extinction is important but not essential if a secure agent is used, and safety of the fire area will depend on the number of lives to be saved, the complexity of the wreck and the time needed for life-saving.

4. MAIN AND SECONDARY AGENTS FOR FIRE-FIGHTING

The agents available for aircraft fire-fighting are:

a) water-based foams

b) dry powders

c) inhibiting liquids or gases

d) water sprays

Of these, only the foams or dry powders are really capable of dealing with large spill fires, and only the foams are capable of securing a fire area against re-ignition. While dry powders are more effective, weight for weight, than foams in controlling spill fires, they have several disadvantages. They do not secure the fire area, so that recurrence of the fire is an ever-present possibility from hot ignition sources. Their mass application tends to obscure the fire area completely, so that it is not possible to see whether complete extinction has been achieved. Their possibly choking effect on occupants already assailed by smoke, fumes and toxic gases cannot be other

than of grave danger in itself. The foams have none of these disadvantages, and since modern foams approach in effectiveness the use of dry powders, their position as the main fire-fighting agent is unassailable except for use with smaller aircraft on the lesser airfields. Dry powders can, of course, be a valuable adjunct to foams, either in initial attack or in mopping-up, but for this use they must be truly foam-compatible.

Dry powders are effective for running-fuel fires from ruptured tanks, and for extinguishing fires in obscure areas which foam cannot reach.

The inerting gases, carbon dioxide and Halons 1211 and 1301, can be used as secondary agents for extinguishing fires in wing-roots, baggage compartments, etc, where their carrying power when injected under pressure, and their inerting capabilities, show to the best advantage. They are not really suitable for large spill fires outside the aircraft. Halon 1211 has been shown to have a particular value in the inerting of windmilling turbine engines.

A possible role for water sprays is in the cooling of hot cabin atmospheres while main fire control is being achieved, although their use does not preclude the possibility of noxious and toxic fumes affecting the occupants.

5. CHARACTERISTICS OF FIRE-FIGHTING FOAMS

These may be classified as:

a) Low expansion air foams made by aerating a solution of foaming agent in water. The

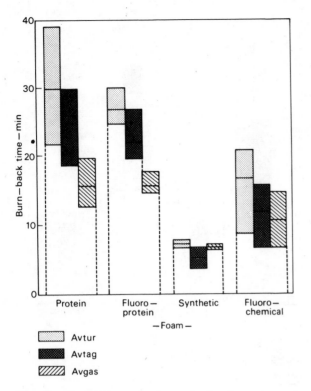

Fig.4. Resistance to burn-back of various foams

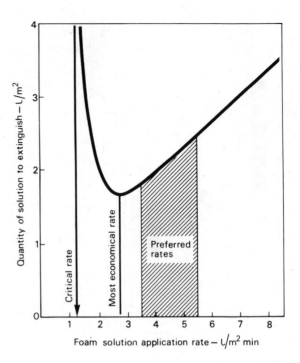

Fig.5. Extinction of 81m^2 Avtur fire (fluoroprotein foam)

modern agents are based on protein
derivatives with stabilising additives,
such as the 'fluoroprotein foams', or upon
synthetic fluorinated agents such as the
'aqueous film-forming foams' (AFFF).
Solution strength varies in the range 3 to
6 per cent, and expansion in the range
6 to 30. They are suitable for surface
application to large non-water-miscible fuel
fires, and can be projected from self-
aspirating equipment up to about 200 feet.

b) Medium expansion airfoams made by aerating
a $\frac{1}{2}$-2 per cent solution of synthetic
foaming agent in water. Modern agents are
usually based upon ammonium lauryl ether
sulphate with stabilisers. Expansion of
these foams is likely to be in the range
30-250, but they are difficult to project
for more than a short distance. Their
application to aircraft fires, for which
they are currently not used, would therefore
need to be from large diameter 'applicators'
from close range. While effective on large
fuel spill fires, medium expansion airfoam
presents a difficult handling problem for
mass application and entirely new equipment would need to be developed.

6. PERFORMANCE OF LOW-EXPANSION AIR FOAMS

The performance of low expansion air foams on a
fire may be expressed in terms of

a) the time to achieve '9/10 control' at
various rates of application

b) the time to achieve extinction

c) the time for the fire to 'burn-back' to
full radiant intensity against an
established foam layer.

Experiments under controlled conditions have
shown the comparative values of these
quantities for the different types of foaming
agent, and how they are affected by such
physical characteristics as expansion, shear
stress (stiffness) and drainage characteristics
of the foam. The results are illustrated in
Figs 2-6, for the four foaming agents, protein
foam, fluoroprotein foam, AFF foam and
synthetic foam (ie medium expansion foam liquid
used at a low expansion), when applied to fires
in kerosene, (AVTUR or JP 1), wide-cut fuel
(AVTAG or JP 4) and gasoline (AVGAS). The
results show a range of values, best, worse
and average, for a number of foams of each of
the different types.

Figures 2 and 3 show that in gaining '9/10
control' and fire extinction, the AFF foams are
quickest, followed closely by the fluoroprotein
foams, then by the protein foams and finally by
the synthetic foams. In Fig.4, for resistance
to 'burn-back', the protein and fluoroprotein
foams are superior to AFF foams, and the
synthetic foams are again the poorest. The fires
which are hardest to control are those in AVGAS,
followed by AVTAG and AVTUR in that order.

When a foam is applied to a fire, the time to
control the fire varies with rate of application
of foam per unit fire area. The time is
generally independent of the 'expansion' of the
foam, but varies with its 'stiffness' or shear
stress. There is a minimum value of rate of
application, (the 'critical rate') below which
the fire cannot be controlled (or extinguished).
If the results are expressed as 'quantity to
control' against 'application rate', (Fig.5),
a 'most economical or optimum rate' appears.
The aim is therefore to apply foam at a rate

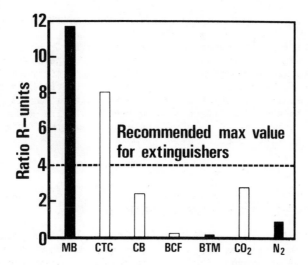

Fig.6. Extinguishing and dangerous concentrations: inerting gases

Agent	Dangerous concentration (DC)		Extinguishing concentration (EC)		Ratio $\frac{EC}{DC}$
	% v/v	lb/1000 ft^3	%v/v	lb/1000 ft^3	
CO_2	10.0	12.0	28.0	33.5	2.8
N_2	50.0	39.0	42.0	32.8	0.8
Halon 1211	24.0	110.0	5.2	24.0	0.2
Halon 1301	50.0	210.0	4.9	20.4	0.1

just above the optimum, or at least to try always to be well above the critical. If the size of the fire is too great for the equipment available, this may be impossible, so that the first tactic would then be to apply foam close to or onto the aircraft fuselage in an endeavour to protect this as long as possible until additional equipment arrives.

The fact that the results are independent of foam expansion (except for very low values where foam stability suffers) means that simple self-aspirating foam equipment can be used without loss of performance. This means that a high proportion of the pumping power is available to project the made foam over a good range, and that the equipment itself is simple, reliable and effective. Gone are the days of vane-type foam pumps of great expense and unreliability, and of pressure aspirated foam-makers with high power absorption. Mr Lodge will be illustrating some of the modern crash tenders which owe their simplicity and effectiveness to this research and development.

7. PERFORMANCE OF SECONDARY AGENTS

It remains to discuss briefly the performance aspects of the supporting agents. Dry powder has already been mentioned, and the important point here is that where it is intended to be used in conjunction with foam, it must be of the foam compatible variety. Powders fall into 4 categories - those for flammable liquid fires (EC powders), those which are foam-compatible BC powders, those which can be used on solid and liquid fuel fires (ABC powders), and those suitable for metal fires (Class D fires). In an aircraft fire, a BC foam-compatible powder is probably what is required since the ABC powders are not necessarily foam-compatible, and other agents can be used for the extinction of fires in upholstery, etc. The Class D powders are a special class by themselves and are usually only used for wheel fires, caused by overheating of brakes, or under crash conditions in dealing with a fire in a wheel or other casting at the final mopping-up stage of a major crash. In either case, the life-risk is probably not affected materially by the metal fire.

The inerting gases are valuable in safeguarding spaces where fire may occur, and in general terms, the Halons are more effective by volume or by weight in inerting a given volume than is carbon dioxide. In their natural state they are also less toxic, but it must be remembered that they operate by breaking down into acid gases and these are of much higher toxicity than the natural agent. Where the Halons can be used to give a quick 'clean' extinction, they are efficient and low in toxicity. On a deep seated smouldering fire, the acid gases produced may alter this picture considerably. A comparison of carbon dioxide, nitrogen and Halons 1211 and 1301 in their natural state is given in the table and a comparison of the values of R = EC/DC is shown in Fig.6. The lower the value of R the safer the material may be considered in its natural state.

8. CONCLUSIONS

The foregoing paper shows briefly the research and development that has gone into improving aircraft fire-fighting agents and techniques. In the accompanying paper Mr Lodge will show how this knowledge has been applied in practice to improve the overall performance of his fire teams and to keep abreast of the ever-increasing difficulties of aircraft crash fire-fighting.

9. ACKNOWLEDGMENT

This paper is Crown Copyright. It is reproduced by permission of The Controller, HM Stationery Office. It is contributed by permission of the Director of the Building Research Establishment (Fire Research Station is the Joint Fire Research Organisation of the Department of the Environment and Fire Offices' Committee).

II. DEVELOPING AERODROME FIREFIGHTING AND RESCUE SERVICES

1. We have heard from Mr Philip Nash how the extinguishing agents have been developed for aircraft fire fighting and rescue by the combined efforts of industry, the research establishments and the users in aerodrome fire services. The greater part of this development and certainly the most effective research has been conducted within the last seven years when those whose responsibility it is to provide and operate aerodrome fire services were able to identify the importance of rapid fire control as a primary objective in their operations. It may appear obvious that fire control, or ideally, fire extinction, should be the immediate objective but aerodrome fire services had tended previously to base their tactics on the equipment which was currently available and this approach contained the seeds of its own ineptitude. We used foams which had no significant knockdown capability, carried on appliances which were constructed on conversions of existing commercial or military chassis, designed to meet operating conditions which were quite different from those likely to be met at an aircraft accident. No-one had clearly understood the importance of response time and rapid intervention and no specification for these factors existed. I speak as one who was involved and therefore equally guilty of any inadequacy which my statement reveals. My self-criticism is possible because of the splendid gift of hindsight, and one can see that we were all too preoccupied in the development of existing scales of provision to meet the constant changes in aircraft types to be able to take an objective look at the bases for these scales.

2. The opportunity for an entirely new approach came when the International Civil Aviation Organisation (ICAO) created its rescue and fire fighting panel (RFFP) in 1969 which, after its first meeting in 1970, became aware of the vast gaps in its statistical knowledge. If one is to specify a level of fire fighting capability it is first necessary to know the probable size and duration of the fire. If one does not know the time-factor in post-accident fire survival there is no basis for specifying the response and fire control objectives. If there are a number of extinguishing agents which can be delivered in a fire fighting operation these must be described in qualitative and quantitative terms and compared, one with another, so that their relative merits can be determined when making the selection. The Panel was fortunate in that a number

of States with representatives in the Panel were able to conduct statistical studies, operational research and large scale tests which together produced much of the evidence required in its considerations. The principal contribution by the United Kingdom was the study commissioned and published by the CAA in 1971 entitled "Aerodrome Fire and Rescue Services". There are, of course, no absolute answers to most of the questions since no two aircraft accidents are the same. It is, however, possible to identify some basic truths and the Panel produced a report in which the following are the key features:-

a for an effective intervention in a post accident fire situation there must be a rapid response by the rescue and fire fighting service and a massive initial attack with effective fire fighting agents;

b "Rapid response", in this context, means within three minutes to any part of the aircraft movement area, and, preferably, within two minutes;

c Aerodrome fire appliances must have the ability to deliver the principal agent, a foam of good quality, at a high discharge rate whilst the foam-producing appliances are in motion. Foam monitors (turrets) must have a range of application appropriate to the longest aircraft using the aerodrome and also have the capability of delivering foam in a dispersed pattern;

d A quantity of a complementary agent must be provided to deal with running fuel fire situations, to suppress fires in screened areas where foams are not fully effective and to inhibit enclosed voids, such as exist in freight holds, and within wings.

e The efficiency of an aerodrome rescue and fire fighting service will depend on a combination of specialised equipment, meticulous organisation and the employment of selected personnel, all of whom receive adequate and continuing training.

3. At this point it is appropriate to observe that during the years which preceded the 8th ICAO Air Navigation Conference many States and aerodrome authorities deferred decisions on re-equipment and re-organisation until the require-

ments and the guidance material for the future were available. This material is now to be published by ICAO in revised versions of Annex 14 to the Convention and in the Aerodrome Manual, Part 5, Volume I so that those who may have needed the advice of this international technical agency now have it for their consideration.

4. The ICAO recommendations define 9 aerodrome categories which are related to aircraft length. The choice of length as a factor in determining scales of fire fighting and rescue equipment may not be immediately understood but if one considers an aircraft as a container of people, crew and passengers, it will be appreciated that a fire in close proximity to this container places the occupants at risk. The ICAO Rescue and Fire Fighting Panel made use of experimental evidence developed at the Federal Aviation Administration's (FAA) National Aviation Facilities Experimental Centre (NAFEC) at Atlantic City and was able to determine critical fire areas for aircraft, using the length and a calculated width, limited in the case of the smaller aircraft by reason of a limited fuel capacity. With the largest aircraft the potential fuel load would be sufficient to support a vast area of fire for a prolonged period but provided that the fire in the critical area is suppressed or extinguished the fire hazard to the occupants of the aircraft can be eliminated. It is on the "critical area" basis and the measured effectiveness of modern extinguishing agents that the quantities of agent and their rates and patterns of application that the ICAO Table of quantities has been devised. The NAFEC experiments also confirmed the advantage of high rates of application of the principal agent, foam, an advantage which can be enhanced by using foams with approved characteristics, which ICAO defines.

5. Foam, applied at these rates, in either straight stream or diffused patterns, is intended to achieve the major part of the fire suppression but certain fire situations, involving running fuel, screened areas or voids, require different types of agent. Carbon dioxide gas, dry powders or one of the halogenated hydrocarbon agents are available for these situations but these agents require refined application techniques to achieve maximum effect. Modern aerodrome fire appliances, with their massive discharge rates and improved extinguishing agents are more demanding on trained personnel if their full potential is to be realised. The amounts of agent to be provided in each category may seem large but they are carefully calculated to achieve 90% control of the fire area within the first minute of the initial attack and to maintain this control or to achieve extinguishment subsequently. It will be obvious that ineffective application of any agent will seriously erode the safety margins built into the calculations. Most modern foam producing appliances have the capability of discharging their contents within two minutes when operating at maximum output. This is a valuable asset in the initial attack, when the rate of effective application is directly related to the time in which fire control can

be achieved. The ICAO scales and output specifications provide for fire control within one minute. Skilled operators can achieve this operational objective but lack of skill will lead to the waste of the limited supply and may result in failure to achieve control. I cannot over-emphasise the importance of training in this respect or the extent to which the ICAO scales of provision are dependent on the efficient delivery of the extinguishing agents.

6. One of the most expensive elements in any aerodrome fire service is the staff required to deploy and operate the equipment. When developing the service required for an aerodrome the planning stage should include the design of appliances which can convey and deliver the extinguishing agents with the minimum number of men consistent with operational efficiency. In this context operational efficiency must include the deployment of the major foam producing appliances so that they achieve a satisfactory response time and can, on arrival at the accident site, deliver their foam at the rate specified for the aerodrome. Additionally, such other appliances as may be operated to achieve rapid response and the conveyance of complementary agents and rescue equipment must be operated and crewed so as to realise their full potential in the critical initial stage of the operation. It may assist you if I quote examples of UK practices in achieving these operational objectives. At one aerodrome, in ICAO Category 9, the authority has decided to employ a Fluoroprotein foam instead of the protein-based foams which have been in use for some years. This decision attracts a one-third reduction in the quantity of water required for foam production when protein-based concentrates are employed. The second policy decision was to construct its foam-producing fleet on chassis capable of conveying 6750 litres (1500 IG) of water, thus providing four major appliances for multiple-point attack around the largest aircraft. The third decision, taken because of the size of this aerodrome and its need to have two stations, was to operate two rapid intervention appliances, each equipped with a quantity of fluorochemical (AFFF) foam and bromochlorodifluoromethane (BCF)(Halon 1211) for the initial attack. These appliances also carry rescue equipment, respiratory protection units, medical first aid kits and lighting equipment. The entire fleet is linked by a comprehensive communications system which links the Fire Service to the Air Traffic Service and provides a channel for direct communication with aircraft captains when an emergency occurs. The ultimate manning for this fleet has still to be decided but it would be possible to deploy these six appliances effectively with about 16 men. Another aerodrome, also in Category 9, has elected to meet its foam-production requirement with only two, very large appliances and whilst this clearly provides the basis for professional debate on tactical grounds there can be no dispute about the ability of these foam tenders to respond quickly and to deliver good quality foam at a massive rate. Here, again, the aerodrome authority has elected to use a fluoroprotein

foam to gain the reduction in its water requirement.

7. The British fire engineering industry has maintained a careful oversight of the developments in ICAO advice and has developed a range of fire appliances and extinguishing agents which can be utilised to meet the new aerodrome requirements effectively and economically. To some extent this happy result has been achieved by liaison with the Civil Aviation Authority's Fire Service and by the use of the Fire Service Training School to evaluate equipment and its tactical use. We intend to maintain this relationship in the future with the aim of further improving the operational capability of aerodrome fire services.

8. Finally, I must spend a moment in linking the aerodrome Fire Service with the total emergency organisation which an aerodrome needs to deal with a major accident.

9. An efficient aerodrome fire service, consisting of modern, effective appliances, extinguishing agents of proven qualities, a comprehensive communications system, trained personnel and competent technical management is only part of the total emergency plan which aerodrome authorities must develop. The design of civil aircraft is constantly being developed to create conditions in which the probability of survival in an accident is increased and the production of commercially-available treated Kerosene fuels will minimise the risk of disastrous post-accident fires. Where successful intervention by aerodrome fire services reduces loss of life by thermal injury the number of persons requiring rescue and/or after-care will increase. In recent accidents the inability of aerodrome and local municipal services to handle the survivors of an aircraft accident has led to serious criticism and in some cases, to litigation. The survivors may be in all conditions, from the grievously injured to the merely alarmed but all will need some kind of treatment and some will require priority if they are to survive. Those who are relatively uninjured are likely to be critical if they, their friends or relatives appear to be neglected and, in addition, there will soon be representatives of the news media to make their contribution to the situation. Most aerodromes have developed an emergency plan of some kind but not all plans are subjected to regular and realistic test to assess their continuing efficiency. Quite often the basic plans are not extended to match the growth in aircraft capacity, a serious matter when one appreciates that the capacity of a Boeing 747 is 2.5 times greater than that of its immediate predecessor, the Boeing 707. The emergency plan will require the mobilisation of aerodrome agencies and the municipal forces responsible for fire fighting, policing, the ambulance service, the hospitals, welfare services and the identification and repatriation of the dead. To produce an effective plan and to maintain this plan at a constant level of readiness and adequacy is a complex task but if efficient fire fighting and rescue is to produce the desired results in the first instance the second phase of an operation, the after-care of all persons involved in the accident, must be equally efficient if the initial advantage is to be preserved.

22. Snow and ice clearing methods:
new techniques and advanced thinking at major airports

R.W. Huson, CD
Vice President, Sales and Marketing, SMI Industries Ltd

The effectiveness of various types of snow and ice clearing equipment is analysed. Economics and suitability are considered in relation to amount of snow and area to be cleared.

1. It is a special pleasure to return to Brighton where I have found memories of a delightful holiday many years ago.

2. I am delighted to have been invited to speak to this illustrious gathering. I have been requested to provide you an insight into the problems of keeping an airport free of ice and snow. So first, let us define the problem!

3. Just what is involved? What is the cost? What is the penalty for not being prepared? These and many other factors must be considered.

4. We must conclude that different airports, have different needs. Then we must ask what are these variables? What are the standards desired? What is the financial limit imposed? Is there a time factor involved. Do we use a standard size runway is it 10,000 feet long and 250 feet wide, or is it larger or smaller? The cost involvement normally will be in direct proportion to the size of the runway, topography, temperature, layout, prevailing winds, volume of traffic, etc., plus all the other factors involved in the answers to the questions which have been posed.

5. As you can see from the outset, it is not easy to obtain an optimum standard because of the variables at each airfield.

6. Careful studies of many aspects of snow removal and ice control have taken place. We have attended many shows, exhibits, trials, symposiums and other allied groups to try and obtain information on this important matter. What we have discovered is that there has been practically no scientific work done on the subject.

7. In spite of many starts such as the Canadian National Research Council meeting of a few years ago and the Snow Removal and Ice Control Research meeting held in Hanover New Hampshire U.S.A. at Dartmouth College in 1970 no real scientific progress has been made. We do know that some important work has been done in the United Kingdom, Germany, Scandinavia, Japan and Russia. However, this work has never been coordinated. The work covers a wide variety of specialties including chemical use, test devices, definition of principles, identification of problem areas, documentation, etc.. Some of the work has been published some has not.

8. One of the major forums on effective use of equipment has been the annual Snow Symposium which is held in Allentown, Pennsylvania U.S.A. annually. This is held usually in early May under the auspices of the N.E. Chapter of the American Association of Airport Managers. This meeting has been attended by experts from Holland, Denmark, Germany, England, Canada, U.S.A., Switzerland and many other countries.

9. As a direct result of the Allentown meeting I had the privilege of meeting a number of people from the New York Port Authority. Executives of the Authority have been kind enough to provide an abbreviated version of their actions in preparation for the winter season.

10. Their Mr. Fred Flags comments are as follows:- quote "We, on this latitude (which includes a large number of major airports between New York - Boston - Washington and points west to Chicago and beyond) cannot hope to "out-experience" our compatriots to the north, whether it be Canada or Scandinavia. The very fact that we cannot, happens to pose a serious problem to us to which our more experienced neighbors seldom give a thought - operator skill and veteran instincts. In this regard, there may be one or two exceptions and it would seem only realistic to cite that Buffalo, New York - in the lee of Lake Erie --- receives an abundance of snow, drift-driving winds, sleet and freezing rain; enough for at least a half-dozen more fortunately located airports in the belt.

11. Since you are looking for fact and since many people with a passing knowledge of airport snow removal can imagine all sorts of snowstorm circumstances never actually encountered, I shall remain purely provincial and address myself to matters we, in New York,

have experienced and hope you can glean something useful from it. Rather than go into a lengthy dissertation on a few aspects of the task, permit me to capsulize a number of variety of conclusions that have become the backbone of our efforts each winter.

a) Consider the season as beginning by November 1 and not ending before April 30 of the following year.

b) Put all rolling equipment on a weekly check for battery life, fuel aboard, tire inflation, chains, and basic lubrication. For attached heads or towed components this inspection should view them as if a snow alert had been declared. They must be accessible, aligned for immediate mounting with lighting and self-contained power supplies at READY.

c) Drivers and assistants (helpers) should be reinstructed in the value of each unit's service to the whole and any variations that are to be tried (experimentation) for evaluation. This training or retraining should go far beyond the mechanical capabilities to start, stop and manoeuver the beasts. Limitations, as well as special capacities, should be clear and unmistakenly printed on the operator's mind. Methods of removal, from identifying the actual people who will be responsible for each facet of the job to special techniques to be employed should receive an "airing" as the season approaches and again as close to actual response as possible.

d) We prefer the 8-hour tour where possible but with prolonged efforts frequently resort to the 12 on-12 off cycle. Absolutely meticulous and scrupulous attention to the fairness of assignments and the impartiality of duties is rewarded handsomely. The snow fighter is first of all a man so it is up to supervisors to know what makes him tick, why he is different from his fellows, where he is alike, when to "stretch" his capacities, how to compensate for his deficiencies.

e) One man must be in charge. Not two or three - just simply and plainly ONE! In the one-horse operation, he may be the whole effort but in the major airport mounted attack, he is, or should be, the most skilled manipulator, with a mind for sorting and filing facts (and separating fiction where possible) and completely knowledgeable of the capacities of those foremen and specialists who will be working directly with him throughout the entire period.

f) Someone in every effort should be well versed on the physical nature of snow (ice) and all its variations. This someone should be conscious of the weather conditions continually (knowing precisely what kind of precip is coming down, temperature, wind velocities, visibilities) and up-date, repeatedly, the forecast information made available to him by the weather service. He should know the significance between wet and dry snow and

advise on numbers and types of brooms, blowers, and plows to employ based on this knowledge.

g) Obviously, equipment maintenance must be of the first order. This involves (as applied before, during and after storm use) a steady, consistent flow of cleaning, checking, greasing, replenishing functions. Keeping the equipment in the best possible condition is axiomatic of the snow removal effort itself, but also has the ancillary benefit of making it more difficult for an vindictive employee to put it out of commission undetected. The latter situation is not prevalent in any but the largest, most sophisticated operations.

h) Every airport management should examine very carefully the actual demand that will be forthcoming when various accumulations of snow or ice occur and base its procurement, its budget allocations, its operations, its maintenance and its recovery of costs on a precise model of performance. Calculated in advance, it is only with such a precise plan that eventual results can be compared and a measure of achievement or failure determined. In either case, adjustments can then be made.

12. The foregoing may give you the gist of our approach to airport snow removal and ice control. In any address, I see an opportunity to stimulate latent energies and imaginations and possibly prod some listener into making a major breakthrough in this, a rather unscientific, yet frequently massive effort to gain the upper hand over nature. unquote"

13. The New York Port Authority also provided me with this computer which they use to establish the team combinations of men and equipment to combat any snow situation.

14. Now let us think about the Economics of Snow & Ice Removal.

15. The Consulting Consortium of Hovey-Sores Ottawa Canada undertook a study of snow and ice removal systems for the FAA Systems Research and Development Service in late 1969. Jointly sponsored by the Canadian and US governments the study was oriented toward airport structures and air traffic of the mid 70's which is just about now. It is interesting to see that their forecasts were quite accurate. The following summary of information from that report is just as valid today as when it was written except for the unforeseen escalation of costs which have risen almost 100 percent. When we take this annual cost increase factor into consideration we can then see how important it is to select the correct equipment, use the correct techniques, and attain optimum use of equipment.

DEFINING COSTS

16. Snow and ice removal system costs, as defined in their study, included the costs of machinery and chemicals, their storage and maintenance, labor involved, and the costs of supervising and controlling the removal

operations.

17. It is important to note that the consultants made no attempt to trade safety considerations against cost; all systems had to satisfy established safety criteria.

18. Effectiveness of snow removal systems was defined as the time period which a given system was required to restore a runway to full operating capacity, with optimum effectiveness resulting from a trade-off between the system costs and the user delay acceptance.

19. Each system differed in both cost and effectiveness. Again it was a question involving several variables including capital cost of equipment, the cost of operating that equipment, the performance characteristics of the machines and chemicals, and the level of skill employed in planning and implementing the removal strategy.

20. Another important factor the consultants took into consideration in evaluating system costs was the degree of adaptability of each piece of equipment in performing tasks unrelated to snow and ice removal. In other words do you choose the equipment for the job or do you attempt to retain multi use equipment even though it is not the optimum for the job.

21. We also find that few airports establish separate accounting or cost control procedures for their winter maintenance operations. The general rule followed at most airports is to allocate such costs to broader categories such as airport maintenance. Therefore, we find no true accounting of the actual price of snow clearance.

22. What we should point out now, are, the many other variables which affect costs. One of the first things we note is that only a very slight correlation exists between the size of an airports investment in equipment and the amount of snow or the area of the airport to be cleaned. We have found that some large airports have an extremely low investment in equipment and a large area to be serviced. We have also found that certain airports were high on investment in equipment compared to the amount of snow or the area of the airport to be cleaned.

23. What we did find out was that almost in every case for all airports, the amount of snowfall has been the decisive factor in reaching most past equipment purchasing decisions. Runway and ramp areas have exerted a marginal influence, while the level of traffic supported by the airport seems to have had no influence on past purchasing decisions whatsoever.

24. Snow plow carriers with reversible, one way, or roll over type of plows dominate the equipment used. The plow carrier best suited is the 4 x 4 high performance heavy duty truck.

However, because of wanting year round utilization we find lighter 4 x 2 carriers employed. We found many opinions indicated greater value can be obtained from the H D 4 x 4 unit. From this you can normally get longer use, better reliability; it is also more flexible in that any type of plow can be used as well as side wings, under body graders, etc.. The chassis can also be equipped with a large dump body or a tank for chemicals, water, or other fluids. It can also be used to plow or to tow a sweeper quite effectively. The 4 x 4 units are normally diesel while the 4 x 2 units are essentially gasoline powered.

25. Three-section, folding-wing plows, measuring 24 to 28 feet in width and mounted on special purpose heavy-duty 4 x 4 carriers of 50,000 GVW, and which cost an average $75,000.00 are used for clearing ramps, runways and taxiways. They are particularly useful for feeding snow to the rotary snowblowers, these units can achieve speeds up to 13 mph in up to 10 inches of snow while clearing a 17 ft. wide path with the plow angled.

26. Three types of rotary snowblowers are now in general use. Newly developed high speed units are used to remove newly fallen snow from priority airfield surfaces, and, in combination with high speed snowplows, pick up and cast snow accumulations entirely off the airfield surface. Average cost of the high speed rotaries is $125,000.00. They are also used for removing deep or heavy windrowed snow.

27. The high capacity low speed rotaries, costing an average of $65,000.00 with some costing $100,000.00 depending upon capacity are designed primarily for removing heavy accumulations of deep or windrowed snow. They are also used in Highway applications and Municipal cleaning. Airports equipped with high speed rotaries normally use the slower units for clearing secondary airfield areas, intersections and for loading snow hauling vehicles.

28. Attachment type rotaries, costing about $17,000.00 for a medium size unit, are available for use on front end loaders, fork lifts and road graders. They are particularly suited for use in medium to light snowfall areas as back-up machines to cover emergency conditions.

29. Runway sweepers designed for all-season airfield maintenance are used to remove snow, slush, excess water, dirt and debris from paved surfaces used by aircraft. Typical average cost of the towed type unit is $38,550.00, self-propelled units costs an average of $95,000.00. When used for dry sweeping, these units operate at a speed of approximately 20 MPH. In deep snow or slush, the excess snow is plowed aside before the sweeper is used. Unless this is done, the broom assemblies become overloaded and the sweeper can no longer maintain speed, especially in accumulations of more than one inch.

30. Another system for clearing runways, now in use at Paris-Orly, employs the Bertin Thermo-Soufflante machine which utilizes the thermal and kinetic energy of exhaust gases from a discarded jet engine. The hot blast from the unit can clear a 130-ft. wide path through fresh snow at 10 mph, slowing to 2-6 mph for clearing compacted snow or slush. The unit is also used for de-icing, runway sweeping and for removing water from runways. The high cost of initial purchase and the high cost of operation have drastically reduced the use of this tool.

31. Runways with electric cables inserted have been discussed from time to time. The obvious advantage of such a system lies in the fact that snow, slush and ice would be prevented from accumulating. The major drawback, at least at the present time, is in the area of economic feasibility. Capital cost estimates covering equipment and runway preparation for 10,000 ft. runway 300 feet wide were in the neighborhood of $8 million. Annual operating costs were estimated at almost 3.3 million. The present escalated costs are not known. Also the problem of drainage for the melted snow has not been overcome in most trial installations.

32. A melting system employing flexible, non-corrodible plastic pipes embedded in concrete through which a heated solution of antifreeze and water is rapidly circulated, may have application for airport parking areas, loading areas and walks. Installation is said to cost about $1.00 per square foot, about a third of the cost of electrical or metal pipe systems, and annual operating cost is estimated at less than $20 per 1,000 square feet.

33. We know that Vienna Airport and Zurich Airport have studied the use of thermal heating for runways. We know that a minimum requirement of 200 watts per square meter is needed to provide the melting effect. We also know that hot water systems have been found to be more effective. However, initial installation costs are oppressive.

34. Thermal heating is now being used and should be effective for certain areas, such as areas around loading docks, walkways, etc., where mechanical equipment cannot manoeuver properly or where snow must be completely removed at all times.

35. In most areas of the world where snow and freezing rain occur; snow clearing equipment must operate in every kind of snow condition from very wet heavy snow to dry powder type of precipitation.

36. The main method of removing ice and snow however is by mechanical means. Most airports maintain a vehicle fleet to meet this challenge and this normally consists of:-
a) High speed rotary sweepers.
b) Single blade snow plows mounted on high powered truck usually 4 X 4 drive.

c) High speed specially designed reversible plows which cast snow long distances. These units are normally mounted on high speed 4 x 4 vehicles.
d) High speed rotary snow blowers designed to operate in concert with the plow and sweeper train combination.
e) Low speed blowers designed to eliminate windrows and for loading trucks.
f) Special thermal plows using aircraft jet engine effluent gases as the snow mover.

37. Now let us think about the various methods or techniques for getting on with the removal job. In our examination we find as many variations as there are airports. Therefore, perhaps we should discuss the methods used at successful airports. We shall now quote from remarks made by Mr. L.M.E. Hawkins, Chief of Mobile Support Services, Canadian Ministry of Transport at a recent snow conference. Quote "Turning to the snow removal activity, three main types of equipment, high speed sweepers, plow mounted trucks and snow blowers, are employed in the clearing of runways and associated taxiways.

38. The quantity of each type of equipment depends upon the area to be cleaned, snowfall, icing and drifting conditions, and the operational commitment or level of service demand. The following is a description of the basic snow control area and the snow control methodology: airport runways in Canada are 200 feet wide and vary from 5 to 12 thousand feet in length. The edges of these pavements are lined with specially designed electric lights spaced 200' apart and 18" high. These units delineate the landing surface for the aircraft pilot. The immediate and continuing objective is to provide a clean pavement surface 75 feet in width for the full runway length which allows a safe aircraft landing or takeoff. The snow removal operation begins with the high speed runway sweeper which has a 14 foot broom, it is angled 30 degrees to the longitudinal axis and clears a 12 foot path at an operational speed of 12-16 MPH. Their use alone is limited to falls of up to 3 inches once several widths have been broomed from the centre of the runway, the plow trucks in conjunction with the sweepers are used to pick up and cast into windrows. The plows have extended mold boards and clear a 16 foot path at effective speeds up to 35 MPH. Blowers, operating at 15-20 mph are then brought into the operation after the plow and sweeper have passed so that the snow can be blown over the runway edge lighting system and moved in the fewest possible stages. Snow is removed a minimum of 25 feet beyond the edge of the runway to allow unobstructed lighting visibility. A recently established aircraft landing aid designed for poor visibility conditions includes, among other things, runway centreline lighting. This system involves a 12" diameter metal fixture imbedded in the runway. The top of the unit is ½" higher than the pavement and contains an optic lens and a 200 watt bulb. A runway contains over 400 of these fixtures and at present are installed in

one runway at six airports across Canada.
This facility is a component of what is known
as a category II instrument landing system and,
as you have now surmised, has complicated snow
removal and ice control to an extreme degree.
Plows and blowers used on runways have category
II ILS facilities are fitted with rubber contact edges. Steel shoes or castors used as
support for flow frames, blades or blower
bankhead assemblies, must be replaced with
pneumatic or semi-pneumatic rubber tires. Much
greater use must be made of the sweepers for
snow removal and of urea for ice control.

39. Moving briefly to aircraft apron areas -
graders with wing blades are used effectively
to clear and windrow the snow for loading by
blowers to trucks for hauling to the dump site.
Because of escalating trucking costs and the
concern expressed by environmentalists relative
to snow dumps, we have examined the merits of
melting versus trucking and dumping snow from
apron areas. Each have their merits.

40. The introduction of category II operations
and increasing frequency of aircraft movements
demands a new approach to the runway snow removal activity which is being phased into our
international airport system. This "team" system involves the use of high speed sweepers and
blowers only, operating at 25 mph or more. The
formation of windrows by plow is omitted.

41. Our objective was to develop a sweeper capable of operating at 25 plus mph, we find that
we have been able to achieve this by replacing
the mechanical drive with a hydraulic drive.
The factor essentially responsible for limiting
the speed of operation has been the amount of
vibration or "bounce" of the broom which has
been largely eliminated through this modification. We now in conjunction with a Canadian
manufacturer have achieved success in eliminating the vibration.

42. The second member of the team, the high
speed blower, has been under development for
some time. We have been working with the manufacturer in developing a single engine hydrosta-
tic drive blower capable of operating at a
constant speed of 25 plus mph. While some difficulty had been experienced in maintaining this
speed, it has now been achieved. A two engine
high speed blower with the same characteristics
has also been developed." Unquote

43. Now let us examine a different method. At
certain other airports a second technique is
used and is called the team approach. It operates as follows:-
The most important runway is selected and a
group of plows operate in a train starting from
the centre line and staggered towards the runway
edge. Normally a single plow will work from the
outer edge of the runway clearing the snow
towards the centre of the runway away from the
runway lights. A rotary blower or blowers removes the windrows at the runway edge. Rotary
sweepers are then employed to clean up the residue snow as a second phase operation.

44. So much for the brief discussion on removal techniques; we now come to another important phase:-
Anti-icing or de-icing? This is a formidable
subject while chemicals have been used with
varying degrees of success at many airports.
We find that in use of chemicals the opinion of
the experts is not always consistant.

45. We note that a number of chemicals are and
have been used. In fact the use of chemicals is
generally increasing. The types of chemicals
include those in liquid form and also the solid
forms such as Urea, Salt, etc..

46. Under certain severe weather conditions
heated sand, small stones, cinders, etc. have
been used to provide a safe landing surface.
However, it is essential to remove these ingredients by use of brushes as soon as practicable
to prevent damage to aircraft engines. This
type of contaminents are easily injested into
jet engines.

47. What do we want or what should we use as
the criteria for chemicals?
a) They must not have any destructive effect
on aircraft.
b) They must act quickly to remove the ice or
snow surface.
c) They must create a friction type surface
and not cause a slippery surface.
d) The chemicals in use must not be injurious
to the environment.

48. The most satisfactory method of keeping
active areas free of ice is anti-icing or
preventive de-icing. The optimum results are
in direct relation to:- humidity, dew point,
temperature of runway surface, air temperature,
wind, type of surface and amount of chemical
used.

49. The method of applying the material is
also quite varied. The use of sprays produces
effective results and spray bars up to 50 feet
have been effectively used. The speed of application varies from 10 km/hr to 30 km/hr.

50. The consumption of liquid varies with the
speed and nozzle size. Solid chemicals mainly
Urea are also used, however, the Urea can be
blown away by the effluent blasts of the aircraft engines. Urea has been coated with clay
to more effectively cause it to remain in position and has also been sprayed with water to
cause better adhesion. Solid chemicals are
normally sprayed on the surface with a sand
spreader of some type.

51. The equipment used varies from the simplest
spinner type of spreader to the modern type of
unit which closely monitors the amount of material used. These units can be calibrated to
compensate for speed, volume, type of chemical,
etc..

52. One of the latest innovations to come on
the horizon for effective monitoring runway
conditions is the new surface systems analyzers.

Many progressive airports have installed one system. The system consists of from one to five sensors connected through cable or radio link to a display unit usually located in the field maintenance supervisor's office or any other place where personnel are on duty for twenty-four hours. The display unit indicates surface conditions by four colored lights on the front panel marked "clear", "wet", "alert" and "ice". In addition, runway surface temperature is displayed by digital readouts for each sensor. There is also an audible alarm that is activated by an "alert" or "ice" condition.

BENEFITS

53. The advance warning supplied by this system allows field maintenance personnel to more efficiently utilize their labor and chemicals because it is possible to utilize an "anti-icing" rather than "de-icing" runway maintenance program. If anti-icing procedures are used, chemical costs in some cases can be reduced by as much as one-half.

54. When using ice control chemicals, this system will allow for more exact use because as the chemical begins to dilute to the point where it is beginning to refreeze, the "alert" light will issue a warning that steps must be taken to either put more chemical on or broom off the solution that is about to freeze on the runway. This also is helpful in the anti-icing situation where an icing situation is predicted. With this system and a high speed liquid sprayer, it is possible to apply a very light application of chemical and then monitor the system to observe when the chemical/water solution begins to freeze. If it doesn't, this means that the smaller amount applied was enough and saved chemical. If it does begin to freeze then it is time to take action and add another light application to keep it in the liquid form.

55. Since this system immediately alerts airport field maintenance when to apply chemicals, it also will indicate when runway traction readings should be taken.

56. Increased safety since the runway can be shut down before a hazardous situation occurs, rather than after.

57. Surface temperature of the runway at the sensor location is very valuable in knowing when to add or remove ice control chemicals. Since this varies considerably from air temperature, it can be very useful in determining whether or not the runway should be treated chemically or whether it can be handled by mechanical means.

58. It is the belief of most effective airport managers that we have only begun to understand the problems and vagaries of the snow removal task. We note that the Western European Airports Association formed a working group in 1970. We have previously mentioned other agencies which have an active interest in keeping airports with a black top runway. What is required is greater international cooperation and exchange of information.

59. Let us all realize that when a major civil airport is not operational the landing fees and concession losses in one day would normally pay the total cost of the snow removal fleet. This does not include the staggering costs to airlines which must land at alternate sites with all the extra costs which this involves.

60. What should we conclude from the remarks which have been made in this summary.
First, we should recognize the importance of effective snow and ice control. Also the monetary costs and possible savings by use of correct equipment and techniques.
Second, the importance of keeping airports open and safe for the traveling public.
Third, the value in cooperation with environmental groups to achieve black top airports without destroying the soil fertility, or bird, and animal habitats.

61. It is hoped that this address will stimulate our thinking and provide further opportunities for study and discussion.

62. I now wish to thank the following business, government, and associations for their ideas and suggestions for this paper.
New York Port Authority, American Snowblast Corp. Denver, Canadian Department of Transport, The Beilhack Co. Rosenheim Germany, SMI Industries Ltd. Montreal Canada, Hovey and Associates Ottawa Canada.

23. Airside servicing vehicles and equipment

G.J. Sweetapple

Manchester International Airport Authority, UK

Airline direct operating costs, including airport costs, can be crucial to an airline's financial viability, and this situation has been exacerbated by the huge increases in fuel costs and the world-wide recession. This paper, therefore, explains in some detail how Manchester International Airport is dealing with the problem of how to minimize their operating costs while, at the same time, safety and operational efficiency is improved. The Airport's policy of rationalisation of ground handling facilities and services is also examined and the paper concludes with a plea for a greater liaison between aircraft manufacturers, airlines, and airports.

INTRODUCTION

1. One of the principal factors which is currently inhibiting the growth of air transport throughout the world is that of rising costs largely brought about by the tremendous upsurge in fuel prices over the last two years. Due to general inflation tendencies, all other costs are also rising, but the proportion of airport costs to total airline costs has remained fairly constant over the years. This varies from about 5% for long haul traffic up to 10% for short haul traffic. However, airports must still strive to reduce their costs to the utmost degree as even the relatively small effect of airport charges can make the difference between profit and loss for an airline. Therefore, the general theme of my paper is to indicate how airports can perhaps achieve a saving in their costs through more efficient operations on the airside and I have used the example of Manchester Airport to illustrate how we think this can best be done.

2. In seeking to achieve our objectives, we meet many problems, but one of the most difficult to overcome at civil airports is that of meeting the opposing requirements of airlines and airport operators. An airline operator has to operate his aircraft efficiently and economically to meet the needs of the passenger and cargo shipper. In order to meet the economic requirements of the airline, the airport is often forced to operate at an inefficient level as regards manpower and equipment as it is impossible for airlines to operate their flights at a constant level throughout the 24 hours in a day.

Traffic Peaking

3. In this day and age, airports face many problems, both technical and operational, which are often exacerbated by environmental considerations including those of aircraft noise, land usage, and pollution. These can all be overcome but only at considerable cost to airport operators, governments, airlines, and aircraft manufacturers. To varying degrees, they all have an effect on the basic and most serious problem of peaking of aircraft and passenger traffic. British Airways have kindly supplied me with copies of diagrams showing the effect of scheduling on their long haul traffic, and it can be seen from this diagram that the effect of night closures and other restrictions seriously reduces the amount by which aircraft movements may be re-scheduled in order to avoid peaking problems. Airports must therefore do all they can to ensure that their operations are conducted in the most efficient way in order to reduce the economic penalties of these irregular traffic patterns. Often, the solution adopted may be extremely unpopular, but experience has already shown that procedures we have adopted can help in reducing both capital and operating expenditure to the absolute minimum, bearing in mind that Manchester Airport probably experiences the most severe peaking problems of any airport in the United Kingdom. Undoubtedly, as our traffic increases over the next few years, these extremes of peaking will be reduced, but at the moment they are at the very worst possible level.

4. The International Civil Aviation Organisation is currently carrying out a world-wide study into the problem of traffic peaking. Information received so far indicates that the problem has to be tackled from two aspects, world-wide and local. They have therefore recommended the setting up, at every major airport throughout the world, of a scheduling committee whose task will be to ensure that the most effective use is made of an airport's facilities by avoiding extreme peaks of traffic and spreading the load as much as possible. However, ICAO have appreciated that the work of each of these local scheduling committees will have an effect on

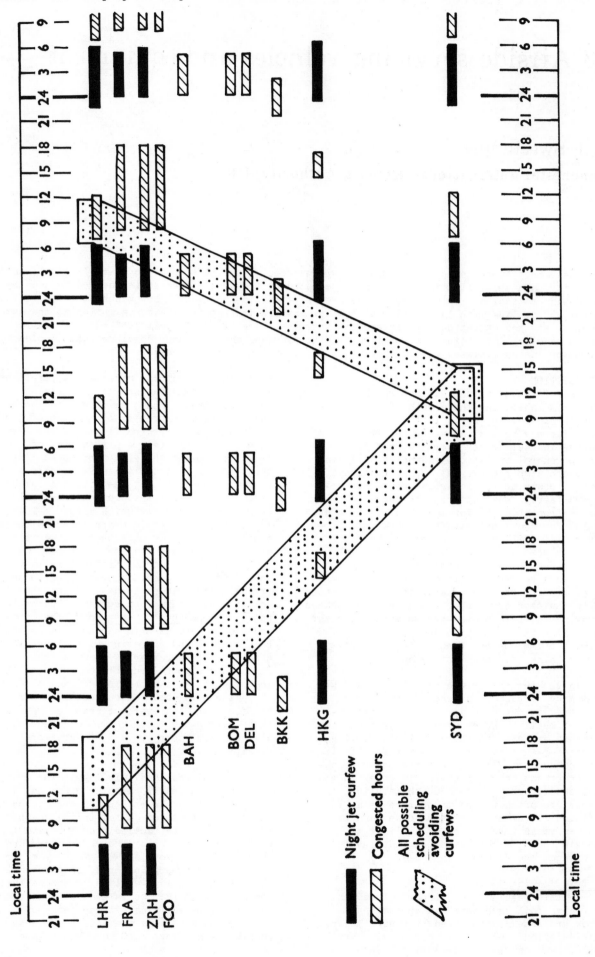

Scheduling limitations: London – Sydney via Hong Kong

Local time

LHR FRA ZRH FCO BAH BOM DEL BKK HKG SYD

■ Night jet curfew

▨ Congested hours

〰 All possible scheduling avoiding curfews

operations at other airports served from that airport. Initially, therefore, the activities of the individual scheduling committees will have only a small effect on the peaking problem, and the real benefits of these committees and their activities will not be seen until they can be co-ordinated on a world-wide or regional basis. The setting up of such a co-ordinated organisation on a world-wide basis presents tremendous problems and would undoubtedly require the use of several computers in various areas around the world. Even if such an organisation can be set up and funded, the improvements to the peaking situation which may result may still only show a minimal improvement in the situation at each individual airport.

5. Airports have had to learn to live with this situation and to run their airports and finances accordingly. However, within the essential operating constraints, it is possible for an airport to adopt various procedures and techniques which will materially improve their own financial situation and therefore the costs applicable to airlines. This paper attempts to indicate how these problems are tackled at Manchester Airport.

Policy Implications

6. For many years, Manchester Airport has been developing a policy of rationalisation applied to all aspects of its operations. This policy covers operations right through the airport from check-in desk to loading of aircraft, and, because it imposes certain limitations on the rights of airlines to employ their own staff, it has not always been universally accepted. As an example, the limitation by the Airport Authority a few years ago on the numbers of check-in desks to be provided in our new Check-In Hall has resulted in a situation in which only two companies are allowed to carry out the check-in operation. This has nevertheless resulted in a most efficient operation where walking distances are reduced and the best possible conditions provided for the passenger. The 'comb' layout of check-in desks allows passengers to walk between the check-in desks thereby avoiding the necessity of having to force their way through queues of other passengers at adjoining desks. Capital costs have also been reduced by keeping the check-in desk area and equipment to a minimum size, with a consequent saving in cleaning, heating, lighting, and maintenance costs.

7. A similar policy has been adopted for all airside operations. The Airport Authority has retained the right to carry out all apron loading operations with the exception of specialised engineering functions. Most Airport Authorities accept that they have the right to decide who should provide operational facilities on the apron, and there must be some acceptance of the view that airlines are best equipped to concentrate on the business of transporting passengers and cargo by air, and leave the ground handling of passengers,

baggage, and cargo to the Airport Authorities. Immediately, the benefits of scale become apparent in that the capital investment in equipment for the ground handling of aircraft can be shared between all airlines operating in and out of a particular airport, coupled with the fact that all the equipment provided is available for use on every airline's aircraft and valuable equipment is not left idle for long periods. Such a monopoly situation also leads to significant savings in manpower costs as the same staff can be used for various purposes, both on the apron and within the terminal building. Such a facility would not be available to airlines employing their own staff for this purpose.

8. Manchester Airport's policy of rationalisation therefore extends to nearly all the airport's activities. Our view is that this policy is the only way in which the many conflicting requirements of the airport's users can be met, although inevitably in the form of a compromise. Passengers' requirements are constantly varying and, indeed, the same passenger will change his views on his own requirements within a relatively short space of time. An Airport Authority also has to cater for the needs of many airlines, which, at Manchester Airport, number 30, together with the essential requirements of Customs, Immigration, and Health Authorities. The ever increasing cost of borrowing money these days means that capital investment in terminal facilities must be optimised as individual airlines can no longer afford the luxury of providing their own facilities which would be utilised for only relatively short periods throughout the working day.

Apron Handling

9. Manchester Airport's policy of rationalisation is best illustrated by the arrangements currently in force for the handling of aircraft on the apron. For many years, the Authority has insisted on their right to provide all loading facilities, equipment, and manpower on the apron. An inspection of our apron immediately illustrates one of the biggest advantages in that apron congestion is minimized and the only equipment seen parked on the apron is that required by individual airlines to carry out their engineering functions. At many airports, the congestion problem caused by aircraft equipment being parked all over the apron area can, and does, result in serious accidents due to lack of manoeuvring space for vehicles and the lack of clear vision on the part of drivers and, sometimes, pilots. Through the implementation of our rationalisation policy on the apron, the number and types of equipment such as cargo lifts, catering vehicles, etc., has been very much reduced, and our staff are trained to handle all types of aircraft expected to use the Airport, thereby ensuring the most efficient use of all resources. It is, incidentally, very apparent that the introduction of nose-in parking of aircraft has also materially improved the safety situation as it has completely resolved

the problem of damage caused by engine blast as aircraft commence to taxi away from a self manoeuvring stand position.

10. This policy is also extended, on the apron, to include the engineering function provided by individual airlines. If every airline were to provide its own engineering facilities and equipment, this would result in a gross under-utilisation of engineering accommodation in the terminal building and piers, and in further congestion on the apron through the parking of engineering equipment such as ground power units and air starters, which are often only used for a few minutes in the day. Individual airlines are therefore encouraged to make use of services provided by the two handling companies at Manchester Airport.

11. The handling of air cargo in the present rather limited accommodation is also restricted in that British Airways provide, on behalf of the Airport Authority, a Common Import Bond so as to make the best use of the area available to them in the import cargo hangar. Any limitations imposed on the export side can be less severe as export cargo needs far less area for storage and therefore the present facilities should prove to be adequate for many years to come. Further, a new cargo terminal complex is being planned and, as soon as cargo traffic shows a sustained increase, final planning will be resumed and construction commenced so that new facilities could be made available within four years. In order to make the most efficient use of the new areas to be provided in this cargo complex, the policy of rationalisation will also be extended to the new facility. This will be covered in more detail later in this paper.

12. A further aspect of the Airport's policy of rationalisation is reflected in our basic philosophy of providing a simplified layout of terminal building, and this is also reflected in the equipment provided within the terminal building and on the apron. We feel that airport equipment has, over the years, lost its basic simplicity of concept and design and therefore, to a large extent, its reliability. This is evidenced in the cost of such equipment coupled with the abnormally high maintenance costs which result from the use of the new sophisticated types of equipment such as automated baggage handling and the very large and complex cargo container lifts and other handling equipment for the handling of Boeing 747 aircraft, etc. A situation now exists where it is impossible to justify the expenditure of nearly £80,000 for a Boeing 747 freighter cargo lift unless the airport can expect to have at least one of these freighters every working day. Admittedly, these new cargo lifts can be used on ordinary freighter aircraft, but they cost over £50,000 more than the equipment used specifically for the Boeing 707 and similar sized aircraft. This difference in cost cannot be justified unless large numbers of Boeing 747 freighters are expected to use the particular airport, and the situation is

made far worse by the requirement to have this specialised equipment available at all times so that a second cargo lift of this type may be required to give reliability and back-up capacity.

13. We therefore feel that there should be a move away from the more complicated type of equipment. Manchester Airport has for many years attempted to provide efficient operating facilities based on the use of the most simplified equipment possible bearing in mind the handling capacity required to meet passenger and cargo throughputs. The use of the most sophisticated equipment has not necessarily demonstrated any greater capacity or reliability, and, in fact, the reverse has often applied. Airside operations at airports always tend to be manpower intensive, at least until that unlikely day when somebody invents a piece of equipment which will physically load baggage or cargo into the aircraft without the use of any manpower whatsoever. Our opinion is, therefore, that the manual loading of aircraft will always continue and that the best system to be provided is a combination of simplified, easily maintained handling equipment together with teams of well trained and conscientious men. The relevance of this philosophy is also highlighted by difficulties which certain airports are bound to experience in the not too distant future when their very sophisticated automated baggage and cargo handling equipment requires major maintenance. Due to the high capital cost of such equipment, it is virtually impossible to provide back-up systems and even minor maintenance can result in the total stoppage of such equipment. There is much to be said for simple collection, distribution, and loading equipment within a terminal building and on the apron to assist the loading crews, and this is the basis of our operations at Manchester Airport. Our view is, and always will be, that the good manual worker is an essential part of an airport's operations.

Apron Equipment

14. Problems arising from the use of apron equipment include its complexity, maintenance, and low utilisation, coupled with the essential requirements of safety and adequate capacity. All these add up to high capital costs, and many manufacturers of such equipment could well price themselves out of the market unless they undertake a critical re-appraisal of airline and airport requirements so that simplified and more rugged equipment can be made available. It is even possible, in the case of Manchester Airport, that our own Engineering Section may be able to design and construct aircraft handling equipment at a cost lower than that of equipment currently available from manufacturers, with the added advantages of simplicity and built-in ease of maintenance. Aircraft manufacturers must also take a large part of the blame for this situation, and they must establish and maintain a much closer liaison with both airport operators and equipment manufacturers. The requirements set by

airlines and aircraft designers are often too severe and complex, and ways must be found to allow the use of more simplified equipment without the added complexity of the many and varied safety devices which airline operators insist must be fitted, and which add so much to the cost. Other ways can surely be found of meeting these essential requirements without unduly increasing the cost of the equipment. One example of our policy of simplification can be seen in the use of the cargo transfer platforms at Manchester Airport which replace transporters, with a saving of many thousands of pounds, and the added advantage of total reliability. Our simplified cargo handling system results in a 35/40 minute turn round for a fully loaded Boeing 707 freighter - a time which is unlikely to be bettered even with the use of the most sophisticated equipment currently available.

15. Manchester Airport Authority is currently investigating the use of electrically powered vehicles and equipment on the apron. The low utilisation of apron equipment means that vehicles and equipment powered by the internal combustion engine, although generally cheaper to purchase initially, are uneconomic both in terms of maintenance and running costs. Electrically powered vehicles or apron equipment therefore seem to be a much better proposition, and the tremendous advances in the design of vehicle batteries and motors in recent years now means that much more powerful motors can be provided at a weight and size compatible with airport equipment and vehicles. Already, one United Kingdom airport has been equipped, on a trial basis, with passenger steps mounted on an electrically powered vehicle chassis. Some years ago Manchester Airport experimented with the use of baggage conveyors into aircraft holds powered from a 50 v. electrical power source installed in the apron. These trials were moderately successful, but the equipment available at that time was not sufficiently reliable or powerful to justify the cost of totally re-equipping. However, the relatively low capital cost, coupled with its simplicity and reliability, now indicates that the use of electrically powered vehicles and equipment should be more carefully considered by Airport Authorities. The added, and very real, advantage is, of course, the fact that electrically powered vehicles can be made intrinsically safe when used while aircraft are being refuelled, etc. Further detailed studies will therefore be carried out at Manchester Airport into the greater use of electrically powered vehicles and equipment, whether supplied from batteries or apron power sources. Already, certain aircraft stands at Heathrow and many other airports are provided with ground power from a fixed source and, if an electrically powered mobile air starter unit can be developed, one of an airport's biggest environmental problems - noise from the use of aircraft APU's - could be resolved. The concept of electrically powered cargo lifts, toilet carts, servicing vehicles, etc., will also be given the fullest consideration during our studies.

16. Finally, on apron equipment, we would commend the use of hydrant fuel systems at modern airports. This concept received little favour years ago due to the limited use of nose in parking at airports, but once this form of aircraft parking has been introduced, then the standard IATA layout of hydrants means that all sizes of aircraft from BAC 1-11 to Boeing 747 can be refuelled from the same hydrant system on any stand. The two biggest advantages of a hydrant system are the great improvement in safety and the very significant reduction in apron congestion which is caused when very large refuelling tanker vehicles are employed.

Cargo Handling

17. The basic concept of a rationalised cargo terminal was developed with our cargo consultants, PE Consulting Group Limited. The basic philosophy rests on the fact that a cargo terminal is divided into three working areas, each of which will, in time, need to be extended or expanded at different rates. Three separate groups of buildings will, therefore, be constructed. One will provide an area for the airside handling of cargo such as the make-up and break-down of containers and pallets; another the bonded warehouse area; and a third group will make up the landside area to include Customs long room, canteen facilities, and non-bonded warehouses, etc. Our policy of rationalisation will also mean that individual airlines and freight agents will be asked to group together for the purpose of renting or leasing accommodation within the new terminal thereby avoiding the situation where individual companies rent small storage and working areas difficult to adminster and operate. By physically dividing the building into its three component parts, we believe a more efficient operation can be assured and any adaptations or extensions to the premises required in the future can be carried out far more easily and with much less disruption to the normal operation of the terminal.

18. In planning a new cargo complex, many problems arise and it is essential that a flexibility of outlook should be retained. Certainly in our new terminal, we shall aim for simplified handling systems, probably coupled with the use of an extended LACES system. However, the whole concept of the carriage of cargo by air is undergoing considerable change and there is a move towards a greater use of containers including those of the intermodal type. The cargo terminal must therefore be capable of adaptation readily as clearance and acceptance procedures can so easily be changed by Customs Authorities, even to the extent of possibly allowing clearance of cargo off the airport at some time in the future. The ever increasing use of the wide bodied aircraft for the carriage of cargo either in the belly hold or on the main deck has also to be taken into consideration in the planning of a terminal complex.

19. To summarise, simplicity and flexibility

should be the keynotes in the design and operation of any cargo terminal.

Conclusions

20. The civil air transport industry has
always been a most dynamic one and subject to
constant change. This same dynamism encourages
the generation of many new ideas, but there has
been a tendency over the years to adopt certain
new ideas without proper consideration being
given to their total costing and, more importantly, their operating costs. Examples which
may be quoted are the use of multiple air
bridges on large aircraft, mobile lounges,
automatic baggage sorting systems, and the so-
called "people movers". No criticism of these
individual pieces of equipment is implied, but
one wonders whether their use in a particular
airport situation has always been given the
proper full financial consideration before
decisions were taken. Certainly, operating
costs are very rarely quoted by the manufacturers of such equipment and yet Airport
Authorities must realise that this is a continuing commitment for the life of the equipment. As any maintenance task must be manpower
intensive, the increasing costs of labour mean
that maintenance and operating costs can only
rise over the years. As a further example, I
would quote the use of the over-wing air
bridges at certain major airports. Undoubtedly,
the use of these over-wing bridges with one or
two bridges to the forward doors can result in
a shorter unloading and loading time for
passengers, and yet it is a well known fact
that the refuelling time on large long range
aircraft is likely to be the critical factor
in any turn round operation. This means,
therefore, that until the refuelling operation
can be refined so as to cut down the present
refuelling time, there is little advantage in
obtaining a slightly reduced passenger unloading and loading time by using an over-wing
bridge, and the considerable capital expenditure involved in the purchase, installation, and
operation of these bridges could well be
largely nugatory.

21. Airport Authorities also have to contend
with high powered sales techniques which tend
to highlight the advantages from obtaining the
new types of sophisticated equipment without
emphasising their inherent disadvantages such
as capital costs and, especially, operating and
maintenance costs. In carrying out an evaluation of such equipment as the mobile lounges,
which are used at certain airports in the
United States, direct cost comparisons as outlined by the manufacturers tend to be restricted to acquisition and operating costs compared
with capital costs of alternative means of
accommodating passengers in terminal buildings.
Other practical factors tend sometimes to be
forgotten, and one can quote the simple example
of the use of mobile lounge against the
traditional terminal concept of a building and
pier layout in which the mobile lounge concept
apparently shows considerable financial
benefits. However, every Airport Authority
knows that terminal buildings are not only
used for the housing and accommodation of
passengers, but also for staff, including such
requirements as those of engineering facilities. With the traditional pier layout,
engineers can be found accommodation on the
ground floor of such structures virtually at
no cost in terms of capital investment. If a
mobile lounge system is used, then special
buildings have to be constructed for engineering staff and other workers. These examples
are merely intended to highlight the
deficiencies which exist in the current
planning and evaluation techniques employed by
many Airport Authorities. Operation and
financial evaluation techniques must be far
more sophisticated and thorough than has been
the case up until now, and the Manchester
International Airport Authority has now commenced a very detailed study of the use of the
mobile lounges against the traditional pier
layout system. Very few totally independent
reviews of this concept have been carried out
by Airport Authorities, and, in our case, a
team of four specialists, led by a finance
officer, will carry out their own appraisal
including in their deliberations every aspect
of the equipment's design, construction,
maintenance, operation, and, most importantly,
its financing.

22. Taking the case of the mobile lounge
concept as an example, I certainly do not
wish to imply that such equipment has no place
in the modern airport system. Even the most
basic of studies will readily indicate that
the mobile lounge can play a very real and useful part in providing increased passenger
facilities without the necessity to construct
new terminal buildings or extend existing
ones. However, we feel that the full potential
of the mobile lounge concept can only be realised if it is incorporated into a terminal
design from its inception.

23. Finally, I would end my paper with a plea
to the industry as a whole. The problems
facing the civil air transport industry at the
present time can only be resolved by a new
approach from the entire industry. Individual
Airport Authorities can resolve some of their
own problems to a degree, but many of the
problems I have highlighted can only be
resolved on a world-wide basis. It is
essential that there should be a much closer
liaison between aircraft manufacturers, airlines, and Airport Authorities, and although
the various airport associations which
currently exist do a good job in establishing
a liaison between Airport Authorities and
aircraft manufacturers, this liaison is in no
way effective enough to resolve the problems
which arise from aircraft manufacturers
continuing to design aircraft which do not fit
existing airports and need specialist equipment
to handle them. We still have the situation
where one of the world's major aircraft
producing companies may build a new freighter
aircraft having a wheel track in excess of 58
feet. Nearly all major airports have constructed their taxiways to a standard width of

SWEETAPPLE

75 feet, and to safely accommodate this
particular aircraft, they would all have to be
widened to 100 feet. The capital investment in
this sort of work is immense and would not only
involve widening taxiways by 25 feet but also
the re-positioning of the centreline lighting
which is incorporated in most taxiway layouts.
If airport costs are to be maintained at anywhere near their present level, or even reduced,
then airline operators must insist that aircraft manufacturers design their aircraft to
fit existing facilities and only require the
minimum of extra capital investment to
accommodate them. The value of equipment
provided at Manchester Airport for the handling
of aircraft is in excess of £1½m at the present
time, and one set of equipment to handle the
Boeing 747 aircraft can cost an airport
operator more than £100,000 to acquire. It is
therefore imperative that all future aircraft
should be designed to make use of the existing
equipment and facilities provided at airports
all over the world. Despite the pleas of
Airport Authorities over the years, aircraft
manufacturers still appear to pay little heed
to the views of these Authorities when they
design their new types of aircraft. Thankfully,
the problem of aircraft noise is being resolved,
but only after Airport Authorities had been
forced to take positive action in the form of
night operating and other restrictions. The
question must be asked whether the tremendous
financial losses which have accrued to airlines
through the imposition of night operating
restrictions could have been avoided if a
closer liaison had been established and
maintained between aircraft manufacturers and
Airport Authorities years ago. My plea must
therefore be that IATA, ICAA, or some similar
organisation, with the least possible delay,
sets up a permanent working party or committee
which will maintain a proper and meaningful
liaison between manufacturers, airlines, and
airports, so that many of our outstanding
problems can be resolved as soon as possible.

24. I sincerely hope that the thoughts which
I have put before this conference will find
some ready acceptance.

Session VIII: Discussion

Mr J. H. DENYER, Airport Director, Newcastle Airport

Papers 21-23 highlight the problem of airport costs. The first, dealing with fire and safety, brings to mind the amount of equipment and men required for general licensing of airports. This equipment is expensive; the problem is to keep up with technology, progress and development and to ensure the equipment purchased is not going to be obsolete within twelve months of obtaining it.

Mr Nash referred to the types of extinguishing media that are required; he mentioned protein foams, fluoro-protein foams and fluoro chemicals but did not mention bromochloride difluoromethane. I think the abbreviation is BCF.

Helicopters have been suggested as extinguishing vehicles. The mind boggles at the cost - the initial cost of the helicopter, the cost of maintaining it, the cost of crewing it. In order to ensure complete cover at least two helicopters would be needed. I wonder whether this concept of fire fighting will ever come into use at airports!

I was privileged to be involved with John Lodge in the UK Committee which examined the recommendations coming from ICAO, discussed them, varied them and put the UK's point of view as to requirements. These have been accepted and now form part of the proposed revision of the CAP 168. By consultation we achieved something.

Regarding the rapid intervention vehicle, Mr Lodge states that the aim is for vehicles with minimum manning. The rapid intervention vehicle is now in use at Heathrow and requires four men to man it. This puts the manning cost up. These vehicles, containing gallons of water producing 200 000 gallons of foam, may not be the answer. Perhaps more money could be spent on research into the power plants for the bigger major applicances which are capable of giving foam on the run, rather than the smaller vehicles which get there 30 s in advance of the main appliance; this critical time factor could be absorbed by the higher powered major applicances.

Snow and ice dealt with in Paper 22, are the airport authorities' nightmare. I told Mr Huson that in the NE of England, situated near the coast with strong northerly and NE winds and 300 miles of sea, it is a frustrating problem for snow clearance operatives, who may go down the runway with equipment, turn around and be unable to see where they have cleared because of fresh snow falls. I asked him what volume of snow was experienced in Canada; he told me that in the far west they had up to 350 in. in the winter - I think if we had that sort of snow in the UK we should all want to hibernate!

I agree with him that there is far too little national and international co-ordination of snow clearance techniques and answers to the problems. In the UK we get together to examine problems which vary according to latitude and to climatic conditions. A lot more would be learnt if everyone got together internationally.

I would like to ask Mr Huson if high pressure steam has been investigated? Slot drains could be heated to ensure that the liquid then flows away freely and does not cause obstructions.

Another suggestion was infra red heaters used underneath lorries. Is this a possibility? Has anyone ever considered this method of snow clearance?

I endorse everything Mr Sweetapple says in Paper 23. What he has not mentioned is the electric vehicle trials. These trials were conducted at Newcastle and have now reached the stage of developing aircraft steps which are currently in use. We have also examined other applications for the electric vehicle on the apron. Some of the advantages relate to cost comparison; with one set of steps, four units of electricity lasted 10 h actual running time. They are very manoeuvrable, and easy to start in the winter - a very important factor; they can be inched forward when operating in the vicinity of aircraft - another important safety factor.

Mr NASH (Paper 21)

I am sure that Mr Denyer will realise that in raising the suggestion of a helicopter fire tender, I am doing so to promote a realization of the crucial nature of the problem of major aircraft fires at their worst. Each of the three factors - safer aircraft, safer fuels and speedier fire tenders - has its place in the scheme of things, and they will need to be used together to get a reasonable solution. It can readily be shown that a helicopter crash tender may well not be any advantage for crashes on the airfield - or up to the $2\frac{1}{2}$ km range that covers the 90% of crashes with fire. Here the answer must surely be in safer fuels, more fire resistant cabin structures and safer furnishings. Outside the $2\frac{1}{2}$ km range, the helicopter comes more and more into its own as the range increases, but I am bound to say that safety fuels and safer aircraft are still of paramount importance, since the increased range actually carries an increased response time penalty. Moreover, this considers only 10% of the crashes with fire, and those which are likeliest to have the highest impact damage. For my part, I would put safety fuels as the prime consideration, with the value of the other two factors to be determined by a more detailed study of the '10%'.

In regard to cost, the world always finds it possible to build - and often reject - new types of aircraft, and in this milieu I find it difficult to believe that the idea of a helicopter crash tender could be rejected on cost alone, since it only requires the adaptation of existing types of helicopter. The Canadians already have a Boeing Vertol in use for this purpose, and the use of helicopters and aircraft for forest fire-fighting is well known. But these matters are not for me to decide - what I can do is to try and stimulate interest by putting forward the salient facts.

As far as halons are concerned (including BCF), I mentioned them only as secondary agents, which I consider to be their role. Foam is the only primary agent, as John Lodge has also said. In regard to the relative merits of foams, I have tried to show that the modern foams - fluoroprotein and fluorochemical - show a distinct advantage over straight protein foams when all the fire-fighting materials have to be brought to the fire. The examples of the Boeing 747 and the Path Finder illustrate this. Should circumstances make a fire difficult to extinguish (an ever-present possibility) the higher foam performance is essential and the virtue of foams which are not only good at controlling a fire but also resist 'burn-back', becomes obvious.

Mr LODGE (Paper 21)

Replying to Mr Denyer's questions about the rapid intervention vehicles and manning and research into the major chassis gives me the opportunity to acknowledge the fine work which he and others have contributed to the development of the scales discussed at ICAO and which have been adopted to a very large extent by member States.

Sometimes people believe that firemen are not conscious of the cost of equipment. I can assure them that if they sat where I do they would soon become conscious of it.

The difference between what one is required to do to get a licence in the United Kingdom, and what one might want to do as a thinking man came out in one of Mr Denyer's points. He does not think the difference in response time between a major fire tender and a rapid intervention vehicle of 30s is very much. It depends where you are at the time. If you are sitting in the aircraft then it is quite a long while.

Reference was made to BAA's new rapid intervention vehicle (RIV) at Heathrow. With respect to the Chief Fire Officer of the BAA I would refer to a demonstration he gave recently at Heathrow where a major foam tender of quite modern design and the new RIV were set stationary side by side 1.4 miles from a fire situation. They were both whistled-up at the same time and the RIV was 40s ahead of the major foam tender after 1.4 miles. This is what it is all about. Rapid intervention is the secret of survival in a post-accident fire.

Mr Denyer has suggested that it is very expensive to man a separate vehicle. It is not my responsibility or role to explain how the BAA, after long and careful consideration and many discussions with the trade union, solved this problem. They have achieved the manning of the vehicle replacing the rescue tender very economically, merely by slipping the No 3 men off their foam tenders, in the belief that if the RIV gets there first and performs its initial task in thirty seconds, then the men who become spare (because there is little more foam to deliver) can fall back if necessary to augment the foam tender manning.

Regarding making the major chassis faster, there is a limit to this. Britain has the fastest major chassis for fire appliances in the world. This vehicle in the form of a 13 500 1 foam tender with a gross vehicle weight of 35t,

can go from 0 to 80km in 35s. It is very hard significantly to reduce that. I believe that if the aim is to get there fast, then there is a definite role for a RIV which provides an initial fire-attack in the most critical areas.

Mr HUSON (Paper 22)

Steam cleaning of runways is possible - anything is possible - but I am not too sure how economic it would be. I have no experience of this. I can see other equipment might be needed, such as brooms to take off the residue so that it would not re-freeze. There may be drainage problems. I have not given thought to this and I do not know anyone who has, but it is an idea and that is what we are looking for - new ideas to have effective snow and ice control.

Mr Denyer's suggestion of infra red heating was supposed to be farfetched, but in fact a great deal of work has been done on this. The work has been done by one of the provincial government agencies in British Columbia, considering not so much airports as mountain pass roads in the Rockies where there are peculiar icing conditions.

In this study a model truck was built with infra red heating on it and tried it out in laboratories for a few years. Some of the problems were ironed out and a working model was made and put on the roads, but I have not any more information about it. I understand that one of the problems came from environmentalists concerned about radio activity created by this. There was also a problem that either the heat was too far away from the road surface and did not work at all or was too close to the road surface and burned it up.

There are other areas of development going on all the time. My organization as a manufacturing firm is trying to keep in touch. Some, or even most, of the work has been in isolation. I would stress that one of the things which is necessary is to have better communication between all the agencies concerned.

Mr SWEETAPPLE (Paper 23)

I was involved with infra red heating some years ago. I am not a scientist but I understand the problem is in converting the wavelengths of the infra red heating to the wavelength which will heat water or snow. The infra red frequencies will go straight through the snow to the surface below, heat it up and then melt the snow by conduction. That takes a long time. I do not think it would work on a road or a runway and it would probably be extremely expensive.

Mr J. R. ADDERLEY, Software Sciences Ltd.

I remember an experiment at a naval base where a jet engine was coupled vertically to a fuel bowser. First it became airborne and pre-empted the Apollo project by several years and, secondly, after taking on a bit more ballast it set fire to the runway and we had to abandon the attempt!

A great deal has been said about the absolute sensitivity of response time and response vehicles and the probability of survival. My question concerns the probability. Most serious accidents occur in the approach phase close to touch-down, or, alternatively, on the departure phase close to the end of the runway. Certainly the analyses I have seen indicate that a high proportion of accidents on the airport occur in a line close to the runways themselves. Therefore, can an advantage be attained - certainly at a major airport which has possibly a duplication of facilities - by deliberately siting the vehicles with one set at the approach end of the runway with very easy access and the others at the departure end? This applies particularly where the airport uses one runway for approaches and one runway for departures. There could be a distinct advantage, instead of siting the fire station in the traditional location, halfway up the runway, well back and with comparatively difficult entry to the runway on a taxi-way system. When an emergency is known to be likely, it is normal to position the vehicles close to the runway. What is the objection to having them there all the time?

Mr LODGE

The Civil Aviation Authority commissioned a study in 1971 which demonstrated beyond reasonable doubt that the best place to have the fire stations is roughly in the centre of the aerodrome.

The real answer is response time. What my organization does as a licensing authority is to go to an aerodrome and require the authority to demonstrate they can get to any part of the aerodrome, that is the licensed area, within 3 mins. Very often this means buying better fire engines, and most people are now doing this.

It is quite impossible to anticipate the location of an accident: 80% of all accidents occur within 5 km of the centre point of an aerodrome. This has been most carefully studied and the best place for the fire station is in the middle of the airport.

There are enormous management problems in having small units of fire equipment dotted around the aerodrome: man management problems and mobilization problems. The reason for going to the runway when there is prior warning of an incident is because the nature of the hazard may well be known. It may be a total lack of flaps, which indicates the aircraft will come in fast and land long. It may be a deficient undercarriage, in which case the plane stops where it touches down. Tactical positions can be taken up according to this information. The worst accidents are those that go 'bump in the night' - accidents without forewarning. For these, the evidence shows that a position mid-point along the runway is the best place to be.

Mr K.WILDE, Chief Airports Section, ICAO

Mr Sweetapple made a proposal that there should be an international group composed of airports, airlines and aircraft manufacturers. One was set up some years ago and meets periodically. It is called the International Industry Working Group. It attempts to coordinate some of the problems he anticipated.

As a result of some of this coordination a vert good series of booklets and documents is pub-

lished by the manufacturers. These give extensive information for each of the aircraft they produce. Called 'Aeroplane characteristics for airport planning' they are available free of charge from the various manufacturers.

Mr SHARP, Civil Aviation Department, Hong Kong

I disagree with Mr Sweetapple on the same point as Mr Wilde. Hong Kong was certainly caught out in 1969 with the 747 but, since then, we have found that the American West Coast manufacturers have been very helpful with their information. Boeing, Douglas and Lockheed publish airport compatibility studies and they are issued very freely. Nowadays manufacturers are generally very helpful although I agree that originally they were not.

Another example further to that given by Mr Wilde is the Airport Operators Council International, which runs technical visits on the West Coast. The last was in 1972. The manufacturers were very helpful and informative.

It is a very brave man who comments on a paper by Sir Peter Masefield. I am sure, however, that there was an omission in Paper 5. He said that no other airport in the world operated the volume and importance of traffic from a single runway than does Gatwick. He should have said 'apart from Hong Kong'.

Mr SWEETAPPLE

I feel that the Industry Working Group is not effective enough at the moment, and more airports need to be more closely linked with it.

Regarding present liaison with manufacturers, I agree that the manuals are first-class, but they are produced after the aeroplane has been built. I know airports get drafts. But the whole question should be turned round so that aircraft are designed and built to fit existing airports and existing facilities.

Mr Walmsley in an earlier session put forward some very novel ideas. They are not capable of being built on to existing facilities. Too much money has already been invested in airports. There must be some return on the capital invested all over the world. Let us improve existing aircraft, as necessary, to make them more economic and make more money with them, but continue to make them fit the existing facilities.

Mr E.REY, IBERIA Airlines, Heathrow Airport

I want to thank Mr Sweetapple for his contribution to the delicate task that the airlines have in scheduling. Figure 1 of his paper shows how complicated it is for an airline to produce a schedule in operations.

The same paper brings out very clearly the answer to an earlier remark that airports should be designed in order to cope with a peak. I disagree with that. We have heard of airports being prepared for a certain number of passengers in a year. If it were for a peak then airports should be prepared for a certain number of passengers in an hour.

The Airports Utilisation Committee sets the number of passengers per hour that the terminal is able to handle. With these figures the airlines produce their schedules, submitted to the

Scheduling Committee of the airport. The schedules go to Geneva for a conference, where they are decided. The airlines coordinate their schedules in order to minimize the problems of peaking at the airports. If an aircraft comes in during a peak period and the capacity of the terminal is already filled then the aircraft is not allowed to come in.

The airlines have no interest in using the airports. After all, our aircrafts are to fly. We want them in the air, not in the airports.

Mr SWEETAPPLE

Terminals are usually designed for certain peak-hour traffic, but it appears to be fashionable to quote a terminal's capacity in yearly figures. I think this is just salesmanship. The only way to design a terminal is for its peak hour rating. That is a figure which will often be given to a scheduling committee, coupled with the number of passenger and cargo aircraft that can be handled at any one time.

Mr J. R. ADDERLEY, Software Sciences Ltd.

I recognize the points about the airlines, including the scheduling at the individual airports. Nevertheless, over the past three years there have been tremendous delays over Europe. The airlines have been the worst sufferers in the economic situation.

What has been happening? There have been a number of independent airport scheduling committees, on which the airlines have fitted in. What was not taken into account were the unfortunate constraints that exist in European airspace and there there was no coordination. With the best will in the world, the airlines were trying to fly their schedules and yet suffering delays, both on the ground and in the air.

My plea was for full coordination of airport, airspace and airline scheduling, to achieve the best interests of all.

Mr E. REY, IBERIA Airlines, Heathrow Airport

The difference is that airline schedules are usually prepared up to two years in advance. In other words, we are now preparing schedules for 1977-1978. It is difficult to guess what is going to happen to air control over Germany or France. What happens if there is a strike?

Mr SWEETAPPLE

The normal airport scheduling committees work on an annual basis.

The problems which arise over Europe change

every day. One may know they are going to be there in advance, but it is Euro-control which has set up an organization to try to resolve some of the problems. I have not much knowledge of it.

Mr R. FERGUSON, Chief Fire Officer, British Airports Authority

The extent of the problem in relation to an aircraft accident situation on any airport has been made very clear by Nash and Lodge. Mr Nash crystallized the situation in scientific terms. If these are evaluated they indicate that to meet them on the airport fire service side requires speeds in excess of 100 mile/h. This is quite obviously not on. I think airports have gone as far as they can in relation not only to the major appliances but the rapid intervention vehicles.

Mr Lodge gave the practical point of view. What I want to do is to emphasise the position on which progress is needed: in building a greater resistance into the aircraft and in making fuels less volatile. These are the two areas where, for various reasons (mainly commercial), there is not a great deal of progress.

There is clear evidence that the airport fire service is making as much progress as it can.

Mr B. TUTTY, Director, Airports, International Air Transport Association, Quebec, Canada

The scheduling problem has not been overlooked, nor has the peaking problem of the airlines. There is at IATA an overall Scheduling Procedures Committee which is examining scheduling procedures on a worldwide basis. This has adopted a guide for airlines and airport authorities, if necessary, whereby local scheduling coordinating committees can be established. They should be established only when absolutely necessary. There is no point in introducing restrictions and coordination rules and regulations which may not apply in more than half a dozen instances.

In London, which is probably the most difficult in the world, there is an extensive scheduling committee. When the IATA Timetables Committee meets twice a year, the London and New York schedules and all other major airport schedules are integrated on a round-the-world route basis. All the various factors are given consideration: peaking, congestion, capacities, so that wherever possible these schedules are operated within the various limits of the particular airports.

It can be seen therefore that IATA airlines are co-ordinating their schedules to the best of their ability and this includes the integration of the European routes.

Summing up

Sir Peter Masefield
Director, British Caledonian Airways Ltd

After the procession of mettlesome horses which have shown their paces here during the past two days, inevitably there must come the dust-cart - the chap with the little spade and shovel, running behind trying to tidy up after them. That's me.

In all seriousness, its been a good Conference and a very wide-ranging Conference, all the way from costs to Concorde - (without perhaps relating the two), from cargo to constant and proper concern about security, from rail links to runways, from mobile lounges to baggage trolleys, and from noise even to snow clearing and fire fighting. At this gathering we have not solved all the problems. But at least we have taken a good look at them.

One of the consoling factors of the difficulties of the recession in air traffic over the past three years, is that they have given a little breathing space in the airports rat race. We have had a couple of years to get organized.

One thing, above all others, seems to me to have shone out, through all 23 papers and the discussions upon them: the central point of the challenges of change in a business which is, at once, in the forefront of innovation and technology and central to the major issues of our times. It is in the middle of the battle against inflation, the drive to promote more trade and the need to climb out of the recession everywhere, in fact of the need to work, and to earn our keep. From the start, this conference has shown - and shown very clearly - that in the world of airports nothing is static. The business as a whole, and even the ideas about the business, are evolving and changing all the time. Surely, one of the most heartening things has been the readiness of everyone to accept the challenges of change and to adapt methods and ideas to a rapidly changing situation.

Compared with 1973, the emphasis has shifted from vastly expensive new sites for vast new airports to the provision of just very expensive new facilities at existing airports, as well as, of course, new airports in developing countries. That is one big change in emphasis which has run right through the conference. There are, I think, two others:
(a) an emphasis on the need to cope with increased passenger numbers much more than an increase in aircraft movements (though, in due course, that will follow also) -
(b) rather less lunatic-fringe bally-hoo about 'environmental' and 'ecological' problems.

I do not suggest that environmental problems no longer exist, but they are being seen in a wider perspective than they were. There are some people who ought to know better who proclaim that traffic through airports should be artificially restricted. In these days the watch-word should be provision and promotion, not restriction. But, perhaps, even some of the restrictionists are beginning to see the overriding requirements of national economics and the need for the development of international trade.

In this context, quieter aircraft are 'making themselves heard'. Instead of the cacophony of the Conway and the jangle of the JT-3D we now have, increasingly, the rumble of the RB-211 and the cadence of the CF-6.

It seems to me that this Conference has been immensely valuable in marking and illuminating a distinctive point in the progress of aviation and its technology: a facing-up to the challenges of change. It has emphasised some particular aspects of those changes, not least in tighter economies, especially costs. It has underlined a new maturity in the business. And it has provided great hopes for future progress, which we can all hope will be fulfilled.

Where that progress should be - and the things on which we ought to concentrate - has been, of course, the meat in the sandwich. One might say, indeed that - through the five world airports conferences, from pre-747 days - we have been seeking that elusive and mysterious beast, the perfect airport with all the trimmings. Senor Dovali tells us this comes in 4000 different varieties, and all you have to do is to pick the winner from a short list of three. However long we continue our quest for the perfect airport, this conference has, most valuably, hacked away at some of the undergrowth around it.

One or two aspects recurred all through. There were four main issues: money, the root of all evil and of the aviation business; the general background - noise and facilities (including aircraft); who is it all about?; and where do we go from here? In fact at the end of the first day of the Conference most of the main areas of discussion had been set. Never have we needed to look more carefully into the future. Never has it been more difficult. What are we going to need?

Taking a cue from Lord Boyd Carpenter the pre-occupation with environmental airports was swept away - in marked contrast with the atmosphere of three years ago.

The first main issue was the problem of who should pay, how much and for what? Should aviation be made, uniquely among all forms of transport to support itself financially in the air and at its airports? Is a 15% target rate of return a fair load to put onto the British Airports Authority, and through the Authority onto the airlines? How much should ratepayers be asked to bear for regional airports? Indeed – what is really a fair financial policy for aviation in general and airports in particular?

We had guidance from many directions – from the Minister, Guy Barnett, from Lord Boyd Carpenter and the merchant banker, Bruno Schroder. I'm not sure we got clarity in the answers. But its a fact that we have a situation in which, in the UK, the British Airports Authority is making a profit, the CAA does not cover its costs, municipal airports are, in general, being supported by the rates, and the airlines (who pay through their revenue earned from passengers and cargo) are making no significant profit on their operating costs at the present – let alone servicing their capital. In fact Knut Hammarskjold said that the bulk of the air carrier industry is teetering on the brink of bankruptcy.

Taking all Britain's airports together, it seems that at present, after crediting BAA's profits against the remaining deficits and at present rates and charges, airport services as a whole are failing to meet their costs by around £50 million plus what is needed to service capital and to provide new facilities.

Broadly, the British government is saying that the users should pay, which means that the 30 million passengers who use the British airports at the present time should eventually, on today's costs, each pay on average an extra £6 or £7, or so, for every journey they make. Alternatively, every transport aircraft movement through the UK's airports should pay, on average, an extra £300, including the servicing of capital. This is just not practicable.

Clearly this means we cannot afford new, expensive airports. We must do the best we can with what we've got.

Secor Browne made it very clear that the United States policy is, and will continue to be – the provision of the infrastructure of air transport, especially FAA Towers, ATC and en route facilities from Federal sources in the US national interest. I believe, most strongly, that the British Government and CAA should recognise this and, in an international competitive business, not penalize British aeronautical facilities by loading all costs directly on the user.

That brings me to the second main point: noise and the general background. Dr Wilkinson gave us an optimistic and encouraging view on the quiet revolution which has already begun. It is, I am sure, one of the really encouraging things about the future – at least for the big aeroplanes flying through the larger airports on the trunk routes. There is clear evidence now that, on the trunk routes, the older narrow-body aircraft are becoming steadily less competitive. In spite of the economic difficulties, I am sure that we shall see a steadily increasing demand for each of the four available wide-body aircraft, B747, DC-10, L1011 TriStar

and A300B. Once the traffic starts building up again there will be a demand for developed versions of these aircraft both upwards, to 800 seats, 1000 and then, perhaps, to 1250 seats, and downwards to 200 seats for thinner routes. One of the significant things which we must never forget about air transport is that reduced costs have come above all else, from the use of larger aircraft, earning more revenue from the same fixed costs. And, of course, the bigger the aeroplane, the fewer the problems of runway capacity, though the greater the problems of providing terminals to adequate standards.

That's another thing this Conference has been about – 'adequate standards'.

Perhaps we did not spend quite enough time talking about regional airports, where the problems may be, I fear, more acute. Because the trend in aircraft size is so predominately upwards, the tendency is for the less heavy routes to get the cast-off smaller aircraft. By the nature of things they are the noisier types, and the cheapest to operate. Nevertheless, contrary to what some people think, I believe that there is going to be a first class market for the best of the new technology aircraft between now and the mid-1980's. And this is a chance for the manufacturing industry to show what it can do in the way of low-drag supercritical wings and low consumption quiet engines.

Because we shall be looking for more passengers through the same number of airports, carried in bigger aircraft, with heavier peaks at convenient times, (which is what transport is all about) we must look also for more passenger terminals, better cargo handling facilities and more and better access, including more rail links. Clearly, as Mr Rockwell stressed, the Piccadilly Tube will be a great thing for Heathrow.

This conference has endorsed the fact that what its really all about is people – and, above all, the customer. Dr Pestalozzi put his finger on it when he talked about the passenger needs and the democratic principle of the most good for the most people. There are indeed seven different sets of people concerned with airports and the standards of their facilities: the travelling public; the airlines, the professionals (who pay most of the bills); general aviation (who often get a raw deal); the staff, also professionals; the community who have come to live around; the taxpayer and the ratepayer (who, at the larger existing airports are getting their money back); the government, the regulating bodies (also professional). The most important of these seven are the travelling public and the shippers of air cargo who are the purpose of the business. Out of the seven four are professionals, but it is the non-professionals for whom we work.

There is sometimes a tendency, though not on the part of the airlines, to look on the customer as a captive market who, once won by the airlines, can be directed, diverted, restricted and generally pushed around. This is a great mistake; it is wrong in principle and it is bad business. They should be encouraged, humoured, cosseted and provided with the best facilities which can be afforded. After all they are paying, on average, a good deal more than for transport by any other means. And if they are pushed around too much, or denied what they seek, they will go away.

Passengers are the purpose of our business, not an interruption of our work, and the more of them, and the happier they are, the better. In these days of recession they are, more than ever, very important persons - not only to the airlines and the airports, but also to international trade and prosperity. There should be no talk of restricting airports, putting artificial ceilings on the numbers of aircraft movements or on the numbers of passengers handled, - and behaving as though national and international trade did not matter. They are, indeed, top priority and must be encouraged in every way possible.

Now the fourth and final theme has had a much broader sense. 'Where do we go from here?' Airports are not ends in themselves. They are means towards ends, and those ends are the safe, and the convenient, and the regular, and the economic, carriage of passengers and goods at fares and rates which they can afford.

Airports exist to give a service - as an interchange between modes of transport. And the most important services, through the air carriers which fly from them and from business associations, are to promote trade, business and travel, nationally and internationally; to hold down inflation by holding down changes; and to create productive employment. Hence, the more traffic which an airport can develop, the more the trade, the more the useful employment and (provided that the charges are right) the more that inflation can be contained (and, hopefully, the nearer the move towards profits). Airports are indeed in the front line of the struggle to beat the recession by the development of business, and for that reason there should be the minimum possible restriction on the development of air traffic.

Where we go from here is to do more business with the good 'historic' assets we possess which we can steadily make better according to strict priorities.

In the very first Paper the Director General of IATA, Knut Hammarskjold, emphasised the importance of a new degree of understanding and co-operation between airports authorities, airline managements, government administrations and consultative committees to get the best for the customer out of the evolving economic situation. Lord Boyd Carpenter crystalized some of these areas for collaboration still further. He emphasised the harm which over-reaction to well-meaning pressure groups could do to the vital need, throughout the civilised world, to promote trade and travel generally in the interests of breaking out of recession and unemployment. This Conference has, I think, put these things in a better perspective than ever before - first things first; economic survival.

Finally, looking at the way ahead, crystal balls have never been more clouded. Even so the concensus of opinion is that we can get through, at least until the 1990's, with getting the most out of existing airports. By then aircraft will be bigger so the pressure on runway capacity may not be more acute. The pressure will be to provide adequate terminal buildings.

There are some of the ways ahead from this Conference. In developed countries no new airports - or almost none, but more effective use out of what we've got. In developing countries, lots of new airports - room for skilled, experienced and enterprising consultants, and room for much more export business, both useful in itself and helpful to the future of trade.

In conclusion, may I on behalf of the whole Conference, pay a most grateful tribute to the Chairmen, for the expert and kindly way in which they have presided over this important conference.